Law and the Media

Law and the Media

Fourth Edition

Tom Crone

Revising authors:
Philip Alberstat
Tom Cassels
Estelle Overs

With expert contributors

Focal Press

OXFORD AMSTERDAM BOSTON LONDON NEW YORK PARIS
SAN DIEGO SAN FRANCISCO SINGAPORE SYDNEY TOKYO

Focal Press
An imprint of Elsevier Science
Linacre House, Jordan Hill, Oxford OX2 8DP
225 Wildwood Avenue, Woburn, MA 01801-2041

First published 1989
Second edition 1991
Third edition 1995
Reprinted 1996, 1999 (twice)
Fourth edition 2002

British Library Cataloguing in Publication Data
Crone, Tom
  Law and the media. – 4th ed.
  1. Mass media – Law and legislation – Great Britain
  I. Title   II. Alberstat, Philip, 1964–   III. Cassels, Tom
  IV. Overs, Estelle
  343.4′1′099

Library of Congress Cataloguing in Publication Data
A catalogue record for this book is available from the Library of Congress

ISBN 0 240 51629 X

For information on all Focal Press publications visit our website at:
www.focalpress.com

Composition by Genesis Typesetting, Rochester, Kent
Printed and bound in Great Britain

Contents

Foreword by Rosie Boycott   ix
Editors' Biographies   xi
Contributors' Biographies   xiii
Acknowledgements   xv
Table of Cases   xvii
Table of Statutes   xxv
Introduction   xxxi

Part I   Protection of Reputation   1

1   Defamation   3
Marietta Cauchi
1.1   Introduction   3
1.2   General principles   3
1.3   Defences   11
1.4   Procedure   26
1.5   Damages   30
1.6   Costs   32

2   Blasphemy, Seditious Libel and Criminal Libel   34
David Green
2.1   Introduction   34
2.2   Blasphemy   34
2.3   Seditious libel   36
2.4   Criminal libel   37

Part II   Intellectual Property   41

3   Copyright   43
Mark Cranwell
3.1   Introduction   43
3.2   Copyright work   44
3.3   Who owns copyright?   50
3.4   Infringement   53
3.5   Defences   55

3.6   No copyright   58
3.7   Duration of copyright   58
3.8   Remedies   59
3.9   Criminal offences   60
3.10   Other rights   61
3.11   The European Copyright Directive   63

4   New Media   65
Estelle Overs
4.1   Introduction   65
4.2   Internet defamation   66
4.3   Copyright   69
4.4   The Data Protection Act 1998   74
4.5   Reporting restrictions   76
4.6   Obscenity and racial hatred   77

5   Rights Clearances   80
Philip Alberstat
5.1   Introduction   80
5.2   Copyright, moral rights and performers' rights   81
5.3   Assignments and licences of copyright   83
5.4   Rental rights   85
5.5   Music   86

Part III   Privacy   87

6   Breach of Confidence   89
Joanna Ludlam
6.1   Introduction   89
6.2   What is breach of confidence?   90
6.3   Defences   97
6.4   Procedure   101

Contents

7   The Data Protection Act 1998   104
Terence Bergin
7.1   Introduction   104
7.2   The Data Protection Act 1998   105
7.3   Access to Personal Files Act 1987   113

8   The 'New' Right to Privacy   114
Peter Grundberg
8.1   Introduction   114
8.2   Common law rights   115
8.3   The Calcutt Committee   120
8.4   The Human Rights Act 1998   123
8.5   The future   126

Part IV   Comment on Court Proceedings   131

9   Reporting Restrictions   133
Jane Colston
9.1   Introduction   133
9.2   The open court rule   134
9.3   The power to postpone the reporting of proceedings   138
9.4   The power to prevent the publication of the names of parties   141
9.5   Restrictions on the publication of information relating to children   142
9.6   Committal proceedings before the magistrates' court   148
9.7   Hearings concerning sexual offences and indecency   150
9.8   Divorce cases   153
9.9   Fraud   154
9.10   Official secrets   155
9.11   Material made available on disclosure   156
9.12   Press challenges to reporting restrictions   156
9.13   Interviewing jurors   159
9.14   Tape recorders, photographs and sketches   160
9.15   Restrictions on reporting in other courts   161

10   Contempt of Court   166
Simon Dowson-Collins
10.1   Introduction   166
10.2   The Contempt of Court Act 1981   167
10.3   Common law contempt   180
10.4   Penalties and injunctions   183

11   Protection of Journalistic Sources   184
Joanna Ludlam
11.1   Introduction   184
11.2   Section 10 of the Contempt of Court Act 1981   185
11.3   Police powers under the Police and Criminal Evidence Act 1984   189

Part V   Prevention of Publication   193

12   Prior Restraint   195
Hugh Tomlinson QC
12.1   Introduction   195
12.2   General principles   195
12.3   Defamation cases   196
12.4   Breach of confidence   197
12.5   Invasion of privacy   200
12.6   Contempt proceedings   201

Part VI   State Restriction on Publication   203

13   Obscenity, Indecency and Incitement to Racial Hatred   205
David Green
13.1   Introduction   205
13.2   The Obscene Publications Acts   205
13.3   Indecent displays   209
13.4   Racial hatred   210

14   Freedom of Information   212
Charles de Fleurieu
14.1   Introduction   212
14.2   Code of Practice on Access to Government Information   213
14.3   The Freedom of Information Act 2000   219

15 Official Secrets   **228**
John Wadham
15.1 Introduction   228
15.2 Section 1 of the Official
     Secrets Act 1911: spying   229
15.3 The Official Secrets Act 1989:
     specific disclosure of official
     information   230
15.4 The Defence Advisory Notice
     system   238

**16 Parliamentary Proceedings and
Elections**   **240**
Tom Cassels and Rebecca Handler
16.1 Introduction   240
16.2 Parliamentary proceedings   241
16.3 Elections   243

Part VII   Media Regulation   **247**

17 Professional Regulatory Bodies   **249**
Tom Cassels
17.1 Introduction   249
17.2 The press: history of
     self-regulation   249
17.3 The Press Complaints
     Commission   252
17.4 Broadcasting: semi
     self-regulation   258
17.5 The Broadcasting Standards
     Commission   258
17.6 The Independent Television
     Commission   260
17.7 The Radio Authority   261
17.8 Other broadcast bodies   261

18 Advertising   **263**
Tom Cassels and Rebecca Handler
18.1 Introduction   263
18.2 The Code of Advertising
     Practice   263

**Part VIII   The Law under the
European Convention on
Human Rights**   **267**

19 The Human Rights Act 1998   **269**
Hugh Tomlinson QC
19.1 Introduction   269
19.2 The basic scheme of the
     Human Rights Act 1998   269
19.3 The Convention rights   275
19.4 The HRA and the right to
     privacy   281
19.5 Other areas of impact on the
     media   282

**Part IX   The Law in Other
Jurisdictions**   **287**

20 The Law in Scotland   **289**
Rosalind McInnes
20.1 Introduction   289
20.2 Defamation   289
20.3 Reporting restrictions   294
20.4 Contempt of court   297

**21 The Law in the United States of
America**   **305**
Estelle Overs
21.1 Introduction   305
21.2 Defamation   306
21.3 Copyright   309
21.4 New media   312
21.5 Invasion of privacy   317
21.6 Reporting restrictions   320
21.7 Contempt of court   321
21.8 Protection of journalistic
     sources   321
21.9 Obscenity and racial
     discrimination   321
21.10 Freedom of information   322

Appendix A   *Glossary of Legal Terms*   325

Appendix B   *Professional Bodies*   330

Appendix C   *Specimen Agreements*   335

Bibliography   355

Index   357

Foreword

Over the last decade much has changed for the newspaper editor, writer or producer. Today's journalist or broadcaster must be aware of an ever-increasing amount of legislation and number of regulatory schemes, as well as a rapidly evolving succession of communication systems. Traditional print media now incorporates new forms of publication such as the internet, news providers rely on videophones to relay instant images from the deserts of Afghanistan to the homes of digital viewers and broadcasters constantly reassess the methods of delivering their product to the public.

Understanding the law is consequently vital to those working in the media at every level. Editors, journalists and broadcasters talk to their lawyers daily about potentially contentious stories and programmes. Much of the daily news is concerned with events in the law courts and Parliament and consideration must always be given to the laws of libel, reporting restrictions and official secrets. All written material and every television and radio programme must conform to the laws of copyright, rights clearance and breach of confidence before publication or transmission, whatever the format.

Of equal importance is the fact that new methods of communication have broken down long-standing international legal barriers. The modern journalist or broadcaster must confront the laws of countries other than their own, or run the risk of legal proceedings for libel, breach of copyright, contempt of court or invasion of privacy in another legal jurisdiction.

This book is therefore to be warmly welcomed. It is written by lawyers prominent in their respective fields of expertise. It sets out the fundamentals of the law most likely to be of concern to those working in the media and provides guidance on the legal issues subject to current debate: new forms of media, the Human Rights Act 1998 and the thorny question of privacy. It sets out the law in Scotland and the United States of America, the two countries where journalists and broadcasters in the United Kingdom are most likely to run foul of different legal principles, and provides invaluable assistance to the busy journalist or broadcastder through comprehensive appendices which include the web sites of relevant professional bodies and specimen agreements. It is a book which deserves to be within easy reach of journalists, writers and broadcasters at every stage of their working day.

Rosie Boycott
Former editor of the *Independent*, the *Independent on Sunday* and the *Express*
Presenter of BBC2's *Life Etc* and BBC Radio 4's *A Good Read*

Editors' Biographies

Philip Alberstat

philip.alberstat@osborneclarke.com

Philip Alberstat is a Partner at law firm Osborne Clarke. He works extensively for companies in the film and broadcasting industries and represents numerous broadcasters, production companies, banks and financial institutions.

Philip is on the editorial board of *Entertainment Law Review* and the advisory board of the British Independent Film Awards. He speaks frequently at seminars and conferences on media-related subjects, and lectures at the Raindance Film Workshop and the European Film Institute. He was the winner of the 1997 HIFAL Lawyer Award as Solicitor of the Year and is the author of the *Independent Producers' Guide to Film and TV Contracts* (Focal Press, 2000).

Tom Cassels

tom.cassels@bakernet.com

Tom Cassels is a Partner in the Dispute Resolution Department of law firm Baker & McKenzie, and is a member of the firm's international media law group. He qualified as a Solicitor in 1994, and has practised in London and Sydney.

Tom acts for a range of media clients including publishers, news agencies, online booksellers and Internet service providers, as well as well-known individuals and companies who attract a high level of media interest. Recent examples of Tom's clients include the challenge by Camelot to the National Lottery Commission's decision to exclude it from competition for the new licence to operate the National Lottery and Transport for London's challenge to the proposed PPP for London Underground.

Estelle Overs

estelle.overs@osborneclarke.com

Estelle Overs qualified as a Barrister in 1994. From 1994 to 2000 she practised as a Barrister at the Chambers of George Carman QC. In 2001, she qualified as an Attorney in the State of California.

Estelle joined the Banking Department of the law firm Osborne Clarke in 2002 where she undertakes all aspects of film finance and international film and television production work. She regularly publishes and lectures on film finance, media-related issues and United States law.

Tom Crone

Tom Crone is Legal Manager of News International plc, publishers of *The Sun*, *News of the World*, *The Times* and *The Sunday Times*. After 5 years as a practising Barrister, he became an in-house lawyer for Mirror Group in 1980 and 'jumped ship' to join News Group, publishers of *The Sun* and *News of the World* in 1985. Since then, he has been at the centre of numerous high profile media cases: Robert Maxwell, Elton John, Ian Botham, George Michael, Sonia Sutcliffe, Bill Roache, Gillian Taylforth, Bruce Grobelaar, Thompson and Venables (the Bulger Killers), and Her Majesty The Queen (twice).

Contributors' Biographies

Terence Bergin

Terence Bergin is a Barrister at the Chambers of Roger Henderson QC, 2 Harcourt Buildings, Temple. He specializes in computer-, e-commerce- and Internet-related litigation, and has a niche practice in entertainment law. Terence was junior counsel in the case of *Anglo Group plc v Winther Browne*.

Marietta Cauchi

Marietta Cauchi is a journalist with Dow Jones Newswires, having previously practised as a media lawyer in London for several years. Her expertise covers all media-related topics, including defamation, intellectual property and human rights issues, and the implication of the Internet in these areas. Marietta has written and spoken on these topics both in Europe and the United States of America.

Jane Colston

Jane Colston is a Senior Associate in the Dispute Resolution Department of law firm Baker & McKenzie. Jane qualified as a Solicitor in 1991 and is a member of the firm's international media law group.

Mark Cranwell

Mark Cranwell is a Senior Associate with international law firm Coudert Brothers. He is a member of the firm's worldwide Telecommunications Media and Technology Group and specializes in domestic and international commercial transactions in the telecommunications and technologies fields, with a focus on digital media. Mark is dual qualified in England and Wales and the Province of Alberta, Canada.

Charles de Fleurieu

Charles de Fleurieu is an Associate with international law firm Coudert Brothers. He is a member of the firm's corporate and Telecommunications Media and Technology Groups, where he works on domestic and international transactions and other corporate and regulatory matters. Charles received his LLB from King's College, London and his Maitrise in French law from the Sorbonne University in Paris in 1996. He is qualified as a Solicitor in England and Wales.

Simon Dowson-Collins

Simon Dowson-Collins was called to the Bar in 1989. He worked at media law specialists Wright Webb Syrett and was made a Partner in 1993 after transferring to the solicitors' branch of the profession. Wright Webb Syrett merged with Davenport Lyons in 1995.

In 1996, Simon joined the BBC legal department where he specializes in all areas of media law, with an emphasis on defamation and contempt. Simon is Director of Legal Services at HarperCollins Publishers.

David Green

David Green is an Assistant Solicitor in the Litigation Department of law firm Herbert Smith.

Peter Grundberg

Peter Grundberg is an Anglo-Swedish Associate with the Worldwide Corporate Group of Wilmer Cutler & Pickering, the international law firm. Based in Wilmer Cutler & Pickering's London office, Peter specializes in corporate commercial work. He graduated from Corpus Christi College, Cambridge in 1996, and is qualified as a Solicitor in England and Wales. He is a regular contributor to various legal journals including *Intellectual Property Lawyer* and *The Legal Mind*.

Rebecca Handler

Rebecca Handler is an Assistant Solicitor in the Dispute Resolution Department of law firm Baker & McKenzie.

Joanna Ludlam

Joanna Ludlam is a litigation lawyer in the Media and Commercial Litigation practice at international law firm Clifford Chance. Joanna has worked on a number of high profile breach of confidence cases, the most notable of which was the defence of Dr Andrew Millar in a breach of confidence claim brought by British Biotech in 1999. Joanna also specializes in defamation.

Rosalind McInnes

Rosalind McInnes received her law degree and diploma from Glasgow University. She worked in Edinburgh as a commercial litigator in private practice for six years before joining the BBC from law firm Maclay Murray & Spens. Rosalind is the co-author of two books, *Scots Law for Journalists* (7th edition) and *Contempt of Court in Scotland*.

Hugh Tomlinson QC

Hugh Tomlinson QC is a Barrister at Matric Chambers in London. He is the author of a number of legal textbooks including *Civil Actions against the Police* (3rd Edn, 2002) and *The Law of Human Rights* (Oxford University Press, 2000). His areas of practice include defamation, privacy law and human rights. Hugh's recent cases include *Loutchansky v Times Newspapers*, a leading case on the operation of *Reynolds* qualified privilege.

John Wadham

John Wadham is a Solicitor and the Director of Liberty (the National Council for Civil Liberties). He has acted for a large number of applicants in cases before the European Commission and European Court of Human Rights. John is the editor of *Your Rights: The Liberty Guides*, the civil liberties section of the *Penguin Guide to the Law* and the case law reports for the *European Human Rights Law Review*. He is the author of *Blackstone's Guide to the Human Rights Act 1998* and *Blackstone's Guide to the Freedom of Information Act*.

Acknowledgements

Philip Alberstat, Tom Cassels and Estelle Overs owe special thanks to all the contributors to this book. They would like to thank Jenny Welham and Beth Howard for their encouragement and patience. They would also like to thank Nancy Peirson for her assistance in editing and compiling the fourth edition, and Dr D. T. McVicar for his general advice and research assistance.

Philip Alberstat would like to thank Carol Hays, Theodora Hays-Alberstat and Alexandra Hays-Alberstat for their support.

Tom Cassels would like to thank the partners of Baker & McKenzie for their support of this project, Dunstan Speight for his assistance and his wife Helen and children Sam and Hannah for their patience.

Estelle Overs would like to thank John and Marian for their support and James Richards and Cassandra Williams for their advice and assistance.

Table of Cases

A v B and C (2001) (unreported)   xxiii, 200, 282
A v United Kingdom (1998) 27 EHRR 611   276
A&M Records Inc v Napster Inc 114 F. Supp 2d 896 (2000)   313
Aga Khan v Times Publishing Co [1924] 1 KB 675   17
A-G v BBC [1981] AC 303   201
A-G v BBC and Hat Trick Productions Ltd [1997] EMLR 76   175
A-G v English [1983] 1 AC 116   180
A-G v Guardian Newspapers [1987] 1 WLR 1248   116, 198, 199
A-G v Guardian Newspapers [1999] EMLR 904   176
A-G v Guardian Newspapers Ltd (No 2) [1988] 3 All ER 545   99, 134
A-G v Guardian Newspapers Ltd (No 2) [1990] 1 AC 109   92, 116
A-G v Hislop [1991] 1 QB 514   177
A-G v Jonathan Cape Ltd [1976] 1 QB 752   92, 97
A-G v Leveller Magazine Ltd [1979] AC 440   142
A-G v MGN [1997] 1 All ER 456   176
A-G v Morgan [1998] EMLR 294   170
A-G v News Group Newspapers [1986] All ER 833   173, 174
A-G v News Group Newspapers Limited [1987] QB 1   139
A-G v News Group Newspapers Ltd [1988] 2 All ER 906   181
A-G v Newspaper Publishing PCC [1987] 3 All ER 276   183
A-G v Newspaper Publishing plc [1988] Ch 333   167
A-G v Punch Ltd [2001] EWCA Civ 403   117
A-G v Sport Newspapers [1992] 1 All ER 503   181
A-G v Times Newspapers [1992] 1 AC 191   196
A-G v Times Newspapers [2001] EWCA Civ 97   198
A-G v Times Newspapers Ltd [1974] AC 273   167
A-G v Times Newspapers Ltd [1991] 2 All ER 398   183
A-G v Times Newspapers Ltd The Times 12 February 1983   176
A-G v Unger [1998] EMLR 280   175
Aitchison v Bernardi 1984 SLT 343   300
Aitken v Preston [1997] EMLR 415   30
Al Megrahi & Khalifa Fhima v Times Newspapers 1999 SCCR 824   301
American Cyanamid v Ethicon Ltd [1975] AC 396   102, 199
Argyll v Argyll [1967] 1 ChD 302   95, 154
Aspro Travel v Owners Abroad Group [1996] 1 WLR 132   9
Associated Newspapers Group Plc v News Group Newspapers Ltd [1986] RPC 515   55
Associated Press v Walker 388 US 130 (1967)   307
Aubry v Les éditions Vice-Versa Inc [1998] 1 SCR 591   120

Baigent v BBC 1999 SCLR 787 — 290, 292, 294
Barry v News Group Newspapers Ltd 1999 GWD 2–66 — 293
Barrymore v News Group Newspapers [1997] FSR 600 — 96, 199
BBC v British Satellite Broadcasting Ltd [1992] Ch 141 — 56
Bell v Bell's Trustee 21 June 2001 Inner House, Court of Session — 290
Beloff v Pressdram Ltd [1973] 1 All ER 241 — 52
Berezovsky v Forbes [1999] EMLR 278 — 27
Berezovsky v Forbes [2001] EWCA Civ 1251 — 284
Berezovsky v Michaels [2000] 1 WLR 1004 — 68
Bergens Tidende v Norway (2001) 31 EHRR 16 — 279
Berkoff v Burchill [1996] 4 All ER 1008 — 8
Bernstein v Skyways [1978] 1 QB 479 — 118
Blackshaw's Case [1983] 2 All ER 311 — 118
Blumenthal v Drudge 992 F Supp 44 DDC (1998) — 312
Bonnard v Perryman [1891] 2 Ch 269 — 197
Boulter v Kent Justices [1887] AC 556 — 164
Bowman v Secular Society [1917] AC 406 — 35
Bowman v United Kingdom (1998) 26 EHRR 1 — 280
Branson v Bower The Times 23 July 2000 — 283, 284
Branzberg v Hayes 408 US 665 (1972) — 321
British Data Management v Boxer Commercial Removals [1996] 3 All ER 707 — 196
Brutus v Cozens [1973] AC 854 — 211
Butler v Michigan 352 US 380 (1957) — 321

Caledonian Newspapers Limited, Petitioners 1995 SLT 1335 — 296
Cambridge Nutrition v BBC [1990] 3 All ER 523 — 198
Camelot Group plc v Centaur Communications Ltd [1999] QB 124 — 187
Campbell v Spottiswoode (1863) 3 B & S 769 — 18
Capital Life v Sunday Mail The Scotsman 6 January 1979 (unreported) — 294
Carroll v BBC 1997 SLT (Sh Ct) 23 — 291
Cassidy v The Daily Mirror [1929] 2 KB 331 — 9
Castells v Spain (1992) 14 EHRR 445 — 279
Charleston v News Group Newspapers Ltd [1995] 2 AC 65 — 8, 118
Cheng v Paul (2001) 10 BHRC 525 — 284
Clibbery v Allan [2001] 2 FCR 577 — 285
Cohen v Daily Telegraph Ltd [1968] 1 WLR 916 — 17
Commissioner of Metropolitan Police v Mackenzie (1987) (unreported) — 192
Cork v McVicar The Times 31 October 1984 — 99
Cossey v United Kingdom (1990) 13 EHRR 56 — 276
Cox & Griffiths, Petrs 1998 SLT 1172 — 303
Creation Records Ltd v News Group Newspapers Limited [1997] EMLR 444 — 90, 116
Cunningham v Scotsman Publications 1987 SLT 698 — 294

Daily Mail v Daily Express (1987) (unreported) — 51
Darker v Chief Constable of the West Midlands Police [2000] 3 WLR 747 — 21
David and Victoria Beckham v MGN Ltd (2001) (unreported) — 125
Derby v Weldon The Times 20 October 1988 — 156
Derbyshire County Council v Times Newspapers Ltd [1993] AC 534 — 6

Designers Guild Ltd v Russell Williams (Textiles) Ltd (Trading as Washington DC) [2001]
  1 All ER 700   48
Douglas v Hello! [2001] 2 WLR 992   124, 125, 200, 274, 281, 283
DPP v Duffield & Another [1977] 1 All ER 519   245
DPP v Luft & Another [1976] 2 All ER 569   245
DPP v Whyte [1972] AC 849   208
Dudgeon v United Kingdom (1981) 4 EHRR 149   276
Duncan v Associated Newspapers 1929 SC14   294

Egger v Viscount Chelmsford [1965] 1 QB 248   20
Elton John v Express Newspapers plc [2000] 1 WLR 1931   187
EMI v Evangelous Papathanassiou [1987] 8 EIPR 244   47
Eric Hvide v John Does (2000) (unreported)   313
Ex parte Central Independent Television Plc [1991] 1 WLR 4   139
Ex parte News Group Newspapers Ltd The Times 21 May 1999   139,159
Express Newspapers plc 1999 SCCR 262   299
Express Newspapers Plc v Liverpool Daily Post & Echo Plc [1985] 3 All ER 680   50
Exxon Corporation v Exxon Insurance Consultants International Ltd [1982] Ch 119   45

Femis-Bank v Lazar [1991] Ch 391   197
Ford v The Press Complaints Commission [2001] EWHC Admin 683   129
Francome v Mirror Group [1984] 1WLR 892   99, 198
Fraser v Thames TV [1984] QB 44   90
Fulham v Newcastle and Journal Ltd [1977] 1 WLR 651   9

Galbraith v HMA 2000 GWD 1223   296
Gardiner v Fairfax (1942) 42 SR(NSW) 172   16
Gaskin v United Kingdom (1989) 12 EHRR 36   276
General Medical Council v British Broadcasting Corporation [1998] 1 WLR 1573   180
George Hensher Ltd v Restawile Upholstery (Lancs) Ltd [1976] AC 64   47
Gertz v Robert Welsh Inc 418 US 323 (1974)   307
Gillick v West Norfolk & Wisbech Health Authority [1986] AC 112   96
GKR Karate (UK) Ltd v Yorkshire Post Newspaper [2000] 1 WLR 2571   23
Gleaves v Deakin [1980] AC 477   38
Godfrey v Demon Internet Ltd [2000] 3 WLR 1020   66, 69, 77
Godfrey v John Lees [1995] EMLR 307   46
Goldsmith v Bhoyrul [1998] QB 459   6
Goodwin v United Kingdom (1996) 22 EHRR 123   186, 280
Greig v Greig [1966] VR 376   117
Groppera Radio AG v Switzerland (1990) 12 EHRR 321   280
Gutnick v Dow Jones (2001) www.austlii.edu.au/au/cases/vic/VSC/2001/305.html   68

Hadley v Kemp [1999] EMLR 589   46
Haig v Aitken [2000] 3 All ER 80   115
Hamilton v Al-Fayed [1999] 1 WLR 1569   21, 242
Hamilton v Al-Fayed [2000] 2 All ER 224   242
Harris v Lubbock The Times 21 October 1971   18
Hassneh Insurance Co of Israel v Mew [1993] 2 Lloyd's Rep 243   162

Hatton v United Kingdom The Times 8 October 2001   277
Hayward v Thompson [1982] QB 47   10
HMA v Caledonian Newspapers Ltd 1995 SLT 926   300
HMA v Little 1999 SLT 1145   295
HMA v News Group Newspapers 1989 SCCR 156   297, 300
HMA v Scotsman Publications 1999 SLT 466   299, 302, 303
HMA v Scottish Media Newspapers 2000 SLT 331   301, 302
HM Attorney General v Associated Newspapers Limited [1993] WLR 74   160
Hoare v Jessop [1965] EA 218   12
Hodgson v Imperial Tobacco Limited [1998] ALL ER 48   138
Holden & Co v CPS (No 2) [1994] 1 AC 22   159
Holley v Smyth [1998] QB 726   197
Hope v Outram 1909 SC230   294
Horrocks v Lowe [1975] AC 135   18, 19
Hubbard v Vosper [1972] 2 QB 84   56, 101
Hulton v Jones [1910] AC 20   10
Hunt v Star Newspaper [1908] 2 KB 309   17
Hunter v Canary Wharf Ltd [1997] AC 655   129

Independent Television Publications Ltd v Time Out Ltd [1984] FSR 64   45
Informationsverein Lentia v Austria (1993) 17 EHRR 93   280

John v Mirror Group Newspapers [1997] QB 586   31, 32
John Reid Enterprises v Bell [1999] EMLR 675   187

Kavanagh v NT News Services [1999] FLR 268   24
Kaye v Robertson [1991] FSR 62   115, 197
Kelly v BBC [2001] 1 WLR 253   283
Kemsley v Foot [1952] AC 345   17

Ladbroke (Football) Ltd v William Hill (Football) UK Ltd [1964] 1 All ER 465   45
Langlands v Leng 1916 SC(HL)102   293
Lennon v News Group Newspapers [1978] FSR 573   91, 95
Lewis v Daily Telegraph [1964] AC 234   8
Liberace v Daily Mirror Newspapers Ltd The Times 18 June 1959   7
Lingens v Austria (1986) 8 EHRR 103   278, 279
Lion Laboratories Ltd v Evans [1985] 1 QB 526   58, 100
London Artists Ltd v Littler [1969] 2 QB 375   16
London Regional Transport v The Mayor of London (2001) (unreported)   199
Lord Brabourne v Hough [1981] FSR 79   197
Loutchansky v Times Newspapers Ltd [2001] 3 WLR 404   23, 119, 283, 284
Loveless v Earl [1999] EMLR 530   18
Lucas-Box v News Group Ltd [1986] 1 WLR 147   13
Ludlow Music Inc v Williams [2001] EMLR 155   48
Lukowiak v Unidad Editorial SA The Times 23 July 2001   284
Macphail v Maclead 1895 3 SLT 137   290
Macpherson v Macpherson [1936] AC 177   134
Magill TV Guide v Independent Television Publications [1991] 4 CMLR 586   45

Mahon v Rahn [2000] 1 WLR 2150 21

Mapp v News Group Newspapers Ltd [1997] TLR 124 12

Marks & Spencer and Others v One In A Million Ltd and Others [1997] Info TLR 316 72

Markt Intern and Beerman v Germany (1989) 12 EHRR 161 279

McArdle v Orr 1994 SLT(J)463 296

McCarey v Associated Newspapers Ltd (No 2) [1965] 2 QB 86 32

McCarten Turkington Breen v Times Newspapers Ltd [2000] 3 WLR 1670 24

McDonalds v Steel [1995] 3 All ER 615 12

McKerry v Teesdale & Wear Valley Justices [2000] Crim LR 594 145

McLauchlan v Orr, Pollock & Co (1894) 22R38 289

McPhilemy v Times Newspapers Ltd [1999] 3 All ER 775 27

McQuire v Western Morning News Co [1903] 2 KB 100 18

MGN v Bank of America [1995] 2 ALL ER 355 139, 140

Miller v California 413 US 15 (1973) 321

Moore v News of the World Ltd [1972] 1 QB 441 61

Morrison v Ritchie (1902) 4F645 290

Muir v BBC 1997 SLT 425 296, 304

Muller v Switzerland (1988) 13 EHRR 212 278, 279

Mutch v Robertson 1981 SLT 217 293

Newspaper Licensing Agency Ltd v Marks & Spencer plc [2001] UKHL 38 54

Newstead v Express Newspapers [1940] 1 KB 377 21

New York Times Co Inc v Tasini (2001) (unreported) 309

Niemitz v Germany (1992) 16 EHHR 97 126, 276

Observer & Guardian v United Kingdom (1991) 14 EHRR 153 198, 278, 279, 280

O'Mara Books Limited v Express Newspapers plc 3 March 1998 (unreported) 187

O'Shea v MGN The Independent 18 June 2001 284

Osborne v BBC 13 August 1999 Inner House, Court of Session 289

Otto-Preminger-Institut v Austria (1994) 19 EHRR 34 279

Oyston v Blaker [1996] 1 WLR 1326 27

P v Liverpool Daily Post & Echo Newspapers Plc [1991] 1 ALL ER 622 164

Panavision International v Toeppen 141 F 3d 1316 (1998) 315

Parvinder Chadha & Osicom Technologies Inc v Dow Jones & Company Inc [1999] EMLR 724 27

Peacock v London Weekend Television (1985) 150 JP 71 201

Philadelphia Newspapers Inc v Hepps 475 US 767 (1986) 307

Polly Peck v Trelford [1986] QB 1000 13

Practice Direction (Contempt: Reporting Restrictions) [1982] 1 WLR 1475 140

Practice Direction (Tape Recorders) [1981] 1 WLR 1526 160

Practice Note: (Contempt of Court: Reports of Proceedings: Postponement Orders) [1983] 1 All ER 64 142

Prager v Times Newspapers [1988] 1 WLR 77 13

Produce Records v BMG Entertainment (Chancery Division, Transcript Beverley F Nunnery, Hearing Date 19 January 1999) 53

Pro Sieben Media AG v Carlton UK Television Ltd [1999] 1 WLR 605 55

Table of Cases

R v A (No 2) [2001] 2 WLR 1546   271
R v Aldred (1909) 74 JP 55   37
R v A Local Authority in the Midlands ex parte LM [2000] 1 FLR 612   124
R v Anderson [1972] 1 QB 304   207
R v Broadcasting Standards Commission [2000] 3 WLR 1327   129
R v Calder and Boyars Ltd [1969] 1 QB 151   206, 207
R v Chief Metropolitan Stipendiary Magistrate ex parte Choudhury [1991] 1 QB 429 36, 37
R v Crown Court at Southwark ex parte Goodwin [1991] 3 All ER 818   143
R v Evesham Justices ex parte McDonagh [1988] 1 ALL ER 371   141
R v Fellows and Arnold [1997] 1 Cr App R 244   207
R v Hicklin (1868) LR 3 QB 360   205, 206
R v Horsham Justices ex parte Farquarson [1982] QB 762   140
R v Hutchinson (1984) 1295 SJ 700   152
R v Independent Television [1994] Fam 192   142
R v Khan [1997] AC 558   115
R v Lambert [2001] 2 WLR 211   271
R v Legal Aid Board ex parte Kaim Todner (a firm) [1998] 3 WLR 925   141
R v Mental Health Review Tribunal, ex parte H [2001] HRLR 752   274
R v Newtownabbey Magistrates' Court ex parte Belfast Telegraph Newspapers Ltd (1997)
    The Times 27 August 1997   138
R v Penguin Books Ltd [1960] Crim LR 176   207
R v Redditch Justices [1885] 2 TLR 193   164
R v Rhuddlan Justice ex parte HTV Limited The Times 21 December 1985   139
R v Runting (1988) 89 Cr App Rep 243   161
R v Secretary of State for Health ex parte Wagstaffe [2001] 1 WLR 292   134
R v Shayler The Times 10 October 2001   94, 231, 232, 233
R v Socialist Worker [1975] QB 637   141
R v Solicitor-General ex parte Taylor and Another Lexis 31 July 1995   178
R v Solicitor-General ex parte Taylor & Taylor TLR 14 August 1994   297
R v Somerset Health Authority ex parte S [1996] COD 244   142
R v Taylor & Taylor TLR 15 June 1993   297
R v Tronoh Mines Ltd & Others [1952] 1 All ER 697   245
R v Westminster County Council ex parte Castelli (1996) 28 HLR 125   158
Rantzen v Mirror Group Newspapers [1994] QB 670   31
Re Applications by Elvis Presley Enterprises Inc [1997] RPC 543   119
Re F (A Minor) (Publication of Information) [1977] 1 All ER 114   144
Regan v Taylor [2000] EMLR 549   22
Re Hooker (Patricia) and the Contempt of Court Act 1981 [1993] COD 190   161
Re L (A Minor) [1988] 1 All ER 418   144
Reno v American Civil Liberties Union 521 US 844 (1997)   316
Re X and Others (Minors) (Wardship: Disclosure of Documents) [1992] 2 All ER 595 143
Reynolds v Times Newspapers Ltd [1999] 3 WLR 1010   23, 119, 197
R (Heather) v The Leonard Cheshire Foundation (2001) (unreported)   270
Riches v News Group Newspapers Ltd [1986] QB 256   6
Rindos v Hardwick (1994) www.law.auckland.ac.nz/research/cases/Rindos.html   67
Robb v Caledonian Newspapers 1995 SLT 631   295, 301
R (on the application of Bright) v Central Criminal Court [2000] UKHRR 796   228
Roth v United States 354 US 476 (1957)   321

Rothermere v The Times [1973] 1 WLR 448 30
Russell v Stubbs 1913 SC(HL)14 290

Saad Al-Fagih v HH Saudi Research & Marketing (2001) (unreported) 284
Savalas v Daily Mail The Times 22 June 1976 31
Schering Chemicals v Falkman [1982] QB 1 91
Scott v Sampson (1882) 8 QBD 491 284
Scott v Scott [1913] AC 417 134
Scottish Daily Record and Sunday Mail Petitioners 1998 SCCR 626 295
Secretary of State for Defence v Guardian Newspapers Ltd [1985] 1 AC 339 60, 187
Shanks v BBC 1993 SLT 326 292
Shelley Films v Rex Features [1994] EMLR 134 90, 116
Shevill v Presse Alliance SA [1995] 2 AC 18 26
Should there be a Law to Protect Rights of Personal Privacy? [1996] EHRLR 450 123
Sim v Stretch (1936) 52 TLR 669 3, 6, 290
SmithKline Beecham Biologicals SA v Connaught Laboratories Inc The Times 14 July 1999 156
South Hetton v North Eastern News Association [1894] 1 QB 133 7
Spiliada Maritime Corporation v Cansulex [1987] AC 460 26
Stein v Beaverbrook Newspapers Limited 1968 SLT 401 290, 292
Stephens v Avery [1988] Ch 449 95, 96
Stern v Piper [1996] 3 All ER 385 12
Stratton Oakmont Inc v Prodigy Services Co 23 Media L Rep 1794 (NY Sup Ct May 24 1995) 312
Sullivan v New York Times 376 US 254 (1964) 293, 307
Sunday Times v United Kingdom (1979) 2 EHRR 245 167, 280
Sunday Times v United Kingdom (No 2) (1991) 14 EHRR 229 280
Sutherland v Stopes (1925) AC 47 12
Sutter v Switzerland (1984) 6 EHRR 272 276

Takenaka (UK) Ltd v Frankl (2000) (unreported) 67
Tancic v Times Newspapers Ltd The Times 12 January 2000 27
Taylor v Director of the Serious Fraud Squad [1999] 2 AC 177 24
Telnikoff v Matusevitch [1992] 2 AC 343 17
The Labour Party v News Group Newspapers (1987) (unreported) 245
Thoma v Luxembourg Judgment 29 March 2001 EctHR 284
Ticketmaster Corporation v Microsoft Corporation (1997) (unreported) 314
Times Newspapers Ltd v MGN Ltd [1993] EMLR 443 101
Tolley v JS Fry & Sons Ltd [1931] AC 333 9, 118
Tolstoy Miloslavsky v United Kingdom (1995) 20 EHRR 442 280
Tsikata v Newspaper Publishing [1997] 1 All ER 655 24

Universal City Studios Inc v Reimerdes 111 F Supp 2d 294 (2000) 314

Venables v News Group Newspapers Ltd [2001] 2 WLR 1038 77, 125, 138, 196, 200, 282

Waddell v BBC 1973 SLT 246 293
Walter v Lane [1900] AC 539 50
Walter v Steinkopff [1892] 2 Ch 489 44
Washington Post Company v TotalNews 97 Civ 1190 (SDNY 1997) 315

Table of Cases

Watts v Times Newspapers [1996] 2 WLR 427   22
West Provident Association v Norwich Union Life Assurance (1997) (unreported)   67
Whitehouse v Gay News and Lemon [1979] AC 617   35
Whiteley v Adams (1863) 15 CB (NS) 392   22
Williams v Settle [1960] 2 All ER 806   60
Williamson Music Ltd v The Pearson Partnership Ltd [1987] FSR 97   53
Wilson v First County Trust [2001] QB 407   274
Wingrove v United Kingdom (1996) 24 EHRR 1   36
Winstanley v Bampton [1943] KB 319   7
Winter v News Scotland 1991 SLT 828   293
Woodward v Hutchins [1977] 1 WLR 760   93
Wray v Associated Newspapers Limited and Another 2000 SCLR 819   291, 293, 294
Wright & Greig v Outram (1890) 17R596   294

X v Sweeney 1982 SCCR 1   303
X v Y [1988] 2 All ER 648   96, 102, 188
X and Y v Netherlands (1985) 8 EHRR 235   277
X Ltd v Morgan-Grampian (Publishers) Ltd [1991] 1 AC 1   185, 188

Z v Finland (1997) 25 EHRR 371   276
Zana v Turkey (1997) 27 EHRR 667   278
ZiaSun Technologies Inc v Floyd Schneider (2000) (unreported)   313

Table of Statutes

Access to Health Records Act 1990   113
Access to Justice Act 1999   143
  s. 72   143
Access to Personal Files Act 1987
    104, 113, 212
Administration of Justice Act 1960
    136, 137, 143, 144
  s. 12   144
  s. 12(1)   137
  s. 12(1)(a)   143
Anti-Terrorism, Crime and Security
  Act 2001   xxxiv, 127

British Nationality Act 1981   214
  s. 44(2)   214
Broadcasting Act 1990   45, 258–61, 296
  s. 175   45
  s. 176   45
Broadcasting Act 1996   258, 259, 260, 261

Children Act 1989   143
  s. 97(2)   143
  s. 108(5)   143
Children and Young Persons Act 1933
    142–5, 147
  s. 37   147
Children & Young Persons Act 1933
    142–5, 147
  s. 39   142–3, 146–7, 158, 163
  s. 44   143
  s. 45   144
  s. 47   145
  s. 49   145
  s. 49(3)   145
  s. 49(4)   145
Civil Evidence Act 1968   14
  s. 13   14

Consumer Credit Act 1974   274
Contempt of Court Act 1981   21, 60, 76,
    103, 137–42, 149, 155–64,
    166–88, 224, 241, 289, 295–7,
    299–300, 304
  s. 1   162
  s. 2   139, 140, 162, 169
  s. 2(2)   168, 173, 296, 300
  s. 3   178, 304
  s. 4   157, 158, 295
  s. 4(1)   179
  s. 4(2)   76, 138, 139, 140, 149, 155,
    157, 163, 164, 295
  s. 5   179, 180, 304
  s. 8(1)   159, 160
  s. 9   160
  s. 9(1)   160
  s. 9(2)   160
  s. 10   60, 103, 184, 185, 186, 187, 188
  s. 11   76, 141, 142, 157, 158, 163, 164
  s. 19   139, 164, 180, 224
Copyright Act 1911   43
Copyright Act 1956   43, 54, 60
Copyright, Designs and Patents Act 1988
    43–63, 69–70, 81–2, 289, 336, 338,
    340, 345–50
  s. 1(1)(b)   48
  s. 3(1)   44
  s. 4(1)   46
  s. 5(1)   48, 49
  s. 31   57, 81
  s. 31(3)   57
  s. 58   57, 82
  s. 77   340, 345, 346, 347, 348, 349
  s. 77(1)   349
  s. 77(8)   349
  s. 78   349
  s. 78(2)(b)   349

s. 79   350
s. 80   340, 345, 346, 347, 348
s. 84   348
s. 85   345, 346, 347
s. 95(1)(b)   346, 347, 348
s. 95(1)(c)   346, 347, 348
s. 180   70, 82
Courts and Legal Services Act 1990   31
s. 8   31
Crime and Disorder Act 1998   150
Criminal Justice Act 1925   161
s. 41   161
s. 41(1)   161
s. 41(2)(c)   161
Criminal Justice Act 1987   154
s. 4   154
s. 6   154
Criminal Justice Act 1988   155–9, 295
s. 159   155, 157, 158, 295
s. 159(1)   156
s. 159(1)(c)   159
Criminal Justice and Public Order
Act 1994   77
s. 4   77
s. 6   77
Criminal Procedure and Investigations
Act 1996   155

Data Protection Act 1984   104, 105
Data Protection Act 1998   xxxi–xxxii, 74–6,
89, 104–13, 122, 126–7, 212, 217,
221, 224–6, 289, 316
s. 3   89
s. 32   106, 112
s. 55   106, 113
Defamation Act 1952   13, 17, 24, 244,
289, 291
s. 1   244
s. 5   13
s. 6   17
s. 7   24
s. 10   244
Defamation Act 1996   3, 11, 21–5, 27, 29,
66–7, 244, 289, 291–2, 294
s. 1   11, 25, 67
s. 2   11, 24
s. 5   27
ss. 5–11   291

s. 6   291
ss. 8–11   29
s. 14   21
s. 15   21, 22, 23, 24
Domestic and Appellate Proceedings
(Restriction of Publicity) Act 1968   144
s. 2   144

Employment Tribunals Act 1996
162, 163, 164
s. 11(6)   163
s. 12   163

Family Law Act 1986   153
s. 68(1)   144
Freedom of Information Act 2000
105, 106, 122, 212–227
s. 4(1)   220
s. 5   220
s. 6   220
s. 21   224
s. 22   221
s. 23   224
s. 23(3)   224
s. 23(4)   224
s. 24   221
s. 26   221
s. 27   222
s. 27(3)   222
s. 28   222
s. 28(2)   222
s. 29   222
s. 30   222
s. 31   222
s. 32   224
s. 32(4)   224
s. 33   223
s. 34   225
s. 35   223, 225
s. 36   223, 225
s. 36(5)   223
s. 37   223
s. 38   223
s. 39   223
s. 40   224, 225
s. 42   224
s. 43   224
s. 50   227

s. 51	227
s. 52	227
s. 53	227
Human Rights Act 1998	xxxi–xxxiv, 3, 34, 89, 92, 94, 98, 101–3, 106, 114, 123–4, 127–8, 133, 138, 195, 200, 217, 221, 232, 234, 249, 269–85, 289, 305
s. 3(1)	xxxii, 123, 271
s. 4	271
s. 4(2)	274
s. 6	123, 124, 128
s. 6(1)	271, 272, 274
s. 6(2)(a)	271
s. 6(2)(b)	271
s. 6(3)	270
s. 6(3)(a)	274
s. 6(3)(c)	270
s. 6(5)	270
s. 7	272
s. 7(1)	272
s. 7(3)	272
s. 7(5)	273
s. 7(7)	272
s. 8	273
s. 8(1)	273
s. 8(2)	273
s. 8(3)	273
s. 8(4)	273
s. 9(3)	274
s. 10	271, 274
s. 12	89, 92, 102, 249, 274, 281, 289
s. 12(3)	102, 199
s. 12(4)	102, 281
s. 12(4)(a)(i)	92, 98
s. 12(4)(a)(ii)	101
s. 12(4)(b)	281
s. 22(4)	272
Indecent Displays (Controls) Act 1981	205, 209, 210
Interception of Communications Act 1985	118, 122
Judicial Proceedings (Regulation of Reports) Act 1926	147, 153–4
s. 1(1)(a)	153, 154
s. 1(1)(b)	144, 153, 154

Law of Libel Amendment Act 1888	23
s. 3	23
Libel Act 1843	38–9, 212
s. 4	39
s. 5	39
s. 6	38
Local Government Act 1972	212
Magistrates' Court Act 1980	143, 148–9
s. 4	148
s. 8	149
s. 8(1)	148
s. 8(2)(a)	149
s. 71(1)	143
s. 71(1A)	143
Matrimonial Causes Act 1973	144, 154
s. 22	144
s. 48	154
Mental Health Act 1959	137
Mental Health Act 1983	274
Newspaper and Libel Registration Act 1881	21
Obscene Publications Act 1959	77, 205, 206, 208, 209
s. 1	206, 207
s. 1(2)	208
s. 2(5)	208, 209
s. 3	209
s. 4	209
Obscene Publications Act 1964	205, 206, 208
Official Secrets Act 1911	189, 228–30, 238
s. 1	228, 229, 230
s. 1(c)	229
s. 2	228, 230
s. 3	229
Official Secrets Act 1920	135, 189
s. 6	189
Official Secrets Act 1989	89, 94, 116, 155, 228–39
ss. 1–6	231, 233, 238
s. 1	231, 233, 234, 237
s. 2	94, 228, 234, 257
s. 3	234, 235, 237
s. 4	231, 233, 234, 235, 236, 237
s. 5	231, 236, 237

s. 6   237, 238
s. 8   238
s. 8(4)   155

Parliamentary Commissioner Act 1967
                                             213, 219
Planning (Hazardous Substances)
   Act 1990   164
Planning (Listed Buildings and
   Conservation Areas) Act 1990   164
Police and Criminal Evidence Act 1984
                                    184, 189, 190–92
s. 8   184, 189, 190
s. 9   184, 189, 190
s. 13   191
s. 15   190
Protection from Harassment Act 1997   117
Public Interest Disclosure Act 1998   94
Public Order Act 1936   210
Public Order Act 1986   78, 205, 210, 211
s. 17   210
s. 18–23   210
s. 19(2)   210
Public Order Act 1994   77

Race Relations Act 1976   210
Regulation of Investigatory Powers
   Act 2000   xxxiv, 122, 127
Rehabilitation of Offenders Act 1974
                                         13, 14, 15
ss. 8, 9   14
Representation of the People Act 1983
                                         240, 243–5
ss. 72–76   244
s. 75   244
s. 93   245
s. 106   243, 244

Security Service Act 1989   236
Sexual Offences (Amendment) Act 1976
                                    149, 150, 151, 152
Sexual Offences (Amendment) Act 1992
                                    146–7, 149, 151–3
s. 1   147
s. 1(2)   146
s. 5(5)   153

Telecommunications Act 1984   262
Theft Act 1981   192
s. 26(i)   192
Trademarks Act 1994   72
Tribunals of Inquiry (Evidence) Act 1921 184

Wireless Telegraphy Act 1949   100, 118, 122
World Intellectual Property Organization
   Copyright Treaty 1996   63, 307

Youth Justice and Criminal Evidence Act
   1999   146–7, 153, 159
s. 44   146, 147, 159
s. 44(11)   159
s. 45   146, 147, 159
s. 45(4)   159
s. 45(5)   159
s. 46   147, 159
s. 46(9)(a)   159
s. 46(9)(b)   159

Scottish Law

Children and Young Persons (Scotland) Act
   1937   296
s. 46   296
Children (Scotland) Act 1995   296
s. 44   296
Criminal Procedure (Scotland) Act 1995   296
s. 47   296

Damages (Scotland) Act   292
s. 3   292

Prescription and Limitation (Scotland) Act
   1973   292
Regulation of Investigatory Powers
   (Scotland) Act 2000   289

Scotland Act 1998   291

United States Law

Anticybersquatting Consumer Protection
   Act 1999   315

Civil Rights Act 1964   322
Civil Rights Act 1991   322
Combating Terrorism Act 2001 xxxiv, 127, 317
Communications Decency Act 1996   312, 316
    s. 230   312
    s. 230(c)   312
    s. 230(e)   312
Copyright Act 1976   309, 310, 313

    s. 201(c)   309
Digital Millennium Copyright Act 1998
       313, 314

Federal Trademark Dilution Act 1995   315
Freedom of Information Act 1966   322, 323

USA Patriot Act 2001   xxxiv, 127, 319,320

Introduction

An understanding of the law is essential for anyone working in the media, whether as a journalist, editor or producer. Media lawyers must be aware of the legal principles that relate specifically to journalism and the broadcast media. It is virtually impossible to present the daily news without reference to events in the law courts or the rules of legal procedure, or to produce a television or radio programme without consideration of the laws of libel and copyright.

The law is not simply a series of rules arrived at indiscriminately. It is a sophisticated and complex system of rules and regulations devised over many years to meet certain social needs and to administer the relationships between individuals, and between individuals and the State. In England and Wales, unlike many other countries where the law originated with a single code or a set of codes, the law is founded on a mix of ancient custom and judge made law, known as the Common Law, and more recently Parliamentary legislation, known as statute.

The common law dates from the twelfth century, when the King's judges were entrusted with the task of setting up a system of laws that would apply throughout the country. The system was based on local customary rules and became the first form of national law. Over the years, the common law has become a body of legal principles and notions of public policy applied and developed by judges from one generation to the next. Over the last few decades, Parliament has rationalized and codified the common law through the enactment of statutes. However, what is passed as law by Parliament is not always as clear as it should be. The result is that statutory legislation also relies heavily on the judiciary for its interpretation and application. Every year there are 'test cases' aimed at setting the meaning and effect of recent legislation.

Since, in general, the law reflects the standards of society, it does (albeit sometimes slowly) move with the times. The three areas that have had the most impact on media law in recent years are new media, the introduction of the Human Rights Act 1998 and the development of new laws relating to privacy.

New media

In the 1990s, the media industry was revolutionized by what became known as 'multimedia' products and 'the information superhighway'. New media is extremely important to those working in the media. Almost all traditional forms of publishing and broadcast are now stored and transmitted in new media formats.

The rapidly changing world of new media presents the law with new challenges. Like most other countries in the world, the law of England and Wales has not kept pace with technological advances.

Introduction

Although Parliament has attempted to incorporate new media elements into recent legislation, the most notable example being the Data Protection Act 1998, it is more often the case that the Courts have incorporated the issues presented by new media into existing legal principles following disputes between individuals that have resulted in litigation. Nowhere has this been seen more than in the case of the Internet, where the existing laws of intellectual property and defamation have been extended by the Courts to encompass online issues. In 1997, the English courts began to use the law of trademarks and passing off in order to provide a remedy for those who have been subject to alleged infringement of a registered domain name or a recognized company or brand name used as a domain name (*Marks & Spencer and Others v One In A Million Ltd and Others (1997)*). In the case of *Godfrey v Demon Internet Ltd (2000)*, the Court ruled for the first time in England and Wales on the issue of Internet defamation in a case involving a defamatory posting to a newsgroup hosted by Demon, the Internet service provider.

However, the global nature of the Internet makes it extremely difficult for individual countries, including England and Wales, to enforce their domestic laws effectively. Countries throughout the world are being forced to move away from traditional notions of isolated and independent domestic legal systems towards a more international outlook. Although there is no international body or Court with the authority to create or interpret the law of the Internet, it comes as no surprise that the greatest influence on domestic new media law has been from European and international organizations. In 2002, the Government is required to give effect to the European Union's Copyright Directive (*2001/29/EC*) and the E-commerce Directive (*2000/31/EC*), which are aimed at ensuring all copyrighted works are adequately protected and at harmonizing electronic commerce throughout the European Union. The World Intellectual Property Organization, a specialized agency of the United Nations which administers international treaties relating to intellectual property protection, is affiliated to the Internet Corporation for Assigned Names and Numbers (ICANN), a non-profit organization based in the United States of America, which adjudicates on ICANN registered domain names such as .com, .net and .org and provides an international remedy for cases involving 'domain name grabbing'.

Moreover, domestic news is now global news. On 25 October 2001, the United States news network CNN won an appeal allowing the broadcast of the second phase of the inquiry into the murders by United Kingdom serial killer Dr Harold Shipman. The inquiry chairman, who had previously rejected an application by the BBC, allowed the appeal on the grounds that there was a 'public interest in seeing television reports of the proceedings'.

The global nature of communications means that it is becoming more important for those working in the media and media lawyers to understand the basic legal principles of other jurisdictions. For that reason, chapters have been included in this edition of the book which set out the basic legal principles of the two countries that interrelate most often with the law of England and Wales; Scotland and the United States of America. The USA is particularly important in the context of new media, as it is at the forefront of developing law and legislation in relation to the Internet.

The Human Rights Act 1998

The incorporation of the European Convention on Human Rights (the 'Convention') into English law by the Human Rights Act 1998 (HRA), which came into force on 2 October 2000, will undoubtedly have a major impact on the media in the future. Under Section 3(1) of the HRA 1998 domestic legislation must, as far as possible, be given effect in a way which is compatible with the Convention. Furthermore, a 'public authority' (although not a private individual) must not 'act incompatibly' with any Convention right.

The Article 6 right to a fair and public trial will impact on court-ordered reporting restrictions, such as the power to postpone the reporting of proceedings and the power to prevent the publication of the names of parties. The Article 10 right to freedom of expression is now the starting point for all cases involving restrictions on expression and will be of considerable importance in cases concerning defamation, breach of confidence, reporting restrictions, contempt of court, prior restraint and 'hate speech'.

The effect of the HRA has already been felt in the 12 months since it came into force. In the case of *Venables v News Group Newspapers Ltd (2001)*, the two notorious child murderers of James Bulger sought injunctions to prevent the publication of confidential information that might lead to their identification. The court felt that there was a 'strong and pressing social need' to maintain the confidentiality of the applicants and to protect their Convention rights. The court granted the injunctions in order to 'protect the applicants from serious and possibly irreparable harm'. The HRA may also put an end of the age of 'kiss and tell' stories. In 2001, a High Court judge granted a preliminary injunction against the *Sunday People* preventing publication of the accounts of two woman who had conducted affairs with an unnamed, married successful footballer (*A v B and C (2001)*). The judge, who had to balance the competing rights of freedom and expression and privacy, ruled that the publication of the material would amount to a breach of a duty of confidence between the footballer and the two women and granted the footballer's application for an injunction. The case is subject to appeal by the *Sunday People* and will have a significant bearing on whether this type of material, as well as less salacious investigative reporting, can be published in the future.

Privacy

The question of an 'express law of privacy' has long been a matter of debate in England. Unlike the law in other countries such as the USA, there is no 'tort of privacy' or statutory right to privacy. A person who claims his right to privacy has been infringed must bring an action for breach of confidence, trespass or defamation. Additional protection is provided by the criminal law and the laws of copyright and confidence in respect of interference with letters and communications, the power of the court to grant injunctions prohibiting or restricting publication of information in court cases, and the Data Protection Act 1998 which purports to enhance a person's right to privacy by safeguarding personal data more effectively.

The debate over a 'law of privacy' always seems to revolve around the activities of the media. Despite the lack of a written constitution in England and Wales, freedom of the press is regarded as the cornerstone of freedom of speech. However, the media are often accused of harassment, inaccurate reporting and intrusion into the lives of private individuals as well as 'celebrities' and the Royal Family. Over the past 40 years, five separate bills have been presented to Parliament aimed at introducing a statutory tort of privacy. All have been unsuccessful because of the difficulty of establishing an adequate definition of privacy. During the same period, various Government committees and Royal Commissions have considered the same question, the most recent being the Government Committee on Privacy and Related Matters chaired by David Calcutt QC which reported in 1990. Each recommended against the introduction of a statutory law of privacy on the basis of an unworkable definition of the tort and the undesirability of such a law, although the Calcutt Report did result in the establishment of the Press Complaints Committee.

The Human Rights Act 1998 establishes for the first time in English law an 'express' right to privacy by reason of the Article 8 right to respect for privacy. The courts must now recognize and determine the inevitable tension between the Article 8 right to privacy and the Article 10 right to freedom of expression in cases involving breach of Convention rights by public authorities. This tension will be of particular concern in cases involving figures in the public eye such as politicians and celebrities. Furthermore, although the Article 8 right relates only to action by public authorities and not private individuals, judicial interpretation of the Human Rights Act 1998 in the 12 months since its enactment seems to suggest that an express right to privacy relating to, and between, private individuals may be developed by the courts in the future. In the much publicized case of *Douglas v Hello! (2001)*, the actors Catherine Zeta-Jones and Michael Douglas signed a contract with *OK!* magazine for exclusive coverage of their wedding. However, rival magazine *Hello!* published photographs of the wedding three days before *OK!*. The Court of Appeal found that Zeta-Jones and Douglas had a 'powerfully arguable' case in respect of the infringement of their privacy based on the tort of confidence and Article 8 of the Convention. However, despite these major developments in the law, there is still no prospect of specific Parliamentary legislation creating a statutory tort of privacy.

Furthermore, the terrorist attacks of 11 September 2001 are likely to impact on the pace and direction of the development of any 'law of privacy'. The Anti-terrorism, Crime and Security Act 2001, which came into force on 20 December 2001, enables communication service providers to retain data (although not content) for reasons of national security or where it may be vital for criminal investigation, gives law enforcement authorities the right to demand passenger details from transport providers and gives financial authorities the power to freeze funds. Although the Government seems for the present time to have backed down on the issue of identity cards, it also proposes increasing the provisions of the Regulation of Investigatory Powers Act 2000 ('RIPA') which only came into force fully at the end of 2001. RIPA, already dubbed the 'e-snooping bill', allows the police and MI5 to collect Internet data without a warrant in certain circumstances. However, freedom of speech will not be further limited by a new offence of incitement to religious hatred, as this was rejected by the House of Lords in December 2001. Although the legislation has been subject to considerable criticism by the media, civil liberties groups and human rights lawyers, the Government insists that the measures are necessary and will not impinge upon the rights of ordinary subjects.

Moreover the Government, standing 'shoulder to shoulder' with the USA in the 'war on terror', will no doubt closely observe the effectiveness in the USA of the Combating Terrorism Act 2001 and the USA Patriot Act 2001. The Combating Terrorism Act 2001, passed by the Senate late at night only two days after the terrorist attack in such haste that Senator Patrick Leahy complained he only read the Bill half an hour before debate began, greatly extends the powers of surveillance by Federal and State governments including the monitoring of communications over the Internet and the installation of FBI Internet surveillance such as the infamous 'Carnivore' system. The USA Patriot Act 2001 allows law enforcement officials to seek court orders placing 'roving wiretaps' on individuals and to subpoena the addresses and times of email messages of those suspected of terrorism. Both Acts have been accused in the USA of trampling over privacy issues in favour of rushing through legislation in order to lessen domestic fears.

Layout of the Book

The book is divided into nine parts, covering the range of topics relevant to those working in the media and as media lawyers. Each part contains individual chapters dealing with distinct areas of the law. Each chapter begins with a short introduction which sets out the basic principles of the law covered in the chapter and makes reference to important concepts and principles contained in other chapters. Web sites mentioned in the body of each chapter are set out in the footnotes. The book also contains appendices: Appendix A sets out a glossary of legal terms, Appendix B the addresses, telephone numbers and web sites of professional bodies, and Appendix C specimen agreements, including interview agreements and moral rights waivers.

The law is stated as at 31 December 2001.

PART I
Protection of Reputation

1 Defamation

Marietta Cauchi

1.1 Introduction

The law of defamation protects the reputation of a person from defamatory statements made about him to a third party without lawful justification. The English common law places great value on the right of reputation. It is less concerned with freedom of expression. The result is that those in the media are in much the same position as other members of the public when it comes to defamatory statements, having only limited special protection.

The common law of defamation in England is based on case law codified by statute, most recently the Defamation Act 1996. The origins of the law of defamation date back as far as King Alfred the Great who, in the ninth century, decreed that slanderers should have their tongues cut out. Over the years the penalties imposed upon those who transgress this branch of the civil law have become financial rather than physical. The categories of defamation have continued to grow. However, until the incorporation of the European Convention on Human Rights into English law by the Human Rights Act 1998, the legal principles have remained virtually unchanged. The Article 10 European Convention on Human Rights right to freedom of expression is now the starting point in all cases involving restrictions on expression.

Of all the legal problems impinging upon the writer or broadcaster bringing news and information to the public it is defamation, specifically libel, which is the most common problem, as well as the most expensive. Any individual whose name has been blackened by a newspaper article or television programme will say that a libel case is a two-year nightmare with massive expense and no prospect of legal aid. The newspaper or television company will complain that libel actions are little more than lotteries in which claimants are unduly favoured by the court and damages are completely unpredictable.

1.2 General principles

1.2.1 What is defamation?

A statement is defamatory if it tends to lower the claimant in the estimation of right thinking members of society generally (*Sim v Stretch (1936)*).

In order to prove defamation, the claimant must show defamatory language by the defendant which:

- Identifies or refers to the claimant, and
- Is published to a third party.

The law presumes that the defamatory statement is false and that the claimant is of good reputation. The claimant is not required to prove any actual damage to reputation or other loss. The burden of establishing the truth of the statement or any other defence is on the defendant.

Defamation actions are heard by a judge and jury. In general, the judge determines issues of law and the jury determines issues of fact. Legal aid is not available in an action for defamation.

The real skill for writers and broadcasters and their editors or producers is determining when statements which may be construed as 'tending to lower the claimant in the estimation of right thinking members of society generally' can be published with a reasonable degree of safety. Consideration should be given to the following:

- Is the piece true?
- Can it be proved to be true?
- If not, is it covered by one of the other defences to defamation?
- Is the subject of the piece likely to sue?

1.2.2 Libel and slander

Defamatory language is placed into two categories. The more common and more serious is *libel*. Libel is defamation in writing or some other permanent form, such as a tape or video recording. Radio and television broadcasts and computer-generated transmissions are defined by statute as libel. *Slander* is spoken defamation or defamatory language in some other temporary form. Although actions against newspaper and television companies for slander are rare, the writer or broadcaster should always be conscious of the risk of making a slanderous statement – particularly the investigative journalist who is checking allegations of wrongdoing or confronting the wrongdoer in person. If the writer or broadcaster makes defamatory statements about the wrongdoer to or in the hearing of a third party, he is exposed to the risk of being sued for slander.

The distinction between libel and slander is relevant only to the issue of damages. Damage is presumed in cases of *libel*. In cases of *slander* the claimant has to prove actual loss, unless the allegation falls within one of four exceptions where damage is presumed:

1. An allegation that the claimant has committed a crime punishable by imprisonment
2. An allegation that the claimant is suffering from a contagious or infectious disease

3. An allegation that the claimant is an unchaste woman or is a woman who has committed adultery
4. An allegation that is likely to damage the claimant's business or profession.

1.2.3 Malicious falsehood

This is a related tort where a false statement does not damage the claimant's reputation but causes or is likely to cause the claimant financial loss. The claimant has to prove that:

- The statement is false
- It was published maliciously, and
- It caused financial loss or, in cases when the statement is written or reflects on the claimant's business or profession, it is likely to cause financial loss.

In practice, proceedings for malicious falsehood are considerably more difficult for a claimant than defamation. The burden is reversed from that of defamation actions. It is for the claimant to establish the falseness of the statement and the malice of the defendant. Actions for malicious falsehood are tried by a judge alone, and are eligible for legal aid.

1.2.4 Who may sue?

All living persons can sue for defamation. This includes children, bankrupts, criminals and those of unsound mind. There is no libel of the dead. Defamatory statements therefore may, and usually are, made with virtual impunity about those who have died. The only risk to the publisher in such circumstances is that the material published is so inflammatory it attracts a prosecution for criminal libel. If the claimant or defendant dies during the action, the action also dies.

In the case of criminals, writers or broadcasters often mistakenly think that the criminal has no reputation to lose and they can publish material about the criminal with impunity. As a general rule, this is not the case. For example, a man with a string of convictions for violence and dishonesty could succeed in a libel action if a newspaper or television programme wrongly accused him of sexual assault. However, there may be cases where a person's reputation in respect of one form of wrongdoing is so bad that one more allegation concerning similar behaviour would cause no damage even if it were untrue. For example, a celebrity may have such a poor reputation for drinking or drug taking that he is unlikely to gain anything from suing over one more story in a similar vein.

An incorporated body can sue if the defamatory statement refers to its business or trading reputation. It cannot suffer from hurt or injured feelings. However, care should be taken when writing in a derogatory fashion about a company, as an allegation of malpractice against a corporation may enable the individual officers of the corporation to sue. In 1993,

Anita and Gordon Roddick and their company Body Shop successfully sued Channel 4 over allegations in a programme questioning the Body Shop's stance against animal-free testing and the sales methods of their staff.

A political party cannot maintain an action for defamation of character, as it would be against public policy (*Goldsmith v Bhoyrul (1998)*). Central and local government institutions cannot sue for defamation in respect of their administrative and governmental functions, but the individual leaders of those bodies can sue if the allegation against the body points to the individual (*Derbyshire County Council v Times Newspapers Ltd (1993)*).

Where a defamatory statement is made about a group of people, the question of whether an individual member of that group can sue depends on the facts of each case. The main factor to be considered by the court is the size of the group and how closely the individuals in that group are associated with the statement. In *Riches v News Group Newspapers Ltd (1986)*, the *News of the World* reported a story concerning a gunman who was holding hostages to publicize his deranged belief that policemen at Banbury CID had raped and beaten his wife. Although the story did not name any individual officer, it identified the group from which the alleged rapist came. There were only 10 members of the Banbury CID. All 10 officers sued the *News of the World* and won.

1.2.5 Who may be sued?

Any person who causes or is responsible for the publication of a defamatory statement can be sued. This includes writers, broadcasters, editors, producers, publishers, programme makers, printers, distributors, newsagents and booksellers. Since each separate communication to a third party is a separate publication and therefore a separate libel, the number of people who may be sued over the same defamatory statement can be considerable.

1.2.6 What is defamatory language?

There is no single, comprehensive definition of defamatory language recognized by law. The determination of defamatory meaning is always an objective test, never a subjective test. This means that the court must give consideration to what the ordinary, reasonable person would think about the defamatory statement, not what the claimant actually thinks.

An allegation by the claimant that the defendant's statement 'tends to lower the claimant in the eyes of right thinking members of society generally' necessarily involves an element of moral blame (*Sim v Stretch (1936)*). Because the test is geared towards what 'right thinking members of society generally' consider to be defamatory language, the proper standard to be applied will adapt with the passage of time to reflect the change in society. A statement found by a jury to be defamatory 75 years ago may be considered perfectly acceptable today. Nowhere is this demonstrated better than in society's attitudes towards sexual matters. An allegation that an unmarried woman spent the night with her boyfriend in a hotel would have lowered her in the eyes of the average person in the 1920s, but would be unlikely to do so today.

Most of the categories of defamatory language are obvious. To suggest that a person is a thief, a fraudster or a cheat will always be defamatory. It is also defamatory to suggest a person is incompetent or unqualified in his trade or profession.

An allegation of criminal or immoral behaviour is usually defamatory, although it must be remembered that the attitude of the 'right thinking member of society' towards morality is likely to change with the passage of time. In 1959 the celebrated *Daily Mirror* columnist Cassandra (in reality the writer William Connor) wrote of the American pianist Liberace:

> He is the summit of sex, the pinnacle of Masculine, Feminine and Neuter. Everything that He, She and It can ever want . . .

The article went on to liken him to:

> . . . a . . . deadly, winking, sniggering, chromium-plated, scent-impregnated, luminous, quivering, giggling, fruit-flavoured, mincing, ice-covered heap of mother-love . . .

Liberace claimed the article suggested he was homosexual, and sued for libel. At the end of the trial the jury agreed with him and awarded the then substantial sum of £8000 in damages (*Liberace v Daily Mirror Newspapers Ltd (1959)*).

The issue of whether an allegation of homosexuality is defamatory was aired before a libel jury again in 1992. Jason Donovan, an unmarried Australian actor and singer with a huge following amongst British teenagers, sued a youth magazine called *TheFace* for suggesting that he was homosexual. Since Donovan had previously gone on record to say that he was not gay, he also sued the magazine for damages for the implicit suggestion that he was a hypocrite. The jury awarded £200 000 to Donovan, which caused an uproar amongst certain sections of society who protested that being thought of as gay is not something that can damage a person's reputation. Ironically, Donovan's reaction was to issue a statement that broadly agreed with this viewpoint. He waived the £200 000 damages and proclaimed that his primary motive in suing the newspaper was to clear his name of the slur of hypocrisy. A decade after the Donovan case the 'right thinking member of society generally' may not agree that it is defamatory to allege a person is homosexual.

It is not defamatory to say someone owes money, but it is defamatory to say that a person cannot or will not pay his debts (*Winstanley v Bampton (1943)*). It is not defamatory to criticize a person's service or product, but it is defamatory to say someone is unfit for his profession or is incompetent in his business. In practice, it may be difficult to distinguish between these points of view (*South Hetton v North Eastern News Association (1894)*).

In a demonstration of the importance modern society places on appearance, the case of *Berkoff v Burchill (1996)* held that calling someone 'horrendously ugly' was defamatory because it might expose that person to ridicule.

1.2.7 The construction and meaning of words

It has long been recognized that the strict rules of construction that may be appropriate for ascertaining the meaning of words in other areas of the law will not do for the purposes of libel. The objective approach is used when construing the meaning of the statement. The court must consider how the statement would be understood by the ordinary, reasonable person, not how it is understood by the defendant.

Where there are conflicting interpretations of the defamatory statement, the court must determine just one 'correct' meaning. Although the meaning intended by the defendant is irrelevant, an 'innocent' defendant can use the 'offer of amends' procedure (see paragraph 1.3.4 below).

It is recognized that a seemingly innocent statement can convey a defamatory meaning to those who have knowledge of certain facts or circumstances that are extraneous to the offending statement. The law of libel therefore recognizes two distinct types of meaning: the natural and ordinary meaning, and the meaning by innuendo.

Natural and ordinary meaning

The 'natural and ordinary meaning' includes both the literal meaning and any obvious inference that could be taken from the statement. It is a question of law to be determined by a judge whether the statement is capable of bearing a particular defamatory meaning. It is a question of fact to be decided by the jury what the ordinary, reasonable person would understand the statement to actually mean.

The ordinary, reasonable person is not unduly suspicious, but can read between the lines (*Lewis v Daily Telegraph (1964)*) and is entitled to assume that there is 'no smoke without fire'. He will be taken to have a reasonable knowledge of contemporary slang and to be aware that words such as 'rip-off' and 'tart' can have meanings that are defamatory today. He will be expected to consider the statement complained of in the context of the whole publication (*Charleston v News Group Newspapers Ltd (1995)*) rather than in isolation, and to attach particular significance to a story appearing under bold headlines on the front page of a newspaper. In the same way that the meaning actually intended by the defendant is irrelevant, the actual interpretation placed upon the statement by the person who reads it is also irrelevant. As a result readership surveys, evidence by actual recipients such as readers or viewers as to their understanding cannot be adduced by either the claimant or the defendant. It is the effect on the ordinary, reasonable person that is relevant.

Defamatory meaning can also be extracted from the manner and sense in which the statement is published. It follows that the publication of rumours and denials can be extremely dangerous. In 1982 the *Sunday People* carried a front-page story about footballer Justin Fashanu under the banner headline 'I am not gay'. The article revealed that rumours about Fashanu's sexuality had been circulating among his team mates. His denial when asked by the *People's* reporter did not legitimize publication of the rumour to millions of newspaper readers who had never heard of it before. The case was settled at the time by payment to Fashanu of substantial damages, although he admitted several years later that he was, in fact, gay.

When the *New Statesman* reported rumours in 1993 that were circulating around Westminster and Fleet Street that the Prime Minister, John Major, had enjoyed a 'secret affair' with a caterer called Claire Latimer, both Major and Latimer issued writs against the magazine publishers, printers and distributors. The magazine publisher asserted that it had not given any credence to the rumours, which it accepted were untrue, but the printers and distributors quickly accepted liability and paid Major and Latimer damages. As it turned out, Major and Latimer decided not to pursue their claim for damages against the magazine publishers.

However, each case depends on its facts, and the Court of Appeal has held that the repetition of rumours without checking can be justifiable in some circumstances (*Aspro Travel v Owners Abroad Group (1996)*).

Innuendo or implication

The law recognizes that in certain circumstances a statement will convey suggestions or imputations over and above their natural and ordinary meaning. This may be because a word or phrase has a technical or slang meaning or because of extrinsic facts known by some of the people to whom the story has been published. In circumstances where the statement has a defamatory meaning that is not obvious to all recipients, the claimant can allege innuendo. It is up to the claimant to prove that at least one recipient of the statement had the necessary special knowledge to understand the innuendo (*Fulham v Newcastle and Journal Ltd (1977)*). The court must decide how the ordinary, reasonable person with that special knowledge would understand the statement.

It is not difficult to think of examples of extraneous matters that convey derogatory imputations to some but not to others. In *Cassidy v Daily Mirror Newspapers Ltd (1929)* the newspaper published a photograph of Cassidy with a woman who it reported was Cassidy's fiancée. Cassidy was in fact married to another woman, although they lived apart. The defamatory implication of the report to whoever knew of the marriage was that Mrs Cassidy was not, as she purported to be, Cassidy's wife but rather his mistress. Mrs Cassidy sued and was awarded £500. In *Tolley v JS Fry & Sons Ltd (1931)* a famous amateur golfer appeared on an advertisement with a Fry's chocolate bar sticking out of his pocket. He had not given permission for his likeness to be used in that way. He sued for libel on the basis that there were a number of people who knew of his amateur status and would believe he was abusing this by becoming involved in commercial sponsorship in circumstances where the rules of amateur golf forbid the commercial endorsing of products.

1.2.8 Identification

The second element the claimant has to prove in an action for defamation is that the ordinary, reasonable person would understand that the defamatory statement referred to the claimant. The claimant does not need to be named in the piece, and can be identified by description, photograph or other characteristic information.

In most cases, claimants will have no difficulty in establishing this element of the tort of defamation, as they will have been named or pictured in the piece. However, in some cases the issue of identity is not so clear. In this type of case the question for the jury is objective. They must consider whether the ordinary, reasonable person would understand the defamatory material to refer to the claimant. A writer or broadcaster may omit the name of the wrongdoer from a piece but give broad hints as to who may be responsible in order to avoid the risk of being sued. This can be a dangerous practice. In *Hayward v Thompson (1982)* the claimant, Jack Hayward, argued that a reference to him in the *Sunday Telegraph* as 'a wealthy benefactor of the Liberal Party' combined with a subsequent report in the *Sunday Telegraph* one week later naming him specifically was enough to establish identification. The court agreed. The risk extends to identification in other publications. As a result, stopping short of identifying a wrongdoer can be problematic where another newspaper or programme carries the same story and publishes the name and picture of the wrongdoer.

Another regular pitfall is the innocent publication or transmission of an accurate piece followed by the discovery that an unknown third party with the same name claims to have been defamed. Such 'gold-diggers' have ample precedent in their favour. The intention of the defendant is irrelevant. What is important is the effect upon the reputation of the claimant (*Hulton v Jones (1910)*). In situations where confusion might arise, writers and broadcasters should take care to make the identification of their subject clear. The particular danger in reporting court cases of confusing the wrongdoer with innocent people is avoided by publishing ages, occupations and addresses.

Television producers should be careful about portraying innocent people on screen as the broadcaster utters a potentially defamatory statement. A London CID officer won £20 000 in libel damages because he happened to be walking out of a police station which was being filmed by a BBC crew for a programme on corruption in the London CID. Although the programme only referred to general allegations of corruption, the particular officer was clearly identifiable from the film.

1.2.9 Publication

A defamatory statement may be thought, written or spoken – even to the person who is defamed – but it does not become actionable until it is published to a third party because reputation exists entirely on the belief of other people about the claimant. Communication of the defamatory statement to the claimant only will not harm the claimant's reputation and is therefore not actionable.

Accordingly, a person may safely write a letter containing any amount of defamatory material about the addressee as long as it remains in an envelope while in transit and is only read by the addressee. The position is different if such a statement is made on a postcard or in an email sent in unencrypted form or in an insecure environment. In such cases the contents are presumed to be transmitted to others between dispatch and arrival. It is irrelevant that the defendant did not intend the defamatory statement to be communicated to any other person.

At the trial of a libel action the claimant must normally call evidence to show that publication of the statement has actually taken place. This is usually unnecessary in cases involving media defendants such as newspapers or television and radio programmes because the law presumes that the material has been published to other persons.

1.3 Defences

The law does not recognize the right to publicize falsehoods. Only the expression of truth is protected. However, freedom to voice an honest opinion is recognized by the court as being in the public interest. The court also recognizes that the free and proper administration of justice in the courtroom and in parliament is in the public interest.

There are seven main defences to libel, of which the first four are most commonly raised by the defendant:

1. Justification
2. Fair comment
3. Absolute privilege
4. Qualified privilege
5. Offer of amends under Section 2 of the Defamation Act 1996
6. Leave and licence
7. Innocent defamation under Section 1 of the Defamation Act 1996.

The burden of proof is on the defendant. It is important to realize that the filing of a defence to a defamation action is a step governed by the formal rules of legal pleading. Under those rules, a defendant is not permitted to plead any point unless there already exists evidence to support that point. Those who publish in the belief that the story is true without any supporting evidence are in danger of being left with no defence at all.

1.3.1 Justification

Justification protects the freedom to tell the truth. In order to raise the defence of justification successfully, the defendant must prove that the defamatory statement is true in both substance and fact, or is substantially true.

In cases where writers or broadcasters are sued over factual pieces, justification will often be the only plausible defence. In principle this should not be something that causes concern, as truth and accuracy are supposed to be bywords for the profession of journalism and broadcasting. In practice, success in raising the defence of justification is measured not by whether the piece is true but whether the defendant can prove that the piece is true. Because the law presumes that the defamatory statement is false, the defendant has the onerous task of overcoming this presumption by proving that the statement is true. A defendant who intends to raise justification should believe that the statement is true and should intend to prove its truth at trial if necessary. The defendant should also have reasonable evidence to support the plea of justification or reasonable grounds for supposing that sufficient evidence will be available at trial (*McDonalds v Steel (1995)*). On average, a libel action comes to trial between one to two years after proceedings have been issued. This significant lapse of time often means that memories have become hazy. Defendants' lawyers often find that some witnesses no longer wish to be involved or cannot be traced. It is vital to have clear and admissible evidence before publication. Notebooks containing rumour and hearsay are insufficient.

The defendant must adduce enough evidence to satisfy the jury on the balance of probabilities that the published statement is true. This means that it is more likely than not that the statement is true. It is a lower standard than the criminal standard of beyond reasonable doubt. In practice, however, where the published allegation is very serious the defendant's evidence will have to be convincing.

Meaning

The judge decides whether the statement complained of is capable of bearing the defamatory meaning pleaded by the claimant. This is a matter of law (*Mapp v News Group Newspapers Ltd (1997)*). The meaning that the statement bears in fact and the issue of whether the defendant has successfully proved the statement to be true in substance or fact or substantially true is a matter for the jury.

It is not enough for the defendant to plead that he believed a defamatory statement to be true because he was repeating rumours elsewhere. The 'rule against repetition' means that it is necessary for the defendant to prove that the subject matter of the rumour itself was true (*Stern v Piper (1996)*).

Substantial justification

In order to succeed in the defence of justification, it is not necessary for the defendant to prove every minor detail of fact, although he must meet the claimant's challenge head on and establish as true those allegations that effectively cause the defamation. This crucial element has been described as the 'sting' of the libel.

The defendant must prove that the words used 'were true in substance and in fact' (*Sutherland v Stopes (1925), Hoare v Jessop (1965)*). For example, if the allegation is that the claimant robbed the National Westminster bank in Chelsea at 11 am last Thursday, the defendant's justification plea will not fail if it is established that the claimant did rob the bank but in fact did so at 3.30 pm last Monday. The 'sting' of the libel is the suggestion that the claimant committed the robbery of the bank. The date and time add nothing to the defamatory content of the published statement.

Partial justification

Where a publication alleges a whole series of allegations against a person, the defendant may have a complete defence under Section 5 of the Defamation Act 1952 even if the defendant cannot prove the truth of all the allegations. In such cases the defendant is entitled to plead partial justification. Under Section 5, the defence will succeed if the unjustifiable matters 'do not materially injure the claimant's reputation having regard to the truth of the remaining matters'. For example, if a television documentary on the music industry portrays a particular disc jockey as being a regular user of narcotic drugs and a heavy drinker and the defendant is able to prove the first allegation but not the second, Section 5 of the Defamation Act 1952 is likely to apply since the taking of narcotics is illegal and considered to be a greater vice than the consumption of alcohol. However, if the unjustifiable allegations have libellous meanings of their own the defendant is likely to have to pay damages to the claimant in respect of those allegations.

A claimant can decide to sue in respect of only some of the allegations made against him in a series of allegations. If the claimant does so, the defendant is unable to justify the other defamatory statements that are not the subject of proceedings in order to mitigate damages or to prejudice the jury against the claimant. However, the defendant is entitled to rely on the statement that is the subject of the proceedings in the context of the publication as a whole as the basis of the plea of justification (*Polly Peck v Trelford (1986)*).

If the defendant wishes to plead that the published statement bears a lesser defamatory meaning than that pleaded by the claimant, the defendant must set out clearly in the defence the defamatory meaning he seeks to justify (*Prager v Times Newspapers (1988); Lucas-Box v News Group Ltd (1986)*).

Aggravation

One of the major concerns a defendant frequently has to face when pleading justification is that the plea itself exacerbates the damages. A claimant is perfectly entitled to argue that the defendant not only published defamatory material and refused to apologize, but also persisted in the damaging and libellous allegations right up to the moment the jury delivered its verdict. In the event that the jury does not accept the plea of justification, the very fact that the defendant chose to enter such a defence can operate as an aggravation of the original libel and become a reason to award a greater amount in damages than would otherwise be called for.

Apart from the limited protection afforded by the Rehabilitation of Offenders Act 1974, there is nothing to stop a defendant relying on previous incidents from someone's past, so long as they are true, to support the defence. In general, the media are free to drag up and publicize any unsavoury incident, however old, from a person's distant past. However, relying on fairly old incidents to support an allegation of present misbehaviour will frequently fail. For example, to call someone a thief on the basis that the person committed minor theft several years ago is actionable as a libel unless the defendant can prove that the person still has dishonest tendencies.

On the other hand, relevant incidents that have occurred after the offending publication can also be relied upon to support the generality of the defamatory allegation and are likely to carry more weight and less likely to backfire than minor misdemeanours from the claimant's distant past. In reality, there is nothing about a person's private life that cannot be published with virtual impunity as long as it is true.

Criminal convictions

The existence of criminal convictions on a claimant's record frequently appears as the cornerstone to the 'particulars' that must be pleaded in support of a defence of justification. Allegations of criminality, for example dishonesty, drug taking or violence, are among the commonest categories of libellous statement.

There was a time when the fact that a person had been convicted and sentenced for a crime was not, for libel purposes, conclusive proof of his guilt. In 1964 Alfred Hinds sued for libel over a *Sunday* newspaper story headed 'They Called Me the Iron Man'. It was the story of Detective Superintendent Herbert Sparks, who, 11 years earlier, had given evidence that led to Hinds' conviction and 10-year sentence for robbery. The newspaper reported Sparks' assertion that Hinds was guilty as charged. The criminal trial that led to the conviction lasted for two days. The subsequent libel action took 26 days to go over precisely the same issue and produced the opposite result. In the event, the jury awarded the claimant £1300.

As a result of Section 13 of the Civil Evidence Act 1968, criminals can no longer secure what amounts to a retrial by bringing a libel action, and the media can refer to convictions without having to worry about proving they are correct. However, by reason of the Rehabilitation of Offenders Act 1974 the media does not have uninhibited reference to previous convictions. Although this Act concerns only the narrow area of old convictions, it represents a significant departure from one of the basic principles of libel law that truth is a complete defence.

In essence, Section 8 of the Rehabilitation of Offenders Act states that where the publication of a 'spent' conviction is 'made with malice', a defendant to libel proceedings shall not be entitled to reply on a plea of justification. In other words, where malice is proved the claimant's crimes will be treated for the purposes of his libel action as if they had never occurred. While there may be good logical and moral reasons for why the past sins of a reformed criminal should not be allowed to wreck his rehabilitation, considerable mental gymnastics are called for on the part of the judge and jury, who must regard information that is true as untrue.

Table 1.1 Rehabilitation periods applicable to the commonest forms of sentence passed by the criminal courts

Sentence	Rehabilitation period
A sentence of imprisonment for a term exceeding 6 months but not exceeding 30 months	10 years
A sentence of imprisonment not exceeding 6 months	7 years
(In each of the above cases the period is cut by half if the offender is under 17 years old)	
A sentence of borstal training	7 years
An order for detention in a detention centre	3 years
A conditional discharge, bind-over or probation order	Either 12 months from conviction or upon the expiry of the discharge, bind-over or probation period, whichever is the longer
An absolute discharge	6 months
Any disqualification, disability or prohibition	To the date upon which the disqualification, disability or prohibition ceases to have effect

Sentences of imprisonment for life or for more than 30 months are never spent.

The Rehabilitation of Offenders Act provides that convictions may become 'spent' after a period of rehabilitation. The length of these periods depends upon the sentence passed on conviction. Once they have elapsed, the criminal becomes a 'rehabilitated person'. This means that the person must be treated as if he has never been charged, convicted or sentenced for a crime.

While the media are still free, provided they are not motivated by malice, to publish spent convictions, by and large they tend to honour the spirit of the Rehabilitation of Offenders Act. In practice, writers and broadcasters are conscious of the provisions of this Act and avoid publicizing the long-past convictions of rehabilitated persons.

1.3.2 Fair comment

Fair comment allows a person to publish a statement of opinion or comment on a matter of public interest provided it is done without malice. It protects the freedom to voice an honest opinion.

In order to raise the defence of fair comment:

- The comment must be on a matter of public interest
- The comment must be recognizable as comment
- The comment must be based upon facts that are true or privileged
- The comment must be fair as judged objectively, and
- The person making the comment must not be motivated by malice.

Public interest

It is for the defendant to prove that the matter upon which he passed comment is one of public interest. The judge, rather than the jury, rules on this question if it is at issue. There is a difference between matters that the public find interesting and matters of public interest. The court has adopted a generous approach in defining the legitimate areas of public interest. In the words of Lord Denning in *London Artists Ltd v Littler (1969)*:

> Whenever a matter is such as to affect people at large, so that they may be legitimately interested in, or concerned at, what is going on, or what may happen to them or others; then it is a matter of public interest on which everyone is entitled to make fair comment.

National and local government and politics, all forms of art, literature and entertainment, and court cases are all matters of public interest. So too are the individuals who appear in those various arenas. Attacks on the individuals involved may be the subject of valid comment so long as they are directed at the work or performance rather than being personal attacks.

Anyone seeking public attention, for example by protesting or writing open letters to newspapers, is a valid subject for comment, as is the conduct of those whose activities affect a significant number of other people, for example employers, charities, managers and directors of companies – and the media.

The comment must be comment

The defence of fair comment undoubtedly gives critics and public commentators a wide licence to write or say whatever they think about matters that are in the public eye:

> A critic is entitled to dip his pen in gall for the purpose of legitimate criticism; and no-one need be mealy-mouthed in denouncing what he regards as twaddle, daub or discord.
>
> *(Gardiner v Fairfax (1942))*

However, critics are not entitled to make derogatory statements in the guise of criticism. If the court deems that what has been said is a factual statement rather than an expression of opinion, fair comment cannot protect the defendant. In 1985 the actress Charlotte Cornwell sued the *Sunday People* and its television critic Nina Myskow over an article in which Myskow reported that Cornwell, 'can't act, she can't sing and she has the sort of stage presence that jams lavatories'. Myskow also candidly remarked of Cornwell, 'her bum's too big'. The defendant argued that the statements were robust comment on the actress's performance rather than assertions of fact. The jury disagreed and awarded Cornwell £10 000 in damages. The defendant successfully appealed the verdict on other points of law, but a second jury awarded Cornwell £11 500. However, it was a classic pyrrhic victory. Cornwell's pride was restored, but she was left with a huge costs bill for the first trial and appeal. Reasonable estimates put her at about £50 000 out of pocket as a result of the litigation.

It can be difficult to distinguish comment from fact disguised as comment. In order to be fair comment, the comment must not be so mixed up with facts that the recipient cannot distinguish between what is a report and what is comment (*Hunt v Star Newspaper (1908)*). Using introductory statements such as 'in my opinion' or 'it is my view that' will help identify the statement as comment, but will not necessarily be conclusive. If there is any doubt, the judge will rule on whether the statement is reasonably capable of being comment and the jury will make the decision as to whether it actually is (*Aga Khan v Times Publishing Co (1924)*).

Based upon facts that are true or privileged

The comment must have an adequate factual basis. The facts must be stated sufficiently clearly in order to enable the recipient to consider those facts. The court takes the view that unless this is done the recipient cannot know that the comment is well founded or even that it is comment rather than an assertion of fact.

In *Kemsley v Foot (1952)* Michael Foot wrote a piece in the *Tribune* newspaper under the headline 'Lower than Kemsley'. In the piece, Foot savagely criticized an article published in the *Evening Standard* the previous week as 'the foulest piece of journalism perpetrated in this country for many a long year'. Kemsley was a well known newspaper proprietor, but in fact had no connection with the *Evening Standard*. Kemsley claimed that the headline suggested his name was a byword for dishonest journalism. However, the House of Lords ruled that the headline was a statement of opinion rather than one of fact, and that the factual basis for this, being the existence and conduct of Kemsley's newspapers, was sufficiently indicated.

If the stated facts upon which the defendant has based the comment are false, those facts must have been published on a previous occasion that was privileged for the law to recognize the piece as fair comment. However, where a piece has set out a number of facts upon which comment is made, some of which are true and some of which are false, the defendant may be able to rely on Section 6 of the Defamation Act 1952 as a defence if the expression of opinion is fair comment having regard to facts that the defendant can prove.

Unlike justification, the defendant may only rely on existing facts in support of his contention, not matters that occur after the publication (*Cohen v Daily Telegraph Ltd (1968)*).

What is fair?

The test of what is fair is an objective one. It does not require the jury to ask themselves whether they agree with the comment; instead, they must ask themselves whether any fair-minded person, however prejudiced or exaggerated in his views, could have made the comment having knowledge of the proved facts. The emphasis is therefore on honesty rather than fairness:

> . . . the observations of an honest man on a matter of public interest may be fairly regarded as comment, so as to attract the defence, even though the essence of his comment was grossly unfair.
>
> (*Telnikoff v Matusevitch (1992)*)

17

It does not matter that the comment was exaggerated or based upon the general prejudices of the writer or broadcaster. It will not even matter if the writer or broadcaster is an unfair and unreasonable person. As long as the opinion expressed is not such that no honest person could have made such a comment, and is not motivated by malice, fair comment will operate as a defence. In 1995, a wealthy Tory from Kent, Mrs Pinder-White, sued Jonathan Aitken for describing her and her husband in a piece in a local newspaper as 'dreadful enough' to play JR and Sue-Ellen Ewing in the TV soap *Dallas*. Pinder-White alleged that she was effectively being compared with a high-class prostitute who was an alcoholic, and called the article 'a dreadful character assassination'. Aitken argued that the criticism contained elements of irony and parody and was not meant to be taken seriously. Pinder-White was cross-examined about the 10 Rolls-Royces owned during their marriage by her and her husband, and was alleged to have travelled in a white one at election time. The jury decided the criticism was harsh, but that it came within the bounds of fair comment.

The view expressed must be honest, fairly called criticism, and relevant to the facts (*McQuire v Western Morning News Co (1903)*). It follows that unless facts exist that raise the question of a man's moral character, a personal attack on that man's character will not be relevant (*Campbell v Spottiswoode (1863)*). A personal attack may form part of fair comment, but only if it is a reasonable inference to draw from the facts (*Harris v Lubbock (1971)*).

Malice

Although the defendant may set up a plea of fair comment, the defence will be defeated if it is shown that the defendant was motivated by malice. Malice is an important concept in the law of defamation. The meaning attributed to malice in the legal context is wider than that given to the word in popular usage. Whilst it includes what most people who understand to constitute malice, being spite and ill will, it also encompasses a dishonest or improper motive, such as personal advantage or gain, provided it is the dominant motive for the publication. The burden of proof is on the *claimant* to show that the defendant did not believe what he published was true, or was reckless as to its truth. If the improper motive is established as the dominant reason for the publication, the fact that the opinion was honestly held will not save the defence. On the other hand, if the defendant can show that the statement complained of has a meaning that was intended to be honest and without malice, the defendant may rely on the defence (*Loveless v Earl (1999)*).

The leading case on malice is *Horrocks v Lowe (1975)*, which involved a Labour local authority councillor who delivered a stinging rebuke against one of this Tory rivals at a council meeting, a forum in which speakers would normally be entitled to qualified privilege against libel suits. The issue was fought all the way to the House of Lords on whether qualified privilege was defeated by malice. The court ruled in favour of the defendant, and laid down the following important principles on the question of malice:

1. In situations where fair comment, qualified privilege or justification in relation to spent convictions would normally apply and an allegation of malice is made, the motive with which the defendant made the defamatory statement is crucial. He will be

entitled to the protection of his defence 'unless some other dominant and improper motive on his part is proved'.

2. 'If it is proved that he did not believe that what he published was true this is generally conclusive evidence of express malice'. The same applies if the defendant published the statement recklessly, in other words 'without considering or caring whether it be true or not'.

3. Even where there is honest belief in the truth of what was published (or, in respect of fair comment, an honest expression of opinion) the defendant will still lose the protection of the defence if it is proved that he misused the situation for some improper purpose, for example to give vent to personal spite or for the attainment of some personal advantage. The improper motive must be the dominant reason for the publication. Where the defendant believed in what he was saying or writing judges and juries should be slow to deprive him of the protection to which he would normally be entitled. Thus, although the Labour councillor was clearly prejudiced and antagonistic towards his Tory rival, his honest belief in what he was saying sustained the defence.

The court held in *Horrocks v Lowe* that 'the motive with which a person published defamatory matter can only be inferred from what he did, or said, or knew'. In order to prove malice, claimants usually rely on the following to substantiate their allegation:

- *Style, manner and prominence of publication*: with media publications the prominence and choice of headline can be taken as an indication of malice. A comparatively trivial matter blown up into a front page or top story or set under screaming banner headlines could suggest an improper motive. The strength of language used might also, in extreme cases, be evidence that the defendant was malicious.

- *Personal grudges or ill will between the parties*: claimants who allege malice can, in support of their plea, adduce as evidence any history of ill feeling between the parties. Anything that might indicate that the defamatory publication was an act of revenge or part of a vindictive campaign is strong evidence of malice. In *Horrocks v Lowe*, the claimant predictably made much of the defendant's political antagonism.

- *Refusal to retract or apologize*: the refusal by the defendant to correct and apologize for the offending publication can be used against him as evidence of malice. Logically, this should only apply in cases where the defendant persisted in his refusal to retract after he was clearly shown to be in the wrong. After all, refusing to apologize can just as properly be interpreted as a continuing honest belief in what was originally published.

Liability for the malice of others

Although the law makes an employer liable for the malice of his employees, fortunately for the media it does not generally make the publisher responsible for the malice of independent third parties. Thus, newspapers and television broadcasters may be answerable for the malicious motives of their own reporters but they will not be infected by those of other people – for example, interviewees or letter writers who appear genuine but are in fact vindictive.

The legal principle governing such situations was expounded by Lord Denning in *Egger v Viscount Chelmsford (1965)*, which involved an allegation of malice against the secretary and 10 members of the Kennel Club who had written a letter that was critical of the claimant. The court held that although the letter was jointly published by all defendants, the malice of some of them did not infect the others. Lord Denning said:

> If the claimant relies on malice to aggravate damages, or to rebut a defence of qualified privilege, or to cause a comment, otherwise fair, to become unfair, then he must prove malice against each person whom he charges with it. A defendant is only affected by express malice if he, himself, was actuated by it; or if his servant or agent concerned in the publication was actuated by malice in the course of his employment.

1.3.3 Privilege

The third category of defence upon which the media relies regularly is privilege. This comes in two forms: absolute and qualified. Both are the result of public policy considerations that recognize that statements and publications made on certain occasions should have immunity from civil proceedings even if they are untrue and damaging.

Absolute privilege

Where absolute privilege applies, no action for defamation may succeed, irrespective of the honesty or motive of the writer or broadcaster. It is the strongest defence available to libel defendants. Where it is applicable it will succeed, no matter how false and defamatory the statement and no matter how malicious the writer or broadcaster. The occasions of absolute privilege are few in number and narrowly defined. The categories most likely to affect the media are:

- Statements made in, or as part of, the course of parliamentary proceedings
- Statements made in the course of judicial proceedings
- Fair, accurate and contemporaneous reports of judicial proceedings.

Other areas of absolute privilege include confidential communications between lawyers and their clients, official reports published by order of either Houses of Parliament, and communications between officers of state in the course of their duty.

Parliamentary statements

Defamatory statements made inside the Houses of Parliament are absolutely privileged. This means that on numerous occasions MPs have used the absolute privilege afforded to them to make allegations that, if uttered in public outside the chamber of the House of Commons, would probably see them on the receiving end of an action for defamation. However, the media should take care when reporting such accusations. If the statement is repeated outside the Houses of Parliament, it only attracts qualified privilege. If a defendant in defamation proceedings is unfairly prejudiced by his inability to challenge statements made in Parliament because of the privilege, the action can be stayed. A Member of Parliament may waive the privilege for the purposes of defamation proceedings (*Hamilton v Al-Fayed (1999)*).

Statements made in the course of judicial proceedings

This covers statements made by witnesses, lawyers and judges, and extends to all documents produced for or during court proceedings or other tribunals that exercise judicial functions such as industrial and employment tribunals. The privilege extends to witness statements, court documents, any statement made as part of the process of investigating crime, and complaints and statements supplied to the Securities Association in its function as regulator of financial services (*Mahon v Rahn (2000)*). It does not, however, extend to fabricated evidence (*Darker v Chief Constable of the West Midlands Police (2000)*).

As the defence only applies to proceedings held in open court, it is not available to those held 'in camera' – in other words, in closed court. The privilege covers court proceedings in the United Kingdom, the European Court of Justice, the European Court of Human Rights, and any international criminal court established by agreement to which the United Kingdom is a party.

Fair, accurate and contemporaneous reports of judicial proceedings

Under Section 14 of the Defamation Act 1996, these need not be verbatim. However, they must be well balanced and materially accurate. More rather than less particulars are desirable, especially in the case of identification. In *Newstead v Express Newspapers (1940)* the newspaper report referred to 'Harold Newstead, a Camberwell man' reporting a conviction for bigamy. Failure on the part of the newspaper to specify the age, address and occupation of the felon enabled another man of the same name living in Camberwell successfully to sue for libel.

If the reporting of court proceedings is banned by court order under the Contempt of Court Act 1981, the requirement that the report be contemporaneous will be met if subsequent reports are published as soon as practicable after expiry of the order.

Court reports that are not published contemporaneously are nevertheless protected by qualified privilege. By virtue of the Newspaper and Libel Registration Act 1881, free newspapers and monthly magazines were also afforded only qualified privilege. However, the distinction is now irrelevant for reports published after 1 April 1999 by reason of Section 15 of the Defamation Act 1996.

Qualified privilege

Qualified privilege is capable of covering a wide variety of statements and communications. Certain occasions to which it attaches are defined with reasonable particularity. Others rely simply on the existence of some duty or interest in the making of a statement that, provided he is acting honestly, will protect the maker against an action for defamation, even if the statement is inaccurate and defamatory. The defence has been developed over the years to encourage and protect open and honest communications both of a public and private nature that are recognized as being 'in the general interest of society' (*Whiteley v Adams (1863)*).

Qualified privilege will arise where a person whose character or conduct has been attacked is entitled to answer that attack. Defamatory statements made by the claimant about the defendant will be privileged, provided that they are published in good faith and are fairly relevant to the accusations made. The privilege extends to the person's agent, for example his solicitor (*Regan v Taylor (2000)*).

What distinguishes qualified privilege from absolute privilege is that the defence fails if the claimant can prove that the defendant was motivated by malice. Unlike those situations where the privilege is absolute, a person who abuses an occasion of qualified privilege will be liable to pay the normal penalty for defamation. The defendant has the burden of establishing the facts and circumstances necessary to create the privilege (*Watts v Times Newspapers (1996)*).

The categories to which qualified privilege will apply are:

- Statements made where there is a moral, legal or social duty or interest in communicating the relevant information
- Fair and accurate reports of parliamentary proceedings and extracts from parliamentary papers
- Fair and accurate reports of judicial proceedings whenever and however made
- Statements made on those occasions specified in Section 15 of the Defamation Act 1996.

Statements made from a moral, social or legal duty

Over the years the courts have developed the defence to protect the many instances in everyday commercial, public and private life where information is passed on either from a sense of duty or in protection of some valid interest of the informant. In order to merit protection, the duty or interest must be shared between the publisher and the recipient of the statement. In order words, the court must recognize that the publisher was acting properly in passing on the information and that the recipient was the valid person to receive it. Examples of such communications include character references by ex-employers, the reporting of suspected crimes to the police, complaints about those with public authority or responsibility, and credit assessments provided by banks. If, in circumstances such as these, damaging statements are made that turn out to be inaccurate the publisher will not be liable provided he has not acted from malice.

In cases of mass publication, the material must concern a matter of public interest. A privileged occasion will exist if:

> ... the public is entitled to know the particular information. That is, if it was the journalist's social or moral duty to communicate it and the interest of the particular public to receive it. This is determined in the light of all the circumstances of the publication.

(GKR Karate (UK) Ltd v Yorkshire Post Newspaper (2000))

In such circumstances, when considering whether the defence of qualified privilege is applicable the court must take into account the circumstances of publication, including the source, status and nature of the material as well as the seriousness of the allegation, the steps taken to verify the information (including any approach to the claimant), and the urgency of the matter. There is no general qualified privilege in the mass publication of political information (*Reynolds v Times Newspapers Ltd (1999)*).

Like the defence of fair comment, but unlike the defence of justification, a defendant who raises qualified privilege may not rely on matters occurring after publication (*Loutchansky v Times Newspapers Ltd (2001)*).

This category of qualified privilege has been developed in recent years becoming increasingly available to mass publication in the media. In *Loutchansky v Times Newspapers Ltd & Ors (No 2) (2001)* the Court of Appeal said that the single test the court has to ask itself was whether the 'duty-interest' question had been satisfied so that qualified privilege attached and if it did this pre-empted a finding of malice.

The interest is that of the public in a modern democracy in free expression and, more particularly, in the promotion of a free and vigorous press to keep the public informed. The corresponding duty on the journalist (and equally his editor) is to play his proper role in discharging that function. His task is to behave as a responsible journalist and in determining whether this standard is reached the court will consider the ten (inexhastive) factors set out in Reynolds including urgency of matter, reliability of source and attempts to corroborate.

Unless the publisher is acting responsibly privilege cannot arise. That is not the case with regard to the more conventional situations in which qualified privilege arises. A person given a reference or reporting a crime need not act responsibly: his communication will be privileged subject only to relevance and malice.

Fair and accurate parliamentary reports

Providing the simple requirements of fairness and accuracy are satisfied, the media is given a good deal of latitude in the reporting of Parliament, safe from the threat of libel lawyers. As long as the reporting itself is accurate and honest, the publisher will not be liable if the original statement that is the subject of the report is incorrect.

Fair and accurate court reports

Section 15 of the Defamation Act 1996 confers a statutory privilege on a wide range of reports. Under the previous law this statutory privilege was confined to publication in newspapers or broadcasts, but the relevant provision, Section 3 of the Law of Libel Amendment Act 1888, is repealed by the 1996 Act. The 1996 Act applies to any publication – for example in a book, periodical, in an Internet message or even on a placard – and oral statements made on radio or in conversation. Such reports do, of course, still need to be fair and accurate reports of the proceedings, and the publisher should be free of malice.

The Defamation Act (1996) creates two categories of statutory protection. Statements that come under Part I are privileged without explanation or contraction. Those under Part II will not be entitled to the protection of the defence if the claimant shows that the defendant was requested by him to publish in a suitable manner a reasonable letter or statement by way of explanation or contradiction and the defendant refused or neglected to do so. Statutory protection is lost under Section 15 if the publication is shown to be with malice.

The protection of qualified privilege may be lost if the publication is misleading in light of subsequent developments, as this may not be in the public interest or may be evidence of malice (*Tsikata v Newspaper Publishing (1997)*).

The reports, copies or extracts must be fair and accurate. Like absolute privilege, they can be summaries and need not be verbatim (*Tsikata v Newspaper Publishing (1997)*). A few slight inaccuracies will not be fatal (*Kavanagh v NT News Services (1999)*). However, unlike absolute privilege there is no requirement that they be contemporaneous.

A press conference is a public meeting. To report the proceedings of such meeting is protected by statutory qualified privilege (*McCarten Turkington Breen v Times Newspapers Ltd (2000)*).

Qualified privilege attaches to defamatory documents prepared as part of a criminal investigation and cannot be used to form the basis of a defamation action (*Taylor v Director of the Serious Fraud Squad (1999)*).

The previous law (by reason of Section 7 of the Defamation Act 1952) restricted the statutory privilege to reports published in newspapers or broadcasts by radio or television. There is no such restriction in the Defamation Act 1996. The privilege applies to any publication, including oral statements, books and the Internet.

1.3.4 Offer to make amends under Section 2 of the Defamation Act 1996

Section 2 Defamation Act 1996 came into force on 28 February 2000. It provides an alternative defence to a defendant who has made an innocent mistake and does not wish to rely on a defence of justification, fair comment or qualified privilege.

An offer to make amends must be made before a defence is served. It must be in writing. The offer may be in relation to the statement generally, or in relation to a specific defamatory meaning that the person making the offer accepts is conveyed by the statement, referred to as a 'qualified offer'. A qualified offer to make amends must set out the defamatory meaning in respect of which it is made.

An offer under Section 2 is an offer to make and publish a suitable correction and apology, and to pay any compensation and costs, the amount of which may be agreed between the claimant and the defendant or, in default of agreement, determined by a judge.

If the claimant accepts the offer to make amends, his defamation action comes to an end. However, he can enforce the terms of the offer against the defendant. If the claimant rejects the offer the defendant can rely on the terms of the offer as a defence, but in such circumstances he is precluded from relying on any other defence. The defendant can rely on the offer in mitigation of damages whether or not it he relied on it as a defence.

1.3.5 Leave and licence

As one would logically expect, if a person consents to the publication of certain statements he is not then entitled to sue for libel because of the publication.

The evidence of consent must be clear and unequivocal. Whatever authorization the claimant is said to have given should be seen to refer to the publication of the defamatory matter. For example, if someone is approached by a reporter and asked about a particular defamatory statement concerning himself he will not, by indignantly denying it, be taken to have authorized the publication of the slur in the form of the denial. Similarly, if during the course of an acrimonious conversation one person challenges another to repeat what he has said in front of witnesses, this will rarely amount to consent for the publication of the slander.

The situation where the defence is most likely to arise is where the claimant has sold his story to a newspaper. The publisher would be entitled to rely on the defence of consent in relation to defamatory statements that had come from the claimant's own mouth.

1.3.6 Innocent dissemination under Section 1 of the Defamation Act 1996

Proceedings for defamation may be commenced against the original publisher of the offending statement and against anyone who publishes it thereafter. However, the potentially disastrous effects of such wide liability are mitigated by the defence of innocent dissemination. Section 1 of the Defamation Act 1996 provides a defence to a distributor who can show that:

- He did not know, and had no reason to believe, that what he did caused or contributed to the publication of a defamatory statement, and
- He took all reasonable care in relation to the publication complained of.

The defence typically applies to those with secondary publication responsibility, such as printers, distributors and retailers or live broadcasters, who can show they had no editorial control over the primary publisher and no knowledge of the offending material.

The statutory defence supersedes the common law defence of innocent dissemination, although it does not abolish the common law defence for distributors and retailers. Distributors and retailers are involved solely in the printing, producing, distributing and selling of publications that contain the defamatory statement.

The common law defence requires the defendant to show he was unaware that the publication contained a libel, defined as an *indefensible* defamatory statement. The statutory defence requires the defendant to show he was ignorant of the defamatory statement, in other words a statement capable of a defamatory meaning that may not be libellous because it may be subject to, or *defensible*, on the grounds of justification or another defence. This may be an inadvertent narrowing of the defence.

1.4 Procedure

1.4.1 Jurisdiction

English courts have jurisdiction whenever there has been publication in England. Jurisdiction can be established on evidence of only a single publication. A libel case can be brought in England even if there is a small circulation in this country and the main readership is abroad (*Shevill v Presse Alliance SA (1995)*).

Service outside the jurisdiction

If the defendant is a foreign person or legal entity with no presence in England, the claimant must first obtain permission from the court to serve proceedings outside the jurisdiction. Permission to serve outside the jurisdiction is not required where the defendant resides in a jurisdiction that is a contracting party to the Brussels Convention or the Lugano Convention, essentially member countries of the European Union.

If permission to serve outside the jurisdiction is required, the application must be supported by the grounds for the application, the whereabouts of the defendant and evidence supporting the merits of the claim. Service outside the jurisdiction can be effected personally or by any method allowed in the jurisdiction where service is to take place.

Forum non conveniens

If a claimant obtains permission from the court to serve proceedings on a foreign defendant and jurisdiction is established in England, the defendant can apply to the court to have the action dismissed on the grounds of forum non conveniens. This fundamental principle was established in order to 'identify the forum in which the case can be most suitably tried in the interests of all the parties and for the ends of justice' (*Spiliada Maritime Corporation v Cansulex (1987)*).

The claimant must demonstrate that he has a substantial complaint against the defendant for defamation in England. This is done by reference to the extent of the claimant's connections with England, his reputation to be protected within England, and the scale of publication by the defendant in England.

There is no presumption that local sales will automatically make the UK courts the most convenient forum where there is publication in England of an allegedly defamatory statement about a person with some connection with England and a reputation in England (*Berezovsky v Forbes (1999)*; *Parvinder Chadha & Osicom Technologies Inc v Dow Jones & Company Inc (1999)*).

1.4.2 Limitation period

Under Section 5 of the Defamation Act 1996, claims arising after September 1996 must be brought within the limitation period of one year. Claims that arose before September 1996 could be brought for a period of three years following the circumstances that gave rise to the claim.

There is no 'single publication' rule under English law. Each and every publication gives rise to a separate cause of action, and it can be difficult to establish when the limitation period has expired. The matter is further complicated by judicial discretion, which allows claims to be brought after expiry of the limitation period. When considering an application by the claimant to extend the expiry of the limitation period, the court will balance the reasons for the claimant's delay and any prejudice to the defendant. In particular, the court will consider the date on which facts enabling the claimant to make a claim were known to claimant, and how promptly he acted. Limitation periods are more easily set aside in defamation cases than other cases, and the judge has a wide discretion (*Oyston v Blaker (1996)*).

1.4.3 The action

The combined effect of the wholesale reform of civil procedure in England, introduced by the Civil Procedure Rules in April 1999, and the Defamation Act 1996, the final provisions of which were brought into force in February 2000, has been to 'streamline' defamation proceedings. The aim is to reduce cost, complexity and delay. In practical terms, this means a move towards a 'cards on the table' approach to litigation.

The court has been vocal in its promotion of these reforms. Extensive pleadings in defamation proceedings are now said to be 'otiose' (*McPhilemy v Times Newspapers Ltd (1999)*). Instead, the pleadings should be limited so as to restrict the parties to the essential issues (*Tancic v Times Newspapers Ltd (2000)*).

Starting an action

The Civil Procedure Rules include pre-action protocols, which outline the steps each party should take to seek information from and provide information to the other about a prospective legal claim. The objectives of the pre-action protocols are to:

- Exchange early and full information about the prospective legal claim
- Enable the parties to avoid litigation
- Support the efficient management of proceedings where litigation cannot be avoided.

Non-compliance with the pre-action protocols may result in an award of costs against either or both parties in any subsequent litigation.

The defamation pre-action protocol came into force on 2 October 2000. The protocol sets out the details that should be included in a claimant's letter before action, including full information about the complaint, factual and evidential matters relating to identification and meaning, and the relief sought. Although there are circumstances in which the protocol allows the immediate issue of proceedings by the claimant without the provision of full information about the complaint, there is no provision for delay by the defendant in providing a full response.

The claim form must contain prescribed details if it does not contain or have attached to it a full Statement of Case. Service of the claim form is effected by the court or the claimant. A defendant must set out whichever defence he relies on in his Defence, and specify defamatory meaning, the circumstances of any privilege claim, details of any matters relied on in support and any statutory offer of amend he relies upon.

Injunctions

As those in the media are aware, before publishing a story in which a person might claim to be defamed it is proper practice to confront the individual concerned and seek his reaction to the allegations. Human nature being what it is, the initial reaction of the person confronted with the prospect of publication of a potentially defamatory statement is to try to work out what can be done to prevent the publication. With that in mind, it is not surprising that such people frequently prefer speaking to their lawyer than the reporter on their doorstep. The first thought that goes through the mind of a lawyer confronted with such a situation is whether it is possible to obtain a court injunction to restrain publication.

The injunction is undoubtedly the strongest weapon in the claimant's armoury. On the principle that prevention is better than cure, it has more practical effect than the issue of proceedings after the damage has been done. Fortunately for the media, the court is generally unwilling to grant injunctions preventing intended publications where the defendant claims that he has a defence to the alleged defamatory statement.

Applications for ruling on meaning

After the proceedings have been issued, the court can, either of its own volition or on application by either party, rule on meaning and strike out or dismiss the action in favour of either party.

Pleadings can be substantially narrowed by applications by the claimant or the defendant for a ruling as a preliminary issue on meaning in the Statement of Case for the Defence. These applications can be heard at any time after service of the statement of case containing full particulars of the claim. The judge will narrow the possible range of meanings and will strike out those that are outside the permissible range. The jury will decide which is the meaning of the statement within the permissible range. Evidence on such an application is minimal, as the court seeks to give the statement the natural and ordinary meaning that would be conveyed to an ordinary, reasonable person.

Summary disposal

Sections 8–11 of the Defamation Act 1996 came into force on 28 February 2000, and provide for consideration by a judge of whether either party is entitled to summary disposal of the claim. The court can, either of its own volition or on application by either party, make such an order at any time after the proceedings have been issued.

The test is whether there is no realistic prospect of success and whether there is no other reason why the case should be tried. The relevant factors include the seriousness of the alleged wrong, including both the content and extent of publication, the extent of conflicting evidence, and whether it is 'justifiable in the circumstances to proceed to a full trial'. Possible relief includes a declaration that the statement was false and defamatory of the claimant, an order that the defendant publishes an apology and be restrained from further publication, and damages of up to £10 000.

1.4.4 Evidence

Both parties must disclose all documents in their control that either support or adversely affect their case or that of another party. This duty is a continuing duty throughout the proceedings. Specific orders can be made if the court considers documents are being withheld.

Witness evidence must be exchanged in the form of witness statements. Both parties can serve Requests for Further Information concerning the pleadings, as well as factual matters.

1.4.5 Protection of confidential sources and information

Both parties are required to serve lists of documents that must include confidential or privileged documents. However, such documents need not be shown to the other party if they are protected by privilege. This form of privilege is different to the defences to defamation of absolute and qualified privilege. It attaches to individual documents because of the particular status or purport of the document, instead of the occasion on which the publication was made.

Legal professional privilege

This extends to all confidential communications between a lawyer and his client, and to all communications between a lawyer or his client and a third party which come into existence for the dominant purpose of pending or actual litigation.

Spouses

A party need not disclose information that may expose him or his spouse to a criminal penalty.

'Without prejudice' communications

These are communications between the parties that explore settlement. They are privileged on the public policy ground of encouraging parties to settle their differences, rather than litigate before the court.

General power

The court has a general power to impose immunity from production on confidential or privileged documents, where to produce such documents would be injurious to the public interest.

1.4.6 Trial

The right to elect trial by judge and jury is preserved in defamation actions, although the parties can agree or the court can order on application that a judge alone should hear the trial.

Where the parties, or one of them, is a public figure or there are matters of national interest in question, this suggests the need for a jury trial (*Rothermere v The Times (1973)*). However, the issue of a person's 'fitness for public office' is one that requires detailed consideration of documents, and in such circumstances a jury trial may not be appropriate (*Aitken v Preston (1997)*).

1.5 Damages

1.5.1 General principles

Of all the unsatisfactory elements in the law of defamation, the one that has attracted most criticism has been the manner of awarding damages. The assessment of damages is solely a matter for the jury.

Prior to 1997 the jury were not told how much other libel claimants had been awarded in the past; nor were they given specific guidance on an appropriate figure or the range they should consider. This led to marked inconsistencies between awards, and outrageously high sums for trivial defamatory statements.

In 1976 the actor Telly Savalas was awarded the sum of £34 000 for unkind things said in an article in the *Daily Mail* (*Savalas v. Daily Mail (1976)*). The foreman of the jury wrote a letter in his own defence to *The Times*, stating that at the time of the trial he and his fellow jurors had '. . . not the remotest idea what compensation is paid for anything . . . Apparently that is why we were asked. If that is so, the court had the outcome it deserved from the appointed procedure' (*The Times*, 22 June 1976).

A surge of high jury awards in the 1980s, including £1.5 million in 1989 to Lord Aldington and £500 000 in 1987 to the writer and politician Jeffrey Archer for an article in the *Daily Star* suggesting that he slept with a prostitute (which famously led to his imprisonment in 2001 for perjury and contempt of court) resulted in the Court of Appeal being given power by reason of Section 8 of the Courts and Legal Services Act 1990 to substitute the jury's award with a sum it considered to be proper.

As a result of this power, the Court of Appeal reduced Esther Rantzen's libel damages award from £250 000 to £110 000 (*Rantzen v Mirror Group Newspapers (1994)*). In reaching its conclusion, the Court of Appeal looked at Article 10 of the European Convention on Human Rights right to freedom of expression and recognized that, although it was not part of United Kingdom law, where 'freedom of speech is at stake the Convention should be regarded as part of the English common law'. The Court of Appeal found that the almost limitless discretion of the jury in awarding damages failed to provide a satisfactory measurement of 'what is necessary in a democratic society'.

In *John v Mirror Group Newspapers (1997)* the Court of Appeal finally ruled that juries could be given specific figures for suggested damages by the trial judge and counsel as guidance, and that comparisons could be made with personal injury damages. In line with this ruling, the Court of Appeal reduced the award made by the jury to the singer Elton John from £75 000 to £25 000 for general damages and from £275 000 to £50 000 for exemplary damages in respect of allegations published in the *Daily Mirror* about his private life.

The combined effect of *Rantzen* and *John* has been to develop a 'tariff' of approved awards and to reduce the level of damages awarded to successful claimants, particularly against newspapers.

1.5.2 Types of damages

Damages for defamation can fall under three possible headings:

1. Compensatory damages
2. Aggravated damages
3. Exemplary damages.

The first two are broadly concerned with compensation, and the third is aimed at punishing the defendant.

Compensatory damages

Compensatory damages aim to put the claimant back in the position he would have been in had the defamatory material never been published. Under this heading the claimant is entitled to recover the monetary equivalent of everything he has lost and suffered as a result of the defamation.

There are two components to the compensatory award. Special damages amount to a sum equal to the actual financial or material loss suffered by the claimant. Damages for distress and injury to reputation are an intangible loss, and are more difficult to calculate. The jury must assess the effect of the defamation on the claimant's feelings (*McCarey v Associated Newspapers Ltd (No 2) (1965)*).

Aggravated damages

Aggravated damages are awarded where the behaviour of the defendant has somehow added to the hurt and injury to the claimant that resulted from the mere publication of the defamatory words. Various factors may give rise to an award under this category of damages. Anything that looks like a campaign of vilification, even if many of the derogatory things said about the claimant are true, might qualify, as would repetition of the defamation after the original complaint is made. Failing to publish the claimant's denial or explanation, or making no attempt to check the defamatory allegations with him, could also be said to aggravate the injury. Similarly, failing to apologize and persisting in a plea of justification are normally put forward with some success as arguments for awarding aggravated damages.

Exemplary damages

In certain circumstances the jury in a libel action may decide that the defendant should be liable not only to compensate the claimant for the wrong committed but should also suffer punishment for the way he has behaved. The appropriate course in such cases is to make an award of exemplary damages. They are a purely punitive measure that will only apply where the jury are satisfied that the defendant showed a cynical disregard for the feelings of the claimant by knowingly publishing the defamatory statement in the hope of profiting from it.

In *John v Mirror Group Newspapers (1997)* Elton John was awarded exemplary damages because the *Mirror* deliberately published for profit a defamatory statement about him.

1.6 Costs

Having to pay damages is, of course, not the only financial penalty an unsuccessful defendant has to bear. He will usually also have to pay the entire costs of the action, including those of the other party. Although the award of costs is a matter for the discretion of the judge, it is invariable practice that the loser in civil litigation must meet the legal costs incurred by the winner. This means that if the claimant is unsuccessful in his action, he must pay the costs of the defendant.

In defamation actions, the question of costs has tended to become the consideration that overrides all others when deciding whether or not to fight a case to the bitter end in court. In Jeffrey Archer's action against the *Daily Star* in 1987 the damages of £500 000 were exceeded by the costs of the action, which, according to reports, amounted to around £750 000.

In an action against Channel Four in 1997, the claimant agreed to pay Channel Four the sum of £765 000, which represented 80 per cent of its costs, as part of an agreement by which he was allowed to discontinue his action after several weeks of trial before a judge sitting alone.

In 2001, Mohammed Al-Fayed obtained a default costs certificate against Neil Hamilton (under Civil Procedure Rules Part 47.11) in the sum of nearly £1.5 million arising out of Hamilton's failed defamation action against Al-Fayed over the 'Cash for Questions' affair.

Early settlement
The Civil Procedure Rules have extended the situations in which parties can make offers to settle. The Civil Procedure Rules Part 36 enables either party to make an offer to settle.

Under the former court rules, only a defendant was able to make an offer to settle, which he did by payment into court. One claimant who gambled against a defendant's payment into court and lost was the actor William Roache. In 1991 he sued the *Sun* for calling him 'smug and boring'. The newspaper paid £50 000 into court several weeks before the start of the trial. Roache declined to take the money. The jury, who had no knowledge of the payment into court, found that Roache had been libelled but awarded him the sum of £50 000, exactly the same amount as the payment into court. Because Roache failed to beat the newspaper's payment into court, he was ordered to meet the *Sun*'s costs from the date it lodged the money with the court. At the end of the case Roache was severely out of pocket.

Statement in open court
Where the other party in a defamation action wishes to accept the 'Part 36 offer', 'Part 36 payment' or other offer of settlement, an application can also be made for permission to make a statement in open court.

Failure to accept offer: costs
If a Part 36 offer to settle is not accepted and the claim results in a determination that is *equivalent* to or *less favourable than* the offer, the party who rejected it is penalized in costs. The court has wide powers in this regard.

2 Blasphemy, Seditious Libel and Criminal Libel

David Green

2.1 Introduction

Those in the media can face criminal prosecution for the ancient offices of blasphemous libel, seditious libel and criminal libel. No modern government would (one hopes) bring these prosecutions. Public interest litigators seeking to punish, and publicize, violations of religious, political or personal sensibilities may, however, pursue private prosecutions. These are rare but not unknown.

The possibility of criminal sanctions against such exercises of free expression appears out of place in the era of the Human Rights Act 1998, which gives full effect in domestic law to Article 10 of the European Convention on Human Rights. However, the European Court of Human Rights held as recently as 1995 that the law of blasphemous libel was a justifiable interference with an individual's freedom of expression. Criminal libel and seditious libel may be similarly protected.

2.2 Blasphemy

The law of blasphemy, or blasphemous libel, which many considered to have been long forgotten as a basis for criminal prosecution, enjoyed a revival in the mid 1970s as a result of the successful private prosecution launched in 1977 by campaigning moralist Mary Whitehouse against *Gay News* magazine.

2.2.1 What is blasphemous libel?

The common law offence of blasphemous libel is traditionally defined, according to Archbold in *The Criminal Practitioner's Handbook*, as:

> . . . to speak, or otherwise publish, any matter blaspheming God, e.g. by denying his existence or providence, or contumeliously reproaching Jesus Christ, or vilifying or bringing into disbelief or contempt or ridicule Christianity in general or any doctrine of the Christian religion or the Bible.

The offence potentially arises where a statement vilifies or denies the truth of the Christian religion. However, for the statement to constitute a blasphemous libel, it must also be crouched in indecent, scurrilous or offensive terms that are likely to shock and outrage the feelings of Christian believers (*Whitehouse v Gay News and Lemon (1979)*). In other words, it must be a religiously charged incitement for a breach of the peace. In 1917, the House of Lords held in *Bowman v Secular Society* that such a statement must 'endanger the peace . . . deprave public morality generally . . . shake the fabric of society . . . and to be a cause of civil strife'. These are clearly difficult requirements to fulfil.

It is clear that the manner and the context of the statement is as important as its content in assessing whether the law against blasphemy has been contravened. A responsible debate or an honest and serious publication in which attacks are made upon Christian beliefs will not constitute the offence.

Leave must be sought from a judge in chambers before a prosecution for blasphemy may be commenced against a newspaper.

2.2.2 The mental element

Once such a statement has been made, the required mental element of the offence is elementary. The offence of blasphemous libel requires only the mere intention to publish the statement. The publisher of the statement does not need to have known that he has published a blasphemous statement (see *Whitehouse v Gay News and Lemon*). It is therefore irrelevant whether he intended the text to be, or to be seen as, blasphemous. Once the fact of publication by the accused is proved, the jury need only consider the meaning and effect of the words.

2.2.3 Penalties

The convicted publisher of a blasphemous libel faces a maximum penalty of a fine or life imprisonment and a fine.

2.2.4 Recent prosecutions

The only successful prosecution for blasphemous libel since 1922 was *Whitehouse v Gay News and Lemon*. The prosecution contended that the magazine and its editor 'unlawfully and wickedly published . . . a blasphemous libel concerning the Christian religion, namely an obscene poem and illustration vilifying Christ in His Life and His Crucifixion'. The poem, written by James Kirkup, contained explicit references to Christ having engaged in homosexual acts with a number of men. It was intended, according to the defendants, to be serious expression of the all-encompassing nature of God's love. The jury found by a majority that it amounted to blasphemous libel. On appeal the House of Lords, again by a majority, upheld the verdict. *Gay News* was fined £1000 and the editor was fined £500, although he successfully appealed a suspended sentence of nine months.

Blasphemous libel only protects the Christian religion, especially in its Anglican form. In 1991 the Court of Appeal held that a prosecution could not be brought for perceived blasphemous libels in *The Satanic Verses* by Salman Rushdie as the common law of blasphemy did not extend to attacks on other religions such as Islam (*R v Chief Metropolitan Stipendiary Magistrate ex parte Choudhury (1991)*).

Article 10 of the European Convention on Human Rights provides for the right to freedom of expression, but this will not necessarily protect those who commit blasphemous libel. In *Wingrove v United Kingdom (1996)*, a video of the erotic story of an early-modern nun, called *Visions of Ecstasy*, was refused a video recording classification certificate by the Video Appeals Committee of the British Board of Film Classification on the grounds that it infringed the criminal law of blasphemy. The decision resulted in an unsuccessful challenge to the European Court of Human Rights. The Court held that the refusal of a certificate did not amount to a violation of the right to freedom of expression under Article 10, as the interference had a legitimate aim in protecting the rights of others and providing protection against offensive attacks on matters held sacred by Christians.

2.3 Seditious libel

In many ways the law against seditious libel, like blasphemy, is a hangover from less tolerant days. The purpose of the crime was to prevent the encouragement of active discontent through attacks on the established order. The authorities and case law for seditious libel are old, and the possible grounds for prosecution appear archaic in modern society.

2.3.1 What is seditious libel?

Seditious libel consists of a statement, in either spoken or written form, which is seditious in content and published with a seditious intent. Seditious content includes promoting hatred or ridicule against:

- The sovereign or his heirs or successors
- The government of the United Kingdom
- The Houses of Parliament, or
- The administration of justice.

Seditious content can also include promoting ill will, discontent or dissatisfaction between the sovereign's subjects, and inciting the sovereign's subjects to use unlawful means to alter any matter relating to church or state or a public issue.

2.3.2 The mental element

Seditious intent is more difficult to establish than seditious content. It is not enough that the accused acted in a seditious way. He must have seditious purpose. The law does not inhibit serious and honest criticism of the law, the government or the sovereign even where the words used are forceful or extreme. There 'must be violence or resistance or defiance for the purpose of disturbing constituted authority' (see *R v Chief Metropolitan Stipendiary Magistrate ex parte Choudhury*).

The accused will avoid conviction if he is able to prove that, although technically responsible for the publication, for example a printer or distributor, he was unaware that the contents were seditious and had no reason to suspect they were.

Newspaper reports of parliamentary proceedings and judicial proceedings are privileged against prosecution providing they are fair and accurate.

2.3.3 Penalties

The convicted publisher of a seditious libel faces a maximum penalty of a fine or (in theory) life imprisonment and a fine.

2.3.4 Recent prosecutions

Prosecutions for seditious libel are extremely rare. In *R v Aldred (1909)* the defendant published statements, aimed at Indian students, which preached the message that political assassination in the cause of Indian independence was not murder. It was held to be a seditious libel. The last prosecution for seditious libel took place over 50 years ago.

2.4 Criminal libel

Criminal libel prosecutions are rare but still possible. The origin of criminal libel appears to lie in the thirteenth century public offence of '*Scandalum Magnatum*'. The objective of this law was to prevent the uttering and dissemination of stories that tended to arouse the people against their masters or cause a breach of the peace.

Despite the availability of the laws of defamation, a person may think it advantageous to pursue his case for libel in the criminal courts instead of, or as well as, the civil courts. The penalties for the maker of a serious libel are harsher for criminal libel than those imposed in the civil courts. An embittered individual may get far more satisfaction from the thought of sending a reporter, broadcaster or editor to jail than from pursuing an action for damages.

2.4.1 What is criminal libel?

A criminal libel must be in permanent form. The words must tend to vilify a person and to bring them into hatred, contempt and ridicule.

Probably because of its public order origins, it was thought at one time that an essential ingredient of criminal libel was a tendency to provoke a breach of the peace. However, more recent cases have shown that for a libel to amount to a criminal offence it must simply be a 'serious' rather than trivial libel. Any remaining doubt about a breach of the peace element in criminal libel was resolved in the case of *Gleaves v Deakin (1980)*:

> A criminal libel must be a serious libel. If the libel is of such a character as to be likely to disturb the peace of the community or to provoke a breach of the peace, then it is not to be regarded as trivial. But to hold . . . that the existence of such a tendency tends to show that the libel is a serious one, is a very different thing from saying that proof of its existence is necessary to establish guilt of the offence.

It was also suggested that a criminal libel might be identified by a comparison between what is deemed to be serious and what would be regarded as trivial:

> It is, however, not every libel that warrants a criminal prosecution. To warrant prosecution the libel must be sufficiently serious to require the intervention of the Crown in the public interest . . . The libel must be more than of a trivial charter: it must be such as to provoke anger or cause resentment.

Criminal libel differs from civil libel in a number of respects. The accuracy or truth of a statement in criminal libel will not necessarily protect its maker from punishment. 'The greater the truth the greater the libel' is a phrase that is rooted in this branch of the law. It has always been recognized that the truth is often more likely to arouse fury than obvious falsehood. Unlike civil libel, those accused of criminal libel must establish that the words were true and that they were published for the public benefit.

2.4.2 Defending criminal libel actions

There are two clearly recognized defences to criminal libel:

1. Under Section 6 of the Libel Act 1843 the defendant will have a good defence if he establishes that the words complained of were true and were published 'for the public benefit'

2. The defendant will also have a good defence if the words were published under absolute or qualified privilege.

In the absence of recent authoritative cases on the point, it is perhaps arguable whether fair comment can be successfully pleaded in answer to a criminal libel charge.

2.4.3 Penalties

A person who publishes a libel knowing it to be false may be sentenced to a fine and a period of imprisonment (Section 4 of the Libel Act 1843). A publisher who did not know a libel was false may also be sentenced to a fine and a sentence of imprisonment (Section 5 of the Libel Act 1843).

PART II
Intellectual Property

3 Copyright

Mark Cranwell

3.1 Introduction

Copyright is an intellectual property right. Intellectual property rights protect things that are created by a person's skill, labour and investment of time and money. The law of copyright prevents a person from copying the work of another without his permission. It is therefore the exclusive right to use material in a certain way. The law of copyright protects two kinds of labour or investment; the labour of the author in his own material, such as articles, programmes, scripts or songs, and the investment of those who provide the technology necessary to publish the material, such as newspapers, broadcasts, films or records.

The law of copyright is important to those working in the media. It determines the extent to which a quotation or the work of a third party can be used in an article or broadcast. It also establishes the right of a writer, newspaper or television company to exploit his own work or the work of the company and prevent others from taking benefit from it.

There is no copyright in an idea, nor is there any copyright in news. However, the law of copyright protects ideas or information expressed in a particular way. Anyone can report the happening of a particular event. However, a newspaper or programme cannot use verbatim another newspaper's report or broadcast another programme's footage of an event.

The English law of copyright is extremely complex. It is based upon the Copyright, Designs and Patents Act 1988 (the 'CDPA') as amended by the Copyright Regulations 1995. The CDPA consolidated and modernized the existing copyright law, which was found in the Copyright Act 1911, the Copyright Act 1956 and case law. The CPDA applies to authors in the United Kingdom, as well as authors from other countries that have given reciprocal protection to copyright by ratification of the two main international treaties on copyright, the Berne Convention and the Universal Copyright Convention. Many countries, including the United Kingdom and the United States of America, are signatories to both conventions. The International Convention for the Protection of Performers, Producers of Phonograms and Broadcasting Organizations 1961, known as the Rome Convention, also provides international protection for performers, broadcasters and authors and producers of sound recordings. The English courts will only hear a copyright dispute if copyright infringement has taken place within England and Wales.

Other important intellectual property rights include trademarks, patents, passing off and the law of confidence. Trademarks prevent a person from taking unfair advantage of the goodwill of established businesses. Patents protect scientific developments. Passing off prevents a person representing the marks, packaging or other features of goods of another as his own. The common law of confidence protects information that is 'confidential', including secret processes, inventions and trade secrets. However, in recent years the law of confidence has been used more and more to prevent the publication of 'confidential' information in the media. This aspect of the law of confidence is considered in Chapter 6.

3.2 Copyright work

3.2.1 General principles

Copyright does not protect ideas, news or information from being copied. Instead, it protects the material form or manner of expression of that idea or information. Infringement of copyright was found where one news service copied verbatim another newspaper's report (*Walter v Steinkopff (1892)*). The law strikes a balance between the right of an author to benefit from his work and the need of the public for a free flow of information.

Although there is no requirement for a notice or mark of copyright under United Kingdom law, there are different requirements under the international conventions on copyright protection. It is therefore prudent to keep a dated copy of the work in permanent form in a safe place and place a prominent copyright notice on all copies of the work to ensure that infringers cannot claim to be ignorant of the existence of copyright in the work.

In order for copyright to exist in a work, it must fall within one of the following categories:

- Original literary, dramatic, musical or artistic works
- Sound recordings, films, broadcasts or cable programmes
- The typographical arrangement of published editions.

3.2.2 Literary, dramatic, musical and artistic works

Literary works
The CDPA does not provide a precise definition of 'literary work'. It is described in Section 3(1) of the CDPA as:

> . . . any work, other than a dramatic or musical work, which is written, spoken or sung.

Literary works therefore include almost any words that are written down or recorded, including newspaper or magazine articles or features, books, plays, song lyrics, poems, film scripts, articles, or features published on the Internet.

44

There is no requirement for literary merit. Letters or emails written to a newspaper are subject to copyright, although where a letter or email is sent to a newspaper or magazine the writer permits publication of it by the newspaper or magazine on at least one occasion. Even computer programs and databases, seemingly without literary 'merit', are expressly included if they constitute the author's own intellectual creation. Railway timetables and logarithmic tables are both literary works. Football fixture lists and pools coupons also qualify for copyright protection (*Ladbroke (Football) Ltd v William Hill (Football) UK Ltd (1964)*). This enables the Football League, which owns the copyright, to charge the pools promoters to reproduce the fixtures, whilst permitting football clubs to do so free of charge.

Television listings are copyright works (*Independent Television Publications Ltd v Time Out Ltd (1984)*). Considerable skill and labour goes into devising weekly schedules. Copyright is owned by the BBC and by the independent television companies. However, as a result of Section 176 of the Broadcasting Act 1990 and the decision in *Magill TV Guide v Independent Television Publications (1991)*, television companies must now make full seven-day listings available to publishers at least two weeks in advance. As well as marketing their own comprehensive weekly guides, these companies also grant licences for their own programme listings.

The CDPA makes it clear that spoken words that are recorded by any means become literary works and therefore qualify for copyright protection. The author of the work – in other words the speaker – owns the copyright. There is an important exception to this rule. Use of a recording of spoken words, such as an interview made for the purpose of recording current events, a broadcast or for inclusion in a cable programme, is not an infringing act subject to its meeting certain criteria under Section 175 of the Broadcasting Act 1990.

Some works may be too short to be protected by copyright. Although much time, money, skill and effort may go into devising a name for a new product or company, copyright cannot exist in a word. 'Exxon', the American industrial corporation, sued to prevent the use of its made-up name by an insurance company on copyright grounds. It failed (*Exxon Corporation v Exxon Insurance Consultants International Ltd (1982)*). Only the law of trademarks or the common law action of passing off can prevent imitators from trading on the established name and goodwill of another.

Dramatic works

Plays, choreographed work, dances, stage musicals and mimes are dramatic works. The scenarios and scripts for films may also be protected under this category. The difference between a dramatic work and a literary work is that a dramatic work has spoken words or some form of action that is to be performed.

Musical works

Copyright exists in an original musical work once it is written down. If music is recorded without being written down, it may only be protected as a sound recording – for example, if a record is made of musicians 'improvising'.

Copyright in a musical work can exist in original compositions, as well as in arrangements of old music or adaptations of existing work. Originality in an arrangement has been described as:

> . . . the manner of expression in permanent form [which] is such that it can be seen to have originated from the arranger.

(Godfrey v John Lees (1995))

Even though copyright may exist in respect of the arrangement, if copyright exists in the original work the arranger must still obtain a licence to use the old music before the new arrangement can be used.

Both the tune and the lyrics in a song have separate copyright. The lyrics are protected as a literary work. The tune is protected as a musical work. One person may own the words and want to use the song in a particular way, while the owner of the music may refuse. Difficulties may also arise where one person writes the basic theme while another adds an improvised and highly significant part to the finished piece. Joint ownership of copyright is a complex area of law. There is great potential for difficulty where members of a band write or record material together without deciding who owns the copyright. Three members of the pop band Spandau Ballet sued a fourth member, alleging joint copyright in the band's songs. The court held that the claim of joint authorship failed *(Hadley v Kemp (1999))*.

Artistic works

An artistic work is defined in Section 4(1) of the CDPA as:

- A graphic work, photograph, sculpture or collage, irrespective of artistic quality
- A work of architecture be it a building or a model for a building
- A work of artistic craftsmanship.

This includes paintings, drawings, diagrams, maps, charts or plans, works of architecture for buildings or models for buildings, cartoons, photographs, sculptures and works of artistic craftsmanship.

As a general rule, a drawing cannot be a graphic work if it is not exclusively pictorial. However, numbers and literary elements can be taken into account when considering whether material is an artistic work.

Skill and labour must go into the artistic work. However, any lack of artistic merit will not deprive the finished work of copyright protection.

The House of Lords has held that the word 'artistic' must be read in the context of the whole phrase 'work of artistic craftsmanship' and given its ordinary and natural meaning. A formula or test cannot be evolved to determine artistic craftsmanship, as this will be a matter for evidence in each case. The court is not the appropriate judge of aesthetic appeal. However, it is the proper function of the court to decide on hearing the evidence whether an object falls within the definition (*George Hensher Ltd v Restawile Upholstery (Lancs) Ltd (1976)*).

Originality

Literary, dramatic, musical and artistic works must be original before they can be protected by copyright. The essence of originality is that the author of the work must have devoted skill and labour to its creation. This is called the 'sweat of the brow' test. There is no aesthetic requirement.

A slavish copy of an existing work will not be protected, nor would the writing out of the letters of the alphabet, or the numbers 1 to 100. However, the creation of a new typeface, or font, of letters and numbers would be a copyright work. A musician who copies a folk tune that has no copyright may have difficulty in showing it to be sufficiently original to prevent others from copying his work. If a person produced logarithmic tables by carrying out all the necessary calculations and work independently, the tables may look exactly like an existing set. However, both works would be entitled to copyright protection. The second set would infringe the first only if copied from it. Similarly, if two people independently painted a picture of the same country scene or still life, the finished works may be very similar but both would be original, having been created by independent skill and effort.

Two photographers may take photographs of the same event from more-or-less the same angle and very similar photographs may appear in rival newspapers. Each newspaper could prevent the copying of its photograph, but could not prevent other photographers from going out to take similar photographs for themselves.

If two literary or artistic works are objectively similar, it may be difficult for the maker of the later work to prove that it is not copied from the first. Articles, books, pictures, songs, storylines and films that have a striking similarity to each other suggest copying. It may be difficult for the author of the work to prove that it was independently created, not copied. It is wise, in such cases, to keep drafting notes and copies of the various stages of development of an idea. Enclosing the work in a letter sent by registered post or enclosing it in an email sent to a trusted person or organization or back to the author himself may assist in establishing the date when the work came into existence.

The difficulties that may arise when two works look or sound alike are illustrated in a case concerning the composer Vangelis (*EMI v Evangelous Papathanassiou (1987)*). The composer of a piece of music called *City of Violets* claimed that Vangelis had heard his music and subconsciously copied in for the theme music for the film *Chariots of Fire*. The court listened to both pieces of music, compared them with the assistance of expert evidence, and concluded that Vangelis had not infringed the earlier copyright. Although the dispute ended in Vangelis' favour, the case took several years to reach trial and involved high legal costs.

In the case of *Designers Guild Ltd v Russell Williams (Textiles) Ltd (Trading as Washington DC) (2001)*, which concerned two designers of a similar fabric, the trial judge reached his conclusion by considering the similarities of the two designs and hearing evidence concerning the opportunity of one designer to copy the other and the independent origin of the defendant's design. On appeal, the court held that it was not right to reach a view on a subjective approach alone. An analytic approach was necessary.

Even where the issue of originality is clear, the case may be complex as a result of issues relating to an application for an injunction or account of lost profits. In the case of *Ludlow Music Inc v Williams (2001)*, a song by pop star Robbie Williams called *Jesus In A Camper Van* was held to have infringed copyright in the lyrics of a song entitled *I Am The Way (New York Town)*. However, the court refused the claimant's application for an injunction. The court held that the claimant had acquiesced to use of the song by Williams because of an agreement to be named as co-writer and because of the delay in taking action for breach of copyright. The court also held that an injunction would be oppressive because it would enable the claimant to demand an excessive price for permitting the continued sale of Williams' album, which included the song.

3.2.3 Sound recordings, films, broadcasts or cable programmes

Copyright also exists in sound recordings, films, and broadcasts by television or radio or cable programme. These works are usually referred to as secondary copyrights or 'derivative works', because they are often based upon other copyrighted works, known as the 'underlying rights'. However, copyright can still exist in derivative works:

> ... originality is not a criterion for the protection of sound recordings, films, broadcasts and cable transmissions.

(Section 1(1)(b) of the CDPA)

Sound recordings
A sound recording is defined in Section 5(1) of the CDPA as:

- A recording of sounds, from which the sounds may be reproduced, or
- The recording of the whole of any part of a literary, dramatic or musical work, from which sounds reproducing the work or part may be produced regardless of the medium on which the recording is made or the method by which the sounds are reproduced or produced.

The copyright in a sound recording attaches to the recording of the music itself, not the compact disc or cassette it is subsequently played back on. The copyright in the song that is recorded is the 'underlying right'.

Copyright in sound recordings is owned by the person who makes the arrangements necessary for the making of the recording. In most cases this will be the record company rather than the artist himself.

Films

A film is defined by Section 5(1) of the CDPA as:

> . . . a recording on any medium from which a moving image may by any means be produced.

This broad definition includes virtually any recorded moving image as a film. Video recordings are included as films. Video piracy is therefore a copyright infringement. As technology advances, the definition should be capable of embracing new forms of media.

A film itself will have copyright protection. Several other aspects of a film will also have a separate copyright as 'underlying works' – for example, the script or the book the film is based upon, and other copyright works integrated into the film, such as clips from other movies or television shows.

Copyright does not exist in a film that infringes the copyright of another film.

Broadcast and cable programmes

These two distinct methods of distributing a work protect the act of transmitting or sending visual images, sounds or other information. The copyright in a broadcast is owned by the person making the broadcast. The copyright in a cable programme belongs to the person providing the cable service. Satellite broadcasts that can be received by members of the public, but not intersatellite transmissions, are also copyright works.

If a television programme is pre-recorded, copyright will exist in the broadcast itself and in the actual film that is broadcast, as well as in the 'underlying rights' such as the script and any music devised for the programme. Making of a video recording of the television programme may therefore infringe all of these copyrights. However, when a broadcast is of a live event, for example the FA Cup Final, the only copyright created is in the broadcast itself. There is no copyright in a live event.

Copyright does not exist in a broadcast or cable programme that infringes the copyright of another broadcast or cable programme.

3.2.4 Published editions of works

The copyright in a 'published edition of the whole or any part of one or more literary, dramatic or musical works' protects the copying of a work that has no copyright but attracts copyright in the typographical arrangement of the edition.

3.3 Who owns copyright?

3.3.1 Literary, dramatic, musical and artistic works

Copyright in literary, dramatic, musical and artistic works belongs to the author of the work. This means the person whose skill and effort produced the work – for example the writer of the book, not the secretary who typed it out.

However, in some cases the person who takes the material down can be the copyright owner. In *Walter v Lane (1900)*, shorthand writers from the *Times* had taken down political speeches of Lord Rosebery. Reports were published in the newspaper. The court held that the *Times* owned the copyright in the reports, which had been produced by the skill and labour of the shorthand writers even though Lord Rosebery was the author of the speech. Other newspapers could have taken down the speeches themselves and published identical reports to the *Times*, but they could not take a short cut by copying from the *Times*. In such cases, copyright protects the material form in which the information is recorded, not the information itself. This principle is of concern to journalists, who are permitted to 'follow-up' stories in other publications but may not 'lift' such stories without permission.

If two or more people jointly create a work and their contributions are indivisible, then, unlike the tune and the lyric in a song, copyright is owned jointly. If a ghost writer produces an autobiography or a newspaper series, the ghost writer owns the copyright subject to any agreement otherwise.

The author has to be a living human being, not a corporation. Where work is produced with the aid of or is generated by computers, the person who undertakes the arrangements necessary for the creation of the work is the author. In *Express Newspapers Plc* v *Liverpool Daily Post & Echo Plc (1985)* the *Daily Express* distributed bingo cards to readers and each day printed a series of winning numbers generated by a computer on a grid. It was not necessary to buy the *Express* in order to take part in the game (at the time this would have been an unlawful lottery). A provincial newspaper reproduced the winning numbers printed in the *Express*. The court ruled that the *Express* was able to prevent anyone else from reproducing its numbers because the numbers and grid were an original literary work. The game had been devised by human skill and labour, not simply generated at random by machines.

Difficulties may arise where computer software is created by the input of several people at different stages. Where such collaboration has occurred, there may be joint ownership of copyright.

3.3.2 Photographs

Before the introduction of the CDPA in 1988, ownership of copyright in photographs had special and different rules. The basic rule was that the person who owned the film in the camera owned the copyright in the photograph. Only photographers who used their own films became copyright owners. A modification applied if the photograph was commissioned. If someone commissioned a photograph and agreed to pay for it, the photograph produced belonged to the person who commissioned it and not the photographer, no matter who owned the film. As a result, a freelance photographer using his own film owned the copyright in photographs taken on the spur of the moment, but he did not own the copyright in photographs commissioned by another person or a publication.

The CDPA brought ownership of copyright in photographs into line with literary works. The person who creates the photograph owns the copyright in it. Even if a photographer has been commissioned or is using someone else's film, he will be the first owner of copyright. As a result, if you ask someone to take a photograph of you on holiday, the person who takes the photograph will become the copyright owner.

The question of copyright ownership in photographs is of fundamental importance to journalists, particularly those in the world of newspapers and magazines. Only the owner can give permission to use a photograph. Permission must be obtained from the right person, whose identity it may not be easy to establish.

In *Daily Mail v Daily Express (1987)*, the *Daily Mail* bought exclusive rights to wedding photographs from a husband whose wife was being kept alive on a life-support system until her child was born. The *Mail* obtained an injunction to prevent the *Daily Express* from publishing the same photographs. The *Express* argued that the husband and the wife owned the wedding photographs jointly. It said that because the *Mail* had only obtained consent from one joint owner, it was not correct to grant an injunction in respect of the copyright until the *Mail* had the consent of both. The court held that the husband and wife did own the photographs jointly, but upheld the injunction. The court said that it was not clear whether the wife was clinically dead and therefore incapable of giving or refusing consent. In such circumstances the *Mail* was able successfully to argue that it had acquired good title to the pictures.

3.3.3 Sound recordings, films, broadcasts and cable programmes

The rules concerning ownership of sound recordings, films, broadcasts and cable programmes were also changed by the CDPA. Under the previous legislation, the rules concerning ownership of copyright in sound recordings were the same as for photographs. The owner of the material on which the recording was made or the person who commissioned it was the owner. Copyright in sound recordings and films is now owned by the person who makes the arrangements necessary for the making of the recording or film. This will be the record company or the producer; not the artist or director.

Under the previous legislation, only the BBC or the Independent Broadcasting Authority could own the copyright in broadcasts. Copyright in broadcasts under the CDPA is now owned by the person who makes the broadcast. Copyright in individual pre-recorded programmes that are broadcast may be owned by the programme maker. The copyright in cable programmes belongs to the person providing the cable service.

3.3.4 Employees

Where someone in the course of his employment produces a work, the normal rule is that the employer owns the copyright. However, there must be a contract of employment or contract of service. This is different from a contract for services or a freelance contract.

Copyright will belong to the employer only it if is part of the employee's duties to produce the work. For example, the employer of a computer programmer will own copyright in all computer programs produced at work, but not in a best-selling novel written by the programmer.

The contract of employment can agree that the copyright position should not follow the general rule.

Anyone who works for himself owns the copyright in any work he produces unless he assigns it to someone else. It is important for anyone working as a freelancer to look carefully at any freelance contract, which may assign copyright.

Newspaper employees

Newspaper reporters are in the same position as all other employees. The proprietor of the newspaper owns the whole copyright.

The right to authorize later use of work and the right to sue for infringement depends on ownership. In *Beloff v Pressdram Ltd (1973)* political journalist Nora Beloff sued the magazine *Private Eye* for breach of copyright when it published a memorandum written by her in the course of her employment with the *Observer*. The original owner of copyright in the memorandum was the *Observer*. An attempt by the editor to assign copyright to Beloff failed because he had no authority to assign copyright belonging to the *Observer*. Beloff had no right to sue. Her claim failed.

3.3.5 Transfer of ownership

Copyright can be transferred from one person to another like any other item of property. Copyright can pass as part of an estate on death or be assigned during the lifetime of the owner. The rules about ownership can be altered by agreement. Any assignment of copyright must be in writing.

3.3.6 Formalities

Under the CDPA, the owner of copyright does not need to go through any formalities such as registration to protect a copyright work. No copyright notice need appear on a work. However, the formula ©, the name of the copyright owner and the date of first publication must be placed on a work for international protection under the Universal Copyright Convention.

3.4 Infringement

The protection of copyright gives the owner of a work the exclusive right to deal with the work in various ways. The copyright owner can permit or prohibit others to deal with the work. A licence can be granted to use the work for one purpose, or generally. Any of the following acts done without the permission of the copyright owner amount to a breach of copyright. However, the consent of the owner is a good defence to an infringing act.

3.4.1 Copying

Copying is an infringement of all types of copyright. If an article in one newspaper is reproduced verbatim in another, it will be a clear infringement. Moreover, the whole article need not be taken. Copying a 'substantial part' of the original will be an infringement of copyright. It is not necessary to take most of the original in quantitative terms in order to be a 'substantial part'. It is enough that the most significant or distinctive part is copied.

The issue of whether the part taken is 'substantial' is always a difficult question of fact. If the first notes of Beethoven's *Fifth Symphony* were taken by a rival composer, but not the rest, that could be an infringement of copyright (if the copyright had not expired). These notes are so distinctive as to amount to a 'substantial part'. In the more modern technique of sampling, very short extracts are taken from a record. If an extract is a distinctive 'riff' or 'hook', it can amount to an infringement of copyright (*Produce Records v BMG Entertainment (1999)*). The same principle applies to written works or film clips. The copying need not be exact. Minor changes will not prevent the infringement from taking place, especially if the changes are intended deliberately to avoid a copyright action.

Even a parody or pastiche may breach copyright. The question is the degree of similarity between the parody and the original. In *Williamson Music Ltd v The Pearson Partnership Ltd (1987)*, an advertising agency took a song from *South Pacific* called *There Is Nothing Like A Dame* and produced a commercial for a bus company praising its waitresses, calling it *There Is Nothing Like Elaine*. The owners of the copyright in *South Pacific* obtained an interlocutory injunction. Although the words were totally different, the tune was the same. The question for the court was whether the parody made use of a substantial part of the expression of literary copyright. The use for which the parody is put appears to be relevant.

The court is more willing to allow parodies that make political or humorous comment than those that are solely for commercial reasons.

There is no precise guidance on what will amount to an infringement. Each case depends on its own facts and a comparison of the original article and the copy. In *Newspaper Licensing Agency Ltd v Marks & Spencer plc (2001)*, Marks & Spencer entered into a contract with an agency for the supply of photocopies of news items appearing in daily and national newspapers. Marks & Spencer then made further copies of the news items for distribution to individuals within its organization. The court held that, when considering whether there had been copying of a 'substantial part' of the typographical arrangement of an edition of each newspaper, the question was whether there had been copying of a sufficient amount of the relevant skill and labour that had gone into producing the edition. A copy of an article on a page, which gave no indication of how the rest of the page was laid out, was held not to be a copy of a substantial part of the published edition of the newspaper as a whole.

Some copying is not a breach of copyright. If a copy is made of a television or sound broadcast for private purposes only it will not amount an infringement of the copyright in the broadcast itself, although it may infringe copyright in a pre-recorded programme or film. Home taping of live programmes to keep in a private collection or to watch at a more convenient time is permitted. However, it would amount to an infringement of copyright if the videotape was sold or hired out.

3.4.2 Other infringements

Copies to the public
Under the CDPA it is an infringement to issue copies of copyrighted works to the public. Under the Copyright Act 1956 the term used is to 'publish' them.

Performances in public
Performing a literary, dramatic or musical work in public is an infringing act, as is playing or showing in public any sound recording, film, broadcast or cable programme. This includes using copyright works in lectures or speeches, or in presentations using films, recordings or broadcasts.

Broadcasts
Broadcasting a literary, musical or dramatic work infringes copyright. However, when an artistic work is publicly displayed it can be included in broadcasts or films, and can be photographed, drawn or painted.

Adaptations
Making adaptations of literary, dramatic or musical works is an infringement of copyright. Turning a play into a book or a book into a play, translating a work or putting it into pictorial form, are all adaptations. Producing a cartoon of a novel would be a breach of copyright.

Giving a tune a new arrangement is also an infringement of copyright in the original work. Translating a program from one computer to another is an infringement of copyright.

Sale, hire and importation
Commercial misuse of copyright work is prevented by making the sale, hire or importation of copyright works an infringement of copyright.

3.5 Defences

The law provides various defences to infringement of copyright, the most important of which is 'fair dealing'.

3.5.1 Fair dealing

The defence of fair dealing acknowledges the wider interest of freedom of speech by allowing considerable latitude in the use of copyright material for certain worthy purposes. The CDPA limits these purposes to news reporting, criticism and review, and research and private study (*Pro Sieben Media AG v Carlton UK Television Ltd (1999)*).

News reporting
With the exception of photographs, use may be made of any sort of copyright work providing it is for the purpose of reporting current events. In the cases of newspapers, magazines and any other sort of print media the reproduction must be accompanied by a 'sufficient acknowledgement', in other words the proper identification of the original work by name and author. However, this requirement does not apply where the reporting of current affairs is by means of television, radio, satellite or cable broadcasting.

Criticism and review
Any sort of copyright work, including photographs, may be copied without liability providing the reproduction is made for the purposes of criticism and review. A sufficient acknowledgement of the original work and its authorship must be given in every case, in other words whether the copying is through the medium of print, radio or television.

Research and private study
Use of copyright works for the purposes of research and private study is permissible. There is no requirement for sufficient acknowledgement.

Identifying fair dealing

There is no definition of what is meant by fair dealing. Each case will depend on what is taken and the reasons for which it was taken. In *Associated Newspapers Group Plc v News Group Newspapers Ltd (1986)* the claimant obtained, for a limited period, the exclusive rights to the letters of the Duke and Duchess of Windsor. The letters were printed in the *Daily Mail*. The *Sun* subsequently published the whole of one letter and part of another. The court granted the claimant an injunction preventing further publication on the grounds that there was no interference with free speech because the aim of the *Sun* had been solely to increase readership. The defendant's argument that the publication was for the purpose of criticism, review or to report current events, failed to impress the court.

The motive of the publisher is also relevant. The court is willing to look behind spurious arguments of the public interest in free speech, when all that a newspaper is interested in is 'spoiling' an 'exclusive' by a competitor.

A genuine review of a work and genuine reports of current events are permitted. The reporting by newspapers of matters obtained from advance copies of magazines is routine practice and is acceptable because the magazine gets free publicity, as long as there is an acknowledgement of the source. However, the amount of material taken must be reasonable. The lifting of a whole article including verbatim quotations could result in an action for breach of copyright. 'Current event' will be generously interpreted to include all varieties of news. In 1991 the court ruled that the use of BBC film footage of World Cup football matches by its satellite station rival, British Satellite Broadcasting, was fair dealing. BSB illustrated its spoken match reports with BBC clips of goals and other highlights of play. It acknowledged the source and confined itself to short, informative excerpts. The court held that contemporary World Cup football matches were 'current events' and dismissed the BBC's copyright claim (*BBC v British Satellite Broadcasting Ltd (1992)*).

In circumstances where a book is published and one media publication has obtained exclusive serialization rights, it is likely to pursue actions against other publications that publish details of the same book. Particular care should be taken by another publication before any extracts are published. Similarly, if an advance copy of a book is shown to a publication to enable it to decide how much to offer for the serialization rights, the publication should not reproduce extracts if it does not buy the rights.

The fair dealing defence permit the reporting of matters of public interest. In *Hubbard v Vosper (1972)*, the founder of the 'cult' of Scientology applied for an injunction to stop publication of a book 'exposing' Scientology written by a former Scientologist. The book quoted from books written by Hubbard and from other writings, including internal memoranda. The court refused an injunction because the defendant showed that he might have a good defence of fair dealing at trial. Although substantial amounts of material were quoted, this did not deprive the defendant of his defence. He was entitled to criticize the philosophy set out in the works, and was not limited to criticizing their literary style.

The fair dealing defence is relevant to investigative reporting in circumstances where documents are obtained. Government documents, local authority reports and private papers are the subject of copyright. However, this defence may justify quotations from them.

3.5.2 Incidental inclusion

Section 31 of the CDPA provides a new defence. Where a copyright work is included 'incidentally' in an artistic work, sound recording, film, broadcast or cable programme, this will not amount to an infringement of copyright.

What is 'incidental' is not defined. However, the defence is aimed at allowing programme makers and news broadcasters to show works that might otherwise breach copyright – for example, capturing background music when interviewing people in the street.

However, Section 31(3) of the CDPA states that any inclusion of a musical work that is deliberate shall not be regarded as incidental. In such circumstances, it will not be possible to rely on the defence.

3.5.3 Spoken words

The CDPA recognizes that spoken words that are in any way recorded become the copyright of the speaker. However, it also allows the media considerable latitude to use or report the words of others without infringing that copyright.

Section 58 of the CDPA provides that where a record of spoken words is made, in writing or otherwise, for the purpose of:

- reporting current events, or
- broadcasting or including in a cable programme service,

use of the record or of material taken from it is not an infringement of any copyright in the words provided certain conditions are met. These are that:

- The record is a direct record of the spoken words and is not one taken from previous record or from a broadcast or cable programme
- The making of the record was not prohibited by the speaker and, where the copyright already subsisted in the work, did not infringe copyright
- The use made of the record or the material taken from it is not of a kind prohibited by the speaker or copyright owner before the record was made
- The use is by or with the authority of the person lawfully in possession of the record.

In essence, this means that newspapers and magazines may quote spoken words as often and as fully as they wish providing their purpose is the reporting of current events. Broadcasters and cable television producers are free to reproduce spoken words for any purpose. If speakers do not wish their words to be used, the onus is on them specifically to prohibit such use. These provisions apply whether the words are spoken in private or in public.

3.5.4 Other defences under the CDPA

Copyright is not infringed if works are copied for the purpose of judicial proceedings or a report of judicial proceedings. The CDPA extended this defence to cover proceedings of Parliament or Royal Commissions.

Taking copies of material that is required by statute to be open to public inspection, including public records and company records, is not an infringement.

There are also detailed rules about copyright where material is reproduced for educational purposes or by libraries.

3.5.5 Public interest

The general public interest defence may also be raised. This is a common law rather than statutory defence, which has been developed by the court in circumstances where published material has been obtained unlawfully. Although there are no firm guidelines, the public interest has been recognized as a defence to a copyright claim. In 1984 the *Daily Express* was permitted by the court to publish copyright material concerning the accuracy of a machine used to test the breath of drivers for alcohol (*Lion Laboratories Ltd v Evans (1985)*). In 1993 an injunction was refused in respect of extracts from the memoirs of Margaret Thatcher on the grounds that the views of the last Prime Minister on certain topics such as contemporary politicians were clearly a matter of public interest (see also Chapter 6).

3.6 No copyright

Public policy may prevent copyright existing in a work. In 1916, the courts held that a novel entitled *Three Weeks* could not be the subject of copyright because it had an immoral theme. The same book would be protected by copyright today, when even so-called 'video nasties' are the subject of copyright. The rule is very limited.

3.7 Duration of copyright

Copyright is a monopoly right. The law of copyright attempts to balance the protection of the author with the need for a free flow of ideas and information in order to allow people free access to works. In order to achieve this balance, copyright is limited in duration.

Duration

The copyright in all literary, dramatic, musical or artistic works under the CDPA lasts until 70 years from the end of the calendar year in which the author dies.

Copyright in sound recordings, films, broadcasts and cable programmes under the CDPA will last for 70 years from the end of the calendar year it was made or released.

Public domain

Once copyright has expired, the work enters the public domain. Anyone is free to deal with the work as they choose. There is no need to pay a licence fee or obtain permission from the owner. This can result in a sudden rush of different editions of the work of a particular author. It can also have financial consequences. For example, the Great Ormond Street Children's Hospital received a large amount of money from the copyright of J. M. Barrie's book *Peter Pan*. This source of money stopped when copyright expired at the end of 1987, and resulted in serious financial consequences for the hospital.

Older works

Older works are subject to transitional provisions in the CDPA. Whether such works can be revived or extended is a complex matter that usually requires specialist legal advice.

3.8 Remedies

3.8.1 Injunctions

Interim injunctions and permanent injunctions are available in actions for breach of copyright. The principles and practice are similar to those applicable in other civil actions (see Chapter 1).

3.8.2 Damages

The calculation for damages for breach of copyright is complicated. Damages are not available from a defendant who did not know or had no reason to believe that copyright existed in the work infringed.

Under the CDPA, three different types of damages are available:

1. Infringement damages
2. Flagrant damages
3. Account of profits.

Infringement damages

Infringement damages are intended to compensate the claimant for the damage done to his interest. It is reparation for the owner to put him into the position he would have been in had the copyright not been infringed. These damages are normally calculated as the reasonable licence fee the defendant would have had to pay the claimant for the right to do what he did.

Flagrant damages

Flagrant damages can be awarded in addition to infringement damages. Under the Copyright Act 1956, if the court was satisfied when looking at the flagrancy of the infringement and any benefit the defendant obtained from it that 'effective relief' was not otherwise available to the claimant, it could award additional damages as it thought appropriate. The CDPA changed the test slightly. Now, the court can award such damages as the justice of the case may require. The court need not consider whether the claimant can obtain effective relief.

Flagrant damages are aimed at deterring the defendant. For example, if the claimant refused the defendant permission to publish something but the defendant did so regardless in order to benefit himself financially, the court might award additional damages to the claimant. If the owner would not have given permission at any price, for example for the publication of private papers, the damages would be higher. A similar situation will arise if publication causes distress to the claimant. In *Williams v Settle (1960)*, a photographer supplied wedding photographs to the press. Because the bride had commissioned the photographs, she owned the copyright under the law prior to the CDPA. The photographer sold them to the press for financial gain after the bride's father-in-law was murdered. The court awarded flagrant damages of £1000.

Account of profits

The claimant may choose to recover an account of profits instead of damages. The amount is calculated by reference to the profit made by the defendant, not the loss suffered by the claimant. Only profit is recoverable. The defendant may set off any expenses incurred in connection with producing the infringing articles against the amount he owes the claimant on account of profits. The calculation of profits can be a long and very expensive task.

3.8.3 Delivery up

Infringing copies of copyright works belong to the copyright owner. Under the CDPA, the owner of copyright can recover infringing copies from anyone who is in possession of them in the course of a business. This enables a copyright owner to demand delivery up, in other words the handing over, of copies of leaked documents. In *Secretary of State for Defence v Guardian Newspapers Ltd (1985)* the Government was granted an order for delivery up of copies of internal documents leaked to the *Guardian* by a government employee, Sarah Tisdall, because the infringing copies belonged to the Government Minister. The privilege against the disclosure of sources of information provided by Section 10 of the Contempt of Court Act 1981 did not protect the *Guardian* from handing over the documents, which identified their source (see also Chapter 11).

3.9 Criminal offences

Certain types of copyright infringement give rise to criminal penalties in addition to a civil claim in damages. The offences are directed at commercial exploitation of copyright.

It is an offence to make for sale or hire, to sell or let on hire, to exhibit in public by way of trade, or to import into the United Kingdom other than for private use, any article that is known to be an infringing copy. It is also an offence to distribute articles that are known to be infringing copies for the purpose of trade, or to such extent as to affect prejudicially the owner of the copyright.

The criminal offences are used mainly in relation to video and DVD pirates, who infringe copyright in films, and compact disc pirates, who infringe copyright in sound recordings. The penalties, which were increased in 1983 to take account of the gravity of piracy, include:

- On trial on indictment, two years' imprisonment and/or an unlimited fine
- On summary trial, two months' imprisonment and/or a fine of £2000.

The police have powers to search premises when criminal offences are suspected.

3.10 Other rights

3.10.1 False attribution of authorship

Damages are available if a person's name is put to a work that he did not author in such a way as to imply that he did. Publishing or selling such a work also gives rise to damages. In *Moore v News of the World Ltd (1972)*, the writer Dorothy Squires recovered the sum of £100 for false attribution of authorship. The newspaper had interviewed her and published an article stated to be by her. She claimed that she had not used the words published.

Publications that make up quotations are therefore at risk of a claim for false attribution of authorship.

The right under the CDPA extends to authors of literary, dramatic, musical or artistic works, as well as film directors, who are deemed to be the author of their film.

3.10.2 Moral rights

Prior to the CDPA, copyright was considered to be an economic right. The CDPA incorporated the provisions of the Berne Convention and the European legal concept of an author's moral right into the English law of copyright. A moral right is not an economic right. It has two aspects: the right of paternity and the right of integrity.

Moral rights actually have little relevance or effect in English law. In European countries moral rights are inalienable – in other words, they cannot be waived. Under the CDPA, an author has the power to waive his moral rights. Such a waiver must be in writing. An author can even consent to an infringement of his moral rights. It is normal for the author of a television programme or film script to agree to waive his moral rights in order for the producer to avoid the risk of overall editorial control by the author. Otherwise, the situation could arise where the author claims minor cuts or additions to his work breach the right to paternity or the right to integrity. Sometimes television programmes or film cannot be sold unless the purchaser, such as a broadcaster or distributor, can adapt the material to fit schedules or markets.

Paternity

The right of paternity is the right of the author of a literary, dramatic, musical or artistic work or the director of a film to be identified as the author. The right does not apply automatically. The identification as author must be clear, reasonably prominent, and in a form that may include use of a pseudonym approved by the author or director. The identification must appear in or on each copy of the work, or in some other way likely to be brought to the notice of people who obtain copies of the work or see the film. The author must also assert in writing the right to be identified in this way whenever the work is made available commercially to the public.

Where a copyright work is subject to fair dealing by film, radio or television for the purpose of reporting current events, identification is not required.

There are limitations to the right. Photographers and journalists do not have a right to credit for their work that is produced for the purpose of publication in a newspaper, magazine or similar periodical.

Damages are available if the author's right to be identified is ignored. There are no guidelines as to the appropriate measure of damages. They are meant to cover any financial loss suffered. An author or director may be able to prove financial loss as a result of a failure to bring his name to the attention of the public in connection with a successful work. No damages can be awarded for hurt feelings.

Integrity

The right of integrity is the right of an author of a literary, dramatic, musical or artistic work or the director of a film not to have his work subjected to 'unjustified modification' – in other words, any addition, deletion, alteration or adaptation. Modification is justified only if 'reasonable in the circumstances, and not prejudicial to the honour or reputation' of the author or director. There are no guidelines about what will be considered reasonable by this definition. Publication to the public of unjustified modified versions of copyright works infringes this right.

Authors who produce work in the course of their employment cannot complain if their employer consents to a modification. The rights of film directors employed under a contract are similarly limited.

There is another exclusion for works produced for newspapers or magazines. Editors and sub-editors need not worry about the author's rights as they cut stories or crop photographs. In such circumstances, there is no right for the author to maintain the integrity of such work.

Damages are available. There are no guidelines as to the appropriate amount. There is no specific exclusion of damages for hurt feelings. The court may order an injunction to prevent the use of an unjustified modified work unless a disclaimer is made at the same time, dissociating the author or director from the modified work.

3.11 The European Copyright Directive

In 2001, the European Union passed a directive aimed at harmonizing certain aspects of copyright and related rights in today's 'information society' and ensuring that all works protected by copyright are adequately protected throughout the European Union (the 'Copyright Directive')[1] (*2001/29/EC*).

The Government and each other Member State of the European Union is required under European Union law to give domestic effect to the Copyright Directive by 22 December 2002. The Copyright Directive will automatically amend the CDPA.

The Copyright Directive gives effect to the World Intellectual Property Organization Copyright Treaty 1996. The World Intellectual Property Organization (WIPO) is a specialized agency of the United Nations, which has taken a leading role in developing global policy and co-ordinates and administers international treaties relating to intellectual property.

3.11.1 Articles 2 and 3

The Copyright Directive extends core copyright concepts to digital media:

- The authorization or prohibition of dealing with copyrighted material is defined in Article 2 of the Directive as the 'reproduction right' and covers 'direct or indirect, temporary or permanent reproduction by any means and in any form, in whole or in part'
- Article 3 of the Directive deals with the right to authorize or prohibit distribution or publication of copyrighted works and provides that 'communication' to the public includes 'making works available to the public in such a way that members of the public may access them from a place and at a time individually chosen by them'.

[1]The Copyright Directive can be found at the European Union On-Line web site at www.europa.eu.int at http://europa.eu.int/eur-lex/en/lif/dat/2001/en_301L0029.html.

Both these Articles are clearly designed to encompass new forms of digital distribution and publication, such as the Internet.

Exemptions

The Directive sets out an exhaustive list of situations by which Member States may provide exemptions or defences to infringement of copyright. This gives national governments the power to adapt the rules to suit national needs. However, it may result in different regulations in different Member States.

Internet service providers

The group most favoured by the exemptions is Internet service providers. This is because they are classed as 'intermediaries' and regarded as having no independent economic significance. Article 5(1) of the Directive states:

> Temporary acts of reproduction . . . which are transient or incidental [and] an integral and essential part of a technological process . . . shall be exempted from the reproduction right.

Berne Convention requirements

The Copyright Directive limits the use of exemption situations by Member States. Exemptions or defences are only permissible if they satisfy the three-part test set out in Article 9(2) of the Berne Convention, which requires that an exemption or defence:

- Must apply only in special cases
- Must not conflict with normal exploitation of the work, and
- Must not unreasonably prejudice the legitimate interests of the author.

The result is that the interests of the copyright owner will always be protected, even where freedom of information is an issue.

Prohibition on exploitation

In addition, Member States are given power under Article 6 of the Copyright Directive to ensure that those who benefit from any exemptions or defences do not exploit them to keep information out of the public domain, for example by the use of technology such as 'firewalls' and encryption systems.

4 New Media

Estelle Overs

4.1 Introduction

New media is extremely important to those working in the media. Almost all traditional forms of publishing and broadcast are now stored and transmitted in new media formats. Newspapers and magazines are widely available on the Internet through personal computers, mobile telephones and handheld products. Television broadcasts are increasingly transmitted digitally via satellite and cable systems and often include Internet access, 'interactive elements' and pay-per-view films. Photographers using digital cameras are able to digitally transmit their photographs back to newspapers and magazines from anywhere in the world almost instantaneously. News reporters and broadcasters the world over use laptop computers, videophones, the Internet and portable mini television studios to send reports and pictures back from the most inaccessible areas of the globe within seconds.

The rapidly changing world of new media technology presents the law with new challenges. Television broadcasts by satellite and cable systems are subject to the same regulations as 'terrestrial' television, considered at Chapter 17. However, the law of England, along with that of most other jurisdictions, has not kept pace with the technology. Instead, the existing law has been developed and extended in order to deal with new issues presented by new media. More often than not these changes in the law are judge-made, brought about as a result of litigation rather than Government legislation.

The Internet poses the most difficult questions for the law. Many users of the Internet consider it to be a regulation-free zone that is not subject to domestic law or international regulation. To a certain extent this is true. The global nature of the Internet makes it difficult for individual countries to enforce their domestic laws. There is no international body or court with the authority to create or interpret the law of the Internet. However, the European Union and the Council of Europe as well as non-governmental bodies such as the World Intellectual Property Organization have taken steps to legislate in respect of the Internet. In addition, the United States of America is at the forefront of developing law and legislation relating to the Internet.

4.2. Internet defamation

4.2.1 General principles

The legal principles of defamation apply to publication in new media formats. In particular, widespread access to the Internet has multiplied the opportunity for publication of a defamatory statement.

Those working in the media should apply the existing legal principles of defamation to any material published in new media format in order to avoid being sued for defamation. In addition, there are four main areas of Internet publication that may give rise to an action for defamation:

1. The world wide web
2. Newsgroups
3. Email
4. Bulletin boards.

The world wide web

The world wide web (the 'Web') is the most important subdivision of the Internet. It is the largest system linking together millions of web sites and documents across the Internet.

Publication on the Web satisfies the requirement of communication to a third party. Each individual or organization is responsible for the documents they author and publish on the Web, whether the documents are published on their own web site or that of someone else.

Online newspapers and magazines are 'publishers' under the Defamation Act 1996, and must avoid defamatory statements in the same way as they would when publishing in traditional formats. The principles of vicarious liability apply, so that an online newspaper or magazine can be sued as well as an individual journalist or author.

Newsgroups

Newsgroups are Internet groups where subscribers post comments and discuss certain subjects. As soon as a message is posted, it is published to a third party.

The first court ruling in England on the issue of Internet defamation involved a posting on a newsgroup (*Godfrey v Demon Internet Ltd (2000)*). Godfrey brought a libel action against Demon, an Internet service provider, alleging that postings about him on a newsgroup hosted by Demon were defamatory. Prior to issuing proceedings, Godfrey asked Demon to remove the postings. Demon accepted that the postings were defamatory but claimed it was not responsible for material posted by its users.

The court accepted that Internet service providers such as Demon are excluded from the definition of 'publisher' under the Defamation Act 1996. This allowed Demon to raise the defence of 'innocent dissemination' under Section 1 of the Defamation Act 1996. However, because Godfrey had told Demon about the defamatory content, Demon was unable to argue that it was ignorant of the alleged defamation, a necessary element of the defence. The case settled out of court in March 2000 with Demon paying Godfrey damages and costs.

Email

Sending an email to any person other than the subject of the defamatory statement will amount to publication to a third party under English law. Great care must be taken when sending and particularly forwarding emails which contain statements that may be defamatory. An email sent in the belief that it will only reach the recipient can easily be very widely communicated, as happened in December 2000 when an email sent from Claire Swires to her boyfriend was forwarded to hundreds of people because of its sexual content. Even if an email is only sent to one recipient, it may be publication to a third party if it is sent from a workplace email account where there is a policy of routine monitoring of emails.

In *West Provident Association v Norwich Union Life Assurance (1997)*, West Provident sued in respect of rumours published in emails sent on Norwich Union's intranet system. The rumours were that West Provident was insolvent and was being investigated by the DTI. West Provident obtained an order for the preservation and delivery of copies of the emails. Norwich Union settled the case out of court by paying West Provident costs and damages.

The court has demonstrated a willingness to order companies to co-operate in identifying the sender of anonymous defamatory emails. In 2000, David Frankl was ordered to pay damages and costs in respect of three emails sent under a false name to his former employer, which contained defamatory statements about the company's managing director. Frankl's former employer obtained court orders forcing Microsoft and Compuserve to co-operate in tracing the defamatory emails to a laptop used by Frankl (*Takenaka (UK) Ltd v Frankl (2000)*).

Bulletin boards

Individuals subscribe to a bulletin board to contribute comments on a particular subject. Bulletin boards are often used in business and academic communities. Every subscriber receives a copy of each posting, thereby satisfying the requirement of publication to a third party. Great care must be exercised when posting on bulletin boards. In an Australian case in 1994, damages for defamation were awarded against a man who posted a message on a science anthropology news bulletin board. The board had a global academic readership. The message alleged that an anthropologist had been dismissed from a university position because of sexual misconduct and lack of professional competence. The court was satisfied that the message had caused serious harm to the anthropologist's personal and professional reputation and had made it more difficult for him to obtain employment (*Rindos v Hardwick (1994)*).

4.2.2 Jurisdiction

One of the major features of Internet defamation is that the defamatory statement will be published to third parties throughout the world. This gives the prospective claimant a choice of jurisdiction in which to issue proceedings, as well as a choice of law.

An action for defamation can arise in the country where the defamatory statement is downloaded and read on screen by third parties. However, countries have different legal principles of defamation. The claimant must therefore consider the legal principles of each country of publication as well as other important matters such as procedure, costs and the likely level of damages in order to decide where best to issue defamation proceedings.

The courts are beginning to recognize the complex issues involved in defamatory statements published on the Internet and read in other jurisdictions. In 2000, the House of Lords held that a Russian businessman could sue a United States magazine called *Forbes* in England in respect of alleged defamatory statements published on the magazine's web site (*Berezovsky v Michaels (2000)*). In the case of *Gutnick v Dow Jones (2001)* the Australian Supreme Court allowed Gutnick, an Australian, to sue Dow Jones, a United States company, for defamation in Australia in relation to an article published by Dow Jones on its web site. The court rejected the contention by Dow Jones that the proceedings should take place in the United States because the article was only intended to be read there.

Publishers must attempt to comply with the laws of every country where an article can be read in order to avoid proceedings for defamation in another jurisdiction that may be less favourable than the publisher's own.

Global publication also raises the issue of enforcement of orders in other jurisdictions. Many courts do not recognize judgments in other jurisdictions because there is no reciprocal mechanism in place or because the law is contrary to their own. Claimants must consider whether it is worthwhile issuing proceedings in a jurisdiction where there is little likelihood of enforcement.

4.2.3 European E-commerce Directive

In order to combat the problems posed by the application of different legal principles in different jurisdictions, the European Union, of which the United Kingdom is a Member State, approved a directive in 2000 aimed at harmonizing certain legal aspects of 'information society services' in Europe – in particular electronic commerce (the 'E-commerce Directive')[1] (*2000/31/EC*). The Government is required under European Union law to give domestic effect to the E-commerce Directive by 17 January 2002.

---

[1]The E-commerce Directive can be found at the European Union On-Line web site at www.europa.eu.int at http://europa.eu.int/eur-lex/en/lif/dat/2000/en_300L0031.html.

The E-commerce Directive will have a impact on Internet defamation. Under Article 12, Internet service providers such as Demon in the *Godfrey v Demon Internet Ltd (2000)* case will not be liable for information transmitted on their sites as long as they do not initiate the transmission, select the recipient or modify the information contained in it. Under Article 15 of the E-commerce Directive they will not be obliged to monitor the information and content they transmit and store. However, under Article 14 they will be required to remove unlawful material such as defamatory statements from their sites if it is brought to their attention. Publishers of online newspapers and magazines do not fall within the provisions.

The situation is different in the United States where no liability is imposed upon Internet service providers for defamatory material.

4.3 Copyright

4.3.1 Original works

General principles

Any media company publishing in multimedia format or on the Internet needs to ensure that its copyright is fully protected. Individual authors must also ensure they have protection for original work. However, complex copyright issues arise where a company or author of an original multimedia product wishes to protect the labour in the work that has been created.

There is no one category under the Copyright, Designs and Patents Act 1988 (the 'CDPA') that can provide overall protection for multimedia products. However, it is possible to protect the various different aspects of a multimedia product such as the text, graphics, images and audio and video on a web site or a CD-ROM under the different categories provided by the CDPA.

Registration

Under the CDPA, the owner of copyright does not need to go through any formalities such as registration in order to protect a copyright work. No copyright notice need appear on a work. However, for international copyright protection under the Universal Copyright Convention the formula ©, the name of the copyright owner and date of first publication must be placed on a work.

Employees and sub-contractors

If employees create an original work for a web site in the course of their employment, the normal rule is that copyright is owned by the employer in the absence of any agreement to the contrary.

Anyone working for himself owns the copyright in any work he produces unless he assigns it to someone else. It is important for freelance journalists to look carefully at any freelance contract, which may assign copyright. If a sub-contractor such as a web-site designer is engaged to create a web site, he will be the owner of the copyright unless there is agreement to the contrary.

In circumstances where a media company commissions work by a freelancer or sub-contractor, the media company must ensure that it obtains full assignment, in other words full ownership, of the entire copyright in order to exploit the work fully in all formats. In the absence of full ownership, the freelancer or sub-contractor may assert that the media company is only able to use the work in a certain way. For example, a media company which commissions a freelancer to write an article for a newspaper may find that it is unable to reproduce the article online in the absence of a full assignment of copyright.

4.3.2 Pre-existing works and contributions by third parties

Rights clearance

Producers or publishers of multimedia products that include or consist of pre-existing rather than original works, or include contributions by third parties, must ensure that they have obtained rights clearance in respect of all the pre-existing works and contributions. This can be a lengthy and expensive exercise.

Rights clearance involves satisfying:

- Copyright – by licence
- Moral rights – by waiver, and
- Performers' rights, such as actors or musicians – by consent to exploit any performers' rights under Section 180 of the CDPA.

For example, an online magazine or a web page accessed via an interactive television service may include pre-existing material such as articles that have previously been published elsewhere, photographs, graphics or other moving images. It may also include contributions by a third party such as interviews or performances by actors or singers. The producer or publisher of the magazine or interactive television service must ensure that he has obtained licences, waivers and consents from each copyright owner and performer for permission to 'copy, adapt and issue copies' to the public.

Producers of live web cams and broadcasts or 'reality TV' programmes must be particularly careful to ensure that those appearing in their programmes do not breach the copyright of others. This can easily occur when photographs or other images subject to copyright are shown or songs or music are played during the broadcast. The problem can be avoided by a slight time delay in the broadcast during which any infringing material can be removed.

Many large media organizations have programme libraries and archives. A producer or publisher can carry out a search in respect of pre-existing material to determine whether the material or clip has been used by the media organization before. If it has been used, there should be a record of the terms of any copyright licence, moral rights waiver and performers' rights payments. If it has not been used, or if there is no archive or library, the producer or publisher must negotiate direct with the copyright owner over use of the material. Use of extracts from copyrighted music and clips of film and television footage can be extremely expensive.

If a multimedia product can only be accessed by using other software, for example to read material stored on a compact disc or CD-ROM, it is also necessary to obtain a licence from the copyright owner of the software so that the viewer of the multimedia product can use the software to read the product.

Infringement

Copying, issuing copies to the public, performing in public, broadcasting, adapting, selling or hiring a work that is protected by copyright without the permission of the owner is an infringement of copyright.

Linking and framing are two additional areas of likely infringement on the Internet. A hypertext link links one web site to another. Framing displays another web site in a smaller window. It has not been established under English law whether linking from one web site to another or framing another web site infringes copyright in the linked or framed web site.

It is possible that a media company publishing online may infringe the copyright of another web-site owner by including a link to or a frame of that web site. Links to and frames of other news stories and web sites are common in online newspapers and magazines. In order to ensure that copyright is not infringed, the ideal situation is to obtain the permission of each web site to which there is a link or frame. However, in practical terms this may be difficult to achieve. An alternative approach is to link to or frame the home page of the web site rather than individual pages, so that the user can see and identify the web site he is entering via the link or frame.

4.3.3 Research on the Internet

The Internet is increasingly used as a research tool. Material that is published on the Internet is subject to copyright and is not in the public domain.

If a member of the media wishes to use material from the Internet whether purchased from an online catalogue or obtained for free from a web site in an article or programme, he must ensure that the relevant copyright and performers' rights clearance have been obtained. This is particularly important when downloading current or archive news stories or video clips.

4.3.4 Domain names

General principles

Domain names are unique names that identify specific Internet web sites. Because a domain name is not recognized as an intellectual property right under English law, it is not possible to bring an action for copyright infringement of a domain name.

However, the English courts have in recent years begun to use the law of trademarks and passing off in order to provide a remedy for those who have been subject to alleged infringement of a registered domain name or a recognized company or brand name used as a domain name. The decision which showed that the English courts will not look kindly on those who 'grab' domain names with the intention of selling them back to the brand owners. *Marks & Spencer and Others v One In A Million Ltd and Others (1997)* in that case, the defendants had registered a long list of domain names including marks&spencer.com, virgin.org, sainsburys.com, thetimes.co.uk, bt.org and bskyb.net.

Registration

Several web companies offer domain name registration services, as do registries in other countries that allocate domain names based on geographical location such as .uk and .fr. However, the so-called 'top level' domain names such as .com, .net and .org can only be registered by registrars accredited by the Internet Corporation for Assigned Names and Numbers (ICANN), a non-profit organization based in the United States. ICANN works with the World Intellectual Property Organization (WIPO), a specialized agency of the United Nations that has taken a leading role in developing global policy and co-ordinates and administers international treaties relating to intellectual property protection.

Disputes

If a dispute arises in relation to a domain name, proceedings should be issued in the English courts for infringement of a trademark under the Trademarks Act 1994 and passing off.

If the domain name has been registered by an ICANN accredited registrar, it is also possible to apply for an adjudication as to whether the domain name should be returned under the Uniform Administrative Dispute Resolution Policy (UDRP). Under UDRP, disputes over the entitlement to a registered domain name must first be resolved by court litigation between the parties claiming rights to the registration. Once the court rules as to who is entitled to the registration, the ICANN accredited registrar will implement that ruling.

If the dispute arises from a registration that is alleged to have been made abusively, such as 'cybersquatting', UDRP provides an expedited administrative procedure that allows the dispute to be resolved without the cost and delay of litigation by one of ICANN's approved dispute resolution service providers. The disputed domain name does not have to be a registered trademark in order to fall within the remit of UDRP. The author Jeanette Winterson was recently granted relief against cybersquatting over jeanettewinterson.com in recognition of her 'character' or 'personality' rights.

4.3.5 European directives and international conventions

European directives

There is little harmonization of copyright laws throughout the Member States of the European Union. In an effort to provide a more uniform system of regulation, the European Union has recently approved two directives that promote and facilitate the exchange of information in new media formats.

The Copyright Directive

The Copyright Directive[2] (*2001/29/EC*) was approved in 2001 and is aimed at ensuring that all works protected by copyright are adequately protected throughout the European Union. It places particular emphasis on new media products and systems and legislates specifically in respect of the 'reproduction right', distribution and the legal protection of anti-copying devices. The Government is required under European Union law to give domestic effect to the Copyright Directive by 22 December 2002. The Copyright Directive will automatically amend the CDPA.

However, the Copyright Directive sets out an exhaustive list of situations in which Member States may provide exceptions or defences to infringement of copyright. This gives national governments the power to adapt the rules to suit national needs, and may result in different regulations in different Member States.

The E-commerce Directive

The E-commerce Directive (*2000/31/EC*) was approved in 2000 and is aimed at harmonizing certain legal aspects of 'information society services' in Europe, in particular electronic commerce. The Government is required under European Union law to give domestic effect to the E-commerce Directive by 17 January 2002.

Article 13 of the E-commerce Directive provides that internet service providers will not be liable for breach of copyright or other intellectual property rights by 'caching', or storing, information on the Internet as long as they comply with any conditions of access to the information imposed by the owner and do not modify the information. In addition, they must act expeditiously to remove or disable access to information if they are informed that the information has been removed from the Internet or a court has ordered that the information must be removed or disabled. However, under Article 15 of the E-commerce directive an Internet service provider is not obliged to monitor the information and content it transmits and stores.

[2]The Copyright Directive can be found at the European Union On-Line web site at www.europa.eu.int at http://europa.eu.int/eur-lex/en/lif/dat/2001/en_301L0029.html.

International conventions

Treaties on copyright

The global nature of the Internet means that international protection of copyright is of considerable importance. Two international treaties on copyright, the Berne Convention and the Universal Copyright Convention, provide for possible world-wide protection of copyright for authors of original material. Many countries, including the United Kingdom and the United States, are signatories to both conventions. In addition, the WIPO co-ordinates and administers international treaties relating to intellectual property protection.

Media companies and authors who are concerned about the global protection of material on their web sites should consider registration under the Berne and Universal Copyright conventions. However, if there is specific concern over copyright infringement in particular countries, specialized legal advice should be sought about the particular country's national copyright registration requirements.

Council of Europe

The Council of Europe is a political organization founded in 1949, which is distinct from the European Union and develops agreements to standardize the social and legal practices of member countries. It has drawn up a convention on cyber-crime,[3] which will create criminal offences in respect of the reproduction and distribution on a commercial scale by computer of copyrighted works. The convention was adopted on 8 November 2001 and will be legally effective when at least five countries ratify it, a process expected to take up to two years. Non-member states, including Japan and the United States, have been invited to become involved with the convention.

In September 2001, the Council of Europe adopted a recommendation concerning protection against piracy in the digital environment. The recommendation sets out measures to protect copyright and combat piracy in the digital environment. It also recommends establishing Europe-wide anti-piracy policies that recognize intellectual property rights and provide appropriate sanctions. The recommendation is unlikely to be incorporated into domestic law in the immediate future.

4.4 The Data Protection Act 1998

From 24 October 2001, every business in the United Kingdom must ensure that it complies with the principles of data protection set out in the Data Protection Act 1998 (the 'DPA'). This includes producers or publishers of multimedia products, web-site operators established in the United Kingdom, and web-site operators established in another country but using equipment in the United Kingdom for processing data.

[3]The convention can be found at http://conventions.coe.int/treaty/en/projets/cybercrime.htm.

The Information Commissioner, who oversees the DPA, has given guidance in relation to the collection and processing of data on web sites.[4]

In addition to compliance with the general principles of data protection, the DPA places an obligation on web-site operators, including the publishers of online newspapers and magazines, to take 'appropriate technical and organizational measures' to prevent the unauthorized or unlawful processing of personal data stored in their software systems, whether by employees or 'hackers'.

'Personal data' refers to data kept on or in connection with a web site, including the collection of visitors' email addresses and forums for the exchange of information by visitors, as well as workplace computer systems and manual records. Data about companies are not subject to the DPA unless named individuals are referred to as points of contact. The appropriate level of security depends on the type of information stored – for example, financial information will require greater security than information relating to visitors' favourite football players.

The DPA also applies if personal information is held for the purposes of marketing, either manually or on a computer system. The use of cookies, software that records a visitor's preferences and page choices, does not fall within the remit of the DPA as such. However, as cookies usually collect personal data about each visitor to the web site, the principles of the DPA will most likely apply. The Information Commissioner is of the view that, in some circumstances, cookies are subject to the provisions of the DPA. In order to avoid any possible breach information obtained by cookies should be regarded as subject to the provisions.

Under the provisions of the DPA personal data must not be transferred out of the European Economic Area (which is the European Union Member States, Norway, Iceland and Liechtenstein) unless the country or territory to which it is transferred ensures an adequate level of protection for rights of the 'data subject' – in other words the person to whom the personal data relates, or the data subject, has consented. This can be problematic because of the global nature of the Internet. Many countries outside the European Economic Area, including the United States, do not have equivalent data protection. However, the United States Government has encouraged companies processing data in the United States to comply with the voluntary data protection provisions of the International Safe Harbor Privacy Principles.

Although it is not a requirement of data protection law to include a privacy statement on a web site that collects personal data, it is regarded by the Information Commissioner as best practice. The privacy statement should be positioned where visitors to the web site are most likely to read it.

[4]The Information Commissioner's web site is at www.dataprotection.gov.uk.

Failure to comply with the DPA can result in an enforcement notice, which may include the deletion of all material stored in a database. Failure to comply with a notice is a criminal offence. Any person whose data has been compromised can sue for compensation.

4.5 Reporting restrictions

Producers and publishers must ensure that any new media publication does not breach reporting restrictions such as a postponement order under Section 4(2) of the Contempt of Court Act 1981, an anonymity order under Section 11 of the Contempt of Court Act 1981, or one of the several other orders that restrict the publication of material arising out of legal proceedings.

Although one of the functions of the media is to report news stories as they happen it has, until recently, been relatively easy for the English courts to prevent and control news coverage by imposing reporting restrictions on the domestic media. However, high profile news stories in England are frequently the subject of media coverage around the world. In the past, publication overseas has resulted in 'leakage' rendering orders imposing reporting restrictions virtually useless. The global nature of the Internet and international 24-hour satellite and cable news channels have increased the risk of pre-trial prejudice and contempt of court in breach of reporting restrictions. It is now easy to circumvent reporting restrictions in England by reading about court proceedings in an overseas online newspaper.

The risk posed by global media coverage is twofold: first, that the media in England will publish the same reports as those published overseas; and second, that jurors will be so influenced by what they have read on the Internet and seen on the news that the defendant will not receive a fair trial.

If the media in England publish information subject to reporting restrictions based on stories broadcast or published overseas they will be in contempt of court and will be subject to sanctions. However, 'hard copy' is much easier for the courts to control than publication on the Internet. In 1995, reporting restrictions were imposed by the court at the beginning of the trial of Rosemary West, the notorious murderer. Details of the committal hearing were posted anonymously on the Internet overseas and subsequently reported by the press in England.

In January 2001, the court attempted to grapple with the issue of publication on the Internet. The two child murderers of James Bulger sought injunctions against the whole world, an extremely wide and unusual order, to prevent the publication of confidential information that might lead to their identification following their release from prison. The court found that there was a 'real possibility' the applicants could be the objects of revenge attacks if information relating to their identities was made public. It therefore considered an injunction to be appropriate but expressed concern about the practical difficulties of enforcing such an injunction because of the risk of publication overseas and on the Internet. The judge concluded that although an injunction might not be:

... fully effective to protect the claimants from acts committed outside England and Wales, resulting in information about them being placed on the Internet ...

If publication on the Internet occurred, the injunction could remain in force in order to prevent wider circulation of the published information.

Although only certain newspapers were defendants to the application, the court granted the injunction against the whole world. The effect of the order was that any person or company anywhere in the world publishing details about the applicants in England, including Internet service providers based in England who hosted or made available such material, would automatically be in contempt of court (*Venables v News Group Newspapers Ltd (2001)*).

In June 2001 the matter came back before the court. The Internet service provider Demon asked the court to 'define the parameters' of its responsibility because the injunction covered all the content on its servers generated anywhere in the world. The court modified the injunction so that Internet service providers would only be in contempt if they had knowledge of the breach but failed to take reasonable steps to prevent publication or to block access to the information.

The modification of the order brings the responsibility of Internet services providers based in England in line with the decision in *Godfrey v Demon Internet Ltd (2000)* and the obligation imposed upon them by the E-commerce Directive. They will be responsible for the information they carry, irrespective of the county of origin, if its unlawfulness is brought to their attention.

4.6 Obscenity and racial hatred

Obscenity

Under the Obscene Publications Act 1959, as amended by the Criminal Justice and Public Order Act 1994, a person who makes obscene material available for transmission or downloads or communicates obscene material by electronic transmission commits an offence.

It is not possible to access the Internet without an Internet service provider. As a result, Internet service providers have been targeted by law enforcement agencies and action groups for providing access to obscene material. For example, in Germany in 1997 the local manager of CompuServe was prosecuted in connection with child pornography on the Internet, which was hosted on CompuServe's servers.

However, the Government and the European Union support self-regulation by Internet service providers rather than the passing of specific obscenity legislation. Under Article 15 of the E-commerce Directive, Internet service providers will not be obliged to monitor the information and content transmitted and stored on their systems, although they will be required to remove unlawful material from their sites if it is brought to their attention.

Racial hatred

It is an offence to incite racial hatred under the Public Order Act 1986. This applies to any material published in new media form.

Internet service providers have been targeted by enforcement agencies and action groups in relation to racial hatred. In 2000, an anti-racism group in Paris sought an injunction in a French court against Yahoo! prohibiting Internet users in France from accessing a web site hosted by Yahoo! that auctioned Nazi memorabilia. Although the site was not available on Yahoo!'s French-language portal Yahoo.fr, it was available on Yahoo.com, which is based in the United States but easily accessible to Internet users in France. Yahoo! defended the proceedings on the grounds that the Yahoo.com service is governed by United States law and, as a result, auctions of Nazi material could not be prevented because of the constitutional right to freedom of speech in the United States.

The French court held that Yahoo! had to respect French laws prohibiting the exhibit or sale of objects that incite racial hatred. It granted the injunction. Yahoo! issued proceedings in the United States, inviting the court to consider whether foreign countries have jurisdiction over the domestic activities of United States companies and material published on American web sites. In 2001, a United States judge ruled that he could hear the case. On 7 November 2001, a District Judge in California held that the First Amendment right to freedom of speech was the dominant legal consideration and ruled that the order made by the French court was inconsistent with United States law. However, the anti-racism group has appealed the judgment, which will have a considerable impact on the issue of foreign jurisdiction over unlawful material on the Internet.

Yahoo! was not prepared to become involved in a similar situation in England. In 2001, following several complaints, it closed down an English web site that advocated racism on the basis that the web site was 'inappropriate'.

Council of Europe

The Council of Europe has drawn up a convention on cyber-crime which was adopted on 8 November 2001 and is likely to become law within the next two years.

The convention will be the first international treaty on cyber-crime. It aims to provide co-ordinated laws on the possession of obscene material as well as 'hacking', the illegal interception of data and computer-related fraud and forgery. It will also regulate in relation to police investigations and enforcement in cases that cross international borders. Non-member states, including Japan and the United States, have been invited to become involved with the convention.

In September 2001 the Council of Europe adopted a recommendation concerning illegal or harmful content on the Internet. The recommendation proposes guidelines for member governments concerning measures that need to be taken in co-operating with the Internet industry. It also stresses the importance of Europe-wide and international co-operation to counteract the distribution of illegal and harmful content, such as obscene and racist material. The recommendation is unlikely to be incorporated into domestic law in the immediate future.

5 Rights Clearances

Philip Alberstat

5.1 Introduction

When producing an original programme, publication, or one that incorporates pre-existing material, it is vital for the producer or editor to 'clear' any rights belonging to third party contributors. Failure to clear such rights will result in infringement of the copyright, moral rights or performers' rights of the contributor, and may result in legal action and financial liability.

The producer or editor must decide whether he wishes to acquire copyright outright, in other words assign it, or clear it for specific use under a licence. If copyright is to be assigned, the lawyers for each party should draw up the terms of purchase at the earliest opportunity. If copyright is to be cleared for specific use, the terms of a licence must be agreed between the producer or editor and the contributor that allow the pre-existing material to be exploited as part of the programme or publication.

The producer or editor must determine at the outset whether the contributor's work is to be exploited in only one form of media, such as television or print, or in all forms of media. This is a particularly important consideration in light of the widespread publication of material in new media formats.

Rights clearance is a time-consuming and costly process. Using extracts from copyrighted music or clips of film, television and radio footage and interviews can be extremely expensive. However, it is important to ensure that all contributor rights are cleared before the programme is broadcast or the article published. Failure to do so risks embroiling the producer or editor in lengthy civil litigation, an even more expensive exercise, or possible criminal proceedings. Broadcasters and distributors should always ensure that producers and editors give appropriate warranties and indemnities.

Several specimen agreements for obtaining rights clearance can be found in Appendix C to this book.

5.2 Copyright, moral rights and performers' rights

The three type of rights the producer or editor must clear are copyright, moral rights and performers' rights. The principles of copyright and moral rights are considered in detail in Chapter 3.

Rights clearance involves satisfying:

- Copyright – by assignment or licence
- Moral rights – by waiver, and
- Performers' rights, such as actors or musicians – by consent to exploit.

Payment of a 'use fee' will also be required.

5.2.1 Copyright

The law of copyright prevents a person from copying the work of another without his permission. A producer or editor must ensure that 'underlying works', such as a script or book upon which a programme is based or music used in the programme, as well as other copyright works integrated into the film, such as clips from films, television programmes, interviews and songs and sound recordings, are all cleared with the copyright owner and an appropriate fee paid.

Fair dealing

Copyright clearance is not required for news reporting and criticism and review under the 'fair dealing' defence provided by the Copyright, Designs and Patents Act 1998 ('the CDPA'). However, there is no definition of what is meant by fair dealing. Each case will depend on what is taken and the reasons for which it was taken.

When reporting current events, no acknowledgement is necessary. However, when material is used for a criticism or review, the work and the author must be given an acknowledgement.

Fair dealing does not apply to use of photographs. Consent for the use of photographs must be sought from the copyright owner, who will be the photographer himself unless he has assigned the copyright to the person or company who commissioned the photograph.

Incidental inclusion

The defence of 'incidental inclusion' under Section 31 of the CDPA is aimed at allowing programme makers and news broadcasters to show works that might otherwise breach copyright. The general rule is that the inclusion of a work is allowed, provided that the maker has no control over the inclusion of the pre-existing copyright work – for example, capturing background music when interviewing people in the street.

Spoken words

Under Section 58 of the CDPA, spoken words in public or private may be quoted for the purpose of reporting current events or for broadcasting or inclusion in a cable programme service, as long as:

- They are not taken from any previous written or spoken recording or broadcast or cable programme
- Any copyright already in existence is not infringed, and
- The person lawfully in possession of the recording gives permission.

As a result, newspapers and magazines may quote spoken words as often and as fully as they wish, providing their purpose is the reporting of current events and permission is given. Broadcasters and cable television producers are free to reproduce spoken words for any purpose, as long as they are a recording original to the broadcaster or cable programme and permission is given.

5.2.2 Moral rights

A moral right has two aspects: the right of paternity and the right of integrity. It is often said that moral rights have little relevance or effect in English law. In European countries moral rights are inalienable – in other words, they cannot be waived. However, under the United Kingdom's CDPA an author has the power to waive his moral rights in writing.

It is normal for the author of a programme or script in the United Kingdom to agree to waive his moral rights so that the producer can avoid the risk of overall editorial control by the author. In order to obtain an effective waiver of moral rights, the waiver should be in writing and signed by the proper owner.

If a work falls out of copyright, the author's moral rights will also come to an end.

5.2.3 Performers' rights

A producer must obtain the written consent of a performer such as an actor, singer, dancer or musician for any recording and/or exploitation of his performers' rights. For example, the broadcast of a commissioned performance, under Section 180 of the CDPA.

Interviews

Interviews should be distinguished from 'spoken words' as defined under Section 58 of the CDPA. Producers should ensure that any person giving a formal interview for a television or radio programme signs an interview agreement permitting the recording and exploitation of the interview in order to ensure that both the copyright and the performers' rights in the interview are assigned.

Editors publishing interviews in written form alone need only obtain assignment of copyright in respect of the recording and publication of the interview, as there is no 'performance'.

5.2.4 Use fees

The payment requirements of 'use fees', in other words the fees to be paid by the producer or editor to the contributor, are generally set out in the assignment or licence.

However, specific industry collective bargaining agreements have been concluded in order to save producers and others having to negotiate individually with each contributor. These agreements exist in the film, television and music industries, and contain certain minimum pay as well as use and exploitation terms in respect of contributors. For example, the Producers' Alliance for Cinema and Television (PACT) has negotiated an agreement with the Writers' Guild of Great Britain Agreement (WGGB), and the actors' union Equity has reached agreements with the BBC, ITV and PACT in respect of performers' rights.

When arrangements with contributors are made under collective bargaining agreements, the accepted form of agreement for payment of fees and for the use and exploitation of the contribution should accomplish the payment requirements and rights consents needed by a producer.

5.3 Assignments and licences of copyright

5.3.1 Assignments

The most complete form of rights clearance is a transfer of the copyright, referred to as an assignment. Taking an assignment of copyright will give the producer or editor the right to use that work in the proposed production or publication and the right to control all further exploitation of the finished product. However, the exploitation will be restricted by the terms on which the copyright was assigned.

The length of time for which copyright is assigned is usually for the full period of the copyright. However, it is possible to agree that copyright should be reassigned to the contributor after a shorter period of time or after a particular event, for example non-payment of use fees, has occurred.

It is essential that an assignment leaves absolutely no doubt that an assignment, rather than a licence, took place. The wording of an assignment must cover *all rights* in the work; not just those rights that presently exist, but also other rights that might be conferred in the future.

5.3.2 Licences

In many cases, a producer will obtain a licence, in other words a form of permission to use certain rights, rather than an outright assignment of a copyright work.

Where pre-existing material such as photographs or film clips are involved, a licence rather than an assignment will be granted.

A licence can include the following rights:

- To copy the work, for example filming or photographing the work or incorporating music or sound recordings
- To make further copies, for example of a finished film or programme
- To present or show the work in public
- To broadcast the work, or
- To adapt the work.

A licence can be as effective as an assignment of copyright. However, a producer or editor should keep in mind that a licence is a form of permission that can be withdrawn or terminated. The producer or editor should try to agree that the licence itself cannot be terminated.

A licence need not be in writing to be effective, except if it is an exclusive licence. In such circumstances it must be in writing and must be signed by the person granting the licence. For example, an exclusive copyright licence granted to a person will give him the right to do whatever he is licensed to do to the exclusion of anyone else, including the copyright owner.

As a matter of law, assignments of copyright must be in writing and must be signed by the person assigning his copyright.

5.3.3 Use and exploitation

Territory

The producer or editor may know at the outset that only certain rights need to be cleared in order to allow specific use of the programme or publication on a 'territorial' basis. For example, a producer may produce a television programme which is to be broadcast in the United Kingdom only and will not be sold to a distributor or broadcaster overseas. In such circumstances, the producer will clear any copyright only for use in the United Kingdom and, depending on the material, pay a small licence fee to the contributor.

If the producer or editor intends to produce material that is to be exploited overseas, for example through sales to distributors or broadcasters, he will need to clear contributor rights for world-wide use in order that the final product can be exploited as widely as possible. In such circumstances, the licence fee will be considerably greater than that paid for domestic exploitation.

Further use and exploitation

In many cases, a producer or editor may only be able to clear certain rights because of budgetary restraints. In such cases, he will clear and pay for specific rights, as well as obtain permission in principle from the rights owner for other uses or exploitation on condition that he pay a specific amount for such additional use or exploitation if and when it occurs.

If the producer or editor does not clear additional uses at the outset, he will need to enter into subsequent, separate negotiations for further exploitation of the rights in order to avoid breaching the contributor's copyright.

5.4 Rental rights

The Rental and Lending Rights Directive (the 'Directive') (92/100/EEC), formulated by the European Commission and incorporated into domestic law by the Copyright and Related Rights Regulations 1996 ('the Regulations') which amend the CDPA, is another issue that must be considered when dealing with rights clearances.

Under the Regulations, exclusive 'rental and lending rights' are granted to authors of literary, musical and dramatic works and most artistic works (as defined under the CDPA – see Chapter 3). Similar rights are granted to performers in respect of recordings of their performances.

When an author and a film producer enter into an agreement, the author's exclusive rental right in the film is presumed to be transferred to the producer unless the contract provides otherwise (Regulation 12). However, authors and performers who transfer their exclusive rental rights in films and sound recordings to producers retain a right to 'equitable remuneration' for rental of the sound recording or film. This right to 'equitable remuneration' cannot be waived by authors and performers (Regulation 14). Unfortunately, there are no payment scales or guidance as to what constitutes 'equitable remuneration'.

A producer of a film or sound recording should always ensure that any agreement with an author, lyricist, scriptwriter, playwright, director, interviewee or composer includes the transfer of rental rights along with the transfer of any copyright, waiver of moral rights or performers' rights consent. The producer must also secure the consent in writing of the individual, that the proposed remuneration is an appropriate payment for their services.

5.5 Music

The use of pre-existing music in a newly created work is an essential part of the rights clearance process. It is important to distinguish between commissioning music, use of pre-existing songs and recordings, and engaging live performers.

Commissioning music

If a piece of music is commissioned for a programme, an appropriate copyright agreement must be reached. A composer may have an existing agreement with a publishing or recording company, which may place restrictions on his ability to compose and record for third parties. In addition, organizations such as the Performing Right Society (PRS), Phonographic Performance Limited (PPL) and the Mechanical-Copyright Protection Society (MCPS) may also control certain rights in a composition or recording.

It is therefore essential that the contractual position of the composer or owner is checked carefully. A 'synchronization licence', in other words a licence granting permission by the copyright owner to use the composition in synchronization with a programme and, in most cases, to exploit the broadcast or programme with the composition, will be required from the music publisher for the use of the composition. In other circumstances, the composer can assign or license copyright in the new composition subject to the payment of a fee.

Use of pre-existing songs and recordings

Incorporating a pre-existing song or sound recording also requires the permission of the copyright owner. The PRS, PPL and MCPS also administer certain rights on behalf of their members, and operate as collecting societies.

The first step in obtaining a copyright clearance of a pre-existing song or recording is to identify who actually owns the rights. In most cases, contacting the PRS, MCPS or PPL is a useful resource for identifying ownership. Once again, a synchronization licence will be required when including a song in a programme that will be broadcast. Because of the complex nature of the industry, it is always best to obtain professional advice.

Engaging live performers

When using the services of a musician, most clearances can be obtained through existing collective bargaining agreements with the Musicians' Union. These agreements enable musicians to be engaged for recording sessions in return for a specific fee and expenses. The payment of these fees also allows certain basic uses of a musician's work. However, in most cases the further use of a musician's works will attract additional payments.

PART III
Privacy

6 Breach of Confidence

Joanna Ludlam

6.1 Introduction

The English law protects an individual from the misuse of personal information about him under common law and statute. The common law of breach of confidence protects information that is 'confidential'. The Data Protection Act 1998, considered in Chapter 7, protects personal data.

The law of breach of confidence is based on a 1848 case in which Prince Albert obtained an injunction to prevent the exhibition of etchings by himself and Queen Victoria in circumstances where the defendant had obtained copies of the etchings without consent. Although the law was subsequently developed to protect secret processes, inventions and trade secrets, its boundaries have been constantly pushed back, and in recent years it has been used more and more to prevent the publication of 'confidential' information in the media.

An action for breach of confidence and an injunction is the most appropriate method for an individual to prevent the publication of confidential information about him. It is relatively easy for a claimant to obtain an injunction restraining publication. Such an order, known as a 'blanket ban', will prevent publication of the confidential information itself as well as the fact that legal action has been taken by the claimant. Because the cost of taking an action to trial frequently deters the defendant from any further resistance, confidential information often never sees the light of day. The result is that an action for breach of confidence has become one of the most significant fetters on freedom of expression in the media.

Actions for breach of confidence are also frequently used by the Government as an effective alternative to a prosecution under the Official Secrets Act 1989.

However, Article 10 of the European Convention on Human Rights, right to freedom of expression, introduced into English law by the Human Rights Act 1998, is now the starting point for all cases involving restrictions on freedom of expression. As a result, the law of confidence may cease to be such an effective tool for restraining the media. Section 12 of the Human Rights Act 1998 prevents hearings made in the absence of the defendant, a common occurrence in breach of confidence applications, unless there are compelling reasons why the defendant should not be notified. Interim injunctions restraining publication are prohibited unless the court is satisfied that the claimant is likely to establish the restraint of publication at trial. Where hearings relate to journalistic material, the court must consider the extent to which the material is available to the public, or whether it is in the public interest to publish it.

6.2 What is breach of confidence?

6.2.1 Elements of the right

In order to establish a breach of confidence, a claimant must show that:

- The information has the necessary quality of confidence
- The information was imparted in circumstances which imposed an obligation of confidence, and
- There has been or will be unauthorized use of the information.

6.2.2 Information having the necessary quality of confidence

It may seem obvious to say that in order to be confidential information must be secret, since that is the whole idea of confidence. However, the 'necessary quality of confidentiality' is not always a straightforward issue.

Any type of information, whether in written or oral form, can be confidential. This even includes ideas. In *Fraser v Thames TV (1984)*, a writer gave a television company an idea in confidence for a television series. The company later made a similar television series without involving the writer. The writer issued proceedings against the company and was awarded damages for breach of confidence for the unauthorized use of his idea. The case demonstrates how important it is to take care when discussing ideas for written articles or television programmes. It can be difficult to show that an idea was independent and original.

The law of confidentiality has recently been expanded to include unauthorized photography. Breach of an obligation not to take photographs will give the claimant a cause of action on the basis of an 'imputed confidential relationship' (see part 6.2.3 below). In *Shelley Films v Rex Features (1994)* the claimant successfully prevented the defendant from using photographs of a film set that the defendant had taken despite signs on the set banning photography. In *Creation Records Ltd v News Group Newspapers Limited (1997)* a photographer from the *Sun* took photographs during a photo shoot for the cover of a new record by the rock group Oasis and published them in the newspaper, inviting readers to purchase a poster version of the photographs. Although the photographer was lawfully at the scene, the court held that the nature of the shoot and the imposition of security measures made it arguable that the shoot was intended to be confidential and the photographer knew he was only entitled to remain on the basis that he refrained from taking photographs. An injunction was granted preventing the publication of the photographs.

Confidentiality will not usually attach to information that is already general public knowledge or in the public domain. The question of whether the information has already been so widely published as to destroy its confidentiality will depend on the facts of each case. In circumstances where the marital secrets of John Lennon and his first wife, Cynthia, had been published by both parties in a number of articles in the past, the court held that the marriage had been placed in the public domain and refused to grant Lennon an injunction to prevent Cynthia selling further stories about the marriage to the *News of the World* (*Lennon v News Group Newspapers (1978)*). Similarly, when Jack Straw attempted to obtain an injunction in 2000 to prevent the publication of a newspaper article in the *Sun* newspaper about the supply of cannabis by his son to the newspaper's reporter, the court ruled that an injunction could not be granted as the information was already in the public domain.

By contrast, also in 2000 Prime Minister Tony Blair and his wife Cherie applied for an injunction to prevent the publication of the memoirs of their former nanny in the *Mail on Sunday*. By the time the application was heard by the court, some 1.5 million copies were off the press and in the distribution chain, firmly placing the information in the public domain. However, the court granted the Blairs an injunction to prevent publication on the grounds that the nanny was in breach of her duty of confidentiality to the Blairs as set out in her contract of employment, despite the fact it was too late to undo the damage. It is arguable that granting the injunction was inconsistent with established law. When information is already in the public domain, the courts are usually not prepared to grant injunctive relief and restrict the claim only to damages.

In some cases, a claimant can even obtain an injunction for breach of confidence to restrain publication of information that is already available to the public from other sources. In *Schering Chemicals v Falkman (1982)*, a television executive who had been asked to train employees of a chemical company in television techniques decided to make a programme about one of the company's drugs, which had been alleged to cause birth defects in children. Although the television executive had been given confidential information by the company as part of the training course, the relevant information for the programme was gathered from public sources. However, the court ordered that the programme should not be shown. It held that the television executive had abused his position of trust and could not be allowed to profit from such an abuse.

The court is faced with considerable difficulty when asked to prevent publication of material in England that has already been published abroad. The English law of confidence is very different to the law of other countries, notably the United States, where it is difficult to regulate reporting restrictions because of the First Amendment to the Constitution, which protects freedom of speech. The *Spycatcher* case is the best-known example. In 1986 the Government obtained interim injunctions that prevented certain newspapers from publishing allegations made by a former senior MI5 officer Peter Wright in his memoirs, *Spycatcher*. In 1987 the House of Lords ordered the continuation of the injunctions, although by that stage *Spycatcher* had already been published in the United States and the major allegations in the book had been reported by the press and television in the United Kingdom, as well as world wide. By the time the case reached trial, *Spycatcher* had also been published in Canada, Australia, Ireland and Europe, and could be freely imported into the United Kingdom. The trial judge, the Court of Appeal and eventually the House of Lords all decided that a permanent injunction should not be ordered against the newspapers, largely because of the widespread distribution of the book (*A-G v Guardian Newspapers Ltd (No 2) (1990)*).

Section 12 of the Human Rights Act 1998 ('the HRA') would, in all likelihood, prevent a recurrence of the *Spycatcher* scenario. Under Section 12(4)(a)(i) of the HRA, the court must have regard to the extent to which the information has already or is about to become available to the public.

However, the English courts can only control what happens in England and Wales. The ease with which information can be communicated across borders in modern society can often make a mockery of English court injunctions relating to confidential material. In 1986 an injunction was granted preventing publication of Joan Miller's MI5 memoirs, *One Girl's War*. However, anyone could obtain a copy of the book by taking a trip to Dublin. The Irish courts refused to grant the Government's application for an injunction because of the free speech provision of the Irish Constitution. In 1988 an injunction was granted preventing English newspapers from publishing certain parts of the autobiography of former MI6 officer Anthony Cavendish. However, as a result of a ruling by a Scottish court, Scottish newspapers were free to publish the material. In 1992 Paddy Ashdown, then the leader of the Liberal Democrat party, obtained an injunction against the *News of the World* preventing publication of information relating to an affair with his secretary on the grounds that it had been obtained from a confidential memorandum prepared by his solicitor. The order was a blanket ban on all facts and all names. In order to ensure universal compliance, a copy of the order was served on every other newspaper. Media reaction ranged from extreme concern to total outrage at the extent of the legal censorship. Within one week, the *Scotsman* had published the full story. As it was a wholly Scottish newspaper, it was not subject to the orders of the High Court in London and Ashdown could do nothing to prevent publication.

Confidentiality can be lost with the passage of time or a change in circumstances. In *A-G v Jonathan Cape (1976)* the Government applied to prevent publication of the *Crossman Diaries*, records of the career of former Cabinet minister Richard Crossman. The Government argued that it was in the public interest to prevent publication of the diaries because publication would deter the frankness required in Cabinet discussions for the effective running of Government. The court refused an injunction. It held that the confidentiality of the discussions had been lost because the information was several years old.

6.2.3 Circumstances imposing an obligation of confidence

Agreement

An obligation of confidence can arise by the terms of an agreement, whether in written or oral form.

Even if there is no term relating to confidentiality, the confidential nature of the agreement may be so obviously intended by the transaction that a duty of confidence will be imposed.

Private employees

A contract of employment may contain terms that expressly prevent an employee from disclosing information learned during the course of his employment. A contractual term imposing a duty of confidence will be more likely if the employee has access to secret information.

Even if his contract of employment does not contain an express confidentiality clause, an employee owes an implied duty of 'fidelity' to his employer. This includes an obligation not to disclose the trade secrets or confidential information of his employer. The duty is often used to prevent an employee setting up in competition with his ex-employer, for example by making use of lists of customers or other information taken from their employer. However, it can also be used to prevent an employee from leaking information about his employer to the media or other body.

The employee's duty of confidence lasts for the whole period of employment. However, it lingers on even after the end of the term of employment. It covers all information learned in the course of employment. In *Woodward v Hutchins (1977)*, the defendant, formerly employed as public relations advisor for pop stars such as Tom Jones, exposed their secrets in a newspaper. Although the defendant was bound by a duty of confidence, in the circumstances of the case the court refused an injunction and allowed him to publish. The court held that the pop stars had courted publicity and tried to create a particular image. If that image was false, it was in the public interest that the record be set straight. The obvious conclusion is that the court is prepared to let those who live by publicity die by publicity.

The court draws a distinction between ex-employees disclosing details that reveal the truth about a false image and those who simply reveal private secrets. Employees of Buckingham Palace who attempt to reveal private details about the Royal Family may be stopped by an injunction. When one newspaper published details in the 1980s, as revealed to it by a Palace servant, about Prince Andrew's then girlfriend, under the headline 'Koo's Sex Romps at Palace', it ended up paying £4000 to charity for acknowledged breach of confidence. Other famous employers have been swift to resort to the courts to preserve their privacy. In 2000, Tony and Cherie Blair obtained an injunction to prevent the *Mail on Sunday* publishing their ex-nanny's story on the front page.

The duty of confidence applies to a member of the media who takes a job in order to find out from the inside how a particular business or company works.

Government employees

An action for breach of confidence can also be used by the government to prevent employees giving information about their work to the media, or to suppress embarrassing or politically sensitive facts.

In theory, criminal sanctions apply to any leak of any official information by a government servant. However, in 1985 the acquittal of Clive Ponting showed that the government cannot trust a jury to convict under what is now Section 2 of the Official Secrets Act 1989 unless genuine national secrets are at risk. Ponting passed documents relating to the sinking of the Argentinian warship the *Belgrano* during the Falklands War to a MP because he believed the Government was positively and deliberately misleading the House of Commons.

Civil actions for breach of confidence are more likely to be effective in keeping official information from the media. Injunctions will be granted where the employee had access to secret information.

Successive governments are especially keen to preserve a blanket of silence about security and intelligence services. Injunctions have been obtained against former Government Communications Headquarters employees Dennis Mitchell and Jock Kane, who wanted to make allegations of inefficiency and wasted money at Government Communications Headquarters in Hong Kong, as well as former MI5 employees Joan Miller in respect of her book *One Girl's War*, which detailed her work as an MI5 agent, and Peter Wright in respect of his book *Spycatcher*. The fact that *Spycatcher* led to legal proceedings in England, Australia, New Zealand and Hong Kong showed the lengths to which the government is prepared is go to keep the work of its employees secret. More recently, David Shayler was charged with breaching the Official Secrets Act 1989 after disclosing information about MI5's activities to the *Daily Mail*. The Government tried, unsuccessfully, to extradite him from France. He returned to England voluntarily in August 2000, confident that the Official Secrets Act 1989 falls foul of the Human Rights Act 1998. However, the Court of Appeal held that there was no such incompatibility (*R v Shayler (2001)*). Shayler has sought leave to appeal the ruling to the House of Lords.

Civil servants and members of the armed forces and secret services do not have written contracts of employment, but do owe a duty of confidence.

Public Interest Disclosure Act 1998

The Public Interest Disclosure Act 1998 redefines to some extent the duty of confidence of an employee. Unofficially known as the 'whistle-blowing Act', the legislation seeks to protect workers from recriminations from employers if they report actual or suspected wrongdoing in good faith and in the public interest. This Act applies to most individual employees, but not to self-employed professionals, the police or the armed forces. It does not protect the public-spirited citizen who discloses corporate wrongdoing to the media in circumstances where he has no connection with the offender.

For disclosure to be protected by the legislation, the employee must have a 'reasonable belief' that a crime, miscarriage of justice or breach of a legal obligation has taken or is likely to take place and that information relating to such matters is likely to be deliberately concealed. An employee who makes disclosure to a third party unconnected with the employer needs to show that he would be subjected to a detriment if he made such disclosure to his employer, and that he is not making the disclosure for personal gain. As a result, an employee who sells information to the media will not benefit from the protection of the Public Interest Disclosure Act. However, an employee who provides information to the media without reward may be protected. In such circumstances, the court will consider the seriousness of the matter in determining whether disclosure was reasonable.

A member of the media who publishes information disclosed under the Public Interest Disclosure Act will not be protected by the legislation. Media publications are subject to the general principles of the law of confidence.

Relationship of confider and confidant

More often, the obligation arises by virtue of a relationship between the 'confider' and the 'confidant'. Whether or not a relationship is confidential depends on all the circumstances. It should be remembered that the issue of confidentiality will only arise if the information exchanged is of a confidential nature.

Husband and wife
The law will not permit the revelation of anything confided by one spouse to the other during a marriage. The protection of matrimonial secrets is based on the sanctity of marriage.

In *Argyll v Argyll (1967)*, the Duke of Argyll intended to reveal secrets of his marriage to the Duchess to the press. The marriage had ended in divorce because of the adultery of the Duchess. Although she had already published allegations of drug-taking about him, she was still granted an injunction. The court held:

> There could hardly be anything more intimate or confidential than is involved in that relationship, or than in the mutual trust and confidences which are shared between husband and wife. The confidential nature of the relationship is of its very essence.

However, matrimonial secrets may be published if the confidence of the whole marriage has been destroyed (*Lennon v News Group Newspapers (1978)*).

Other sexual relationships
The protection afforded to matrimonial confidences has been extended to other sexual relationships. In *Stephens v Avery (1988)* the claimant, a married woman, successfully sued her friend Mrs Avery, the editor of the *Mail on Sunday* Stewart Steven, and *Mail Newspapers plc* for damages for breach of confidence after the *Mail on Sunday* published details of her sexual relationship with another woman who had been the victim of a sensational murder. The court held there was no reason why information relating to sexual matters should not be the subject of an enforceable duty of confidence. Most people would regard information relating to their sex lives as high on their list of confidential matters.

In the past, 'kiss-and-tell' revelations, particularly those concerning a married person in an adulterous relationship, were unlikely to enjoy the protection of the law of confidence. In 1988 a male barrister tried to prevent publication in the *Sun* of letters he had written to his male lover. The court held that there was no confidentiality in a 'transient homosexual relationship'. However, in 1997 the television personality Michael Barrymore succeeded in obtaining an injunction against the *Sun* restraining further publication of information regarding his previous relationship with a man (*Barrymore v News Group Newspapers (1997)*). The court followed the reasoning in *Stephens v Avery*, and said:

> . . . common sense dictates that when people enter into a personal relationship of this nature it is not done for the purpose of publication in newspapers; the information about the relationship was for the relationship and not for some wider purpose . . . when people kiss and later one of them tells, the second person is almost certainly breaking a confidential arrangement, although this might not be the case if they merely indicate that there had been a relationship and do not go into detail. In this case the article went into detail about the relationship and therefore crossed the line into arguable breach of confidence.

Doctor and patient

The court has emphasized the public interest in preserving the confidentiality of medical records. In *X v Y (1988)*, the *News of the World* obtained information from local health authority medical records that showed that two of its doctors were suffering from AIDS but were still in practice. The information had been provided by an employee at the hospital treating the doctors.

The health authority issued proceedings in order to prevent publication of its confidential information. The court granted a permanent injunction to restrain publication of the confidential information. It held that discussion of the issues of public importance was permissible, for example whether there was any danger to patients who were being treated by a doctor with AIDS. However, it ruled that the doctors and their places of work could not be identified. If people suffering from AIDS decided not to seek medical assistance because of a fear that their condition would be made public, that would be detrimental to the public interest. Medical confidentiality prevents a doctor from revealing that a patient has AIDS, even to another member of the patient's family who may be affected by the illness.

The issue of whether information provided by a child to a doctor should be kept confidential from a parent was considered in *Gillick v West Norfolk & Wisbech Health Authority (1986)*. In particular, the House of Lords considered whether a doctor must tell the parents of a child if their daughter under the age of 16 years sought contraceptive advice. The court held that if a girl under 16 years of age had sufficient maturity and intelligence to understand the nature and implications of the proposed medical treatment, she had the legal capacity to consent to such treatment. The parental right to control a minor child would therefore depend on the degree of intelligence of the particular child.

The court also held that there may be exceptional cases where it might be desirable for a doctor to give a girl contraceptive advice and treatment, if necessary without the consent or even knowledge of her parents, if it was in her best interests and the doctor could not persuade her to inform her parents or allow him to inform her parents that she sought contraceptive advice.

Other confidential relationships

Information given by clients to their lawyers is confidential and will be protected by legal privilege. Information provided by a parishioner to a priest is also confidential. A member of the Cabinet owes a duty of confidence to other members of the government (*A-G v Jonathan Cape (1976)*). It is open to question as to whether information provided by a child to a teacher is subject to an obligation of confidence, or whether the media can try to obtain private information from teachers about children of famous people.

Third parties

A third party who is in receipt of confidential material that he knew or ought to have known was subject to confidence may also be prevented from publishing the information.

The media and sources

The obligation of confidence extends beyond the original parties involved to any third person who receives the information knowing of the breach of confidence. Liability of a third party often arises where information of confidential information is provided to the media and published in breach of that confidence. The newspaper or television company will often be party to the proceedings, along with the person who broke the confidence.

If a person says 'I shouldn't tell you this, but . . .', the writer or broadcaster will be put on notice of a potential breach of confidence but may be able to establish a defence to any action for breach of confidence. However, in cases involving information provided by current or former employees about their employers or information concerning a person's medical history, there is a danger the court will take the view that the writer or broadcaster should have known a confidence was being broken simply by the confidential nature of the information itself. In such circumstances, a defence will be much more difficult to establish.

6.3 Defences

Several defences are available to an action for breach of confidence:

- The information is not 'confidential' because it is in the public domain
- The owner of the information has permitted its publication
- The information discloses 'iniquity'
- The public interest requires publication.

6.3.1 Public domain

Confidentiality will not generally attach to information that is already general public knowledge or in the public domain. The question of whether the information has already been so widely published as to destroy its confidentiality will depend on the facts of each case.

It may not be enough for the defendant to show that the information is already available to the public in some form. Just because information has been published in an obscure journal does not mean that it can be broadcast on national television. However, if confidential information about private individuals is available in a form that is generally available to the public, it is much less likely that a claimant will bring an action for breach of confidence. The Internet has had a profound effect on the availability of information to the public, and may assist a defendant who defends on the basis of public domain.

In contrast, government information that has only been published in a small circulation newsletter abroad has not in the past prevented the Attorney General commencing proceedings for breach of confidence.

Section 12(4)(a)(i) of the Human Rights Act 1998 will make it more difficult to obtain an injunction to prevent the publication of confidential information which has been, or is about to be, published.

6.3.2 Consent

If the owner of information consents to its publication, he cannot later attempt to restrain its disclosure. Once the owner of information has consented to its going into the public domain, any rights in confidence are lost.

It is important to obtain consent from the right person. Any consent must be given by the owner or 'confider'. Although a lawyer may be happy to reveal the sordid secrets of a client, this consent is insufficient because the information belongs to the client.

6.3.3 Iniquity

The defence of 'iniquity', sometimes referred to as the defence of 'public interest', is one of the most important defences for the media. The court will not intervene to prevent the publication of information that concerns an iniquity. The public interest in publication of information about an iniquity outweighs the public interest in confidentiality. There is no confidence in the disclosure of an iniquity.

Iniquity is only a defence for an action for breach of confidence. It will not be a good defence to an application for an injunction.

There is no exact meaning for iniquity. It is a wrongdoing or an act of wickedness. It includes crimes, suspected criminal conduct, financial malpractice and police corruption. In *Cork v McVicar (1984)* a journalist conducted an interview with a former officer of the Metropolitan Police about police corruption. Unknown to the former officer the journalist had a concealed tape recorder, which he used to tape 'off the record' parts of the conversation. Despite the breach of confidence, the court refused to prevent publication of the story based on the secret tapes because the information clearly revealed allegations of police corruption and miscarriages of justice. However, it is not clear how far the concept extends to lesser wrongs.

In some cases, it may be difficult for the defendant to prove actual iniquity on the part of the claimant. The defendant may be assisted by the disclosure of relevant documents in the course of the proceedings for breach of confidence. For example, if a television programme alleges financial malpractice by a company and proceedings are issued, it will be entitled to disclosure of the claimant company's relevant accounts and records. However, in cases concerning the government the court may not order the disclosure of certain documents.

Fortunately, the defence does not depend upon proof by the defendant of the iniquity of the person who alleges breach of confidence. Rather, the issue before the court is the weighing of the public interest in allowing publication of information relating to wrongdoing against the public interest in confidentiality. In *A-G v Guardian Newspapers Ltd (No 2) (1988)*, certain newspapers wished to publish allegations by Peter Wright, a former senior officer, about the activities of MI5. The Court of Appeal found that some of the allegations clearly revealed iniquity, namely that the former Director General of MI5 had been a Soviet agent and that MI5 officers had conspired to overthrow the government of Harold Wilson, but it could not reach a unanimous view as to whether every 'bugging and burglary' would amount to iniquity. However, it held that it in cases of iniquity it was not necessary for the defendant to *prove* that the allegations were true, although before publication the media should:

- Assess the authenticity of the source
- Carry out any possible investigations to corroborate the allegations
- Give due weight to the findings of any investigations that had already taken place into the allegations.

In effect, this case demonstrates that editors and producers must act 'responsibly' and must consider the possible harm that may be done if a confidence is broken. The guidelines relieve the media of the need to be able to prove the truth of their publications by legally admissible evidence, and are particularly helpful to investigative reporters.

There is a limitation on the defence of iniquity, which impacts on the media. The court may find that a breach of confidence is justified on the grounds of iniquity, but only to the extent that the information may be handed to the appropriate authority, such as an employer or the police, and not published to the general public. In *Francome v Mirror Group (1984)* a newspaper was given transcripts of the telephone conversations of a leading jockey. The newspaper claimed that the conversations showed misconduct on the part of the jockey. The court held that despite the enormous interest of the public in horseracing and bookmaking, the newspaper could not publish articles based on the transcripts. It ruled the material should be handed to the Jockey Club or to the police, but could not be published to the public at large.

In the *Francome* case the court was influenced by the fact that the tapes had been obtained by committing a criminal offence under the Wireless Telegraphy Act 1949. If the conversations had been overheard on a crossed line, they could have been published. There would have been no breach of confidence. This is because anyone who talks on the telephone takes the risk that they may be overheard accidentally.

Any member of the media who intends to publish a story obtained in breach of confidence in reliance on a defence of iniquity should carefully consider the nature of the defence in advance. The following factors should be considered in order to assess whether the defence of iniquity can be raised successfully:

1. What is the nature of the misconduct?
   ▪ Can it be proved conclusively?
   ▪ Is the source credible?
   ▪ Is any independent evidence available?
2. Has the misconduct been investigated by anyone else?
   ▪ What was the result?
   ▪ Should the finding be disbelieved?
3. Is there a necessity to publish the information to the public at large, beyond publishing a good story, rather than to a 'responsible authority'?

6.3.4 Public interest

There is a separate defence of publication in the public interest, even if there is no iniquity. There are many types of information that, arguably, it is in the public interest to publish, as opposed to being merely interesting to the public. The definition of public interest in the Press Complaints Commission Code of Practice includes not only detecting or exposing crime, but also protecting public health and safety and preventing the public from being misled by some statement or action by an individual or organization.

In *Lion Laboratories Ltd v Evans (1985)*, an employee gave information to the press about defects in a breathalyser manufactured by his employer which was used to test the breath of drivers for alcohol in the police station. The accuracy of the machine was vital because the liberty of members of the public who were tested by it was affected. There was no iniquity because no one in the company had lied or was guilty of misconduct or inefficiency. However, the court allowed the newspaper to publish the information provided by the employee. It was clearly information that the public ought to know.

The Church of the Latter Day Saints failed to prevent publication of information relating to Scientology. The court found that the public is entitled to information about 'cults' (*Hubbard v Vosper (1972)*).

In 1993 the court decided it was in the public interest for the views of the former Prime Minister Baroness Thatcher about current government ministers to be published. The *Daily Mirror* obtained an early copy of Thatcher's autobiography and published selected extracts before the official release of the book and its 'exclusive' serialization in the *Sunday Times*. Both the *Sunday Times* and the publishers of the book, Harper Collins Publishers Ltd, tried and failed to obtain an injunction against the *Daily Mirror*. The Court of Appeal found that the opinion of the former Prime Minister about her successor and his colleagues was clearly a matter of public interest (*Times Newspapers Ltd v MGN Ltd (1993)*).

Although difficulties do exist in raising the defence of public interest, under Section 12(4)(a)(ii) of the Human Rights Act 1998 the court must now have regard to the public interest when considering whether or not to grant an injunction to restrain publication.

The issues the media should consider before publication in respect of the defence of public interest are similar to those raised by the defence of iniquity:

- How grave is the matter revealed?
- How likely to be true is the information?
- Ought the information to be published to the public at large?

6.4 Procedure

6.4.1 The action

The procedure in an action for breach of confidence is, for the most part, the same as an action for defamation (see Chapter 1).

6.4.2 Interim Injunctions

Importance

It is normal for a claimant in an action for breach of confidence to apply for an interim injunction under the Civil Procedure Rules Part 25.1(1)(a). An interim injunction is usually the most important aspect of a claim for breach of confidence. Once information is published by the media, its confidentiality is gone for ever. No damages can properly compensate its former owner. The court is therefore often prepared to prevent publication by way of an interim injunction pending trial. In such circumstances, the interests of the publisher take second place to the interests of the owner of the confidential information.

In fact, very few actions for breach of confidence actually proceed to trial. Victory at the interim injunction stage is usually decisive, which is why evidence and arguments should be ready at the earliest possible moment. If the claimant fails to obtain an injunction and the information is published, the action is likely quietly to go away. If an interim injunction is granted, it is seldom economically worthwhile for a media organization to incur the expense of proceeding to trial just to publish a story. The costs of litigation are prohibitive, and the risk of an order to pay the successful claimant's costs as well as the defendant's own costs is often the ultimate deterrent. In *X v Y*, the case concerning publication of information relating to doctors diagnosed with AIDS, the cost of the trial was more than £200 000. The costs of the *Spycatcher* trials around the world ran into millions of pounds.

The publisher in possession of confidential information is faced with a dilemma. On the one hand, he may wish to confirm the authenticity of the information with the owner of the information for editorial or legal reasons. However, this may put the owner on notice and lead to an action for breach of confidence and an application for an interim injunction. There is no easy answer. Failure to check the information may lead to an incorrect story and an expensive defamation action. Checking may lead to an interim injunction. However, at the least the issue is then addressed correctly by the court.

Impact of Human Rights Act 1998

Prior to the enactment of the Human Rights Act 1998, it was relatively straightforward for a claimant to obtain an interim injunction restraining publication on an *ex parte* basis, in other words without giving notice of the application to the defendant. A simple telephone call to the duty judge at the High Court in London, even as the presses were rolling or the programme was about to be broadcast, could be sufficient to obtain an *ex parte* injunction in situations regarded by the court as sufficiently serious. The first the defendant would hear of the court order would be a phone call warning that the injunction had been issued. The television presenter Anne Diamond obtained an injunction preventing a story sold by her ex-nanny from appearing on the front page of the *Sun* in precisely this way.

In the normal course of events, if the defendant wished to discharge the *ex parte* injunction an *inter partes* hearing would take place, where both parties would appear before the court, call evidence, and argue as to whether the confidential information should be published pending trial. The court would balance the interests of both parties until the full facts could be investigated at trial using the principles set out in *American Cyanamid v Ethicon Ltd (1975)*.

The Human Rights Act ('the HRA') 1998 has changed the procedure for *ex parte* and *inter partes* interim injunctions. Under Section 12 of the HRA, injunctions made in the absence of the defendant are now prohibited unless there are compelling reasons why the defendant should not be notified. Furthermore, the principles in *American Cyanamid* no longer apply. Section 12(3) of the HRA provides that no relief is to be granted to restrain publication before trial 'unless the court is satisfied that the applicant is likely to establish that publication should not be allowed'. Section 12(4) of the HRA provides that the court must have particular regard to freedom of expression, and must consider the extent to which the material is available in the public domain or whether it is in the public interest to publish it.

The provisions of the Human Rights Act 1998 are mandatory. They will force the courts to approach the issue of interim injunctions in a different way, by balancing the right to privacy with the right freedom of expression.

6.4.3 Differences between breach of confidence and defamation

There are three significant differences between an action for breach of confidence and an action for defamation:

1. The truth of the information being published is irrelevant. It is not open to a defendant in a breach of confidence action to argue that it intends to justify the publication. The court may grant an interim injunction regardless of the truth of the information, as long as the elements necessary for a breach of confidence action are made out.
2. Historically, the courts have been more willing to grant injunctions to restrain breaches of confidence rather than to prevent damage to a person's reputation. Once a secret has been published, it cannot be made confidential again. By contrast, damages are regarded as an adequate remedy for an injured reputation.
3. Any damages for breach of confidence will be decided by a judge rather than a jury.

6.4.4 Other remedies

The claimant is usually more interested in an injunction than any other remedy. However, the other available remedies are:

- *Damages*. Damages are not normally applicable to most media cases because no amount of money can compensate for the revelation to the public of confidential matters. However, in breach of confidence actions concerning trade secrets or business information the claimant may recover damages for the market value of the information. There are no useful guidelines to assess the likely awards for loss of non-commercial confidences.
- *Account of profits*. An account of profits is most relevant to book publishers. The claimant can recover all profits generated by the defendant by use of the claimant's secrets. A publisher could forfeit all profits from the sale of a book as a result. In circumstances where a newspaper contains one story in breach of confidence or a television company broadcasts one offending story, the difficulties of apportioning part of the profits to the breach of confidence will be considerable.
- *Delivery up*. The court can order that the defendant return to the claimant all the claimant's confidential documents. Any defendant who is ordered to hand back material should bear in mind Section 10 of the Contempt of Court Act 1981, which protects the identity of sources (see Chapter 11).

7 The Data Protection Act 1998

Terence Bergin

7.1 Introduction

The English law protects an individual from the misuse of personal information about him under statute and common law. The Data Protection Act 1998, which replaces the Data Protection Act 1984, protects personal data whether it is stored in manual or computerized form. The common law of confidence, which protects against the disclosure of 'confidential' information, is considered in Chapter 6.

Any person or organization holding personal data about a living individual who can be identified from the information, or from consideration of personal data in conjunction with other information in the possession of the person or organization, is subject to the provisions of the Data Protection Act 1998 (the 'DPA').

'Personal data' does not just mean private information such as medical records or financial details. Under the DPA, it includes automatically processed information, as well as information recorded as part of a filing system or forming part of a record. For example, this will include the names and addresses on a newspaper or magazine subscription list, or information derived from a library of newspaper clippings or a card index. Even a person's shopping habits or favourite television programmes will be included if such information, used in conjunction with other information held by a production company or broadcaster, can identify the person concerned.

The person or organization holding the personal data is required to register with the Data Protection Commissioner. This will include media organizations such as newspapers and television companies.

Under the DPA, the subject of personal information has several rights in relation to the personal data, including the right to be informed as to whether personal data is being processed about him.

A person also has a very limited right to access his own personal information held in manual format under the Access to Personal Files Act 1987.

The right to information and access to personal information should be distinguished from the obligation on public bodies to provide freedom of information under the Code of Practice on Access to Government Information 1997 and the Freedom of Information Act 2000, both of which are considered in Chapter 14.

7.2 The Data Protection Act 1998

7.2.1 History

The common law was slow to keep up with developments in the technology of acquiring, storing and processing data. Even in the 1970s it was recognized that an action in breach of confidence, the only realistic common law remedy, was inadequate to address the use of data in the computer age. The increased use of computers and, in recent years, the Internet to acquire and store information has made it increasingly important to protect against abuse of personal data.

Domestic legislation in the United Kingdom concerning data protection has been shaped by European legislation. In 1984, the Data Protection Act 1984 was passed to comply with the provisions of the European Convention for the Protection of the Individual with regard to the Automatic Processing of Personal Data. In 1998, the DPA was passed in order to comply with the European Union's directive on the processing of personal data and the free movement of such data. The majority of the DPA's provisions came into force on 1 March 2000, replacing the Data Protection Act 1984.

7.2.2 General principles

The DPA significantly extends the obligations imposed under the Data Protection Act 1984 on 'data controllers'. The data controller must:

- Register with, pay a fee to and provide certain information to the Data Protection Commissioner
- Obtain and process personal data in accordance with the data protection principles under the DPA.

Information about deceased individuals is not subject to the DPA. Information about companies is not subject to the DPA unless named individuals are referred to as a point of contact.

The DPA also extends the rights of individuals who are the subject of personal data. Such a person is entitled to write to the data controller asking whether any personal data concerning him is being processed. He is also entitled to ask the data controller to stop processing such information if it is causing or is likely to cause him substantial damage. He may also apply to the court for an order to rectify, block, erase or destroy personal data, and he is entitled to compensation if he suffers damage as a result of a contravention of the DPA by the data controller.

There are a series of exceptions to some of the provisions of the DPA. The most important exception for those working in the media is that found in Section 32 of the DPA, which concerns 'journalism, literature and art'.

Section 55 of the DPA creates a number of criminal offences, including unlawfully obtaining or disclosing personal information or offering to sell personal data. Those working in the media must be particularly careful when obtaining personal information about the subject of an article or programme in order to avoid committing such an offence.

The DPA also extends the powers of the Data Protection Commissioner, who, along with the Data Protection Tribunal, is authorized to deal with disputes relating to data protection law. However, the DPA has been amended by the Freedom of Information Act 2000. The Freedom of Information Act 2000 will be enforced by a newly established Information Commissioner, who will also oversee the DPA, along with an Information Tribunal. In the future, the Data Protection Commissioner will therefore become the Information Commissioner. Because the Data Protection Act 1998 and the Freedom of Information Act 2000 both relate to information policy, this double supervisory role should allow the Information Commissioner to provide a coherent approach to the handling of and access to information. Some of the changes brought about by the Freedom of Information Act 2000 will not take effect until 2005.

There has been very little judicial consideration of the provisions of the DPA. Moreover, the DPA will now have to be construed in the light of the Article 8 European Convention on Human Rights right to privacy introduced into English law by the Human Rights Act 1998. Under the Human Rights Act 1998, information must not provided if it amounts to unwarranted disclosure to a third party of personal information about any person, including a deceased person, or any other disclosure that would constitute or could facilitate an unwarranted invasion of privacy.

7.2.3 Definitions

Data controller
A data controller 'determines the purposes for which and the manner in which' personal data is processed. The DPA applies to any data controller who is 'established' in and processes data in the United Kingdom. 'Established' means:

- An individual who is 'ordinarily resident'
- A body that is incorporated
- A partnership or other unincorporated association that is formed

- Any of the above maintaining and regularly using an office, branch or agency
- Any of the above using equipment in the United Kingdom for processing data, unless the data is merely in transit

in and under the laws of the United Kingdom.

Data

'Data' includes data on computer systems as well as manual paper-based records, for example a card index, if it is recorded for a 'relevant filing system'.

The notion of a 'relevant filing system' is a complex one. It encompasses any set of information relating to individuals that is structured, either by reference to individuals or by reference to criteria relating to individuals, in such a way that specific information relating to a particular individual is readily accessible.

Personal data

As well as information that can identify a person by itself or in combination with another source that is in the possession of, or is likely to come into the possession of, the data controller, 'personal data' also includes any expression of opinion about the individual and any indication of the intentions of the data controller or any other person in respect of the individual. This is a very wide-ranging provision. It will include notes of interviews about prospective employees, and internal memoranda about an employee's promotion prospects.

Sensitive personal data

'Sensitive personal data' consists of personal data relating to such matters as race, political opinion, health, sexuality and criminal proceedings.

Processing

Processing is a very broad concept. It extends to obtaining, recording or holding data, or carrying out any operation or set of operations on the data. This includes organizing, adapting, altering, retrieving, consulting, using, disclosing or even erasing the data.

It should be assumed that this definition is capable of extending to any of the many things that can be done with data, including simply retrieving data to a computer screen. It clearly extends to storing, adapting and retrieving data on a desktop, laptop or palmtop computer.

7.2.4 Obligations on the data controller

The data controller is subject to three main obligations. He must:

1. Notify the Data Protection Commissioner of his identity and provide a description of the personal data to be processed and the purpose of that processing
2. Process personal data in compliance with the data protection principles
3. Provide the person who is the subject of the data with access to it.

Notification

The notification procedure is straightforward. It can be undertaken by post, over the telephone, or online at the Data Protection Commissioner's web site.[1] The notification lasts for one year but is automatically continued on payment of the fee, currently £35.

The data controller must provide the 'registrable particulars', which include his name and address and information relating to the personal data being processed, as well as a general description of the measures to be taken for the purpose of complying with the seventh data protection principle concerning security measures.

Data protection principles

The primary obligation on the data controller is that all processing must be fair and lawful. In addition, there are eight data protection principles:

1. Personal data shall be processed fairly and lawfully and shall not be processed unless at least one of the conditions in Schedule 2 is met or in the case of sensitive personal data at least one of the conditions in Schedule 3 is also met
2. Personal data shall be obtained only for one or more specified and lawful purpose, and shall not be further processed in any manner incompatible with that purpose or those purposes
3. Personal data shall be adequate, relevant and not excessive in relation to the purpose or purposes for which they are processed
4. Personal data shall be accurate and, where necessary, kept up to date
5. Personal data processed for any purpose or purposes shall not be kept for longer than is necessary for that purpose or those purposes
6. Personal data shall be processed in accordance with the rights of data subjects under the DPA
7. Appropriate technical and organizational measures shall be taken against unauthorized or unlawful processing of personal data and against accidental loss or destruction of, or damage to, personal data
8. Personal data shall not be transferred to a country or territory outside the European Economic Area, which is the European Union Member States, Norway, Iceland and Liechtenstein, unless that country or territory ensures an adequate level of protection for the rights and freedoms of data subjects in relation to the processing of personal data.

Fair and lawful processing

All personal data must be obtained fairly and without deception. Certain information, including the identity of the data controller and the purpose for which the data is to be processed, must be provided to the subject of the personal data at the time the data is obtained. This applies whether the personal data has been obtained from the subject himself or from another person or organization.

---

[1]The web site can be found at www.dataprotection.gov.uk.

An exception applies if providing this information would involve a 'disproportionate effort'. 'Disproportionate effort' is not defined, but will be measured against the prejudice to the subject of the personal data. When the DPA was at the Committee stage, much time was spent discussing whether a florist asked to deliver flowers must spoil the surprise by notifying the proposed recipient.

Schedules 2 and 3

The Schedules provide minimum standards only. Compliance with the Schedules will not automatically render any processing fair and lawful, nor will it affect whether any processing breaches other statutes or common law principles such as the law of confidence.

For example, in 1997 British Gas wanted to notify its customers about its own and third party products and services and pass on customer information to other companies in the British Gas Group. The Data Protection Tribunal held that British Gas had processed data unfairly despite the fact that it had sent an 'opt-out' form to all customers. The Tribunal said that the form should have been an 'opt-in' form. In 1999, Midlands Electricity plc ran into similar difficulties with a direct marketing campaign.

Schedule 2

Schedule 2 provides that processing will be unlawful under the DPA unless the subject of the personal data has given his consent to the processing; it is necessary in order to perform a contract, comply with a legal obligation or the administration of justice or protect the vital interests of the subject of the personal data.

Schedule 3

At least one of the conditions set out in Schedule 3 must be met when processing personal data:

1. The data subject has given his explicit consent to the processing of the personal data
2. The processing is necessary under employment legislation
3. The processing is necessary in order to protect the vital interests of the data subject or another person, usually relied on by the data controller if consent cannot be given by or on behalf of the subject of the personal data
4. The processing is carried out in the course of legitimate activities by a non-profit political, philosophical, religious or trade union body or organization in relation to members of the body or those connected with it
5. The information contained in the personal data has been made public as a result of steps deliberately taken by the subject of the personal data
6. The processing is necessary in connection with legal proceedings, legal advice or legal rights
7. The processing is necessary for the administration of justice
8. The processing is necessary for medical purposes
9. The processing is of sensitive personal data consisting of information relating to racial or ethnic origin necessary for identifying equality of opportunity or treatment.

Data Protection (Processing of Sensitive Personal Data) Order 2000

The Order provides a further 10 conditions to which regard must be had in addition to Schedule 3.

The most important conditions for media organizations and journalists are:

- Condition 3, which concerns the disclosure, with a view to publication, of sensitive personal data connected with unlawful acts, dishonesty or malpractice, unfitness or incompetence, or for the purposes of journalism, literature or art, in circumstances where the data controller reasonably believes such publication is in the public interest
- Condition 9, which relates to the processing of certain limited types of data for research purposes.

7.2.5 Rights of the subject of the personal data

Right of access

A person who is the subject of personal data is entitled to apply to the data controller in writing, on payment of a fee (which at present can be no more than £10), for information as to whether personal data about him is being processed by or on behalf of the data controller.

The information must be provided within 40 days. However, the data controller may reasonably request further information in order to satisfy himself as to the identity of the person making the request and to locate the information sought by that person. The data controller need not comply with the request until receipt of the further information.

The data controller is obliged to provide a copy of the personal data in a permanent form unless doing so would involve disproportionate effort, or the applicant agrees otherwise.

An applicant may apply to the court for an order if the data controller fails to comply with a request.

Right to prevent processing: damage or distress

A person is entitled at any time to write to a data controller requesting that the controller cease or does not begin to process personal data concerning him, because it is causing or is likely to cause unwarranted substantial damage or distress to him or another person. However, the right does not apply if the applicant has consented to the processing or it is necessary for the performance of a contract, to comply with legal obligations, or to protect the vital interests of the data subject.

The data controller must inform the applicant in writing within 21 days as to whether he has or will comply, or whether he thinks the request is unjustified.

The applicant may apply to the court for an order if the data controller fails to comply with the request.

Right to prevent processing: direct marketing

'Direct marketing' is communication by whatever means of any advertising or marketing material directed to particular individuals. A person is entitled at any time to write to a data controller requesting that the controller cease or does not begin to process personal data concerning him for the purposes of direct marketing to him. This is an absolute right, and is not subject to a requirement of damage or distress.

The applicant may apply to the court for an order if the data controller fails to comply with the request.

Right to prevent automated decision taking

A person is entitled at any time to write to the data controller requiring that he ensure that no decision is taken by or on behalf of the data controller that significantly affects the individual based solely on the automatic processing personal data. For example, this would include a person's performance at work, his creditworthiness, his reliability or his conduct.

The data controller must reply within 21 days. The applicant may apply to the court for an order to reconsider or make a new decision if the person taking a decision in respect of him has failed to comply with his obligations.

Right to rectification, blocking, erasure and destruction

A person may apply to the court for an order that the data controller rectify, block, erase or destroy inaccurate data. If the inaccurate data accurately reflects information passed to the data controller by the data subject or a third party, the court may instead make an order requiring the data to be supplemented by a statement approved by the court of the true facts relating to the matters dealt with by the data.

Right to compensation

If a data controller contravenes any requirement of the DPA and a person suffers loss as a result, he is entitled to compensation from the data controller for that loss and for any distress caused.

Media organizations may be liable to pay compensation even when no damage has been caused. Compensation for distress without damage may be claimed where the processing is for the purposes of journalism, literature or art.

In proceedings brought against the data controller, it is a defence for him to prove that he took such care as was reasonably required in all the circumstances.

Right to an assessment

A request for an assessment as to whether processing is being carried out in compliance with the DPA may be made to the Data Protection Commissioner by or on behalf of any person who is, or believes himself to be, directly affected by any processing of personal data. Upon such a request being made, the Data Protection Commissioner is obliged to carry out the assessment.

7.2.6 Exemptions

There are a series of exemptions to the DPA. For media organizations and journalists, the most important exemption is found in Section 32 of the DPA, which concerns journalism, art and literature.

The processing of personal data that concern journalism, art or literature is exempt if *all* of the following apply:

- The processing is undertaken with a view to the publication by any person of any journalistic, literary or artistic material, and
- The data controller reasonably believes, having regard to the importance of freedom of expression, that publication would be in the public interest, and
- The data controller reasonably believes, in all the circumstances, that compliance with the provision of the DPA with which the data controller does not wish to comply is incompatible with journalism, art or literature.

An example of when the exemption might apply is the use of details of the previous sexual history of a convicted sex-offender in a documentary about his crimes.

When considering whether the data controller's belief that publication would be in the public interest is reasonable, it is possible to consider whether he complied with any relevant code of practice for the publication in question, such as the National Union of Journalists' Code of Practice, the Press Complaints Commission's Code of Practice or the Broadcasting Standards Commission's Fairness, Privacy and Standards Codes.

In circumstances where the exemption under Section 32 of the DPA applies, a media organization or journalist is not required to comply with:

- The data protection principles, except the seventh principle concerning appropriate technical and organizational measures to be taken against unauthorized or unlawful processing of personal data
- The right of access
- The right to prevent processing causing damage or distress
- The right to prevent automated decision taking
- The right to rectification, blocking, erasure and destruction, and
- The conditions in Schedules 2 and 3 of the DPA.

If a person issues court proceedings against a media organization or journalist in relation to personal data concerning journalism, art or literature which is:

- being processed only for the purpose of journalism, art or literature with a view to publication, and
- had not been published by the data controller at any time other than within the 24 hours before the claim of exemption

the court will stay the proceedings until the Data Protection Commissioner can determine the application, or the data controller abandons the claim to exemption. This provision is intended to prevent the granting of injunctions that prevent the publication of personal or sensitive personal data.

7.2.7 Criminal offences

Section 55 of the DPA creates a number of criminal offences, including unlawfully obtaining or disclosing personal information or offering to sell personal data. Those working in the media must be particularly careful when obtaining personal information about the subject of an article or programme in order to avoid committing such an offence.

7.3 Access to Personal Files Act 1987

Files that are held manually are subject to the provisions of the Access to Personal Files Act 1987. However, this Act is of extremely limited application. The provisions of the Access to Personal Files Act only apply to files held by social services and housing departments. The relevant authority that holds such files has an obligation to provide access to the records and to maintain accurate records as provided for by prescribed regulations.

It is also possible to obtain access to personal medical records under the Access to Health Records Act 1990 and to environmental information under the Environment Information Regulations 1992.

8 The 'New' Right to Privacy

Peter Grundberg

8.1 Introduction

It has long been recognized that a general right to privacy exists in English law. However, there is no express common law 'tort of privacy' or statutory right to privacy. Prior to the enactment of the Human Rights Act 1998 ('the HRA'), the 'right' could only be established by combining several different common law and European law strands. A person who claimed his right to privacy had been infringed could bring an action against the defendant for breach of confidence, trespass or defamation. The English courts also attempted to give effect to the provisions of the European Convention of Human Rights (the 'Convention'). However, these common law causes of action provided only indirect protection against invasion of privacy. Furthermore, the effect of the Convention was limited, as it did not prevail over English law if a conflict arose between the two.

As a result, there has been considerable debate over the past 40 years as to whether Parliament should legislate to make privacy expressly enforceable through the courts. The question always seemed to focus on the activities of the media. Not surprisingly, it produced strong arguments from both sides. Freedom of the press is the cornerstone of freedom of speech. However, infringements of 'privacy' have usually been committed by a prying or intrusive press. Since 1961, five separate bills have been presented to Parliament aimed at introducing a statutory tort of privacy. All have been unsuccessful because of insurmountable problems in connection with establishing adequate definitions of the civil offence of privacy and acceptable defences. During the same period, there have also been various Government committees and Royal Commissions that have considered the same question, the most recent of which was the Government Committee on Privacy and Related Matters chaired by David Calcutt QC, which reported in 1990. All recommended against the introduction of a statutory law of privacy on the basis of an unworkable definition of the tort and the undesirability of such a law.

An express right to privacy finally found its way into English law in October 2000. The Human Rights Act 1998 incorporated the Convention into English law, including the Article 8 right to privacy. The HRA only applies to government action and not that of private individuals. Despite the introduction of the Article 8 right to privacy, there is still no specific government legislation creating a statutory tort of privacy. Furthermore, the Article 8 Convention right to privacy can often be at odds with the Article 10 Convention right to freedom of expression. However, in view of recent judicial interpretations of the HRA it is reasonable to speculate that an express right to privacy will soon develop that will encompass the activities of private individuals as well as the government.

8.2 Common law rights

8.2.1 No 'tort of privacy'

Historically, the common law has been somewhat ambiguous when it comes to the protection of privacy. An example of the inability of the courts to find a cogent legal footing to maintain an individual's privacy can be found in the case of *Kaye v Robertson (1991)*. A well-known British television actor, Gordon Kaye, had undergone extensive surgery following a car accident when he was photographed and allegedly interviewed by journalists from the *Sunday Sport*, the tabloid newspaper, whilst still in hospital. Since he had in no way consented to the interview or the taking of photographs, and indeed was not in a condition so to do, he applied for an injunction to restrain publication of the journalists' material. Although the Court of Appeal refused his application, it noted that the case:

> . . . highlighted, yet again, the failure of both the Common law and of statute to protect in an effective way the personal privacy of individual citizens.

In the case of *R v Khan (1997)*, a case involving the admissibility of evidence secured through the use of covert police surveillance equipment in relation to the defendant's suspected heroin importation, the House of Lords noted that the Article 8 right to privacy would only be of relevance in order to assist the construction of the law in a case of ambiguity or doubt. The House of Lords did not lament this lacuna in the law. It was more a case of 'relief' on the part of the House of Lords that it concluded, in spite of the element of trespass, that the evidence was not rendered inadmissible even though it could be said to have contravened Article 8. Lord Nolan said:

> . . . it would be a strange reflection on our law if a man who has admitted his participation in the illegal importation of a large quantity of heroin should have his conviction set aside on the grounds that his privacy has been invaded.

It is interesting to note that when Lord Nolan heard the case in the Court of Appeal he, along with Lord Taylor, highlighted the fact that the Convention had not been incorporated into English statutory law. It remains open to speculation whether a decision similar to that given by the House of Lords in *R v Khan* would be adopted quite so easily today, or whether the same result would be achieved in a more roundabout way on the basis of national interest.

There have been occasions where the court has recognized privacy over and above other legal provisions, although this recognition has not been consistent. In *Haig v Aitken (2000)*, the trustee in bankruptcy of Jonathan Aitken, ex-Conservative MP and Cabinet member, wished to 'realize' valuable papers belonging to Aitken that were personal to him in a variety of ways. The papers ranged from letters to heads of State and former ministers through to so-called 'intimate' correspondence. As a matter of insolvency law, it was recognized by the court that, because Aitken was a bankrupt, his estate should be transferred to the trustee in bankruptcy for him to 'realize' it – in other words sell it – for the benefit of Aitken's creditors. However, the court upheld Aitken's arguments that, given their personal nature, the documents ought not to be sold because they were protected by Article 8.

8.2.2 Breach of confidence

The law of confidence offers some protection against abuse or unauthorized use of confidential information. Breach of confidence may give rise to a claim for an invasion of privacy. This has been the case in the taking of unauthorized photographs or film of a person or his home. Founded on a 'confidential relationship' as found by the court in the *Spycatcher* case (*A-G v Guardian Newspapers Ltd (No 2) (1990)*), it has been held that a breach of an obligation not to take photographs may allow a claimant to bring action for breach of confidence. In *Shelley Films v Rex Features (1994)*, the defendant was prevented from using photographs taken on a film-set that had signs prohibiting photography. In *Creation Records v News Group Newspapers Limited (1997)*, a photographer from the *Sun* published photographs taken during a photo shoot for the cover of a new record by the rock group Oasis. Although the photographer was lawfully at the scene, the court found that the security measures at the shoot made it arguable it was intended to be confidential. An injunction was granted preventing the publication of the photographs.

However, in other areas it has been a difficult task for the courts to balance the absolute protection of privacy with the public interest. In the past, authors of books containing confidential government material, such as Peter Wright, who retired from MI5 to Tasmania and authored *Spycatcher*, faced litigation by the Government in order to prevent publication and the possibility of prosecution under the Official Secrets Act 1989.

In its first decision in the *Spycatcher* affair (*A-G v Guardian Newspapers (1987)*), the House of Lords upheld an injunction (by a majority of only three to two) against several newspapers who wished to publish serializations of *Spycatcher* on the eve of the book's publication in the United States. In its second decision (*A-G v Guardian Newspapers Ltd (No 2) (1990)*), the House of Lords decided not to grant a permanent injunction. It is doubtful whether the House of Lords preferred to safeguard free speech over maintaining confidentiality, since this decision was largely based on the fact that the confidentiality had already been broken and no such duty was owed by third parties. The House of Lords adopted a pragmatic stance and found that a permanent injunction in the United Kingdom was rendered futile in view of the fact the material had already been published abroad. However, the court noted that:

> . . . the right to personal privacy is clearly one which the law should in this field seek to protect . . .

and that an injunction would have been granted in relation to the publication if it had first been made in the United Kingdom:

> ... there is no room for discrimination between secrets of greater or lesser importance, nor any room for close examination of the precise manner in which revelation of any particular matter may prejudice the national interest.

More recently, in *A-G v Punch Ltd (2001)* the court considered confidentiality in relation to David Shayler, a former MI5 officer who used information gathered in the course of his employment to contribute to articles, material and a column in *Punch* magazine. The Court of Appeal granted the appeal of *Punch* and its editor, James Steen, against their convictions for contempt of court since, amongst other things, it could not be shown that the disclosure by them of information provided by Shayler defeated, in whole or in part, the purpose of the court in granting an injunction.

By contrast, in 2001 Dame Stella Rimington, who had been Director General of MI5 for four years, published her memoirs *Open Secret*, which contained confidential government material. Although the Home Office said that the Government 'regretted' Rimington's decision to publish the book, it said that it would not resist its publication largely, it seems, because the memoirs were edited to appease both MI5 and the Government itself.

The difficulty faced by the court of balancing the absolute protection of privacy with other public interests is likely to continue in the future following the incorporation into English law of the conflicting rights to privacy in Article 8 and freedom of expression in Article 10. In September 2000 celebrity couple David and Victoria Beckham sued Andrew Morton over his 'unauthorized biography', which revealed intimate details about their personal and professional lives. Morton had gathered the information from a former bodyguard who had signed a confidentiality clause on commencing employment with the Beckhams. The matter settled out of court on the basis that 200 offending words were removed from the manuscript. However, if the claim had proceeded to trial, the court would have had the difficult job of weighing Morton's right to express himself under Article 10 with Beckhams' right to privacy under Article 8.

8.2.3 Trespass

A particularly common area of complaint relates to individuals who are kept under constant observation. Claimants have often sought remedies from the court for harassment, which is now a statutory offence under the Protection from Harassment Act 1997.

However, other remedies can be found in trespass. Trespass to land or property may be claimed in a variety of situations. Any person entering on to another's land to observe him or to plant a listening device will be guilty of trespass (*Greig v Greig (1966)*). However, in recent years the 'protection' provided by an action in trespass in this respect has been diminished by the development of surveillance devices that enable such activities to take place without any physical trespass onto land. Trespass by interference with letters and communications is afforded wide protection through the criminal law and the laws of copyright and confidence. The Wireless and Telegraphy Acts and the Interception of Communications Act 1985 now apply criminal sanctions against those who plant listening bugs or who intercept postal or telephone communications.

The usefulness of trespass to maintain privacy may also be limited in other ways. In *Bernstein v Skyways (1978)* the court held that aerial photography that had been taken over the claimant's land was not trespass because the rights of a landowner in the airspace above his property are limited to a height necessary for the 'ordinary use and enjoyment' of the land. However, the court intimated that relief might be granted in circumstances where a person was subjected to the 'harassment of constant surveillance of his house', accompanied by the photographing of his 'every activity'.

8.2.4 Defamation

A publication that is defamatory will give rise to a cause of action and damages. A publication is defamatory if it tends to lower the claimant in the estimation of right thinking members of society generally. This can include the publication of an image. In *Tolley v JS Fry & Sons Ltd (1931)*, the image of a famous amateur golfer appeared on an advertisement with a Fry's chocolate bar. He had not given permission for his image to be used. His action for defamation was successful on the basis that people who knew of his amateur status would believe he had abused it by becoming involved in commercial sponsorship.

However, even if the images in themselves are defamatory, there will be no cause of action if the publication read as a whole clarifies the real position. In *Charleston v News Group Newspapers Ltd (1995)*, two actors who played the characters Madge and Harold in the Australian television programme *Neighbours* were unsuccessful in their action against the *News of the World*, which had published photographs showing their faces superimposed on bodies in pornographic poses, because the article made it clear that the photographs had been produced without the consent of the claimants.

Furthermore, statements that may appear to be defamatory and hence encroach upon a person's privacy may be tolerated where the maker of the statement enjoys a privilege of some description. The grounds of such privilege are generally rather narrow. The maker of the statement would have to be acting upon knowledge rather than mere inference and have a legitimate interest in or duty in publishing such information. In light of the tragedy that befell those in New York's World Trade Centre on 11 September 2001, the dicta of the court in *Blackshaw's Case (1983)* may be particularly pertinent. In that case, a journalist published what was more conjecture than solid fact about a civil servant's incompetence and mal-administration. The court said that there might be circumstances where:

... urgency of communicating a warning is so great, or the source of the information so reliable that publication of a suspicion or speculation is justified.

The court proposed the examples of facing danger from suspected terrorists or the distribution of contaminated food or drugs.

In *Loutchansky v Times Newspapers Ltd (2001)*, the court shed further light on the parameters of an individual's 'right of reputation' and its interrelation with freedom of speech and reporting by newspapers and journalists. In that case, the defendant newspaper, its editor and two of its journalists were found to have defamed the claimant by referring to investigations concerning money laundering and inferring that he was closely involved with the Russian mafia. The defendants claimed that the public was entitled to be informed of allegations that were of such a serious nature. The court noted that:

> ... great services [have been] rendered to the public by skilled and fearless investigative journalists in uncovering fraud and corruption and incompetence, in high places as well as in low.

However, in finding against the defendants, the court referred to the often cited dicta in the case of *Reynolds v Times Newspapers Ltd (1999)*:

> ... reputation is an integral and important part of the individual ... Protection of reputation is conducive to the public good.

8.2.5 Trademarks

Unlike the law in the United States, English law does not protect 'personality' or 'character' rights. However, in order to prevent interference with 'right to one's image', several celebrities in the United Kingdom have registered their names as trademarks in order to guarantee some sort of protection. Trademarks identify products or services. They use the symbol ™ if the trademark is not registered or ® if the trademark is registered to demonstrate protection. If the trademark is registered, special rules apply simplifying the way in which it can be protected. A trademark must be capable of being represented graphically, and must distinguish the product or services of one business from another.

However, it is difficult to register a famous name as a trademark. In the case of *Re Applications by Elvis Presley Enterprises Inc (1997)*, an application by the Estate of Elvis Presley in 1989 for registration of the names 'Elvis' and 'Elvis Presley' was opposed by a man called Sid Shaw. Shaw had been trading under the name 'Elvisly Yours' for the previous few years. He opposed the application on the basis that Presley had been dead for several years, many different companies produced Elvis products, and his name could not be associated with any one particular company or brand. The trademark registry rejected Shaw's opposition. The High Court upheld his opposition, as did the Court of Appeal. Other celebrities who have been more successful than the Estate of Elvis Presley are David and Victoria Beckham, who registered as trademarks the nicknames 'Becks' and 'Posh'.

Individuals in other jurisdictions enjoy more tangible rights to privacy than in the United Kingdom, which in some cases are premised upon the right to one's image. For example, in *Aubry v Les Éditions Vice-Versa Inc (1998)* the Chief Justice in Quebec, Canada, dismissed an appeal against a decision of the Court of Appeal made by a photographer and the publisher of a magazine found to have transgressed the right to one's image by taking and publishing a photograph of a 17-year-old student without her permission. The Chief Justice observed that the protection of privacy 'must include the ability to control the use of one's own image'. Furthermore, it was held that the girl's right to protection of her image was more important than the appellants' freedom of expression and right to publish the photograph without her consent.

In Germany the law does not use the expression 'personality', nor does it recognize a general right to personality. However, an individual has the statutory right to contest another person's use of his name. If there is a threat that such use will continue, it is possible to obtain an order requiring the person infringing the right to stop. Provisions also exist relating to the right to one's likeness. However, there is an argument in Germany that these special remedies need to be diversified because they run counter to what appears a deep-rooted German suspicion of monetary remedies.

8.3 The Calcutt Committee

The Government Committee on Privacy and Related Matters chaired by David Calcutt QC, which reported in 1990, was the most recent committee to consider the issue of whether a statutory tort of privacy should be introduced into English law.

8.3.1 General principles

Any proposed new law, especially one that would have the effect of curtailing freedom of speech and freedom of information, ought to satisfy two basic criteria before it is allowed to pass onto the statute books:

1. Can the proposed law work efficiently, in other words with certainty and consistency? This is a question of definition and scope.
2. Is there an overriding social need for legislative control?

Definition and scope
The Calcutt Committee had to consider what privacy itself encompassed and the circumstances in which the public interest in disclosure would override a person's right of privacy. The Committee concluded that difficulties over adequate definitions did not

necessarily rule out the formulation of a limited tort directed towards the publication of personal information towards the world at large. It specifically excluded from the suggested definition any material concerning corporate entities, individuals in relation to their business or employment, and information that was available for public inspection. It also set out what it considered might be an acceptable form of public interest defence.

In the event, the Calcutt Committee recommended against the introduction of a statutory tort of privacy, although not because definition would be an insurmountable problem.

Overriding social need

Like the earlier commissions of inquiry, the Calcutt Commission's consideration of whether a statutory right of privacy was necessary focused upon two questions:

1. How large is the problem?
2. How adequate is the existing legal protection?

In relation to the first question, Calcutt's report stated at paragraph 4.8 that his committee:

> ...found no reliable evidence to show whether unwarranted intrusion into individual privacy has or has not risen over the last twenty years.

In relation to the second question concerning the extent of existing legal protection, Calcutt explored the range of remedies available to the individual against the press. As noted above, there are laws offering protection in the following areas:

- *Untruths.* The libel law and those relating to malicious falsehood are available against many forms of published untruths, especially those of a personal or damaging nature.
- *Confidential information.* The law of confidence offers some protection against abuse or unauthorized use of confidential information, whether of a personal or business nature. This area of the law has seen its parameters extended in recent years and can be very effective, particularly at restraining a publication.
- *Private property.* The law of trespass, although not very effective against the occasional incursion, is there to enforce the individual's right to decide who remains on his property.
- *Private correspondence.* Interference with letters and communications is afforded wide protection through the criminal law and the laws of copyright and confidence.
- *Family matters.* Under the courts' inherent powers relating to wardship and the guardianship over minors, judges are usually willing to protect children and their families against publicity and press intrusion. Blanket injunctions against all sections of the media can be obtained very quickly. Reporting of family cases, including divorce matters, is also severely restricted.

121

- *Interception and bugging.* The Wireless and Telegraphy Acts and the Interception of Communications Act 1985 apply criminal sanctions against those who plant listening bugs or who intercept postal or telephone communications. However, the Regulation of Investigatory Powers Act 2000 ('the RIPA'), Part 1 Chapter 1 of which came into force in October 2000 and Part 3 of which came into force in September 2000, has amended and indeed augmented the Government's powers to intercept, so much so that as a bill it was dubbed the 'e-snooping bill'. It remains to be seen how the RIPA will sit with the Freedom of Information Act 2000 and the Data Protection Act 1998 (the 'DPA'), which purports to enhance a person's right to privacy by safeguarding personal data more effectively (see Chapter 7).

Following its review, the Calcutt Committee report concluded that a law of privacy was both practicable and justifiable, particularly in view of the absence of sufficient protection for the individual against intrusion by the press. It found that there was a particularly 'pressing social need' to protect individuals vulnerable to exploitation by virtue of age, immaturity, infirmity, grief or the need to undergo medical treatment (paragraph 12.6). The Committee expounded the view that a well-drafted tort of privacy would not unduly inhibit either freedom of speech or investigative journalism.

Despite reaching the above conclusions, the Committee recommended against legislation to create an enforceable general right of privacy. However, it said that the press had to clean up its own house (paragraph 12.5):

> We have concluded that an overwhelming case for introducing a statutory tort of infringement of privacy has not so far been made out and that the better option lies with the measures set out elsewhere in this report. We therefore recommend that such a tort should not presently be introduced . . . We have come to our conclusion from a variety of standpoints and for different reasons. No single argument has prevailed for us all. Our grounds for deciding against the proposed tort include arguments of principle, practical concerns and the availability of other options for tackling the problems which we have identified. We make our recommendation on the assumption that the improved scheme for self-regulation recommended [in this report] will be made to work. Should this fail, the case for a statutory tort of infringement of privacy might have to be reconsidered.

The 'improved scheme for self-regulation' proposed by Calcutt was the Press Complaints Commission, which came into existence on 1 January 1999 (see Chapter 17).

8.3.2 Post-Calcutt

Two years after the Calcutt report, David Calcutt QC was asked to review the behaviour of the press in relation to privacy and self-regulation during the intervening period. In the wake of the report, published in 1993, the constitution of the Press Complaints Committee was altered so as to contain a non-industry (in other words independent) majority.

In the last decade, many more voices have advocated express, although not necessarily statutory, protection of privacy. In 1993 the Lord Chancellor's Department published a consultation paper called *Infringement of Privacy*, which proposed the introduction of legislation to create a civil right to privacy. In 1996, Lord Bingham of Cornhill advocated strongly the need to import a statutory protection akin to the United States of America model (*Should there be a Law to Protect Rights of Personal Privacy? (1996)*). He maintained that even if the development of a statutory tort of privacy was not imminent, the courts would probably be forced to construct one where the 'need to give relief is obvious and pressing'.

However, despite these recent developments there is still no specific government legislation creating a statutory tort of privacy. The position is different in the United States, where there is a long-established and well-recognized tort of privacy (see Chapter 21). Ironically, in the United States the concepts of confidence, trespass and harassment, which were largely imported from England, were found wanting when it came to protecting privacy. The gap in the law was noted and 'the desirability – indeed of the necessity of such protection' was strongly advocated in the often-cited article written by Samuel Warren and Louis Brandeis for the *Harvard Law Review* in 1890. Even in the 1890s the authors noted the unpleasant effect of pernicious gossip that 'is pursued with industry as well as effrontery'. This sentiment is just as applicable today.

8.4 The Human Rights Act 1998

8.4.1 General principles

The introduction into English law of the Convention's Article 8 right to privacy by the HRA has propagated a more tangible right to privacy. Article 8 states that everyone has the right to respect for his private and family life, home and correspondence.

The HRA is starting to trigger a new culture whereby the courts determine whether the acts of public authorities and Parliament are compatible with the Convention. Under Section 3(1) of the HRA, subordinate and primary legislation must, so far as is possible, be read and given effect in a way that is compatible with the Convention. Incompatible subordinate legislation will, accordingly, be struck down or disapplied by the court. Although primary legislation cannot be struck down, the higher courts are empowered to declare the incompatibility of a provision. Following such a judicial declaration of incompatibility, Parliament may utilize a fast-track procedure with a view to amending the statute if it so chooses.

Public authorities
The HRA imposes a duty on public authorities to observe the right to privacy. Section 6 of the HRA renders it unlawful for a 'public authority' to 'act' incompatibly with any Convention right. The definition of 'act' also encompasses 'a failure to act'. Although it is not entirely certain what constitutes a public authority, it seems that the net will be cast

wider than has previously been the case for judicial review cases, in which the phrase 'public functions' is equated with governmental functions. However, for immediate purposes any decision having 'public effect' is likely to bring the relevant body within the scope of Section 6.

Private parties

Although the HRA creates clear privacy rights against public authorities, it does not, in general, entitle the court to create new causes of action between private parties in litigation. Nevertheless, the HRA seems to have bolstered the development of the common law based on existing causes of action, particularly breach of confidence, and may spawn a more tangible common law right of privacy for individuals between themselves. In view of recent judicial interpretations it is reasonable to speculate that the widely anticipated development of an express protection of the right to privacy will spread to the private sector. Some of the decisions are explicitly premised upon the HRA, whereas others are premised upon an amalgamation of common law doctrines such as the law of confidence. Regardless, the courts seem to be interpreting privacy as a right that is readily available to those who seek redress, and from which derogation is only permitted in exceptional circumstances.

8.4.2 Recent decisions

In *R v A Local Authority in the Midlands ex parte LM (2000)*, the Court of Appeal, applying the HRA, held that the police or local authorities could disclose to a third party allegations of sexual abuse of children if they genuinely and reasonably believed that it was desirable to do so in the interests of protecting children and preventing crime. However, the so-called 'pressing need' for such disclosure would have to outweigh the need to safeguard an individual's right to privacy.

On the facts of the case, the court held that mere allegations of sexual abuse were insufficiently 'pressing' to justify the local authority's education department, acting on information disclosed by the social services department and the police in response to its inquiries, terminating the applicant's contract to provide school bus services. The applicant had no criminal record and had never been cautioned or bound over. He therefore had the right to be presumed innocent. The allegations, made 10 years earlier, were not proved either to the criminal or civil standard of proof, and had not been the subject of criminal or civil proceedings. The court found a breach of Article 8, and quashed the decision of the police and the local authority to disclose the allegations.

The Court of Appeal appears to have extended an individual's right to privacy in the much publicized case of *Douglas v Hello! (2001)*. The actors Catherine Zeta-Jones and Michael Douglas signed a £1.2m contract with *OK!* magazine for exclusive coverage of their wedding. The agreement provided for the couple's right of veto over publication of *OK!*'s photographs. However, although Zeta-Jones and Douglas operated a tight security system at the wedding it was infiltrated by rival magazine *Hello!*, which published photographs of the wedding three days before *OK!*. Zeta-Jones and Douglas were granted an injunction, but it was too late to stop the distribution of the 15 750 copies already on sale.

The Court of Appeal subsequently dismissed the injunction, but found that Zeta-Jones and Douglas had a legal right in respect of the infringement of their privacy for which the remedy was to be damages. The court found the right of privacy under English law to be based on the tort of confidence and Article 8 and Article 10(2) of the Convention. Article 10(2) qualifies the right to freedom of expression in favour of other rights, which in this case was the right to privacy. The court held the couple had a 'powerfully arguable' case that they 'have a right of privacy which English law will today recognize and protect'. The law had to protect those 'who find themselves subjected to an unwarranted intrusion into their lives'. Even though the major part of the couple's privacy rights had become the subject of a commercial transaction, they had retained privacy in the shape of editorial control over *OK!*'s pictures. *Hello!*'s photographs had violated this aspect.

The *Douglas* case was followed by *David and Victoria Beckham v MGN Ltd (2001)*. The Beckhams were granted an injunction preventing Mirror Group Newspapers publishing photographs of their new home. They gave a cross-undertaking that they would not publish photographs of their new home themselves. However, they later sought to extend the injunction against Mirror Group Newspapers on the basis of invasion of privacy and security risks. When they told the court that they were in discussions with another publication with a view to publishing the photographs, Mirror Group Newspapers sought another undertaking that the Beckhams would not publish the photographs without giving it an opportunity to address the court on the sale. The court extended the injunction, but refused to grant the additional undertaking on the basis that it would be an unjustified restriction on their freedom to determine the extent of any interference with their privacy.

The High Court has followed the lead of the Court of Appeal and has seemingly broadened the ambit of the right of an individual to privacy. The two murderers of James Bulger sought an injunction protecting their identity following their release from prison. The court again considered the *Douglas* case and decided to grant the injunction in order to protect the identity and preserve the anonymity of the applicants on the basis that the provisions of the Convention and the law of confidentiality could, exceptionally, be extended to protect individuals who were seriously at risk of injury or death if their identity or whereabouts became public knowledge.

Initially, the injunctions granted were to terminate on the eighteenth birthdays of the applicants. The court extended the injunctions indefinitely to restrain publicity of the applicants' identities, changes in their physical appearance since their detention, their new identities upon their release into the community, information concerning their existing placements, and all specific information that related to their time in secure units. The court premised its decision to extend the injunctions on the right to life as enshrined in Article 2 of the Convention as well as the English common law of confidentiality (*Venables v News Group Newspapers Ltd (2001)*).

In a pilot case under the DPA, Norman Baker, the Liberal Democrat MP for Lewes, successfully applied his right under the DPA to force MI5 to open its top-secret files for the first time. Following an original request from Baker to see his file, Jack Straw, then Home Secretary, issued a certificate exempting MI5 under the DPA from having to reveal whether it even held the information. Baker successfully argued that this was 'unreasonable'. The certificate was quashed by the Data Protection Tribunal, which applied the 'reasonableness' test applicable in judicial review cases and the 'proportionality' test required under the DPA (contained in the 8th principle) and found that the exemption was 'wider than is necessary to protect national security'.

Even though the decision has been termed a 'landmark ruling' because MI5 can no longer rely on a blanket policy of refusing to confirm or deny if it holds particular information on individuals, it seems likely that the decision will not give terrorists immunity from investigation. Nor will it unduly hamper the security services, which will still be able to refuse access or even refuse to make comment if to do so would 'actually threaten national security'. The main difference brought about by the decision is that these considerations will have to be made on a case-by-case basis.

8.5 The future

The recent developments by the English courts may only be the thin end of the wedge. The courts may interpret the laws of privacy further to cover an even wider range of scenarios.

8.5.1 Companies

Companies, businesses and firms may one day be able to assert a right of privacy. Although the European jurisprudence has not expressly recognized that firms may be able to invoke the right to privacy, the European Court has found that privacy should not be excluded in relation to professional or business activities. In *Niemitz v Germany (1992)*, the court held there was:

> . . . no reason in principle why this understanding of the notion of 'private life' should be taken to exclude the activities of a professional or business nature since it is, after all, in the course of their working lives that the majority of people have a significant, if not the greatest opportunity of developing relationships with the outside world.

In that case, the European Court found that a search of a German lawyer's office for incriminating evidence conducted by the German police in the absence of any independent observer constituted a violation of Article 8. Although it remains to be seen whether firms and companies will be able to assert a right to privacy, there are likely to be imminent and significant ramifications for them in their capacity as employers, particularly in their attempts to monitor staff emails and telephone conversations.

8.5.2 Surveillance and interception of communications

The right to privacy pervades all areas. Long-range photos and closed circuit television would seem to cross the boundary of what is acceptable as evidence before the courts. Recently, some tribunals have displayed their increasing discomfort about accepting such surveillance as evidence. Similarly, police video-surveillance activities could also fall within the scope of the HRA. The police in the United Kingdom may have to adopt the position of their European counterparts and take particular care to comply with principles of proportionality. In order to ensure that freedom of movement and conduct are not unreasonably impinged upon, the use of video surveillance may be restricted to the prevention of 'real danger' or the suppression of a specific criminal offence.

However, one complicating factor is the interrelation of the right to privacy with the DPA and the RIPA. The DPA was introduced to implement the European Union Data Protection Directive, and was never envisaged as being a civil liberties measure. It is more a mechanism for facilitating the collection, storage, regulation and possible trade in personal data within the European Community. The DPA may complement the HRA. However, if the DPA fails to protect personal privacy in accordance with the European Union Data Protection Directive, the United Kingdom is likely to be in breach of its community obligations.

The RIPA makes it illegal to intercept communications such as telephone calls or email unless it is necessary for a specific purpose such as national security, preventing or detecting crime or preventing disorder or in the interests of public safety. This will allow the police and MI5 to collect Internet data without a warrant, to pick up emails of people suspected of serious crimes with a warrant, and to demand encryption tools with a view to unscrambling data. One school of thought is that the RIPA follows a long tradition of government snooping and cements the state's right to 'tap' emails and any other forms of communication in order to prevent crime, maintain national security and economic well-being. It is equally arguable that the RIPA delineates the state's powers of interception and actually safeguards a person's right to privacy. It remains to be seen whether the Government will accept the proposals made by the Deputy Director General of the National Criminal Intelligence Service that Britain's police and intelligence services should be allowed unrestricted access to records of every telephone call, email and Internet connection made in the United Kingdom. The events of 11 September 2001 in New York and Washington may well impact on any decision made in this area. The Government has already brought about sweeping security measures in response to the terrorist attacks in the form of the Anti-Terrorism, Crime and Security Act 2001, some of which impacts on surveillance and interception of communications. The Government will also no doubt closely observe the effectiveness of the Combating Terrorism Act 2001, passed by the United States Senate two days after the terrorist attack, and the USA Patriot Act 2001, passed by the Senate in October 2001 (see Chapter 21).

The terrorist attacks may also impact on other areas of surveillance and privacy. Immediately after 11 September 2001, the Home Secretary David Blunkett suggested that the British Government was sympathetic to the introduction of identity cards in order to combat the threat from terrorists and bogus asylum seekers. It was suggested that the card, which would include a computer chip to hold detailed information about the bearer's physical characteristics, age, address, social security data, health records and, in all probability, traffic offences, outstanding warrants for arrest and criminal offences, could also function as a driving licence, credit card and store card to make it more acceptable to consumers.

It has been argued in several quarters that the impact of such a card would be to stunt the embryonic right to privacy and transgress data protection rights. For identity cards to be effective, the police would have to be granted powers to stop people at random to demand sight of the card. Although proponents of the system argue that those with nothing to hide have nothing to fear, the real danger is that each individual will be allocated a central number around which will accumulate a huge amount of personal information from each and every arm of the State. In view of the power that the card would confer, some commentators have suggested that at stake is the very nature of our society and the power and authority of the State over the individual and his privacy. The Government seems to have backed down on the idea of identity cards in the weeks following the terrorist attacks, although some commentators believe that it has simply been put on hold.

8.5.3 Impact on the media

It seems likely that the HRA will have a major impact on the media. It is arguable that the Press Complaints Committee and the Broadcasting Standards Committee are 'public authorities'. If they are, they must conduct themselves within the provisions of the HRA. Failure to supply a system that provides complainants with proper protection for their Article 8 right may amount to unlawful action under Section 6 of the HRA, and entitlement to damages or an injunction.

8.5.4 A 'Privacy Act'

The difficulty in drafting a statutory right of privacy lies in producing a coherent and infallible definition of privacy that sits comfortably with any possible defences to the tort – such as, for example, a 'public interest' defence. Any analysis of the 'public interest' defence must take into account the concept of 'proportionality' to the legitimate aim to be achieved – after all, a sledgehammer should not be used to crush a nut. Defences of 'innocent infringement', consent, privilege, legal authority and protection of property and legitimate business interests have also been suggested. As noted above, this is not a new problem. The various Royal Commissions have grappled with this difficulty over the years, and have not as yet managed to produce a satisfactory legal definition of privacy.

Although the right to privacy seems in the absence of legislation to be evolving via judicial interpretations, as mentioned above, the courts have adopted a fairly piecemeal approach and have been careful not to maintain the privacy of individuals in all circumstances. In the case of *Ford v The Press Complaints Commission (2001)*, the High Court rejected newsreader Anna Ford's application for a judicial review of the Press Complaints Commission's decision not to uphold a complaint or grant an injunction restraining the publication of photos taken of herself and her companion, David Scott, on a beach. The court made it clear that its role was not to make a factual evaluation of the circumstances and decide whether the privacy rights of Ford and Scott had been transgressed. Rather, it was to determine whether Ford had an arguable case to pursue her complaint by invoking the court's limited supervisory jurisdiction over the Press Complaints Committee.

It is open to debate whether the *Ford* case will actually have any bearing on the development of a law of privacy. The court maintained that:

> . . . the courts will be deferential to and not be keen to interfere with decisions of the Commission . . . unless . . . clearly desirable to do so.

In reaching this decision, the court drew support from the case of *R v Broadcasting Standards Commission (2000)*, in which is was said that:

> . . . it is very important that where you have a body such as the Press Complaints Commission, if the court has any jurisdiction it is reserved for cases where it would be *clearly desirable* for this court to intervene.

However, the court:

> . . . could not conclude that a publicly accessible Majorcan beach was a place where the Complainant could have had a reasonable expectation of privacy . . . even if there was much less deference due by this court to the determination than appears appropriate in the authorities to which I have referred, there still would not be even an arguable case that there was any justification for this court to interfere on this ground as there was adequate material to justify the decision of the Commission that there had not been a breach of Clause 3 (ii) of the Code.

Moreover, previous case law may not be sufficient to develop a law of privacy. For example, the definition of 'private nuisance' in English law may change in the light of Article 8 of the Convention. In *Hunter v Canary Wharf Ltd (1997)*, the House of Lords dismissed a claim for nuisance arising out of interference with television reception by large buildings at the new Canary Wharf development. It was held that an owner of land was entitled to build on his land as he pleased, subject to planning control, and was not generally liable if a building interfered with his neighbour's enjoyment of his own land. Although the court observed that 'the presumption is for freedom in the occupation and use of property', the court concluded that because the defendant had been granted planning permission, no action lay in private nuisance. In the future, there may be a difficult balancing act between an occupier's right to do as he pleases on his own land and his neighbour's right to enjoy his land to the fullest extent.

It remains to be seen whether the courts will be able to develop the law of privacy as fully as other jurisdictions such as the United States. The courts will be mindful of some of the concerns highlighted by the Calcutt Report and in recent cases before the courts. The right to assert privacy is also complicated by the need to consider other recently introduced legislation such as the RIPA. Only time will tell whether the embryonic right to privacy develops fully or is rendered subservient to other, more politically charged, legislation.

PART IV

Comment on Court Proceedings

9 Reporting Restrictions

Jane Colston

9.1 Introduction

It has long been established in English law that the proper administration of law in accordance with the rules of natural justice requires that court proceedings should be held openly and in public. Although the principle may not be universally observed, it is undoubtedly recognized throughout the world as being a basic standard by which the quality of a legal system is judged. The principle has been incorporated into numerous other national constitutions and parliamentary statutes. Article 6 of the European Convention on Human Rights (the right to a fair and public trial) which has been incorporated into English law by the Human Rights Act 1998, echoes the principle precisely.

Although the open court rule is the norm for legal proceedings, there are numerous common law and statutory exceptions. In circumstances where the interests of national security or justice demand it, the court may sit behind closed doors 'in camera', meaning in private. Although the public and the media are not permitted to attend these hearings, the media may be able to publish limited reports on the proceedings. In other situations, while the proceedings may be open to the public and the media the court may order that the media are prevented from reporting on the case. The most important of these orders preventing reporting by the media are:

- The power to postpone the reporting of proceedings
- The power to prevent the publication of the names of parties
- Restrictions on publication of information relating to children.

There are also automatic bans that restrict reports relating to, for example:

- Committal proceedings before magistrates' courts
- Hearings concerning sexual offences and indecency
- Divorce cases
- Documents made available on disclosure.

There have been occasions over the years where judges have taken it upon themselves to clear their courts of the public and the media in order to conduct cases in private. Unless there is legal authority at common law or by statute to take such a step, conducting the case in this way will be improper and will amount to grounds for appeal. For example, the controversial decision to hold an inquiry into the murders committed by Dr Harold Shipman in private was held to be irrational (*R v Secretary of State for Health ex parte Wagstaffe (2001)*) because it was contrary to the principle of freedom of expression and the expectation that the hearing would take place in public.

Breach of reporting restrictions is a serious criminal offence and/or contempt of court. It is punishable by a fine and, in extreme cases, the penalty is imprisonment.

9.2 The open court rule

9.2.1 General principles

The fundamental principle that court proceedings should be held openly and in public so that justice is seen to be done and the public can be informed about the justice administered in their name was considered by Lord Halsbury in the case of *Scott v Scott (1913)*:

> ... publicity is the very sole of justice ... and the surest of all guards against improbity. It keeps the judge himself, while trying, under trial.

To facilitate the process of open justice, the media are permitted to sit in the courtroom itself and even to be present on occasions when the public are excluded. This is:

> ... not because of any special wisdom, interest or status enjoyed by proprietors, editors or journalists. It is because the media are the eyes and ears of the general public. They act on behalf of the general public. Their right to know and their right to publish is neither more nor less than that of the general public. Indeed, it is that of the general public for whom they are trustees.
>
> (*A-G v Guardian Newspapers Ltd (No 2) (1988)*)

The majority of hearings in criminal proceedings are heard in public. The Civil Procedure Rules, which came into force in April 1999, govern the conduct of civil proceedings. The general rule set out in Part 39.2(1) of the Civil Procedure Rules is that hearings are to be in public.

A court is not 'open' if the judge takes deliberate steps to prevent the public or the media attending. In *Macpherson v Macpherson (1936)* the trial took place at lunchtime in the judge's library, to which the only access was through a door marked 'private'. On appeal it was held that, in effect, the hearing had been held in private. As there was no jurisdiction at that time for a court to do so, it was held that the order made at the end of the trial was voidable.

9.2.2 Obtaining information

One consequence of the rule that hearings should generally be in public is the automatic right to obtain copies of any civil judgment or order made in public on payment of the appropriate fee. There is no standard fee. Initially requests for copies of judgments or orders should be made to the appropriate court. If the hearing took place in private, an application for leave must first be made to the hearing judge to obtain a copy of the judgment or order (Practice Direction 39 supplementing Part 39 of the Civil Procedure Rules paragraph 1.12). If permission is granted, the prescribed fee for each copy must be paid.

Copies of civil court judgments are also published on the Internet. A unique number is allocated by the official shorthand writer to each approved civil judgment in the High Court, which is placed in front of the case citation. Many of these cases appear on the Court Service web site[1] and are available to download free of charge. The Court Service web site also includes the current daily cause list for the High Court in London. This list sets out the scheduled hearings for that day. To check when a case is likely to be heard, enquiries will have to be made to the listing officer at the relevant court. The daily cause lists for the district registries and county courts are not on the Court Service web site, but are available for inspection at each individual court. The daily cause lists can be a valuable source of information about hearings, including those held in private, as they include the name of the parties and judge, the court room and the action number. However, sensitive cases and applications that do not require notice to the other party are not listed.

On payment of the prescribed fee of £20 per hour it is also possible to inspect the claims list held by the various divisions of the High Court. As the claims list is only computerized in the Commercial Division of the High Court, searches usually have to be done manually, which can be very time consuming and expensive.

The claims list provides the names of the parties, the date the proceedings began and the names of the solicitors acting on behalf of the parties. By using this list it is possible to obtain a copy of the claim form filed in the case once it has been served and notification of this has been given to the court. The particulars of claim may also be obtained, but only if they are recorded in the body of the claim form. The claim form and the particulars of claim set out details of the claimant's case. Until the county courts install facilities for computer searches of court records, it is not possible to carry out a similar inspection of the records of these courts.

9.2.3 Proceedings held in private

At common law the court has the residual power to sit in private if it is necessary for justice to be done or, possibly, in order to prevent the proceedings being disrupted by disorderly conduct. However, in general the authority to sit in private is governed by the rules of the court and by statute.

Only a small portion of criminal court work is held in private. For example, the Official Secrets Act 1920 allows the judge in an official secrets trial the power to clear the public from the court

---

[1] The web site can be found at www.courtservice.gov.uk.

if he considers it necessary to avoid prejudice to national security. A much greater portion of civil court work takes place in private. The authority to sit in private in civil proceedings is found mainly in the Civil Procedure Rules and the Administration of Justice Act 1960.

Civil Procedure Rules

Part 39.2(3) of the Civil Procedure Rules sets out when a hearing, or part of it, may be held in private – for example when:

- Publicity would defeat the object of the hearing
- It involves matters relating to national security
- It involves confidential information and publicity would damage that confidentiality
- It is necessary to protect the interests of a child or patient
- It is a hearing made without notice and it would be unjust to any respondent for there to be a public hearing
- It involves uncontentious matters arising out of the administration of a trust or estate
- The court considers it necessary in the interests of justice.

The decision whether to hold a hearing in private will be made by the judge having regard to any common law or statutory power he may have, any representations made to him by the parties or the media, and Article 6 of the European Convention on Human Rights (Practice Direction 39 supplementing Part 39 of the Civil Procedure Rules paragraphs 1.4 and 1.4A). There are 11 categories of case that should, in the first instance, be listed by the court as hearings in private (Practice Direction 39A supplementing Part 39 of the Civil Procedure Rules paragraph 1.5), such as applications for possession of premises by mortgagees or landlords.

If the court or room in which the proceedings are taking place has a sign on the door stating that the proceedings are 'private', members of the public who are not parties to the proceedings, including the media, will not be admitted unless the court gives permission (Practice Direction 39 supplementing Part 39 of the Civil Procedure Rules paragraph 1.9).

Even if proceedings are held in private under this rule, they are not secret proceedings. Other than in exceptional circumstances (for example, where it would prejudice the administration of justice or where the court has made an order restricting reporting) or cases governed by the Administration of Justice Act 1960, it is still possible for the media to pass comment on what happened during the proceedings. The practical difficulty is that the media are not allowed to be present during the hearing itself. They must, therefore, rely to a great extent upon interviewing those directly involved in the proceedings outside the door of the court and carrying out the searches referred to in Section 9.2.2.

Administration of Justice Act 1960

The general rule is that the publication of information relating to proceedings before any court sitting in private shall not, of itself, be contempt of court except in cases:

- Relating to minors, wardship, adoption, residence, guardianship, maintenance, or rights of access to a child
- Involving applications made under the Mental Health Act 1959
- Where the court sits in private for reasons of national security
- Where information relates to a secret process, discovery or invention that is in issue in the proceedings
- Where the court expressly prohibits publication of information relating to the proceedings.

Publication of information relating to these proceedings will not *in itself* incur liability for contempt of court. However, because it is not 'a fair and accurate report of legal proceedings held in *public*' it may amount to an offence under the Contempt of Court Act 1981 (see Chapter 10) if it involves publication of a seriously prejudicial matter. For the same reason there will be no automatic defence to libel proceedings following publication, since absolute privilege does not attach to reports of proceedings that are not held in open court. Extreme caution should be exercised when giving consideration to publishing information relating to such cases, and legal advice should be taken before publication. However, it is lawful to publish the whole or part of any order made at such a hearing unless such publication is expressly forbidden by the judge. In addition, the prohibition may be relaxed by the judge if, on hearing representations by the parties, he believes it is in the interests of justice to do so, for example, to trace a missing child.

9.2.4 Proceedings held in chambers

A small amount of criminal court work and an enormous amount of civil court work is conducted in chambers. Most hearings in chambers are concerned with pre-trial procedural matters, and are dealt with in this way purely for reasons of speed and administrative efficiency. Most matters dealt with by the family courts are also held in chambers.

The average hearing in chambers is unlikely to be of particular interest to the media since it is likely to be primarily concerned with technical points of procedure and pleading. Nevertheless, there are occasions when the media will want to report on hearings in chambers, for example, injunctions and residence applications. Generally, what happens during proceedings in chambers is not confidential or secret and can be the subject of a media report provided that it does not substantially prejudice the administration of justice, fall foul of Section 12(1) of the Administration of Justice Act 1960 or any order the court might make restricting reporting.

Provided that there is no sign on the door of the court or judge's room indicating that the proceedings are private, members of the media may be admitted where practicable. The requirement for hearings to be in public does not require the court to make special arrangements for accommodating members of the public (Part 39.2(2) of the Civil Procedure Rules). However, if members of the public or the media wish to attend a hearing in chambers but cannot be accommodated, the judge should consider adjourning the proceedings in whole or in part into open court or allowing one or more representatives of the press to attend the hearing (*Hodgson v Imperial Tobacco Limited (1998)*; Practice Direction 39 supplementing Part 39 of the Civil Procedure Rules paragraph 1.10).

9.2.5 The court as a public authority under the European Convention on Human Rights

The incorporation of the European Convention of Human Rights into English law by the Human Rights Act 1998 will have an impact on reporting restrictions. The effect of the Convention has already been felt in the case of *Venables v News Group Newspapers Ltd (2001)*. The two notorious child murderers of James Bulger sought injunctions to prevent the publication of confidential information that might lead to their identification. Given there was a 'real possibility' that the applicants could be the objects of revenge attacks if their new identities and whereabouts were made public, the court was of the view there was a 'strong and pressing social need' for their confidentiality and Convention rights to be protected, and granted the injunctions 'to protect the applicants from serious and possibly irreparable harm'. The court acknowledged that injunctions had not previously been granted in such circumstances, but emphasized that the claimants were 'uniquely notorious' and their circumstances 'exceptional', and stressed that the case created a 'strictly defined exception'.

9.3 The power to postpone the reporting of proceedings

9.3.1 General principles

Under Section 4(2) of the Contempt of Court Act 1981, the court may order the postponement of publication of any report relating to proceedings. The postponement may be for any period of time the court thinks necessary in order to avoid a substantial risk of prejudice to the administration of justice. The risk may relate to the proceedings in question or any other pending or imminent proceedings. The authority of the court to postpone the publication of information under Section 4(2) of the Contempt of Court Act 1981 is exhaustive, and there is no inherent power beyond this provision (*R v Newtownabbey Magistrates' Court ex parte Belfast Telegraph Newspapers Ltd (1997)*).

Since the implementation of Section 4(2), its use by the courts has frequently led to criticism and challenge. There seems to have been a tendency, especially in the lower courts, to make an order on inappropriate grounds or in the form of a permanent ban rather than simply for the postponement of reporting on the proceedings. The Court of Appeal has acknowledged that orders restricting publication are commonly made in situations where they should not be made. It also acknowledged that the problem is often exacerbated where the story is one that local newspapers would wish to publish but is not of such great public interest that the newspaper restrained by the order would incur the expense of applying to have the order revoked. The Court of Appeal has, therefore, emphasized the need for the court to give 'very serious consideration' to the issues before making an order under Section 4(2) (*Ex parte News Group Newspapers Ltd (1999)*).

Once an order is made under Section 4(2), the media are usually subject to major inhibition. The following key ingredients of Section 4(2) are, therefore, of considerable importance.

The court
In this, as in every other provision of the Contempt of Court Act 1981, the reference to court 'includes any tribunal or body exercising the judicial power of the State' (Section 19). Thus, all the regular courts from the magistrates' court upwards may make orders under Section 4(2), as may the coroners' court, employment tribunals, mental health tribunals and any other tribunal established by statute to perform a judicial function.

Necessary
The court must consider that the order is 'really needed' rather than just expedient or useful because any other order would undermine Article 10 of the European Convention on Human Rights (the right to freedom of expression). 'Necessary' in the context of Section 4(2) implies more than 'merely convenient', and must be 'specifically related to the avoidance of the described risk'. In *Ex parte Central Independent Television Plc (1991)*, the banning of reports on a trial when the jury retired overnight to consider its decision was held to be unnecessary because the jurors could have been instructed not to switch on their televisions or radios.

Substantial risk
The risk must be substantial. Unlike the strict liability rule in Section 2 of the Contempt of Court Act 1981 (see Chapter 10), the prejudice does not have to be 'serious' but it must be more than minimal. In considering whether the risk of prejudice is 'substantial', the court will consider the length of time between the publication and the proceedings (*A-G v News Group Newspapers Limited (1987)*) and give credit to jurors' ability to consider only the evidence before them (*MGN v Bank of America (1995)*).

Proceedings
The proceedings may be those actually before the court, or any other case that is 'pending or imminent'. The power to postpone is limited to reports of legal proceedings held in public (*R v Rhuddlan Justice ex parte HTV Limited (1985)*).

For any period of time
Any postponement order should be for a specific period of time that should be defined by reference to the test of necessity. The media should be in no doubt that the Section 4(2) order is a powerful gagging weapon. The postponement may run for a considerable time, although it is often until the conclusion of the trial or a series of trials. However, the court may not

prohibit reporting for all time under the guise of postponement, nor may it make an order for any reason other than to avoid prejudice in the proceedings or pending proceedings. In addition, 'blanket bans' on reporting are likely to be inappropriate (*R v Horsham Justices ex parte Farquarson (1982)*).

9.3.2 Discretion

The court has an overriding discretion whether to make a postponement order. The exercise of the court's discretion will be in response to the particular facts and circumstances of each case. However, there are three situations in which a postponement order is regarded as normal practice, often because the strict liability contempt rule in Section 2 of the Contempt of Court Act 1981 might not apply unless there is an order for postponement. The three situations are as follows:

1. Where a prejudicial matter is heard by the court while the jury is absent, known as a 'trial within a trial'. The admissibility of particular pieces of evidence, such as confessions and submissions on points of law, are usually made during a trial within a trial.
2. Where the accused is awaiting a further trial or trials for other matters. Here, there is a risk of prejudice to 'other proceedings' rather than those in which the order is made. Obviously, the publication of damning evidence or a conviction is likely to influence a future juror against the defendant. However, only other proceedings which are imminent or pending may be taken into account under Section 4(2), which effectively means any other case in which the accused has already been charged or where it is known that he is about to be charged.
3. Where the separate trial or trials of other people, for example co-defendants, are likely to be prejudiced by material arising during the proceedings. It is not uncommon for evidence to be given in one trial, which is highly prejudicial to separate proceedings against other parties. If the judge considers the risk to be substantial he may make an order postponing publication. Again, the other proceedings must be imminent or pending.

9.3.3 Terms of the order

Orders made under Section 4(2) must be formulated in precise terms, committed to writing and kept in permanent record for later reference (*Practice Direction (Contempt: Reporting Restrictions) (1982)*). The order must be crystal clear in scope, and no wider than is necessary (*MGN v Bank of America (1995)*). It must also state the reason why the order was made and the time at which it shall cease to have effect.

The court must give notice to the press that a postponement order has been made. It must also state that it is prepared to answer any queries about specific cases. However, failure on the part of the media to discover the existence or precise terms of a particular order will not result in avoiding liability for contempt of court (*Practice Direction (Contempt: Reporting*

Restrictions) (1982)). Although court staff should give every assistance to the media who wish to find out what was ordered, it is clear that the responsibility remains with the media to make all necessary enquiries and ensure that no breach of the order occurs.

9.4 The power to prevent the publication of the names of parties

Under Section 11 of the Contempt of Court Act 1981 the court has the power to restrict the publication of material, including the names of participants, arising out of proceedings held in open court. Section 11 states:

> In any case where a court (having power to do so) allows a name or other matter to be withheld from the public in proceedings before the court, the court may give such directions prohibiting the publication of that name or matter in connection with the proceedings as appear to the court to be necessary for the purpose for which it was so withheld.

Section 11 does not give the court any particular powers it did not already possess under the common law. Significantly, however, it does confirm that in circumstances where there is power to impose partial secrecy inside the courtroom itself by withholding a 'name or other matter from the public', it may impose the same secrecy upon media reporting of the case. In order to make such an order, the court must have first exercised a valid power to withhold the relevant information from the members of the public sitting in court.

Orders for anonymity under Section 11 cannot be made in respect of a 'name or other matter' that has already been spoken in open court. Further, Section 11 should only be invoked in circumstances where the interests of justice would be harmed if the name or other matter were made public. It is a draconian measure, and must not be used simply to spare the embarrassment of defendants or witnesses. In *R v Evesham Justices ex parte McDonagh (1988)*, magistrates trying an ex-MP on a motoring charge allowed his address to be kept secret because he feared harassment from his former wife. The Divisional Court ruled on appeal that Section 11 orders should be made only where to do otherwise would '. . . frustrate or render impracticable the administration of justice' because the power to restrict publication 'was not enacted for the comfort and feelings of defendants'. The need for objective justification was confirmed in *R v Legal Aid Board ex parte Kaim Todner (a firm) (1998)*.

A common instance where names will be withheld are blackmail proceedings and cases under the Official Secrets Act. The apparent justification for orders in blackmail cases is to ensure that victims of blackmail will not be frightened about reporting the crime. In *R v Socialist Worker (1975)*, the judge in a blackmail case directed that the victims should be referred to as Mr X and Mr Y. A subsequent article written by Paul Foot in the *Socialist Worker* headed 'Y, Oh Lord, Oh Why?' named the two men. Both Mr Foot and the magazine were successfully prosecuted for contempt of court.

An individual can apply to court for an order under Section 11 to protect himself or another interested party (*R v Somerset Health Authority ex parte S (1996)*).

An order under Section 11 should be in writing and should state its precise scope, the time at which it shall cease to have effect, and the specific purpose of making the order. There must be a clear ruling expressed as a formal order before the media can be held in contempt for disobeying it (*A-G v Leveller Magazine Ltd (1979)*). Courts must normally give notice to the media that an order has been made, and court staff should be prepared to answer any queries about the order (*Practice Note: (Contempt of Court: Reports of Proceedings: Postponement Orders (1983))*).

9.5 Restrictions on the publication of information relating to children

The court has a general power to restrict publication of information relating to children. Although children do not have any special right of confidentiality (*R v Independent Television (1994)*), the court will prevent publication in order to protect the administration of justice. There are also numerous statutes designed to prevent the identification of children and young people in court proceedings.

9.5.1 Section 39 of the Children and Young Persons Act 1933

Section 39 of the Children and Young Persons Act 1933 states:

(1) In relation to any proceedings in any court . . . the court may direct that . . .
   (a) no newspaper report of the proceedings shall reveal the name, address, or school, or include any particulars calculated to lead to the identification of any child or young person concerned in the proceedings, either as being the person by or against or in respect of whom the proceedings are taken, or as being a witness therein;
   (b) no picture shall be published in any newspaper as being or including a picture of any child or young person so concerned in the proceedings as aforesaid;

except in so far (if at all) as may be permitted by the direction of the court.

Orders restricting publication of information identifying children under Section 39 are discretionary. There is no guidance in Section 39 as to when it will be appropriate for the court to exercise its discretion to make an order.

Section 39 is applicable to any proceedings in any court, and a Section 39 order may be made in respect of any child who is a claimant, defendant or witness in proceedings. However, such orders are routinely made in family cases and education cases in the county court. They are also routinely made in criminal proceedings in the magistrates' court and crown court where the child is the defendant, although they are not automatic where the child is simply a witness.

When considering such an order in regard to a young person who is a defendant, the court will balance the age of the young person and the potential damage to him of public identification as a criminal against the general proposition that there is a strong and proper public interest in identifying criminals, particularly of serious and detestable crimes. In weighing this balance the court must also have regard to the welfare of the child, but not to the exclusion of all other factors (Section 44 of the Children and Young Persons Act 1933). Section 39 does not give the court an express power to restrict the publication of the name of a defendant in criminal proceedings who is not a child or a young person (*R v Crown Court at Southwark ex parte Goodwin (1991)*).

The trial judge should give reasons for his decision, and it will only be in 'rare and exceptional cases' that an order under Section 39 will be discharged by the Court of Appeal.

9.5.2 Children Act 1989

Family proceedings often commence in the magistrates' court. Restrictions on the reporting of family proceedings in the magistrates' court are automatically imposed by Sections 71(1) and (1A) of the Magistrates' Court Act 1980 and Section 97(2) of the Children Act 1989. The automatic restriction imposed by Section 97(2) of the Children Act 1989 has been extended to the reporting of any family proceedings before a county court and the High Court by Section 72 of the Access to Justice Act 1999.

9.5.3 Wardship proceedings

Wardship proceedings are heard in chambers. In general, the media may not attend or report on such hearings (Section 12(1)(a) of the Administration of Justice Act 1960 as amended by Section 108(5) of the Children Act 1989).

The purpose of the prohibition is to protect the wardship proceedings, not the confidentiality of the child himself:

> . . . the mere status of being a ward does not confer on a child any right as such to have its affairs cloaked in secrecy. The privilege of confidentiality is that of the court, not of the child, and the primary purpose of that privilege is to protect the court in the exercise of its paternal functions.
>
> *(Re X and Others (Minors) (Wardship: Disclosure of Documents) (1992))*

143

The prohibition extends to matters such as statements of evidence, reports and accounts of interviews (*Re F (A Minor) (Publication of Information) (1977)*). As it does not extend to information about the ward himself, a minor can still be the subject of published stories even if he is a ward of court. However, the story must not rely on or reproduce anything that was said in or produced for the wardship proceedings. In *Re L (A Minor) (1988)*, the *Daily Mail* was held not to be in contempt of court by publishing a ward's reaction at the funeral of her parents who had been passengers on the Herald of Free Enterprise, which sank in Zeebrugge in 1987.

When dealing with stories about wards of court the media should, however, take care to check whether an injunction is in force that affects publication. Judges often reinforce the general provisions of Section 12 with an injunction specifically prohibiting identification of the child. Since the penalties for breach of an injunction can be severe, checks should be made with the court or the child's lawyers before any publication.

The reporting restrictions imposed under Section 12 can be lifted in whole or part by the judge, as frequently happens when there is a fear the child will be forcibly removed from the jurisdiction. At such times, especially when the whereabouts of the child is unknown, the courts are generally quick to recognize that publicity in the media may be helpful.

9.5.4 Legitimacy and maintenance proceedings

Section 2 of the Domestic and Appellate Proceedings (Restriction of Publicity) Act 1968 (as amended by Section 68 Schedule 1 of the Family Law Act 1986) restricts the reporting of proceedings that relate to declarations of legitimacy.

The reporting of applications for maintenance are restricted to those matters that may be reported under Section 1(1)(b) of the Judicial Proceedings (Regulation of Reports) Act 1926, namely:

- The names, addresses and occupations of the parties and witnesses
- A concise statement of the charges, defences and counter-charges in support of which evidence has been given
- Submissions on any point of law arising in the course of the proceedings, and the decision of the court thereon
- The judgment of the court and observations made by the judge in giving judgment.

Maintenance is an order requiring either party to a marriage to make periodical payments to the other for his or her maintenance (Section 22 of the Matrimonial Causes Act 1973).

9.5.5 Young offenders

Youth courts

Young people under the age of 18 who are the subject of criminal charges appear before 'youth courts' (Section 45 of the Children and Young Persons Act 1933 (as amended)).

Although youth courts are closed to the general public, they are open to 'representatives of newspapers and news agencies' (Section 47 of the Children and Young Persons Act 1933). However, there are strict controls over what may be reported. Section 49 of the Children and Young Persons Act 1933 states:

> . . . no report shall be published which reveals the name, address, or school of any child or young person concerned in proceedings [in a youth court] or includes any particulars likely to lead to the identification of any child or young person concerned in the proceedings and no picture shall be published as being or including a picture of any child or young person so concerned in [such] proceedings.

The youth court is one of the few types of court where all reporting is automatically restricted. The limitations extend to defendants as well as witnesses under the age of 18 and apply to reports, broadcast by radio or television (Sections 49(3) and 49(4)). It is frequently not sufficient to simply leave out the name of the young person and his parents. Section 49 makes it unlawful to reveal any matter that is likely to lead to the young person being identified. For example, to name an adult present at court as the aunt of the defendant could amount to an offence.

Only the proprietor, editor or publisher of a newspaper, or any broadcaster who has corresponding functions to a newspaper editor, can be held liable for an unlawful report. It is a defence for such a person to prove that at the time of publication he was not aware nor suspected that the publication included material that contravened Section 49.

Reporting restrictions may be relaxed if the court believes it is in the interests of justice to do so. The court may give detailed reasons for its decision to lift the reporting restrictions, but it is not required to do so. The restrictions may also be relaxed after the young person has been convicted. However, before relaxing any restrictions the court must hear representations from the parties to the proceedings or any other person. The power to dispense with anonymity under Section 49 should be exercised with 'very great care, caution and circumspection'. In *McKerry v Teesdale & Wear Valley Justices (2000)* the court went on to say as follows.

> It will be wholly wrong for any court to dispense with a juvenile's *prima facie* right to anonymity as an additional punishment. It is also very difficult to see any place for 'naming and shaming'. The court must be satisfied that the statutory criterion that it is in the public interest to dispense with the reporting restriction is satisfied. This will very rarely be the case.

Other courts

On occasion, young offenders are dealt with in other courts. If they are co-charged with an adult, they will initially appear before a magistrates' court. The magistrates may send the case to the crown court or remit it for hearing to the magistrates' court. In such cases, the media may publish the young person's identity unless there is a specific order to prevent this.

The Youth Justice and Criminal Evidence Act 1999

The relevant sections of this Act, known as 'the Youth Justice Act', are not yet in force. Once in force, Section 39 of the Children and Young Persons Act 1933 will only apply to civil proceedings and those criminal proceedings instituted before the Youth Justice Act came into force (Schedule 2 Section 2 of the Youth Justice Act).

Under Section 44 of the Youth Justice Act, as soon as a criminal investigation conducted by the police (or any other charged with the duty of investigating offences) has begun there will be an automatic prohibition on identifying a person under 18 involved in the investigation, whether as the accused, a victim or a witness. The automatic prohibition will cease to have effect when proceedings relating to the offence have begun. Under Section 44 reports may not include the young person's:

- Name
- Address
- School or place of work, or
- Any still or moving picture of the young person.

A magistrates' court or crown court will be able to lift reporting restrictions under Section 44 if they believe it is in the interests of justice to do so and unrestricted reporting will not prejudice the welfare of the young person. Reporting restrictions may nevertheless apply in regard to cases involving sexual offences.

Once proceedings have begun, under Section 45 of the Youth Justice Act, a magistrates' court or crown court will be able to prohibit any media reports that identify young persons under the age of 18 if they are the accused, the victim or a witness. The court will be able to restrict reporting on the same matters subject to restriction under Section 44. The prohibition is discretionary and will be made only if it is in the interests of the young person to do so, and will not impose a substantial and unreasonable restriction on the reporting of the proceedings. The power should not be used as a matter of routine, and it will cease to have effect when the young person reaches the age of 18. The court will also be able to prohibit reporting after proceedings have commenced under other legislation, such as Section 1(2) of the Sexual Offences (Amendment) Act 1992 (see part 9.7 below).

Any person who is party to the proceedings, or any other person with leave of the court, will be able to appeal to the crown court against the decision of the magistrates' court to make or refuse to make an order lifting the restriction.

Breach of Sections 44 and 45 of the Youth Justice Act will be an offence. Only the proprietor, editor or publisher of a newspaper, or a broadcaster with the function of a newspaper editor, will be liable. The Attorney General must consent to proceedings for an offence under Section 44 or 45.

A member of the media will have a defence to a charge of breaching Section 44 if the young person is not the accused or a witness to an offence under Section 1 of the Sexual Offences (Amendment) Act 1992 and if he can show that the restrictions imposed a substantial and unreasonable restriction on reporting the offence or he held the written consent of the young person or his guardian at the time of publication. A member of the media will have a defence to a charge of breaching Section 44 or 45 if he can show that he did not suspect or have reason to suspect that a criminal investigation had begun or that his report contained material that would breach any restriction.

Section 46 of the Youth Justice Act will allow criminal courts, on application by any party to the proceedings, to prohibit media reports that will identify an adult witness by:

- Name
- Address
- Identification of any educational establishment attended by the witness
- Identification of the place of work of the witness, or
- Any still or moving picture of the witness.

The prohibition will last during the person's lifetime. The prohibition is discretionary, and will be granted where the court believes the quality of the evidence or level of co-operation by the witness is likely to be improved by a grant of anonymity. When exercising the discretion, the court must take into account the following:

- The nature and circumstances of the offence
- The age of the witness
- The social and cultural background and ethnic origins of the witness, the domestic and employment circumstances of the witness and any religious beliefs or political opinions of the witness if the court considers it to be relevant
- Any behaviour towards the witness by the accused, the family or associates of the accused, or any other person who is likely to be an accused or a witness in the proceedings
- The views expressed by the witness, and
- The public interest in avoiding unreasonable restrictions on the reporting of proceedings.

Cases involving indecency or immorality

The public may be excluded when children give evidence in any proceedings in relation to an offence involving conduct contrary to decency or morality (Section 37 of the Children and Young Persons Act 1933). However, Section 37 expressly confers on the media the right to remain in court. Reporting restrictions may still be imposed in such circumstances under Section 39 of the Children and Young Persons Act 1933 or, in the future, Section 45 of the Youth Justice Act.

9.6 Committal proceedings before the magistrates' court

9.6.1 General principles

Generally, all criminal proceedings start in the magistrates' court. In the case of offences triable only on indictment or either way (see part 9.6.3 below) where the magistrates choose to send the case to the crown court, there will be a preliminary hearing (known as committal proceedings) whereby the magistrates examine the evidence against the defendant to determine whether there is a case to answer and whether the case should be committed for trial to the crown court. Committal proceedings are always conducted in open court unless 'the ends of justice would not be served by their sitting in open court' (Section 4 of the Magistrates' Court Act 1980).

Until 1967, a full report of committal proceedings in the magistrates' court could be published or broadcast to the general public. However, the publication of material at the committal hearings of the murder trials of Dr Bodkin Adams in 1957, accused of murdering his elderly patients, and the Moors murderers in 1966 led to strict limits on the reporting of committal proceedings.

9.6.2 Section 8(1) of the Magistrates' Court Act 1980

Section 8(1) of the Magistrates' Court Act 1980 governs reporting restrictions at committal hearings. It also applies to remand hearings, which are preliminary hearings in the magistrates' court that take place prior to committal. It is only lawful to publish the following details:

- The identity of the court and the names of the examining justices
- The names, addresses and occupations of the parties and witnesses, and the ages of the accused and witnesses
- The offence or offences, or a summary of them
- The names of counsel or solicitors engaged in the proceedings
- Any decision of the court to commit the accused, or any of the accused, for trial, and any decision of the court on the disposal of the case if any accused is committed
- The charges on which the accused is committed or a summary of them, and the court to which the accused was committed
- If there is any adjournment, the date and place of the next hearing
- Any arrangements regarding bail – for example, the amount of any surety, and
- Whether legal aid was granted.

The reasons given by the police for opposing bail, the magistrates' reasons for refusing bail and the defendant's previous convictions cannot be reported.

Anonymity can, of course, be conferred by the court on young persons (see sections 9.5 above and 9.7 below), and in cases concerning sexual offences under the Sexual Offences (Amendment) Acts of 1976 and 1992 (see part 9.7 below).

There are exceptions to the rule. Full reporting of committal proceedings is permitted:

- If the magistrates decide not to commit the accused for trial at the crown court and dismiss the charges
- After the accused is tried, or
- If the court lifts the restrictions (even then the media should be cautious about the nature and scope of the information they report to avoid being in contempt of court).

Whenever any one of these exceptions apply, the media are free to report full details of the committal proceedings. They are also free to publish the details at the conclusion of the trial, but may not wish to do so given the passage of time.

When considering an application to lift reporting restrictions the magistrates must be satisfied that it is in the interest of justice to do so (Section 8(2)(a) Magistrates' Court Act 1980). Where there are two or more defendants and not all wish to lift the reporting restrictions, they will only be lifted if the court is satisfied that it is in the interests of justice to do so after hearing representations from all defendants. If reporting restrictions are lifted, the magistrates may postpone reports of the proceedings until after the trial under Section 4(2) of the Contempt of Court Act 1981 (see part 9.3 above).

Section 8 of the Magistrates' Court Act 1980 places restrictions only on reports of the actual proceedings. It would not be a breach of Section 8 to publish, for example, the fact that the defendant was driven to court by his wife in the family car, or that large crowds assembled outside the courthouse to witness his arrival. The media should not report, however, information that carries a risk of serious prejudice to any trial, such as any admissions of guilt or previous convictions.

Only the proprietor, editor or publisher of a newspaper, or a broadcaster with executive power, will be liable for breaching Section 8 of the Magistrates' Court Act 1980. A prosecution for breach may only be brought with the Attorney General's approval.

9.6.3 Applications to dismiss summary offences and offences triable either way

Some offences, known as 'summary offences', are generally heard in the magistrates' court. In some circumstances summary offences may be heard in the crown court if the defendant has also been charged with a related offence that must be heard in the crown court. Both charges will be sent to the crown court in order to avoid two trials. Some offences can be tried either in the magistrates' court or in the crown court. These are known as offences that are 'triable either way'. In such circumstances, the magistrates decide whether to try the offence themselves or send it to the crown court for trial.

If the defendant has been committed to the crown court on a summary offence or an offence triable either way and feels that he should not have been sent to the crown court, he can apply to the crown court for the case to be dismissed on the grounds of insufficiency of evidence. An application to dismiss is subject to reporting restrictions (Regulation 3 of Schedule 3 of the Crime and Disorder Act 1998). The only matters that may be reported are:

- The identity of the court and the name of the judge
- The names, ages, home address (past and current) and occupations of the defendant and any witnesses
- The offence or offences
- The names of counsel and solicitors engaged in the proceedings
- Where the proceedings are adjourned, and the date and place to which they are adjourned
- The bail arrangements
- Whether legal aid was granted to the accused.

The media may publish a full report if the application is successful and the proceedings against the defendant are dismissed. If the application is not successful, a full report may be published at the end of the trial. The judge hearing the application to dismiss has the discretion to lift the reporting restrictions. If two or more defendants are jointly charged and both apply for the proceedings to be dismissed, a full report can only be published if all the applications are successful or at the end of all the trials. Where there are two or more defendants and one of them objects to the lifting of the restrictions, the judge may only lift the restrictions if he is satisfied, after hearing representations from the defendants, that it is in the interests of justice to do so.

9.7 Hearings concerning sexual offences and indecency

9.7.1 General principles

The Sexual Offences (Amendment) Act 1976 introduced the unique concept of anonymity in the reporting of rape cases. However, the protection only commenced at the issue of a warrant for the arrest of the defendant or the defendant's first appearance in court. This loophole in the law was brought to the fore in 1985 when the victim of the 'Ealing Vicarage Rape' was identified by the press and subjected to massive media coverage whilst her assailants remained unknown and at large. Successive amendments to the Sexual Offences (Amendment) Act 1976 resulted in the complete removal of anonymity of the defendant in rape cases, and the protection of the identity of victims of rape from the time the complaint is first made.

The Sexual Offences (Amendment) Act 1976 and the Sexual Offences (Amendment) Act 1992 (together 'the Sexual Offences Acts') are applicable only to England and Wales. The prohibition applies to all written and visual media that publish in England and Wales.

The Sexual Offences (Amendment) Act 1976 applies to:

- Rape
- Attempted rape
- Aiding or abetting either of the above
- Conspiracy with intent to rape, and
- Burglary with intent to rape.

The Sexual Offences (Amendment) Act 1992 applies to:

- Indecent assault on a man or woman
- Buggery and assault with the intent to commit buggery
- Incest by a man or a woman
- Intercourse with a girl under the age of 13 or between 13 and 16
- Intercourse with or procurement of a mentally handicapped person
- Indecent conduct towards a child
- Procurement of a woman by threats or false pretences
- Administering drugs to obtain intercourse with a woman
- Incitement by a man of his granddaughter, daughter or sister under the age of 16 to commit incest with him, and
- Attempts to commit any of the above offences.

There are special rules relating to cases involving incest and buggery; that is to say, if the victim of an offence of incest or buggery is accused of the same offence, he or she will only have anonymity up to the time he or she is accused of such an offence.

9.7.2 Levels of protection

The Sexual Offences Acts provide that anonymity runs from the time the complaint is first made. However, there is a distinction on the reporting restrictions between the time of the first complaint and the time the defendant is accused. The Sexual Offences Acts provide that from the moment when an allegation has been made that a sexual offence has been committed neither the victim's name nor address nor a still or moving picture of that person may be published during their lifetime if it would be likely to lead members of the public to identify him or her as the victim. The prohibition applies irrespective of whether or not criminal or civil proceedings follow. The prohibition applies to a victim of male rape.

Once a person is accused of a sexual offence, no matter likely to lead members of the public to identify a person as the person against whom the offence is alleged to have been committed can be published during the victim's lifetime. This means, for example, publication, as part of a crime report, of the victim's job, place of work or name of any family member would be prohibited if it would lead to the victim's identification. The reason for the less stringent restrictions prior to the defendant being accused is to allow the publication of information that might bring forward witnesses or otherwise help the police investigation.

The Sexual Offences Acts do not define 'an allegation', but it is reasonable to assume the court will interpret this to mean a complaint to the police. The complainant does not, however, have to be the victim.

There is no prohibition on reporting the court proceedings provided that the anonymity of the victim is protected. Nor is there any prohibition on identifying the defendant, provided the victim is not thereby identified. However, the media should exercise extreme caution when publishing pictures of the defendant if the identification of the defendant as the perpetrator of the offence is an issue at trial.

9.7.3 Lifting the prohibition

The prohibition about identifying victims of sexual offences does not apply if the victim, who must be over 16 years of age, consents in writing, freely and without any undue influence, to being identified. Further, judges (or magistrates if the matter is before them) have the discretion to lift the anonymity rule if:

- The trial judge is satisfied that the prohibition would 'impose a substantial and unreasonable restriction' upon the reporting of the trial and it would be in the public interest to remove or relax the restriction, or
- The defendant applies to the court to lift the restriction to encourage witnesses to come forward and there is a likelihood the defence or any appeal will be 'substantially prejudiced' if the reporting restrictions are not lifted.

Judges are likely to be sympathetic to the plight of the press where the matter being tried goes beyond a sexual offence. For example, in the case of *R v Hutchinson (1984)* the defendant was charged with the murder of three members of a wealthy Sheffield family and the rape of another family member who survived. The victim of the rape, whose name was the same as her deceased relatives, was also the chief prosecution witness on the murder charges. It was suggested to the judge by some members of the press that proper reporting of the murder trial could not take place if the name of the murdered family was not made public because of the rape charge. The judge ruled that it was in the public interest for the restriction to be lifted in respect of the rape victim.

9.7.4 Defences

It is a defence to a charge of breaching the anonymity rule to prove that at the time of publication the accused was not aware nor suspected that the report contravened the Sexual Offences Acts.

It is also a defence to a charge of breaching the anonymity rule that the victim gave his or her written consent to the relevant publication. However, written consent will not be a defence if it is proved that '. . . any person interfered with the peace or comfort of the person giving the consent with intent to obtain it' (Section 5(5) of the 1992 Sexual Offences Act).

Only editors, proprietors and publishers of newspapers and their equivalents in broadcasting will be criminally liable if a report is published which contravenes the Sexual Offences Acts. The Attorney General must consent before a prosecution is brought.

9.7.5 Youth Justice Act 1999

When the relevant sections of the Youth Justice Act 1999 come into force, all restrictions relating to the identification of victims of sexual offences will be contained in one act – namely, the Sexual Offences (Amendment) Act 1992.

9.7.6 Cases involving indecency

The Judicial Proceedings (Regulations of Reports) Act 1926 automatically restricts publication of any indecent, medical, surgical or physiological information that would be calculated to injure public morals (Section 1(1)(a)).

It is not easy to define the sort of matters arising from legal proceedings that would be so indecent as to injure public morals. Public morality is hardly constant in each generation, and society today is certainly exposed to matters that are likely to have caused offence in 1926. There have been few prosecutions brought under this Act in recent years.

9.8 Divorce cases

Husband and wife disputes have always been a source of good copy for reporters who work at the popular end of the media market. However, the steady flow of lurid stories from the divorce courts has been reduced in recent years as a result of the change in society's attitude to divorce and new legislation that means that the element of fault is rarely applicable in divorce proceedings today. The vast number of divorces are now uncontested. However, those that are defended in open court are subject to reporting restrictions.

Section 1(1)(b) of the Judicial Proceedings (Regulation of Reports) Act 1926 as amended by the Family Law Act 1996 restricts the publishing of information relating to divorce, nullity or judicial separation proceedings to:

- The names, addresses and occupations of the parties and witnesses
- A concise statement of the charges, defences and counter-charges in support of which evidence has been given
- Submissions on points of law and the rulings of the court thereon
- The judgment of the court and observations by the judge in giving judgment.

Of course, the above-mentioned information should not offend Section 1(1)(a) of the Judicial Proceedings (Regulation of Reports) Act 1926. Also, charges and counter-charges can only be reported if evidence has already been given in support of them. For example, if an allegation is made about which no evidence is given at the hearing, the allegation cannot be reported unless it is referred to by the judge in his judgment.

The court may grant an injunction to prevent reports arising out of divorce proceedings. In *Argyll v Argyll (1967)*, the Duchess was granted an injunction to prevent publication of an article in the *People* by her former husband that reported details of charges in their divorce proceedings other than those permitted under Section 1(1)(b) of the Judicial Proceedings (Regulation of Reports) Act 1926.

Only editors, proprietors and publishers of newspapers and their equivalents in broadcasting will be criminally liable if a report is published that contravenes the Judicial Proceedings (Regulation of Reports) Act 1926. The Attorney General must consent before a prosecution is brought.

In any proceedings for nullity of marriage evidence on the question of sexual capacity will be heard in private unless it is in the interests of justice not to do so (Section 48 of the Matrimonial Causes Act 1973).

9.9 Fraud

In serious or complex fraud cases, magistrates can dispense with committal hearings and transfer the case to the crown court (Section 4 of the Criminal Justice Act 1987). When notice of transfer has been given, the defendant may apply to the crown court for the case to be dismissed on the basis that there is no case to answer (Section 6 of the Criminal Justice Act 1987). Automatic restrictions are imposed on the reporting of applications for dismissal. Only the following matters may be reported:

- The identity of the court and the name of the judge
- The names, ages, home addresses and occupations of the accused and witnesses
- Any relevant business information, for example, the name and address of any business partnership or company in which the accused was involved at the time of the fraud
- The offence or offences or a summary of them with which the accused is charged
- The names of counsel and solicitors in the proceedings
- Where the proceedings are adjourned, the date and place to which they are adjourned
- Any bail arrangements
- Whether legal aid was granted to the accused.

Where the issues are complex and the defendants are numerous, the judge may decide to split the indictments and order sequential trials. In those circumstances, defendants often seek an order postponing reporting. Section 4(2) of the Contempt of Court Act 1981 (see part 9.3 above) permits such an order where it is necessary to avoid a substantial risk of serious prejudice to any trial.

The Criminal Procedure and Investigations Act 1996 imposes automatic reporting restrictions until the conclusion of the trial on pre-trial hearings of cases that are long or complex. The judge may lift the restrictions in the interests of justice. Unless the judge does so, the media may only report on:

- The identity of the court and the name of the judge
- The names, ages, home addresses and occupations of the accused and witnesses
- The offence or offences or a summary of them with which the accused is charged
- The names of counsel and solicitors in the proceedings
- Where the proceedings are adjourned, the date and place to which they are adjourned
- Any bail arrangements
- Whether legal aid was granted to the accused.

9.10 Official secrets

The court has an inherent power to order the exclusion of the public from proceedings involving national security. Additionally, under Section 8(4) of the Official Secrets Act 1920 the court may exclude all or any portion of the public, including the media, during any part of the trial if the publication of any evidence would be prejudicial to national safety. However, any sentence must be given in open court (Section 8(4) of the Official Secrets Act 1920).

The prosecution must give notice of any intention to apply for the exclusion of the public at least 7 days before the trial is due to begin. The court must display a notice in a prominent place within the precincts of the court stating that the application is to be made (Crown Court Rules 1982 Statutory Instrument 1982/1109 as amended by Statutory Instrument 1989/1103). Such prior notice is to allow time for the media to challenge the decision.

If a notice is displayed and a media company wishes to report on the trial, it will have to apply in writing in Form 20 (Criminal Appeal Rules 1968 1968/1262 as amended by Statutory Instrument 1989/1102)) to the Registrar of the Criminal Appeal Office within 7 days of the notice's display for leave to appeal to the Court of Appeal under Section 159 of the Criminal Justice Act 1988. At the same time a copy of the application must also be served on the crown court, the prosecution, the defendant and any other interested person. The application for leave will be determined by a single judge of the Court of Appeal without a hearing, that is to say it will be a 'paper hearing', meaning that no formal court hearing will take place. The decision of the Court of Appeal is final (Section 159(1) Criminal Justice Act 1988).

Where an order to exclude the public is made at the trial itself, the media may apply for leave to appeal against the order by notice in writing as prescribed in Form 20 within 24 hours of the order and the court must adjourn the trial for 24 hours to allow any appeal (Criminal Appeal Rules 1968).

9.11 Material made available on disclosure

Documents that have been disclosed by parties in civil proceedings can only be used for the purpose of the proceedings in which they were disclosed, unless:

- The document has been read out to or by the court or referred to at a hearing that has been held in public
- The court gives permission, or
- The party who disclosed the document and the person to whom the document belongs agree to its wider use.

(Civil Procedure Rules Part 31.22(1))

This duty of confidentiality means that documents that have been disclosed between parties to litigation can only be copied to the media if one of the exceptions apply. Documents are to be treated as read to the court if they are read only by the judge but subsequently referred to in his judgment which is given in open court (*SmithKline Beecham Biologicals SA v Connaught Laboratories Inc (1999)*). Documents will also be treated as read to the court if they are referred to in open court by the judge or the lawyers although not read out or referred to in counsels' skeleton arguments (*Derby v Weldon (1988)*).

The court may make an order restricting or prohibiting the use of a document that has been disclosed even where the document has been read to or by the court or referred to at a hearing that has been held in public. An application for such an order may be made by any party or any person to whom the document belongs (Civil Procedure Rules Part 31.22(2) and (3)).

9.12 Press challenges to reporting restrictions

The court sometimes makes orders restricting the reporting of proceedings on inappropriate grounds. They are frequently made following an application from defence counsel, and are occasionally nodded through unopposed. There are other instances where, although it is appropriate to postpone publication of certain material, the order is too wide and amounts to a 'blanket ban' or a permanent restriction.

Faced with an imperfect order, the options open to a media company are limited. It can publish or broadcast in defiance of the order and hope to escape punishment. However, until an order is varied or set aside on appeal, a person who knowingly breaches it may be liable to be committed for contempt of court. Defiance is, therefore, not recommended at all.

There are three ways to challenge an inappropriate order:

1. Application to the originating court
2. Judicial review
3. Appeal under Section 159 of the Criminal Justice Act 1988.

9.12.1 Application to the originating court

The cheapest, quickest and often most effective way to challenge an order restricting publication is to raise the matter with the court that made the order. The media do not have an absolute right to be heard, but there is plenty of guidance from the higher courts to the effect that magistrates and judges should allow representations to be made by or on behalf of the media. In 1993 the High Court overturned a stipendiary magistrate's ruling that he had no power to hear media representations against an order under Section 4(2) of the Contempt of Court Act 1981 during the committal for trial of Larry Trachtenburg, one of the accused in the Robert Maxwell affair. The court held that although the power to hear representations by the media was discretionary, it would '. . . expect that the power will ordinarily be exercised when the media ask to be heard either on the making of an order or in regard to its continuance'.

If the reporter in court believes that an order restricting reporting has been wrongly made, the following two options exist:

- Informal note
- Legal representation.

Informal note
The media company can set out its relevant objections and arguments in a note and hand it to the court clerk to pass to the magistrates or judge. The note might for example, point out that an order under Section 11 of the Contempt of Court Act 1981 has been made to ban reporting of a name which came out earlier in the trial, or remind the court that an order under Section 4 of the Contempt of Court Act 1981 has no time limit on it. This informal route is frequently very effective. Upon receipt of such a note, the court is likely to look carefully at what the statute allows it to do.

Legal representation
Alternatively, or additionally if the first option fails, the media company might instruct its lawyer to make representations to the court on the propriety of the order. It is usually possible

to organize such an application within 24 hours of the order being made. Although the media do not have an absolute right to be heard, the court will usually exercise its discretion to allow representations to be made.

9.12.2 Judicial review

Under common law, the High Court has always had the power to review the workings and orders of inferior courts. This power is now found in the Civil Procedure Rules Part 54, which sets out the limits of and procedure in relation to applications for judicial review.

There are two drawbacks to an application for judicial review. First, it is not available to challenge orders of the crown court relating to trials on indictment. Second, the process can be slow, so that by the time such an application is heard the relevant report might be stale.

An application for leave for judicial review is separate to the hearing of the application itself although in urgent cases they might be heard at the same time. When hearing an application for leave, the court does not have jurisdiction to make an order under Section 11 of the Contempt of Court Act 1981 (*R v Westminster County Council ex parte Castelli (1996)*).

9.12.3 Appeal under Section 159 of the Criminal Justice Act 1988

Section 159 of the Criminal Justice Act 1988 gives 'any person aggrieved' the right to appeal to the Criminal Division of the Court of Appeal against the following orders made by a crown court judge:

- Under Sections 4 and Section 11 of the Contempt of Court Act 1981
- Which restrict public access to all or part of a trial of an indictable offence, or
- Which restrict reporting of all or part of the proceedings, for example under Section 39 of the Children and Young Persons Act 1933.

The media are clearly within the definition of 'aggrieved persons'. However, the procedure under Section 159 relates to the crown court only and has no application to the magistrates' court or the county court.

An application for leave to appeal must be made within 14 days after the making of the order restricting reporting. The media company must serve on the Registrar of the Court of Appeal (Criminal Division) a Form 20 notice (Statutory Instrument 1989/1102) seeking leave of a single judge. Notice must also be served on the trial judge, his clerk, the prosecutor, the defendant and any other interested person. If the matter is urgent, an expedited hearing of the appeal may be possible. In urgent cases, the leave stage and the appeal may be dealt with at the same time.

At the hearing of the appeal the Court of Appeal can stay any proceedings until after the appeal is disposed of, or confirm, reverse or vary the order. The Court of Appeal's decision is final (Section 159(1)).

The Court of Appeal may also make an order for costs as it thinks fit. In *Holden & Co v CPS (No 2) (1994)*, the Court of Appeal held that the costs of a newspaper could not be paid from central funds but might be made against the prosecution. However, an order for costs against the prosecution will usually only be made where it has failed to object to an order that was manifestly wrong or departed from its proper role and became in some way partisan (*Ex parte News Group Newspapers (1999)*).

9.12.4 Youth Justice Act 1999

When the relevant sections of the Youth Justice Act 1999 (see part 9.5.5 above) come into effect, it will be possible to challenge orders under Sections 45 and Section 46 of the Youth Justice Act in the following ways:

1. By seeking that the order be lifted or modified by an 'excepting direction'. An exceptions direction will be made if the court:

   - Is satisfied that it is necessary in the interests of justice to do so (Section 45(4) and Section 46(9)(a)), or
   - The effect of the reporting restrictions 'is to impose a substantial and unreasonable restriction on the reporting of the proceedings' and it is 'in the public interest' to remove or modify the reporting restrictions (Section 45(5) and Section 46(9)(b)).
2. By appealing the order under Section 159(1)(c) of the Criminal Justice Act 1988.
3. By appealing to the crown court after the refusal of a magistrates' court to lift or modify an order under Section 44 (Section 44(11)) of the Youth Justice Act. There is no appeal to the crown court in relation to orders made by the magistrates' court under Section 45 or Section 46 of the Youth Justice Act 1999, although any such orders would be susceptible to judicial review.

9.13 Interviewing jurors

Under Section 8(1) of the Contempt of Court Act 1981 it is contempt of court:

> ...to obtain, disclose or solicit any particulars of statements made, opinions expressed, arguments advanced or votes cast by members of a jury in the course of their deliberations in any legal proceedings.

This applies to the media and the jurors equally.

'Disclosed' in Section 8(1) of the Contempt of Court Act 1981 is given a wide meaning and covers the reporting of jury room deliberations by a member of the jury as well as by a person such as a publisher, editor or journalist who has received such information.

In *HM Attorney General v Associated Newspapers Limited (1993)*, the *Mail on Sunday* was fined £30 000 for publishing an article that revealed the opinions of the jurors in the year long Blue Arrow fraud trial because the 'free, uninhibited and unfettered discussion by the jury in the course of their deliberations is essential to the proper administration of justice'.

9.14 Tape recorders, photographs and sketches

As well as the limitations placed on the content of court reports, there are also certain restrictions on how those reports are gathered.

9.14.1 Tape recorders

Section 9(1) of the Contempt of Court Act 1981 makes it contempt to:

- Use in court, or bring into court for use, any tape recorder or other instrument for recording sound, except with the permission of the court
- Use any such recording in contravention of any permission granted by the court, or
- Publish a recording of legal proceedings made by any instrument or any recording derived directly or indirectly from such an instrument, by playing it in public or to any section of the public or disposing of it or any recording so derived with a view to publication.

Tape recorders are rarely seen on court press benches. However, the court has discretion to grant permission for the use of tape recordings in court subject to restrictions that it considers appropriate (*Practice Direction (Tape Recorders) (1981)*). For example, the discretion could be exercised to allow reporters to check their court notes. When deciding whether to give leave the court should consider 'any reasonable need on the part of the applicant', but permission should not be granted if there is a risk that the recording will be used for briefing future witnesses or where the sight of or noise from the machine could distract the court.

Once permission has been granted, the court may amend or withdraw it in relation to part or all of the proceedings (Section 9(2) of the Contempt of Court Act 1981).

Sound recordings made for the purposes of official transcripts of the proceedings are exempt from the restrictions.

If permission has not been given, a member of the media takes a risk even entering the courtroom in possession of a tape recorder. It remains unclear whether an intention to commit the offence is a necessary component of contempt under Section 9(1) (*Re Hooker (Patricia) and the Contempt of Court Act 1981 (1993)*). Offenders can be sentenced to imprisonment or fined. Section 9 of the Contempt of Court Act 1981 also allows the court to order forfeiture of the offending items.

9.14.2 Photographs and sketches

Photographs may not be taken in court, nor may sketches be made if they are intended for publication. The prohibition includes televising proceedings. Under the Criminal Justice Act 1925, Section 41(l):

> No person shall (a) take or attempt to take in any court any photograph, or, with a view to publication, make or attempt to make in any court any portrait or sketch of any person, being a judge of the court, or a juror or a witness in, or a party to, any proceedings before the court, whether civil or criminal, or (b) publish any photograph, portrait or sketch taken or made in contravention of this Section or any reproduction thereof.

For the purposes of Section 41, 'court' is deemed to cover the area within the courthouse and its precincts. Although it is almost common practice and seems to go unpunished, it is also an offence to photograph or film defendants or witnesses while they are entering or leaving the courtroom and its precincts (Section 41(2)(c)). However, hindering, jostling, threatening or persistently following defendants and witnesses as they go to and from court can amount to contempt (*R v Runting (1988)*).

Sketching inside court is not forbidden in itself. However, it will be a breach of Section 41 if it is done with the intention of publishing the sketch. Making a sketch of a trial or its participants from memory after leaving the court and publishing it is lawful.

9.15 Restrictions on reporting in other courts

9.15.1 Arbitration proceedings

It is a basic principle of arbitration proceedings that they take place in private. In order to give effect to this principle, all parties to arbitration proceedings are under an implied obligation to respect the confidence of the proceedings. If the public or the media are allowed to attend, they are not able to make public what was said and done at the hearing.

The duty of confidentiality of the recipient of any information obtained during arbitration proceedings is subject to a number of exceptions:

- If disclosure is necessary under compulsion of law
- If disclosure is reasonably necessary in the public interest
- If disclosure is reasonably necessary for fulfilling the recipient's duties to other persons, or
- If disclosure is reasonably necessary for protecting or pursuing the recipient's rights against other persons.

(Hassneh Insurance Co of Israel v Mew (1993))

9.15.2 Inquests

Inquests are held in open court unless the coroner orders that it is in the interest of national security to exclude the public (Coroners Rules Statutory Instrument 1984 552 Rule 17). The decision of the coroner can be challenged by judicial review.

There is no statutory right to be informed of the details of a forthcoming inquest. However, a Home Office circular (Number 53/1980) urges coroners to make suitable and formal arrangements to ensure that the media, particularly local newspapers, are properly informed of all inquest arrangements, including the date, time and place of any formal resumption of an adjourned inquest.

Rule 37 of the Coroners Rules allows a coroner to receive documentary rather than oral evidence from any witness. The Rule provides that coroners must announce publicly at the inquest the name of the person giving documentary evidence and a brief account of the document.

The Contempt of Court Act 1981 applies to inquests. For the purposes of the strict liability rule under Sections 1 and the 2 of the Contempt of Court Act 1981 (see Chapter 10), an inquest is 'active' as soon as it has been opened even if the opening was a formality and the proceedings were then adjourned indefinitely.

9.15.3 Employment tribunals

The media can freely attend and report on hearings before employment tribunals and the employment appeal tribunal, unless the tribunal considers that a private hearing is appropriate on the following grounds:

- National security
- Disclosure would lead to contravention of a prohibition imposed by legislation
- Disclosure would otherwise break a confidence
- Disclosure would cause substantial injury to the employer's undertaking
- A witness would be seriously prejudiced.

(Employment Tribunals Act 1996; Employment Tribunals Act 1996 (Constitution and Rules of Procedure) Regulations 2001))

Pre-hearing assessments, at which the tribunal considers the prospects of success of the applicant, are not open to the public.

Advance information about forthcoming employment cases is given in a weekly press notice issued by the Department for Work and Pensions. Case lists exhibited at each tribunal give the names of the parties and the towns in which they live, together with the date, time and place of the hearings. Tribunal staff will give the full addresses of the parties to the media on request. They will also provide the media, on application, with a copy of a reserved decision in any case.

An employment tribunal is a 'body exercising the judicial power of the State'. As a result, it qualifies as a 'court' under the Contempt of Court Act 1981 and has the power to make an order under Section 4(2) or Section 11 (see sections 9.3 and 9.4 above). It can also make an order under Section 39 of the Children and Young Persons Act 1933 (see part 9.5.1 above) banning the identification of young persons under the age of 18 years.

To avoid lurid reporting deterring potential applicants from bringing valid claims, tribunals have been given further significant powers to curtail reporting. Section 16 of the Employment Tribunals Act 1996 (Constitution and Rules of Procedure) Regulations 2001 enables tribunals to make orders banning the publication of the identity of a person involved in the proceedings in which allegations are made of sexual misconduct or conduct relating to sex or sexual orientation. 'Sexual misconduct' is defined by Section 11(6) of the Employment Tribunals Act 1996 as:

> ... the commission of a sexual offence, sexual harassment or other adverse conduct (of whatever nature) related to sex, and conduct is related to sex whether the relationship with sex lies in the character of the conduct or in its having reference to the sex or sexual orientation of the person at whom the conduct is directed.

An order restricting reporting may be made in cases involving allegations of discrimination where an individual has been diagnosed as HIV positive or has AIDS. The tribunal may also restrict reporting in a disability discrimination case where evidence is likely to be heard of a personal nature (Section 12 Employment Tribunal Acts 1996 and Section 16 Employment Tribunals Act 1996 (Constitution and Rules of Procedure) Regulations 2001).

The order restraining publication under the Employment Tribunals Act 1996 may last up to the time when the tribunal hands down its decision on the case. The tribunal can also order that the relevant name or names are permanently removed from all records of the case that are available to the public. To report a case in contravention of an order will be an offence punishable by a fine. It is a defence to prove that at the time of the alleged offence the person charged with the offence was not aware and did not suspect the publication included the matter subject to the restriction.

The same restrictions under the Employment Tribunals Act 1996 apply to proceedings before the employment appeal tribunal.

9.15.4 Mental health review tribunals

The Mental Health Review Tribunal Rules (Statutory Instrument 1983/942 Rule 21) require that mental health tribunals sit in private. The tribunal may admit any persons to the hearing if it considers it appropriate to do so (Rule 21(3)). Rule 21(5) bans publication of:

> . . . except in so far as the tribunal may direct, information about proceedings before the tribunal and the names of any persons concerned in the proceedings.

As a result, the media may only publish the bare fact that an application has been made to a tribunal, and the formal order. To the extent that the recorded reasons for the decision disclose the evidential and other material on which it is based, it too will fall within the prohibited areas (*P v Liverpool Daily Post & Echo Newspapers Plc (1991)*).

A mental health tribunal is a 'court' for the purposes of the Contempt of Court Act 1981 (Section 19), and has the power to make an order under Section 4(2) or Section 11 (see sections 9.3 and 9.4 above).

9.15.5 Licensing justices

Licence applications for public houses and clubs are heard by the magistrates' court. The magistrates must hear applications and any objections to them in public. When magistrates exercise a licensing power they are not acting in a judicial capacity (*Boulter v Kent Justices (1887)*). Press reports are not constrained by the Contempt of Court Act 1981 (*R v Redditch Justices (1885)*).

9.15.6 Planning enquiries

Local authority hearings concerning applications for planning permission, enforcement notices and compulsory purchase of land take place in public. Any evidence filed in documentary form is open to inspection. However, an order may be made that that it should not be open to inspection if it relates to national security and the measures taken or to be taken to ensure the security of any property (Planning (Listed Buildings and Conservation Areas) Act 1990, Schedule 3 Paragraph 6 (5–7); Planning (Hazardous Substances) Act 1990).

The findings of a local authority public planning enquiry are usually made available to the media.

9.15.7 Medical disciplinary hearings

A disciplinary complaint against a doctor is first considered in private by the Preliminary Proceedings Committee of the General Medical Council. If the Preliminary Proceedings Committee finds there is a case to answer, the matter is referred to the Professional Conduct Committee. The Professional Conduct Committee sits in public, although it can exclude the press and the public if it is satisfied that undue prejudice would be caused if it did not make such an order. The Professional Conduct Committee must deliver its decision in public (General Medical Council Preliminary Proceedings Committee and Professional Conduct Committee (Procedure) Rules 1988 (Statutory Instrument 1988/2255)). The media may publish a fair and accurate report of the proceedings.

Similar provisions apply to opticians (Statutory Instrument 1985/1580), nurses (Statutory Instrument 1993/893), pharmacists (Statutory Instrument 1978/20) and veterinary surgeons (Statutory Instrument 1967/659).

10 Contempt of Court

Simon Dowson-Collins

10.1 Introduction

Contempt of court is the improper interference with the administration of justice. Its origin lies in the rule of law that the court must be free to decide on the matters before it, unhindered by any outside influence. Its purpose is to ensure respect for the legal process and compliance with the remedies ordered by the court. The contempt laws are therefore aimed at those who undermine, obstruct or interfere with the workings of the court.

Contempt of court is the area of the law in which the press and broadcast media are most likely to exercise care in their day-to-day publication of news and features. Publishing a contempt is a serious offence. The penalty can be an unlimited fine or a sentence of imprisonment. Whereas actions for defamation may drag on in the civil courts for many months, ending in a quiet out of court settlement, contempt proceedings are dealt with quickly and vigorously. In cases of criminal contempt, the proceedings are prosecuted by the Attorney General.

Publication of a contempt can be either a criminal or a civil contempt. The distinction does not depend on whether the reporting is on proceedings in the criminal court or the civil court. However, reporting on the criminal courts usually carries a greater risk of falling foul of contempt law.

At common law there are three offences of criminal contempt:

1. Interfering with 'pending or imminent' court proceedings
2. Contempt in the face of the court
3. Scandalizing the court.

Parliament has also legislated in the area of contempt. The Contempt of Court Act 1981 ('the CCA') introduced a statutory offence of interfering with active court proceedings. Although the CCA has not codified or replaced the common law offence of interfering with 'pending or imminent' court proceedings, it has introduced a single rule by which it is now possible to judge potentially dangerous features. This rule, known as the strict liability rule, is the most significant and relevant area of contempt law for those working in the media today.

Other offences that may amount to contempt are:

- Failing to comply with a court order
- Improper use of documents disclosed during proceedings.

The law of contempt places a considerable restriction on freedom of expression. However, the courts must now give weight to the Article 10 European Convention on Human Rights right to freedom of expression introduced into English law by the Human Rights Act 1998 when considering restrictions on publication.

10.2 The Contempt of Court Act 1981

Although it might not always appear to be the case, the CCA came about in order to:

> ... effect a permanent shift in the balance of public interest away from the protection of the administration of justice and in favour of freedom of speech.
>
> (*A-G v Newspaper Publishing plc (1988)*)

The CCA was brought into force as a result of a report on contempt by the Phillimore Committee in 1974 and the European Court of Human Rights decision in *Sunday Times v United Kingdom (1979)*. Both arose out of proceedings for contempt in respect of a report in the *Sunday Times* about the drug thalidomide.

In 1972 the manufacturers of the drug were in the process of settling legal claims brought by some of the victims of the drug when the *Sunday Times* published an article criticizing the proposed court settlement and announcing a further article about the tragedy. Proceedings were brought against the newspaper by the Attorney General for contempt under the common law of interfering with active court proceedings. The House of Lords concluded that it was in the public interest for the *Sunday Times* to be restrained from publishing further articles about the proceedings because:

> ... anything in the nature of a prejudgement of a case or of specific issues in it is objectionable ... [and may lead to] ... disrespect for the processes of law.
>
> (*A-G v Times Newspapers Ltd (1974)*)

The decision by the House of Lords that 'anything' that 'prejudged' the case amounted to a contempt imposed a greater limitation under the common law on the media than before without clarifying precisely what the media could or could not publish. An application was made to the European Court of Human Rights. The European Court disagreed with the 'prejudgment' test, and declared that restriction on freedom of expression was not outweighed by a sufficiently pressing social need.

10.2.1 The strict liability rule

Under Section 2(2) of the CCA, strict liability applies to any publication that:

> ...creates a substantial risk that the course of justice in the proceedings in question will be seriously impeded or prejudiced.

The CCA limits the period during which strict liability applies. The only publications that are subject to the rule are those occurring while proceedings are 'active' within the meaning of the CCA.

The four elements to the rule are:

1. Strict liability
2. A publication
3. Active proceedings
4. A substantial risk of serious prejudice.

10.2.2 Strict liability

Strict liability means that a publisher may be found in contempt of court irrespective of whether or not he intended to cause a substantial risk of serious prejudice.

In criminal law, the prosecution must usually prove that the defendant committed the physical act of the offence and did so with *mens rea*, or a guilty mind. Thus, for a man to be guilty of murder the prosecution must prove that he fired the gun and did so with the intention of killing the victim or causing the victim serious harm. For a man to be convicted of theft, the appropriation of property by the defendant must be established as well as the defendant's dishonest state of mind.

However, for some offences Parliament has dispensed with the need to prove a guilty mind. In these cases liability is said to be strict.

In the case of contempt under the CCA, if the publisher creates a substantial risk of serious prejudice to proceedings that are active, it is no defence that this was not what he intended. The prosecution does not need to prove intent, recklessness or even negligence. For example, an editor or producer summoned before the court for contempt will not escape conviction by pleading that the feature was published only after he took great care, took extensive legal advice and pondered long and hard over the rights and wrongs of publication. Such a plea may establish that he did not have personal culpability, but would still only amount to mitigation and not a defence.

It follows that motivation is irrelevant in contempt proceedings. Newspapers or television programmes may be able to establish convincingly that they are performing a public service in exposing the other wrongdoings of a person already facing charges, but that will be to no avail if their publication creates a substantial risk of serious prejudice to that person's trial.

The only concession made by the CCA to a publisher's innocent intent is in relation to genuine and blameless ignorance of the existence of proceedings that might be prejudiced.

10.2.3 Publication

Section 2 of the CCA provides that the strict liability rule applies only to publications. 'Publication' as defined includes any:

> . . . speech, writing, broadcast or other communication in whatever form which is addressed to the public at large.

It is clear, therefore, that strict liability applies to all the usual output of the media, including newspapers, magazines, television and radio programmes and the Internet. Plays, concerts and speeches at public gatherings are also publications for the purposes of the CCA.

10.2.4 Active proceedings

For the strict liability rule to apply, the proceedings in question must be 'active' within the meaning of the CCA. Conversely, if the proceedings are not active there is no danger of the publisher being found to be in contempt of court under the CCA.

Whether a case is active under the CCA is not open to argument. Schedule 1 to the CCA lays down specific periods as to the commencement and conclusion of the active period.

Criminal proceedings

Commencement
Criminal proceedings become active on:

- Arrest without a warrant
- The issue of a warrant for arrest
- The issue of a summons to appear before the court
- The service of an indictment or other document specifying the charge, or
- Oral charge (except in Scotland).

In practical terms, this represents a considerable tightening of the old law. Before 1981, the fact that an arrest was made or a warrant was issued would almost invariably provoke the publication of background and speculation in the press rather than inhibit it. Such stories ceased only when the police let it be known that charges were imminent.

When proceedings first become active, the reporting of some matters clearly will be objectionable. For example, publication of the previous convictions of the defendant, the fact that the defendant is well known as a criminal or the 'fact' that the police have arrested the person who committed the crime is likely to be objectionable. This is because the court is of the view that the question of whether the defendant committed the crime is for the jury, and not the media or the public.

In recent years it has become the practice of some sections of the media to publish prejudicial material immediately proceedings become active. These media companies are prepared to take the risk of a prosecution for contempt because, in most cases, the longer the period of time between publication and hearing the less likely there will be a 'substantial risk of serious prejudice'.

However, in 1997 the *News of the World* was found to be in contempt of court by publishing prejudicial information the day after an arrest had been made. The case involved a 'sting' in which the newspaper's journalists set up and recorded criminals producing counterfeit currency. The day before publication of the feature, the newspaper tipped off the police and the suspects were arrested. The headlines the following day said 'We smash £100 million fake cash ring'. The court held that published material was prejudicial. Because the proceedings were active by the time the newspaper went to press, the court convicted the newspaper of contempt (*A-G v Morgan (1998)*).

Arrest

Those in the media must exercise caution and restraint in coverage of arrests. While it will normally be unobjectionable to report the fact of the arrest, the name of the person held and general background about the suspect and the crime, other matters such as facts linking him with the crime should not be published. Even information provided by the police at a press conference following arrest can amount to a contempt. In 1995, the BBC broadcast information given by the police at a press conference, which included details of the defendant's previous convictions. Although the defendant had been charged with unrelated matters, the BBC was held to be in contempt and was fined.

Although the same principles apply the situation may appear to be different where information is provided to the media by the arrested person himself. In August 2001, Neil and Christine Hamilton were arrested in connection with alleged sexual offences against a woman. They were cautioned and released on bail pending further investigation. Immediately following their release, the Hamiltons decided to 'go public'. They gave several press interviews in which they denied the offence and gave a detailed account of their whereabouts on the day of the alleged offence, producing documentary evidence to the media that they claimed showed they were elsewhere at the time. Huge media coverage ensued, with the *Mail on Sunday* even taking the unprecedented step of publishing a verbatim transcript of the police interview with the Hamiltons. In such unusual circumstances, the media may be prepared to publish prejudicial material on the assumption that prosecution is less likely where the material has been provided by the arrested person himself.

Problems can arise when a person is arrested but charges do not follow within a reasonable time. Suspects are frequently arrested and then later released from police custody without being charged. The CCA states that proceedings that become active upon arrest cease to be active if the suspect is released on anything other than bail. When the arrested person is freed unconditionally, the media are not inhibited by the strict liability rule.

Bail

The media face real difficulty when the suspect is released without being charged but on police bail. The proceedings remain active. The terms of bail may be that the suspect has to report back to the police station on a date in the future. Such people are often never charged. In the meantime, however, the proceedings remain active and media coverage of the suspect is still subject to the strict liability rule.

Warrants

Similar difficulties may occur with warrants. The person named in the warrant may not be apprehended for many months. The police and media may be aware that the suspect has fled the country and is unlikely to return. However, media coverage is severely restricted from the moment the warrant is issued.

Two factors exist that mitigate the problem for the media. The first is the provision in the CCA that provides that proceedings that become active on the issue of a warrant cease to be active 12 months from the date of the warrant if the suspect has not been arrested during that period. The second is that the Attorney General made it clear before the CCA became law that he would not use it to institute contempt proceedings where the media assist the police with publicity in a 'hue and cry' situation.

In practice, therefore, the media has nothing to fear from publishing pictures of wanted men or prejudicial descriptions of them – for example 'armed and dangerous' – if they are clearly acting for the protection of and in the interests of the public.

Conclusion

Criminal proceedings are concluded by:

- An acquittal or by sentence
- Any other verdict or finding or other decision which puts an end to the proceedings, or
- Discontinuance or operation of law.

In general terms, this means that the active period ceases when the proceedings are brought to an end for whatever reason. This includes instances where charges are dropped or an order is made by the court that they should 'lie on the file', which means no further action will be taken on them.

It is important to note that proceedings remain active until sentence is passed. There will often be a gap between a finding of guilt and the passing of sentence. The judge may postpone sentence to await sentencing reports. The strict liability rule continues to apply until sentence.

However, in practice the media are free to publish extensive background material on the assumption that judges are experienced enough not to be influenced by such publicity. A great deal more care needs to be exercised in cases where sentence will be passed by magistrates.

Civil proceedings

Commencement

The CCA provides that civil proceedings are active from the time when arrangements are made for the hearing of the case or from when the hearing begins. As a result of the introduction of the Civil Procedure Rules in 1999 dates are now set for the trial at an earlier stage of proceedings. The active period, therefore, commences sooner than was previously the case.

The majority of civil proceedings are heard by a judge sitting alone. On the assumption that a judge is experienced enough not to be influenced by publicity, the risk of proceedings for contempt following the publication of information during proceedings is not so great as during criminal proceedings. However, the strict liability rule does apply, and care must be exercised if consideration is given to publishing a feature during the course of civil proceedings. Libel and some civil actions against the police are still heard by a jury. In these cases extreme caution must be exercised because of the increased risk of serious prejudice to the proceedings.

Conclusion

The active period ends when the proceedings are disposed of by settlement or judgment, or are discontinued or withdrawn. In the case of pre-trial applications or interim remedies, the proceedings cease to be active when the specific matter before the court is disposed of. They may then become active again at a later date.

Inquests

Proceedings in the coroner's court are active from the time the inquest is opened. The active period ends when the proceedings are disposed of.

Appeals

Appeal proceedings are active from the time of application for leave or the lodging of a notice of appeal. This means that during the period between the end of a trial and the application for leave or the lodging of a notice of appeal, the media are not prevented from reporting under the strict liability rule.

Retrials

If an appeal in criminal proceedings is successful and a retrial is ordered, the proceedings become active again from the date of the order for retrial.

10.2.5 Substantial risk of serious prejudice

Section 2(2) of the CCA states that the strict liability rule only applies to publications that create a substantial risk of serious prejudice to the course of justice in the relevant proceedings. Those in the media are well advised to remember the relevant test for contempt: is there a substantial risk of serious prejudice?

The court has made it clear that this a twofold test. The risk must be substantial and the likely prejudice has to be serious:

> First there has to be some real risk that the proceedings in question will be affected at all. Second there has to be a prospect that if affected the effect will be serious. The two limbs of the test can overlap but they can be quite separate.
>
> *(A-G v News Group Newspapers (1986))*

The threshold is not a high one. 'Substantial' risk does not mean 'weighty', but merely more than minimal or remote risk. The time at which the risk is to be assessed is the time of publication.

At the time of writing, the trial against the Leeds United footballers, Lee Bowyer and Jonathan Woodgate, has been halted because of an article published in the *Sunday Mirror* newspaper. An order of the court is currently in force restricting discussion of this case. It is possible to say, however, that the Attorney General is considering whether the contents of the article created a substantial risk of serious prejudice to the proceedings. That matter will be determined at a later date.

Prejudice can include stopping the hearing, moving the hearing elsewhere, or discharging the jury.

The following factors should be among those considered by the media when assessing whether a feature is likely to be a contempt:

- The court
- Date of hearing
- Place of trial
- Content
- Circulation
- Undermining or intimidating of witnesses, the parties or a juror
- Anticipating the verdict
- Civil proceedings.

The court
The issue of whether there is a real risk that a publication will affect the course of justice in proceedings frequently depends upon the type of court hearing the proceedings, or the mode of

trial. While there may be an enormous risk that a feature might prejudice a jury trial, the same story may be assumed to have no effect at all on proceedings heard by a judge alone.

Court hearings fall into four main categories: by jury, by judge alone, by district judge, or by lay magistrates.

Jury trials

The greatest care needs to be taken in jury trials. Jurors are selected from the public at large. Although in some cases jurors are considered to be capable of disregarding what is said in newspapers or on television, and a strong direction from the judge to disregard any comment by the media may reduce the risk of serious prejudice, the court is diligent in protecting them from the influence of prejudicial publicity.

Judge alone or district judge (formerly stipendiary magistrate)

Judges and district judges are fully trained lawyers and can be expected to use their legal training to disregard almost any sort of material not adduced in evidence or argument in their court. However, it is still possible for proceedings to be prejudiced, so those in the media should still exercise care about features that may be grossly prejudicial.

Lay magistrates

Lay magistrates have comparatively very little legal training and, although the risk may be less than in the case of jurors, extreme caution must still be exercised before publishing material concerning hearings before them.

Date of hearing

The proximity in time between publication and hearing is a crucial factor that can affect both the degree of risk and the seriousness of the prejudice.

This issue is particularly relevant to jury trials. Jurors exposed to prejudicial material are far more likely to have it at the front of their minds after one month than after a year. The Court of Appeal dealt with precisely this point in *A-G v News Group Newspapers (1986)*. The well-known cricketer Ian Botham sued the *Mail on Sunday* for libel over allegations of drug taking. Eleven months before the trial was due to take place, the *News of the World* announced its intention to publish similar allegations about Botham. The Attorney General applied for an injunction to prevent publication on the grounds that the *News of the World* article would be in contempt of the existing libel action, which was already active. The Court of Appeal held that it was not satisfied the publication of the article by the *News of the World* so far in advance of the trial date would create a substantial risk of serious prejudice, and refused to grant an injunction.

In 1996 the *Daily Mail* published an article about a woman who had been charged with theft. Next to photographs of the woman taken in secret was the headline 'The home help who was busily helping herself'. The judge found that there was a clear case of 'trial by newspaper', which amounted to contempt. However, a crucial factor was that the publication was made nine months before the woman's trial was likely to take place. The judge felt that by the time of the trial the contents of the article would have faded sufficiently from the minds of the public for there to be no serious prejudice to the defendant. This is sometimes known as 'the fade factor' (*A-G v Unger (1998)*).

By contrast, in the same year the BBC satirical news quiz *Have I Got News For You* called Kevin and Ian Maxwell 'heartless scheming bastards' whilst they were awaiting trial for fraud. Although the programme was broadcast some six months before the trial was due to take place, both the BBC and the independent producers of the programme were fined £10 000 (*A-G v BBC and Hat Trick Productions Ltd (1997)*).

Although the degree of risk and the seriousness of the prejudice will depend on the circumstances of each case, published features will pose the most risk when they are published close to or contemporaneously with a hearing or a trial, or contain information that must not be heard by the jury.

Place of trial

The location of the trial is an obvious consideration when assessing the element of substantial risk. For example, a story published in a local newspaper in Cornwall is unlikely to cause a real risk of prejudice to a trial taking place in Newcastle. Place of trial will have no impact on features published in national newspapers, national broadcasts or on the Internet.

Content

The content of the feature is always the major factor when considering serious prejudice. Whether a feature is seriously prejudicial will depend on the particular facts of each case and the specific issues the court will have to decide. The prominence or publicity given to the article or programme will have an impact on the degree of risk and seriousness of the prejudice. However, the following matters are relevant in considering contempt:

- Photographs
- The defendant's character and record.

Photographs

There is a duty to refrain from publishing photographs of a defendant or describing his appearance where identity is an issue. Before publishing photographs of a person who has been arrested or is the subject of a warrant, the media should check with the police or defence lawyers to see whether identity is an issue. In 1994 the *Sun* published a photograph of a man charged with murder shortly before he was to appear in an identification parade. Both the paper and editor were found to be in contempt and fined a total of £100 000. However, where the publication of a photograph is likely to assist the police in arresting a suspect and the photograph has been issued by the police, there will be no contempt even though the proceedings are active.

The defendant's character and record

It is a basic rule of criminal law that a defendant's bad character or previous convictions cannot be used against him. Evidence of bad character or previous convictions is only admissible in exceptional circumstances. Since this rule of evidence would be meaningless if the jurors or magistrates were to learn of such matters through the media, their publication usually amounts to contempt.

However, not every derogatory feature about a defendant will create a substantial risk of serious prejudice. In 1983 the publicity following the arrest of an intruder called Michael Fagan inside Buckingham Palace led to five national newspapers being charged with contempt. Stories published in the *Sun* and the *Sunday People* alleged that Fagan was a liar and had been 'a junkie'. In the circumstances of the case, the court found that the risk of serious prejudice to Fagan's trial was not substantial (*A-G v Times Newspapers Ltd (1983)*).

In 1997 Geoff Knights, the boyfriend of the well-known television actress Gillian Taylforth, was charged with assault. Shortly thereafter, the *Daily Mirror, Daily Star, Sun, Today* and *Daily Mail* newspapers published articles referring to Knights' violent past and previous convictions. The court held that Knights could not have a fair trial, and the criminal proceedings against him were dropped.

Contempt proceedings were brought against the newspapers. However, the court held that it was difficult in the circumstances of the case to find that any one of the tabloid headlines had created a greater risk of serious prejudice because Knights' criminal past was already public knowledge as a result of a libel trial brought by Taylforth some months earlier. The court found that although it had been proper to discontinue the criminal proceedings because Knights could no longer receive a fair trial, no individual newspaper was guilty of contempt (*A-G v MGN (1997)*).

In 1999 the artist Anthony-Noel Kelly was charged with theft of body parts from a hospital, which he used to make moulds for works of art. During the course of the trial, the *Observer* published an article comparing the defendant to well-known mass murderers. Although the article was a criticism of the work of the defendant, it also amounted to a scathing attack upon his character. The trial judge held that the article was highly prejudicial. In fact, only one juror had read the article, and she informed that court that she would disregard it when reaching her verdict. The *Observer* was prosecuted for contempt. The court hearing the contempt proceedings held that there had been a risk of prejudice. However, it took the view, albeit reluctantly, that there was insufficient evidence to establish a *substantial* risk of prejudice, bearing in mind the 'unusually responsible' reaction of the juror (*A-G v Guardian Newspapers (1999)*).

Although these cases demonstrate that the court may be prepared to interpret the strict liability rule liberally, the media should think carefully before publishing details of the defendant's bad character. Anything that shows he is the type of person who would commit the crime with which he is charged or suggests he should not be believed is likely to attract a charge of contempt.

Circulation

If the circulation of the publication is small, the risk and seriousness of the prejudice is reduced. This may have limited relevance as a result of the increasing availability of the Internet.

Undermining or intimidating witnesses, the parties or a juror

If a publication suggests that a witness or party is untruthful, this may prejudice the trial at which he is to give evidence. A publication that seeks to persuade a witness or party to refrain from giving evidence or change his evidence would probably constitute a serious interference within the meaning of the strict liability rule. A publication that seeks to undermine or intimidate a juror is likely to produce the same result.

Articles written to deter the other party from pursuing a claim will amount to a substantial risk of serious prejudice to those proceedings. In *A-G v Hislop (1991)*, the defendant published material in the magazine *Private Eye* that the court held was for the purpose of persuading the wife of the 'Yorkshire Ripper' to discontinue her action for defamation against the magazine.

Anticipating the verdict

There is an obvious danger of contempt in media features that predict the outcome of a case or comment on the worth of particular pieces of evidence. This is especially so in cases heard by a jury.

Civil proceedings

In civil proceedings, there is a particular danger in revealing details of communications that are protected against disclosure to the court – for example, documents to which legal professional privilege attaches, or offers of settlement.

10.2.6 The role of the Attorney General

Criminal proceedings for contempt of court under the strict liability rule can only be instituted by the Attorney General. The Attorney General carries out his duties 'on behalf of the Crown as the fountain of justice', not in his capacity as a member of the government.

The CCA prevents a private individual from bringing proceedings for strict liability contempt. The issue was considered in the case involving Michelle and Lisa Taylor, two sisters who were convicted of murder in 1992. There was extensive media coverage of the proceedings, which the trial judge referred to as 'unremitting, extensive, sensational, inaccurate and misleading'. The Court of Appeal quashed the convictions and agreed with the trial judge about the sensational and inaccurate nature of the media coverage.

The Attorney General was requested to consider a prosecution of various newspapers for contempt. However, he declined to prosecute. The Solicitor General, acting on behalf of the

Attorney, concluded that the defendants had not been prejudiced in any significant way, and proceedings for contempt against the newspapers would be unlikely to succeed. The Taylor sisters sought judicial review of the decision. The court hearing the application for judicial review said the inaccurate reporting of the trial had caused it great concern:

> ... some of the coverage crossed the acceptable limits of fair and accurate reporting by a substantial margin. In some instances ... neither of those adjectives were in any way applicable.
>
> (*R v Solicitor-General ex parte Taylor and Another (1995)*)

However, it held that the institution of proceedings for contempt under the strict liability rule was a matter under the CCA for the Attorney General alone. The court held that if the Attorney General decided not to bring proceedings for contempt, he could not be compelled to do so. As a result there was no effective remedy for the inaccurate reporting.

10.2.7 Defences

The CCA provides three defences to strict liability contempt:

- Innocent publication
- Fair and accurate contemporary reports
- Discussion of public affairs.

Innocent publication

Section 3 of the CCA provides that a publisher is not guilty of contempt under the strict liability rule:

> ... if at the time of publication (having taken all reasonable care) he does not know and has no reason to suspect that proceedings are active.

A similar defence is available to distributors who take all reasonable care and have no reason to believe nor any reason to suspect that the publication they distributed contained material in contempt of court.

The burden of proof is on the publisher or the distributor. The defence may be of limited application. It is unlikely to assist a media company when publication occurs in the days following an arrest or the issue of a warrant. A member of the media always has the opportunity to telephone the police, the court or the lawyers of the accused to determine whether proceedings are active. A court is likely to find that if he has not done so, he has not taken 'reasonable care' and will be unable to rely on the defence.

However, the defence may be of assistance to a media company in circumstances where the person was arrested or the warrant was issued just as the presses were rolling or the programme was broadcast. Cogent evidence will be needed to show that all reasonable care had been taken by the publisher to try to discover the true position. Section 3 requires a high standard of care.

The existence of negligence will, of course, destroy this defence.

Fair and accurate contemporary reports

Section 4(1) provides that:

> ... a person is not guilty of contempt of court under the strict liability rule in respect of a fair and accurate report of legal proceedings held in public, published contemporaneously and in good faith.

The elements of the defence are that the report must:

- Be fair and accurate
- Relate to proceedings held in public (in other words that the public are freely entitled to attend)
- Be published 'contemporaneously' (in other words during or as soon as practical after the hearing)
- Be published in good faith (in other words honestly and without ulterior motive).

Reports published in this way are also safe from libel proceedings (see Chapter 1).

The same section of the CCA gives the court powers to postpone reports of the proceedings or any part of them if otherwise the administration of justice in those proceedings is likely to be prejudiced (see Chapter 9).

Misreporting what was said in court, for example by including in a report elements that were not put to the jury, may be a contempt under Section 4.

Discussion of public affairs

Section 5 of the CCA provides:

> ... a publication made as, or as part of, a discussion in good faith of public affairs or other matters of general public interest is not to be treated as a contempt of court under the strict liability rule if the risk of impediment or prejudice to particular legal proceedings is merely incidental to the discussion.

This defence did not exist before 1981. Its introduction was recommended in the 1974 report by the Phillimore Committee, which concluded that it was wrong to bring to a halt publicized debates about matters of general public interest simply because legal proceedings had arisen which reflected the issues being debated. The purpose of the defence is to comply with the Article 10 European Convention on Human Rights right to freedom of expression.

The leading authority on this defence is *A-G v English (1983)*, in which the House of Lords held that an article in the *Daily Mail* by Malcolm Muggeridge that argued for a Pro-Life election candidate and referred to an alleged practice among doctors of allowing deformed babies to die was not in contempt of the contemporaneous trial of a doctor on a charge of murdering a baby with Down's Syndrome. The House of Lords held that Section 5 was intended to prevent the:

> . . . gagging of *bona fide* discussion of controversial matters of general public interest merely because there are in existence contemporaneous legal proceedings in which some particular instance of those controversial matters may be in issue.

The court found that although the article was likely to create serious prejudice in the doctor's trial, it met the requirements of Section 5 and was not, therefore, a contempt. In other words, the report was part of a *bona fide* discussion of a matter of public interest, and the prejudice was merely incidental to that discussion.

However, if a publication concentrates on the specific issues of a particular case that is active, there will be a risk of prejudice to particular legal proceedings and Section 5 will not provide a defence.

10.2.8 Scope of the Contempt of Court Act 1981

Section 19 provides that the strict liability rule applies to the proceedings of 'any tribunal or body exercising the judicial power of the state'.

This has led to discussion as to what qualifies as a tribunal or body under the CCA. Apart from all cases heard in criminal and civil courts, employment tribunals, coroner's courts, mental health tribunals and courts martial are courts included in the rule. However, the General Medical Council is not a body exercising the judicial power of the state (*General Medical Council v British Broadcasting Corporation (1998)*).

10.3 Common law contempt

10.3.1 Interfering with 'pending or imminent' court proceedings

The common law offence is unaffected by the CCA. The position at common law is that a person is guilty of contempt if he publishes material that is calculated to prejudice or interfere with proceedings that, at the time of publication, were 'pending or imminent'. For a prosecution to succeed, it is necessary to establish that the publisher intended to cause the prejudice or was at least reckless in that he was aware of the future proceedings and knew the nature of what he published.

While there is plenty of uncertainty about the precise meaning of 'imminent', it is reasonably clear that criminal proceedings are 'pending' when a person has been arrested and is about to be charged.

Although prosecutions under the offence are unusual, they do take place. In 1986 the *Sun* newspaper announced that it was funding a private prosecution against a doctor who was alleged to have raped a child. Although there was medical evidence that the girl had been raped, the only evidence against the doctor was the word of the child. Because she was only nine years old, the Director of Public Prosecutions thought a conviction was unlikely and decided not to prosecute. Unfortunately, by announcing that it was going to finance the private prosecution the *Sun* gave the clear impression that the doctor was guilty. In fact, the doctor was not arrested and charged until 53 days after the report in the *Sun*. Despite the significant passage of time between the report and the arrest, the court held that in the circumstances, taking into account the fact that the *Sun* was funding the prosecution, the proceedings were imminent. The court went on to say that:

> . . . the common law is not a worn out jurisprudence rendered incapable of further development . . . it is a lively body of law capable of adaptation and expansion to meet fresh needs all for the exertion of the discipline of law.

The *Sun* was fined £75 000 for contempt (*A-G v News Group Newspapers Ltd (1988)*).

The decision extended the restraints imposed upon the media by the contempt laws. Few would have thought that a report published more than seven weeks before a person was arrested could be punishable as a contempt. Indeed, doubts about the validity of the court's decision were openly expressed by the court in a case involving charges of contempt brought against the editor and publishers of the *Daily Sport* following the publication of the previous convictions of a man sought by police in connection with a missing schoolgirl (*A-G v Sport Newspapers (1992)*). The prosecution failed because the court was not satisfied that the defendants had the necessary intent to cause prejudice. Even though the decision of the court did not turn on whether the proceedings were 'pending or imminent', one of the judges declared his belief that the case involving the *Sun* was wrongly decided and the other judges expressed reservations about it.

As a result, unless an editorial decision is made to publish material with the intention to prejudice proceedings, it is difficult to imagine circumstances where common law contempt would apply.

Recent guidance has been issued which provides that a contempt at common law is likely to be committed where a report of proceedings is published where the jury has been asked to withdraw from court. Publishing a report in such circumstances would defeat the object of the jury's withdrawal. (See *Reporting Restrictions in the Crown Court*, published by the Judicial Studies Board.)

181

10.3.2 Contempt in the face of the court

It is an offence to behave in a courtroom in a manner that undermines the authority of the court, for example by throwing missiles at the judge, carrying out a demonstration or directly insulting the judge to his face.

10.3.3 Scandalizing the court

'Scandalizing the court' is an oral or written statement that is designed to bring the court or the judge into contempt or lower his authority. Such an offence is not affected by the CCA. In any event, even if there are active proceedings, a statement that scandalizes the court creates a risk of prejudice to the administration of justice rather than particular proceedings.

The most common form of scandalizing the court is publishing an attack on the integrity of a judge by accusing him of being biased, taking bribes or being asleep in court. Prosecutions for scandalizing the court are very rare. It has been said recently that the offence is 'virtually obsolescent'. In recent years such attacks on a judge are met with a libel action or a request for an apology.

10.3.4 Failing to comply with a court order

Failure to comply with an order of the court can lead to serious repercussions. If the failure was inadvertent and the effect on proceedings minimal, a speedy and honest apology to the court may result in leniency. The court may, for example, warn that any further breach would lead to a fine or reference to the Attorney General to consider prosecution.

If the breach were deliberate, however, and had a serious effect on the conduct of the proceedings, again the matter may be referred to the Attorney General for him to consider taking contempt proceedings.

10.3.5 Use of documents disclosed during proceedings

When documents are disclosed during civil proceedings under an obligation to the court or other party to those proceedings, then any use of the document for a purpose collateral to those proceedings is a breach of the Civil Procedure Rules. This is the position except in specified circumstances such as where the document has been read to or by the court or referred to at a public hearing. Care should therefore be taken when considering documents that have come into the possession of a journalist via a party to litigation when those documents have been disclosed as part of the court process and belong to the other party to the action.

10.4 Penalties and injunctions

10.4.1 Penalties for contempt

As well as controlling pre-trial publicity, the court's inherent power to punish for contempt is the key to enforcement of court orders. Disobedience to an order of the court will lead to punishment. There is *no limit* to the fines or term of imprisonment that can be imposed for a contempt. As a result, the court can impose whatever form of punishment it feels is appropriate. Contempt is the court's ultimate weapon and can even result in a term of imprisonment up to a maximum of two years.

10.4.2 Injunctions

An injunction applying prior restraint to publication is the court order most commonly encountered by the media. It can take many forms. For example, an author or photographer whose copyright has been infringed by a newspaper might obtain an injunction to prevent further infringement. If a breach of confidence is apprehended, the person with rights in the confidential information can ask the court to prevent its proper disclosure. In the family courts, it is extremely common for injunctions to be granted against the media in order to protect minors against publicity that might be harmful. Less common but by no means infrequent are injunctions banning the publication of libellous material.

Most editors and producers understand the importance of an injunction that has been granted in respect of his newspaper or programme. Once the order has been served or proper notice of its existence has been given, which can be by telephone, letter or fax, any breach of its terms will almost certainly result in punishment for contempt of court.

However, although an injunction may be granted against one particular publisher, it can bind all other publishers with knowledge of the injunction. Breach of such an order by another publisher will be contempt. The principle of 'third-party contempt' arose from the *Spycatcher* litigation in the 1980s. In 1986, injunctions were granted pending trial against the *Guardian* and the *Observer* to restrain them from publishing extracts from *Spycatcher*. Knowing of the existence of the injunction, the *Independent* and the *Sunday Times* each carried stories that included parts of the banned material. The rationale for the decision was that by publishing the material at the heart of the injunction, the *Independent* and the *Sunday Times* destroyed its confidentiality and negated the central issue in the forthcoming trial between the government and the *Guardian* and the *Observer* (*A-G v Newspaper Publishing PCC (1987); A-G v Times Newspapers Ltd (1991)*).

Injunctions can also be made 'against the world'. These injunctions bind all publishers within the jurisdiction of England and Wales subject to notice.

Injunctions are often served on the Press Association by the party obtaining the injunction in order for the information to be widely disseminated.

11 Protection of Journalistic Sources

Joanna Ludlam

11.1 Introduction

Of all the valuable commodities cherished by the media, particularly those working as journalists, a long contact list of reliable sources is one of the most important. The system by which sources of information and contacts are built up is based on mutual trust and co-operation. In circumstances where a person provides accurate information on the understanding that he will not be compromised or named, it is a cardinal rule of journalism that his identity remains confidential.

However, people who speak to reporters on this basis frequently break a duty of confidence that they themselves owe to a third party. As a result, the journalistic principle of protecting sources can sometimes clash with the different principles held by the court.

The outcome of such a clash will vary depending on the circumstances of each case, but courts have been known to take a hard line. Journalists do not have an absolute privilege against disclosure like that of lawyers and their clients. The issue of whether a journalist will be ordered to reveal the identity of his source is a matter of discretion for the judge.

Under the common law, the court was reluctant to force journalists to betray their sources unless the interests of justice or of the state demanded it. The protection of journalistic sources is now provided for under Section 10 of the Contempt of Court Act 1981. In addition, special protection is given to material acquired or created for journalism in circumstances where the police search for and seize material under Sections 8 and 9 of the Police and Criminal Evidence Act 1984.

In general, a person will not be compelled to divulge names or other information unless ordered to do so by a court of law, a Tribunal of Inquiry (set up under the Tribunals of Inquiry (Evidence) Act 1921) or a Parliamentary Committee. Similarly, a person will not be obliged to supply information requested by the police because the duty of a citizen does not require active co-operation. However, a charge of obstruction may follow if the police are deliberately misled.

11.2 Section 10 of the Contempt of Court Act 1981

11.2.1 General principles

Section 10 of the Contempt of Court Act 1981 ('the CCA') provides:

> No court may require a person to disclose, nor is any person guilty of contempt of court for refusing to disclose the source of information contained in a publication for which he is responsible, unless it is established to the satisfaction of the court that it is necessary in the interests of justice or national security, or for the prevention of disorder or crime.

Section 10 of the CCA recognizes the need for protection of journalists' sources in a free and democratic society, and creates a presumption in favour of journalists who wish to protect their sources. However, the presumption is subject to four exceptions where disclosure of the source of information will be deemed to be necessary:

1. In the interests of justice
2. In the interests of national security
3. For the prevention of disorder, or
4. For the prevention of crime.

11.2.2 In the interests of justice

The meaning of 'in the interests of justice' was explained to some extent by *X Ltd v Morgan-Grampian (Publishers) Ltd (1991)*. William Goodwin, a journalist working for a trade magazine called *The Engineer*, had obtained highly confidential information from a missing copy of the claimant's corporate business plan. Goodwin's telephone calls to the company's offices prior to publication alerted the company to the fact that he was in possession of information that must have come from the missing document. The claimant obtained an injunction restraining publication of the confidential material, and Goodwin was ordered to hand over his notes so that the person who stole the business plan could be identified.

On appeal, the House of Lords ruled that 'in the interests of justice' should be given a wide meaning and need not necessarily be confined to situations where court proceedings were already in existence or about to be commenced. The phrase should be construed so that:

> ... persons should be enabled to exercise important legal rights and to protect themselves from serious legal wrongs whether or not resort to legal proceedings in a court of law will be necessary to protect these objectives. Thus, to take an example, if an employer of a large staff is suffering grave damage from the activities of an unidentified disloyal servant, it is undoubtedly in the interests of justice that he should be able to identify him in order to terminate his contract of employment, notwithstanding that no legal proceedings may be necessary to achieve this end.

The court emphasized that:

> The judge's task will always be to weigh in the scales the importance of enabling the ends of justice to be attained, in the circumstances of the particular case on the one hand, against the importance of protecting the source on the other hand. In this balancing exercise it is only if the judge is satisfied that the disclosure in the interests of justice is of such preponderating importance as to override the statutory privilege against disclosure that the threshold of necessity will be reached.

Among the factors affecting the balancing exercise would be the nature of the information obtained from the source:

> . . . the greater the legitimate public interest in the information the source has given to the publisher or intended publisher, the greater will be the importance of protecting the source

and the manner in which the source obtained it:

> . . . if it appears to the court that the information was obtained legitimately this will enhance the importance of protecting the source. Conversely, if it appears that the information was obtained illegally, this will diminish the importance of protecting the source unless, of course, this factor is counterbalanced by a clear public interest in publication of the information, as in the classic case where the source has acted for the purpose of exposing iniquity.

This definition allows the 'interests of justice' exception to be argued in all situations where a claimant can show some prejudice. This broad interpretation is difficult to reconcile with the limitations imposed by Section 10 of the CCA, which specifically provides only four exceptions to the presumption in favour of journalists who wish to protect their sources.

On the facts of the case in *Morgan-Grampian*, the court found that it was necessary 'in the interests of justice' to order the disclosure of the source, even though the distribution of the confidential information had been restrained by the injunction. Despite the ruling against him, Goodwin continued to refuse to surrender the documentation and was fined £5000 for being in contempt of court.

The law remained largely unchallenged until March 1996, when Goodwin's application for review came before the European Convention of Human Rights (*Goodwin v United Kingdom (1996)*). The court held that the order forcing Goodwin to disclose his source breached Article 10 of the Convention. It noted that without protection, journalists' sources could be deterred from assisting the public by informing the press of matters of public interest. This would undermine the role of the press as public watchdog. The court also found that the interest of the company in identifying the disloyal employee who had given Goodwin the information and in preventing damage to the company by disclosure of confidential information was not enough to outweigh the public interest in protecting Goodwin's source.

The issue of 'necessary in the interests of justice' came before the court again in *Camelot Group plc v Centaur Communications Ltd (1999)*. A Camelot employee copied Camelot's draft accounts to Centaur, who published them a week before they were to be made public. Centaur refused to agree to Camelot's request for delivery-up of the documents, as this would identify the source. It offered to destroy them instead. The Court of Appeal found that there was an 'ongoing threat' to Camelot to which it had to attach great weight. It held that Camelot's wish to identify a disloyal employee outweighed the public interest in protecting sources, and ordered disclosure. In making its decision, the court failed to follow the approach of either the House of Lords in *Morgan-Grampian* or the European Court of Human Rights in *Goodwin*, but attempted to reconcile the two by stating that the courts had taken 'substantially the same' approach to the issues. Any difference, it stated, was attributable to a 'different view [being] taken on the facts'.

The differing approaches taken by the court was emphasized in two subsequent cases. In the case of *John Reid Enterprises v Bell (1999)*, the defendant journalist provided information and documents leaked from the claimant company to a newspaper. The claimant obtained an *ex parte* order for disclosure of the source in order to identify the disloyal employee. The defendant appealed. Although his case was dismissed on the facts, the court applied the methodology of *Morgan-Grampian* and took into account the lack of public interest in the information. The judge noted that for disclosure to be ordered, the importance of a free press needed to be outweighed by the importance to the claimant of exercising his rights. In contrast, in *O'Mara Books Limited v Express Newspapers plc (1998)* the court applied the 'ongoing threat' test laid down in the *Camelot* case, holding that on the facts of the case there was no public interest in protecting the source.

In the most recent case on the issue to come before the court, the Court of Appeal held that it was necessary to demonstrate it was in the public interest to reveal journalistic sources before such an order could be made. The protection of journalistic sources remained the most important principle, unless it was overridden by the necessity of disclosure (*Elton John v Express Newspapers plc (2000)*). Before the courts will require a journalist to reveal his sources, other means of identifying the source must be explored. The absence of such an attempt to explore other means will be a powerful, even decisive, factor against the intervention of the court.

When deciding whether a source should be identified, the most appropriate legal test remains unclear. With the introduction of the Human Rights Act 1998, it may be that the approach taken by the European Court of Human Rights in *Goodwin* will be adopted by the English courts in the future.

11.2.3 In the interests of national security

The strength of the protection afforded by Section 10 of the CCA in cases where national security is involved was considered in *Secretary of State for Defence v Guardian Newspapers Ltd (1985)*. On 31 October 1983, under the headline 'Heseltine's Briefing to Thatcher on

Cruise', the *Guardian* published a confidential memorandum prepared by the Secretary of State for Defence, which dealt with the question of the arrival of cruise missiles in Britain. When the Government issued proceedings demanding the return of the document, the *Guardian* realized that the marks on their copy would identify their source. It cited Section 10 of the CCA and refused to return the document. The court had to consider the conflict between national security and the protection of a journalistic source. The House of Lords ordered the *Guardian* to disclose the memorandum:

> The maintenance of national security requires that trustworthy servants in a position to mishandle highly classified documents passing from the Secretary of State for Defence to other Ministers shall be identified at the earliest possible moment and removed from their positions. This is blindingly obvious. Whether or not the Editor acted in the public interest in publishing the document was not the issue. The Secretary of State's concern was quite different. It was that a servant of the Crown who handled classified documents had decided for himself whether classified information should be disseminated to the public. If he could do it on one occasion he might do it on others, when the safety of the state would be truly imperilled.

The *Guardian* was forced to hand back the document, revealing the source to be a junior civil servant in the Foreign Office called Sarah Tidsall, who was subsequently sentenced to six months imprisonment.

It is clear that where interests of national security are concerned, the necessity of disclosure will be 'almost automatic' (*X Ltd v Morgan-Grampian (Publishers) Ltd (1991)*).

Moreover, even though the court may have sympathy for a journalist who does not wish to divulge information carried in his head, it will not look kindly on a journalist who refuses to hand over physical property such as documents that belong to someone else. After the sentencing of Tisdall, the *Guardian* admitted that it should have destroyed the document before the Government issued proceedings.

11.2.4 For the prevention of disorder or crime

The public interest in preventing disorder or crime is of such 'overriding importance' that disclosure will usually be 'almost automatic' (*X Ltd v Morgan-Grampian (Publishers) Ltd (1991)*).

In *X v Y (1988)*, a *News of the World* reporter was provided with information from local health authority medical records that showed that two of the doctors employed by the health authority were suffering from AIDS but were still in practice. The information had been provided by an employee at the hospital treating the doctors. The health authority issued proceedings in order to prevent publication of its confidential information and to force the reporter to reveal the name of his source. The health authority argued that the interests of justice demanded the identification of the person who had wrongly divulged the medical records because he had committed a criminal act. The health authority also argued that disclosure was necessary in order to prevent any further dissemination of confidential information. The court granted a permanent injunction to restrain the publication, but refused to order that the reporter name his source. It held that the prevention of crime was not the responsibility of the health authority, and that the health authority had not established disclosure was necessary in the interests of justice.

11.2.5 Section 6 of the Official Secrets Act 1920

There is an exception to the general rule that journalistic sources are protected. Section 6 of the Official Secrets Act 1920 states:

> Where a chief officer of police is satisfied that there is reasonable ground for believing that an offence [of 'espionage'] under Section 1. . .(of the Official Secrets Act 1911) . . . has been committed and for believing that any person is able to furnish information as to the offence or suspected offence, he may . . . with the permission of the Secretary of State, authorize a senior police officer to require the person to reveal the relevant information, or, in a case 'of great emergency' he may require that the information be revealed without first obtaining the Secretary of State's permission.

Any person who fails to comply with such a requirement or knowingly gives false information commits an offence.

11.3 Police powers under the Police and Criminal Evidence Act 1984

The provisions giving the police the power under Sections 8 and 9 of the Police and Criminal Evidence Act 1984 ('the PACE') to search for and seize material are complex. Special protection is given to material acquired or created for journalism.

The police often treat applications for orders to seize material as routine. However, when considering applications involving journalistic material, the court should weigh carefully the public interest in investigating crime and the public interest in the freedom of the press.

11.3.1 Section 8 Police and Criminal Evidence Act 1984

Under Section 8 PACE, a justice of the peace may authorize a police constable to enter and search premises for material if there are reasonable grounds for believing that:

- A serious arrestable offence has been committed
- There is material on the premises specified in the application that is likely to be of substantial value to the investigation of the offence
- The material is likely to be relevant evidence, and
- It does not consist of or include items subject to legal privilege, excluded material or special procedure material.

In addition, the police must satisfy the justice of the peace of any of the following:

- It is impractical to communicate with any person entitled to grant entry or access to the premises
- Entry to the premises will not be granted unless a warrant is produced
- The purpose of the search may be 'frustrated or seriously prejudiced' unless the police can secure immediate entry.

Section 15 PACE stipulates that every warrant must specify the name of the officer who applied for it, the date of its issue, the statutory authority for its issue, the premises to be searched, and, so far as practicable, the articles or persons sought. Each warrant authorizes one search only. A return visit will therefore require a fresh application to a justice of the peace. The person whose premises are searched should be supplied with a copy of the warrant.

The normal search warrant procedure under Section 8 PACE will not apply if the items the police wish to see consist of material which is subject to:

- Legal privilege
- Excluded material, or
- Special procedure material.

11.3.2 Section 9 Police and Criminal Evidence Act 1984

The police may apply to a circuit judge for a production order or a search warrant under Section 9 PACE for access to:

- Excluded material, or
- Special procedure material

for the purposes of a criminal investigation if they satisfy the requirements set out in Schedule 1 PACE.

The person who is the subject of the application should be given notice of the application, and has a right to be heard.

11.3.3 Legal privilege, excluded material and special procedure material

Legal privilege

Material that is subject to legal privilege is effectively off limits to the police. Legal privilege, or legal professional privilege as it is better known, attaches to:

- Communications between a lawyer and his client or his client's representative for the purpose of giving legal advice or in connection with, and for the purpose of, legal proceedings
- Communications between either a lawyer, his client or his client's representative on the one side and other persons on the other side in connection with, or in contemplation of, legal proceedings and for the purposes of such proceedings.

With one exception, items that are subject to legal professional privilege are totally exempt from police powers of search and seizure. The exception is if the relevant material is held 'with the intention of furthering a criminal purpose'.

Excluded material

Excluded material means:

- Personal records that a person has acquired or created in the course of any trade, business, profession or office and which he or she holds in confidence
- Human tissue or tissue fluid samples held under a duty of confidence for medical purposes
- 'Journalistic material' consisting of documents or records, which is, and since its acquisition or creation has always been, held under an 'undertaking, restriction or obligation of confidence' – in other words, *confidential* material.

Section 13 PACE defines 'journalistic material' as 'material acquired or created for the purposes of journalism' and in the possession of the person who acquired or created it for those purposes.

Special procedure material

Special procedure material is either of the following:

- Business or professional records, but not personal records which come within excluded material, held under a duty of confidence
- 'Journalistic material' other than 'excluded material' which is in the possession of the person who acquired or created it for journalistic purposes – in other words, *non-confidential* material.

11.3.4 Schedule 1 Police and Criminal Evidence Act 1984

If the circuit judge is satisfied that one of the 'sets of access conditions' concerning excluded material or special procedure material set out in Schedule 1 PACE exists, he may make an order that the person in possession of the relevant items produce them to a constable to take away, or give a constable access to them. The order must be complied with within seven days or such longer period as the judge may specify. Failure to comply with an access order is punishable as a contempt of court.

Excluded material

The police must establish that:

- There are reasonable grounds for believing excluded material exists on the premises specified, and
- A search warrant would have been granted under any legislation prior to the PACE.

A search warrant would have been granted under the previous law in only a very limited range of circumstances – for example in respect of stolen medical records under Section 26(i) of the Theft Act 1981.

Special procedure material

The police must establish that there are reasonable grounds for believing that:

- A serious arrestable offence has been committed
- There is special procedure material on the premises
- The material is likely to be of substantial value to the relevant investigation
- The material is likely to be admissible evidence, and
- Other methods of obtaining the material have failed or have not been tried because they were bound to fail.

The police must also show that it is in the public interest for the order to be made.

11.3.5 Case law

An understanding of these extremely complex statutory provisions is not helped by the fact that there have been few cases to illuminate the law and procedures involved.

In *Commissioner of Metropolitan Police v Mackenzie (1987)*, the Vice Squad wanted to obtain statements and other documents gathered by the *Sun* during an investigation into underage homosexual prostitution. The application was issued against the *Sun's* editor in person, Kelvin Mackenzie. Since the police were unable to establish that Mackenzie himself had ever been in possession of the evidence, their application failed. The application should have been brought against the newspaper company as the employer of Mackenzie, or the person who actually had possession of the material. In any event, Mackenzie was able to show that most of the statements sought by the police had come into existence for the purposes of defending libel proceedings against the *Sun*. The statements were therefore covered by legal privilege and were wholly exempt from the access provisions of the PACE.

PART V
Prevention of Publication

12 Prior Restraint

Hugh Tomlinson QC

12.1 Introduction

The power of the courts to prevent publication in the media is the most stringent form of restricting freedom of expression. The basic principle is that jurisdiction to grant injunctions to restrain publication should only be used in 'the clearest cases' – cases in which the claimant can demonstrate that publication is wrongful and likely to cause irreparable harm. Prior restraint is extremely rare in defamation cases, but is much more readily granted where a breach of confidence or contempt of court is threatened. Since the Human Rights Act 1998 came into force on 2 October 2000, the courts have, increasingly, been prepared to grant injunctions to restrain the publication of information about a person's 'private life'.

12.2 General principles

12.2.1 Applications for interim injunctions

An application for an interim injunction to restrain publication can only be made when a claimant becomes aware of an impending publication to which he takes objection. Applications are often made 'without notice' to the defendant. It should be borne in mind that in such a case:

- The claimant has a duty of 'full and frank disclosure' – all points that undermine his case and support that of the defendant must be disclosed to the court. If this duty is breached, the defendant is entitled to have the injunction set aside for this reason alone.
- The claimant must give an 'undertaking in damages' to the court. If what is sought is an injunction that prevents the publication of a newspaper or magazine, the loss to the defendant is likely to be very substantial and the claimant must satisfy the court that he can cover this loss if it turns out that the injunction was wrongly granted.

Any media organization that receives an injunction should check that both these requirements have been complied with. If not, either could form the grounds for an immediate application to discharge the injunction.

12.2.2 Compliance

Once the order has been served or proper notice of its existence has been given, which can be done by telephone, letter or fax, any failure to comply with its terms will be a serious contempt of court, which could result in a substantial fine or even, in some cases, a sentence of imprisonment. If the defendant believes that the injunction was wrongly granted, an application should be made to discharge it. The injunction cannot be ignored.

12.2.3 The defendant

Injunctions are usually directed to specific defendants – the publisher, editor or journalist. However, in some limited cases injunctions may be granted against the 'whole world' as happened in *Venables v News Group Newspapers Ltd (2001)*. In such cases, it will be a contempt of court for anyone to publish the information covered by the injunction.

In other cases, injunctions are often served on the Press Association in order for the information to be widely disseminated. It will be a contempt of court if a third party with knowledge of the injunction publishes the information covered by the injunction. This is because, even though the injunction is not directed at the third party, the publication of the material means that the purpose of making the order was intentionally frustrated (*A-G v Times Newspapers (1992)*). If a third party wishes to publish the information, an application must first be made to discharge or vary the injunction.

12.3 Defamation cases

12.3.1 Applications for interim injunctions

The courts have always been extremely reluctant to restrain the publication of material that is said to be defamatory. In order to obtain an interim injunction in a defamation case, the claimant must show that:

- The defendant intends to publish a statement
- The statement is unarguably defamatory of the claimant
- Any defence of justification on which the defendant relies is bound to fail, and
- There are no defences that might succeed.

Intention to publish a statement
The claimant must not only show the general terms of the statement that he intends to publish, but must also be able to set out with 'reasonable certainty' the actual words about which he complains (*British Data Management v Boxer Commercial Removals (1996)*). In practice, this requirement will be very difficult to satisfy unless a claimant has obtained an advance copy of the publication complained of.

Statement is defamatory

The court must be satisfied that a jury would be bound to conclude that the words that the defendant threatens to publish are defamatory (*Kaye v Robertson (1991)*). If the words are capable of non-defamatory meanings, it is unlikely that an injunction will be granted.

Defence of justification will fail

An injunction will not be granted if the defendant asserts that the words complained of are true (*Bonnard v Perryman (1891)*). Provided that the defendant advances some evidence to support a proposed plea of justification, an injunction will be granted only in the extremely rare case in which the claimant can satisfy the court than the plea of justification is bound to fail. The rule in *Bonnard v Perryman* applies whatever the defendant's motive and the manner in which publication is threatened. For example, the court refused an injunction even where a defendant sought to extract money from the plaintiffs on threat of publication of what he said were damaging but true allegations about them (*Holley v Smyth (1998)*).

No defences

The claimant must rebut any other defences that might properly be raised – for example, fair comment or qualified privilege. If the publication is on a matter of public interest and appears to be the product of 'responsible journalism', the claimant must show the defendant would be bound to fail in establishing a defence of qualified privilege as set out in the case of *Reynolds v Times Newspapers Ltd (1999)* (see Chapter 1).

12.3.2 Conclusion

Each one of these is a stringent test that is difficult to satisfy. Taken together, their practical effect is that interim injunctions are not often granted in any defamation case, and injunctions restraining the media from publishing defamatory material are extremely rare.

12.4 Breach of confidence

12.4.1 Claims relating to non-confidential material

The rule restricting the availability of interim injunctions in defamation cases also extends to similar torts, such as trade libel and injurious falsehood (*Lord Brabourne v Hough (1981)*). Therefore a claimant attempting to restrain the publication of material he believes to be damaging will often seek to do so on other grounds, such as conspiracy to injure, breach of copyright, trademark infringement and, most importantly, breach of confidence.

However, attempts to avoid the rules that apply in defamation cases are unlikely to be successful. The courts have made it clear that, whatever the cause of action, freedom of speech is an important factor to be taken into account in the exercise of the discretion of the court (*Femis-Bank v Lazar (1991)*). The court will not allow claims for trademark infringement, breach of copyright or breach of confidence to be a 'vehicle' for what is, essentially, a defamation claim. If the essence of the complaint is that an attack on the claimant's reputation is threatened, the court will not grant an injunction unless the strict criteria that apply in defamation cases are satisfied, as was the case in *Francome v Mirror Group (1984)*.

Even where there is a claim for a breach of a contract not to publish the material complained of, the court will not grant an injunction simply on the basis of an arguable claim. Instead, it will assess the relative strengths of the parties' cases (*Cambridge Nutrition v BBC (1990)*).

12.4.2 Breach of confidence

General principles

The most important basis upon which a claimant may obtain 'prior restraint' of publications is a claim of breach of confidence. Proceedings for confidential information are in a special category because:

> . . . if, pending the trial, the court allows publication, there is no point in having a trial since the cloak of confidentiality can never be restored. Confidential information is like an ice cube . . . Give it to the party who has no refrigerator or will not agree to keep it in one, and by the time of the trial you just have a pool of water.
>
> (*A-G v Guardian Newspapers (1987)*).

Interim injunctions to restrain breaches of confidence can have a serious effect on the freedom of expression of the media. In the well-known *Spycatcher* litigation, the Government obtained injunctions to restrain the publication of a book by a former intelligence officer, Peter Wright. The interim injunctions were continued by the House of Lords despite the fact that book had been published in Australia and the United States (*A-G v Guardian Newspapers (1987)*). In *Observer & Guardian v United Kingdom (1991)*, the European Court of Human Rights held that this was a breach of Article 10 of the European Convention on Human Rights. Although the grant of the interim injunction at the outset was in accordance with Article 10, the continuation of the injunction after the publication of the book in the United States was unnecessary.

Public domain

The court will not, of course, grant an injunction in a breach of confidence claim to restrain the publication of information that is already in the public domain. Any injunction should be qualified to exclude such information.

Even in a case involving 'national security', a newspaper cannot be required to seek confirmation from the Attorney General that facts that it intends to publish are in the public domain (*A-G v Times Newspapers (2001)*).

Applications for interim injunctions

Before the Human Rights Act 1998 the ordinary *American Cynamid* principles that governed the grant of interim injunctions applied (*American Cynamid v Ethicon Ltd (1975)*). All the claimant needed to show was that:

- There was an arguable claim for breach of confidence, and
- The 'balance of convenience' favoured the grant of an injunction.

This was a very easy test to satisfy, and interim injunctions were regularly granted to restrain publication of confidential information, for example:

- Information about a sexual relationship provided by one of the parties (*Barrymore v News Group Newspapers (1997)*)
- Information from former employees of the security services concerning their activities (*A-G v Guardian Newspapers (1987)*).

The position has now been changed by Section 12(3) of the Human Rights Act 1998. This provides that an interim injunction that might affect the exercise of the right to freedom of expression should not be granted unless the applicant is 'likely to establish that publication should not be allowed'. This is a stricter test than that in *American Cyanamid*.

The principles to be applied when considering whether or not to grant an injunction restraining the publication of confidential information were considered in the case of *London Regional Transport v The Mayor of London (2001)*. In that case, the Court of Appeal stressed the importance of the Article 10 right to receive and impart information:

> Whether or not undertakings of confidentiality have been signed, both domestic law and Art 10(2) would recognize the propriety of suppressing wanton or self-interested disclosure of confidential information; but both correspondingly recognize the legitimacy of disclosure, undertakings notwithstanding, if the public interest in the free flow of information and ideas will be served by it.

It was suggested that, at least in cases involving public authorities, disclosure should only be restricted if such a restriction:

- Meets a recognized and pressing social need
- Does not negate or restrict the right to freedom of expression more than is necessary, and
- The reasons given for it are logical.

This approach applies whether the court is considering an express confidentiality undertaking or an implied obligation.

In other words, in order to obtain an interim injunction, a claimant will now have to show that:

- The information is confidential
- There is unlikely to be any 'public interest' defence, and
- The injunction sought is in clearly defined terms that provide the minimum restrictions compatible with protection of the confidence.

12.5 Invasion of privacy

The coming into force of the Human Rights Act 1998 has meant that the English courts have further developed the doctrine of 'breach of confidence' towards a full blown tort of 'invasion of privacy' (see Chapter 8).

When considering whether to grant an injunction to restrain the publication of 'private' information, the court will take into account relevant privacy codes such as that of the Press Complaints Commission (see Chapter 17) (*Douglas v Hello! (2001)*).

Interim injunctions have been granted to restrain the publication of 'private information' concerning the claimant in a number of cases, for example:

- An injunction to restrain the publication of information that might lead to the identification of the two young men convicted of the murder of James Bulger (*Venables v News Group Newspapers Ltd (2001)*)
- An injunction to restrain the publication of the fact and detail of adulterous affairs (*A v B and C (2001)*).

On the other hand, the court will take into account the likelihood of harm to the claimant and whether he can be compensated in damages. An injunction was refused where an exclusive agreement made between Michael Douglas and Catherine Zeta-Jones and a magazine to publish photographs of their wedding was breached when another magazine published them (*Douglas v Hello! (2001)*).

It now seems likely that a claimant will be able to restrain the publication of information about his or her private life by the media unless:

- The information is trivial or is already in the public domain, and/or
- There is a clear public interest in publication involving, for example, the detection or exposure of crimes or misdemeanours, protection of public health and safety and preventing the public from being misled (see the Press Complaints Commission Code, paragraph 3), and/or
- The claimant can clearly be compensated in damages because, for example, he is prepared to sell the relevant information about his private life, as was the case in *Douglas v Hello!*

12.6 Contempt proceedings

The court has jurisdiction to grant an injunction to restrain the publication of any material that may constitute a 'criminal contempt' (see Chapter 10). An application for such an injunction is usually made by the Attorney General; however, it appears that anyone with a sufficiently proximate interest may also apply for an injunction. For an example, in one case the Police Federation was granted an injunction to restrain a TV programme on grounds that it would prejudice a pending inquest concerning a death in custody (*Peacock v London Weekend Television (1985)*).

Because the prior restraint of a publication is a very serious interference with press freedom, an injunction on grounds of contempt will only be granted where the publication would, manifestly, be a contempt of court (*A-G v BBC (1981)*). However, an application to restrain a manifestly contemptuous publication will not be refused simply because the defendant seeks to argue that the statement is true.

PART VI

State Restriction on Publication

13 Obscenity, Indecency and Incitement to Racial Hatred

David Green

13.1 Introduction

English law imposes restrictions on freedom of expression by regulating and prohibiting the publication and distribution of material that is considered to be obscene, indecent or racially offensive.

Any law based upon prevailing attitudes towards morality and aimed primarily at literature and images may encounter controversy. It is perhaps difficult to reach any sort of consensus about which words or images are so harmful to society that their production and distribution should be punishable under the criminal law. Parliament has, however, devised tests of obscenity, indecency and racial hatred and legislated against their publication in:

- The Obscene Publications Acts of 1959 and 1964
- The Indecent Displays (Controls) Act 1981
- The Public Order Act 1986.

Despite the implementation of legislation, the extent to which material published in newspaper articles or television programmes should be considered obscene, indecent or racially offensive remains the subject of debate. Nowadays, the law is usually used to prevent only the more disturbing or dangerous publications.

13.2 The Obscene Publications Acts

13.2.1 General principles

Until 1959, the offence of publishing obscene matter was dealt with under the common law charge of obscene libel. The test applied in such cases was formulated in *R v Hicklin (1868)*:

> ... whether the tendency of the matter charged as obscene is to deprave and corrupt those whose minds are open to such immoral influences and into whose hands a publication of this sort may fall.

The old common law offence was supplemented but not abolished by the introduction of the Obscene Publications Acts in 1959 and 1964, which maintained the test of tending to deprave and corrupt but otherwise went some way to liberalizing the law. These Acts were introduced as a result of a number of prosecutions of serious literary works in the 1950s. It is still possible for a prosecution to be brought under the common law, although any prosecution is likely to be brought under the 1959 Act. An offence can be tried before the magistrates or a judge and jury.

13.2.2 What is obscenity?

Obscenity is a question of fact, not opinion. The test of obscenity is set out in Section 1 of the Obscene Publications Act 1959:

> . . . an article shall be deemed to be obscene if its effect or (where the article comprises two or more distinct items) the effect of any of its items is, if taken as a whole, such as to tend to deprave and corrupt persons who are likely, having regard to all the relevant circumstances, to read, see or hear the matter contained or embodied in it.

The 1959 Act modifies the common law test set out in *R v Hicklin*. It changes the type of person likely to be depraved from those into whose hands it 'may fall' to those to whom the material is likely to be given or sold. For example, 'adult' material sold in a sex shop will not be obscene under the 1959 Act just because its effect would be to 'tend to deprave' a child, because in normal circumstances this sort of adult material will not be sold to children. On the other hand, adult material published in a national newspaper that is available and likely to be read by almost every section of the community, including children, is likely to be obscene.

The law of obscenity cannot be used to prohibit what society considers to be 'bad taste'. To be obscene, the material must go beyond questions of lewdness. It must tend to be harmful to those who are likely to read, see or hear it.

Obscenity is not limited to sexual matters. Depictions of brutality and violence aimed at young people and drug abuse have been held to be capable of 'depraving and corrupting'. However, if material is so unpleasant or disgusting that it would actually dissuade a person from indulging in the material activity, it will not 'deprave and corrupt' and cannot be considered obscene. This was the case in *R v Calder and Boyars Ltd (1969)*.

Article

'Article' means 'any description of an article containing or embodying matter to be read or looked at or both, any sound record, any film or other record of a picture or pictures'. This wide definition includes anything that can be read, viewed or otherwise appreciated, including books, magazines, audio and video recordings, pictures and new media. It also includes negatives or information kept in electronic form (*R v Fellows and Arnold (1997)*). However, television and radio transmissions are specifically exempted.

Taken as a whole

The court must consider the article as a whole. It is wrong to judge it by reference to isolated extracts. The magistrates or jury will read a book from cover to cover in order to establish its effect. However, where the material consists of a number of separate and independent items, such as that found in newspapers and magazines, the court may convict if any single item satisfies the test of obscenity, despite the fact that the rest of the publication is harmless. In *R v Anderson (1972)* the magazine *Oz* was successfully prosecuted because the Court of Appeal confirmed that although some parts of the magazine were unobjectionable, the publication taken as a whole was tainted by those parts that were objectionable.

Deprave and corrupt

In order to convict for obscene publication, the court must be satisfied that the effect of the matter would be to 'tend to deprave and corrupt'. The prosecution is not required to prove the specified effect by reference to any resulting sexual or other physical act by a reader or viewer. It is enough to establish a tendency to deprave and corrupt by acting upon the mind or emotions of the likely recipient.

The words 'deprave and corrupt' are plain English terms and have no technical meaning. The prosecution of *Lady Chatterley's Lover*, by D. H. Lawrence, was the first major case for the Obscene Publications Act 1959, and produced the authoritative working definition of the key words in Section 1 of the Act:

> Deprave means to make morally bad, to pervert, to debase or corrupt morally.

> Corrupt means to render morally unsound or rotten, to destroy the moral purity or chastity, to pervert or ruin a good quality, to debase, to defile.
> (R v Penguin Books Ltd (1960))

The test is stringent. It is not enough that the publication would simply shock or disgust, or even that a reader or viewer would be led morally astray.

Persons who are likely to read, see or hear

The court must identify the likely readers or audience of the material. Once the court has done do, it must be satisfied that the effect of the material was to deprave and corrupt 'a significant proportion' of those readers or viewers (see *R v Calder and Boyars Ltd (1969)*). In other words, the effect does not have to be upon all the likely readers, nor upon the average reader, nor even upon the majority of readers.

In *DPP v Whyte (1972)*, the defendants argued that the target audience was middle-aged men whose morals were already depraved and corrupted and that, as a result, the effect of the material would be negligible and they could not have committed an offence. The argument was accepted by the magistrates' court but rejected by the House of Lords, who said that it was wrong to consider the effect only upon the category of the *most* likely reader, in this case people who were already corrupted. All categories of likely reader must be included. The House of Lords also held that the Obscene Publications Act 1959 protects not only the innocent likely reader but also those whose morals are already corrupted, because they may still be capable of further corruption.

13.2.3 Contemporary standards must apply

In deciding whether an article tends to deprave or corrupt, the magistrates or jury must judge an article by the standards of the day. The law recognizes that society's views about what constitutes obscenity changes with time, and that material which would have been judged as unacceptable 20 years ago would not necessarily be so today.

13.2.4 Publication

Section 1(2) of the Obscene Publications Act 1959 states:

> . . . any person who, whether for gain or not, publishes an obscene article or who has an obscene article for publication for gain (whether gain to himself or gain to another)

commits an offence.

'Publishes' means 'distributes, circulates, sells, lets on hire, gives or lends'. It also includes offering an article for sale or for letting on hire. Having an obscene publication for gain is also an offence. A person 'has' an article if it is in his ownership, possession or control.

13.2.5 Intention irrelevant

The offence is one of strict liability. The test for obscenity will be satisfied if the prosecution establishes the *fact* of the publication and the *effect* of the published article. The *intention* of the author or publisher is irrelevant.

However, the degree of *knowledge* possessed by those who publish obscene material is relevant to establishing the statutory defence under Section 2(5) of the 1959 Act.

13.2.6 Defences

Although an article may be found to be obscene, the publisher will escape conviction if he establishes one of the statutory defences under the Obscene Publications Act 1959. The burden of proof is on the defendant.

Public good

Under Section 4 of the 1959 Act, a publisher shall not be convicted if the article is justified as being for the public good on the grounds that it is in the interests of science, literature, art or learning, or another object of general concern. Another object can include justifying the article on 'ethical' merits.

If the article is a film or film soundtrack, Section 4 provides that there will be no conviction if the publication is justified as being for the public good in the interests of drama, opera, ballet or any other art or literature or learning.

It is always for the magistrates or jury to decide whether an obscene article is justified as being for the public good. However, Section 4 allows the prosecution and the defendant to call evidence as to the literary, artistic, scientific or other merits of an article.

Knowledge

Under Section 2(5) of the Obscene Publications Act 1959, a person shall not be convicted if he proves he had not examined the article and had no reasonable cause to suspect that the article was obscene.

Penalties

The publisher can be liable to either a fine or up to three years' imprisonment. However, imprisonment is generally reserved for the commercial exploitation of pornography.

Under Section 3 of the 1959 Act a court may issue a warrant for the police to enter a premises, stall or vehicle to seize offending material if there are reasonable grounds to suspect that obscene articles are kept there for publication for gain. Where offending articles are seized, the occupier of the premises may be summoned to court to show cause why they should not be forfeited. The owner, author, maker or another person through whose hands the material had passed before being seized may attend court to oppose a forfeiture order.

13.3 Indecent displays

Under the Indecent Displays (Controls) Act 1981, it is an offence for a person to display or cause or permit to display any indecent matter. 'Indecent matter' is not defined in the Act. A matter is displayed if 'it is visible from a public place'. Public place means any place to which the public have or are permitted to have access, except:

- A place where the public have to pay in order to see the display, or
- A shop or any part of a shop to which the public can only gain access by passing beyond the following warning notice:

WARNING
Persons passing beyond this notice will find material on display which they may consider indecent. No admittance to persons under 18 years of age.

The exceptions above only apply if persons under 18 years of age are not permitted access to the display.

The Indecent Displays (Controls) Act 1981 does not apply to displays by way of television broadcast, museum, theatre, or cinema. Also exempted are displays that are authorized by and on the premises of the Crown or any local authority, and displays at art galleries.

The police may seize any article upon reasonable suspicion that it is an indecent matter on display constituting an offence under the Indecent Displays (Controls) Act 1981.

A prosecution could also be brought under the common law offences of conspiracy to corrupt public morals, and outraging public decency.

13.4 Racial hatred

13.4.1 General principles

Incitement to racial hatred was criminalized by the Race Relations Act 1976, which amended the Public Order Act 1936. The relevant legislation is now found in Part III of the Public Order Act 1986. 'Racial hatred' is broadly defined in Section 17 as:

> . . . hatred against a group of citizens in Great Britain defined by reference to colour, race, nationality (including citizenship) or ethnic or national origins.

The three main offences of inciting racial hatred under the Public Order Act 1986 are:

1. Using threatening, abusive or insulting language, or displaying abusive or insulting written material
2. Publishing or distributing abusive or insulting written material, or performing plays, distributing or presenting visual images or sounds or producing a programme containing abusive or insulting written material, or
3. Possessing written material or recordings of images or sounds that is threatening, abusive or insulting with a view to displaying or publishing it

with the intention of stirring up racial hatred or in circumstances where racial hatred is likely to be stirred up (Sections 18 to 23). A prosecution can be brought by the Crown or as a private prosecution.

13.4.2 Meaning of threatening, abusive or insulting

The language or material must be sufficiently extreme. The words 'threatening, abusive or insulting' are to be given their ordinary meaning. The issue of whether the language or material was threatening, abusive or insulting is a question of fact for the court. To be insulted is to be more than annoyed. Rudeness does not constitute an insult. It has been said that 'an ordinary sensible man knows an insult when he sees or hears it' (*Brutus v Cozens (1973)*).

The requirement that the language of the offence be 'inflammatory' has been criticized in recent years in light of racist publications written in a 'pseudo-academic' style. This has been particularly prevalent in publications concerned with what has been coined 'holocaust denial'. Although there have been attempts to make 'holocaust denial' a criminal offence, they have not been successful.

13.4.3 Defences

It is a defence under Section 19(2):

> . . . for an accused who is not shown to have intended to stir up racial hatred to prove that he was not aware of the content of the material and did not suspect, and had no reason to suspect, that it was threatening, abusive or insulting.

The burden of establishing the defence is on the defendant.

Responsible members of the media will of course not be at risk of intentionally inciting racial hatred under the Public Order Act 1986. However, inadvertent incitement of racial hatred may amount to an offence if racial hatred is a likely consequence of the material having regard to all the circumstances. In addition, the reporting or broadcasting of racially extreme speeches or literature in news reports may itself attract a prosecution if the effect is that racial hatred is likely to be stirred up.

14 Freedom of Information

Charles de Fleurieu

14.1 Introduction

Historically, the Government has always exercised strict control over the disclosure of information related to government activities and public authorities. Over the years, the suppression of this type of information has led to political controversy and public outcry, such as the 'Arms to Iraq' affair and the BSE scandal.

As a result of this type of controversy, the Government has been under increasing pressure to move towards a more 'open' form of government. The development of freedom of information legislation in other counties has contributed to the debate. In addition, modern society is now fuelled to a greater extent by the 'information market', which is heavily reliant on governmental and public authority sources. The result of all these factors is a gradual change in the regime that governs access to information held by government departments, their agencies and public authorities.

Limited rights to freedom of information were first granted in the early 1970s under the Local Government Act 1972, which enables members of the public to inspect and take copies of local authority minutes, reports and background papers.

However, it is only in the last decade that the issue of widespread freedom of information has really been pushed to the forefront of the political agenda. In 1994 the Code of Practice on Access to Government Information (the 'Code') was introduced. Finally, on 30 November 2000 the Freedom of Information Act 2000 (the 'FIA') was passed. The FIA, the first such in the history of the United Kingdom, is an extremely important piece of legislation. When it comes into force, it will give individuals and organizations a general right of access to information held by public authorities, as well as the right to be told whether certain information exists. However, there are a number of exemptions to the general right of access to information, which are also set out in the FIA.

The FIA will gradually replace the existing regime under the Code by phased introduction. It will be fully implemented by 30 November 2005.

The obligation on public bodies to provide freedom of information under the Code and the FIA should be distinguished from the right of an individual to access their own personal information under the Data Protection Act 1998 and the Access to Personal Files Act 1987, both of which are considered in Chapter 7.

14.2 Code of Practice on Access to Government Information

14.2.1 General principles

The Code was introduced in 1994 and revised in 1997. It governs access to information held by almost all central Government departments and their agencies, as well as many public bodies that are subject to investigation by the Parliamentary Ombudsman – for example, the Arts Council of England, the Biotechnology and Biological Sciences Research Council, parts of the Cabinet Office, the Commission for Racial Equality, and various State Departments.

The Parliamentary Ombudsman regularly updates a list that sets out the departments and bodies subject to the Code.[1] The Parliamentary Ombudsman is appointed by the Queen as an independent officer of the House of Commons. He remains separate from the Government and the State, and generally receives and deals with complaints from members of the public who have suffered 'maladministration' by government departments or public bodies. His powers and responsibilities are set out in the Parliamentary Commissioner Act 1967.

The Code will continue to regulate these departments and bodies until they fall under the jurisdiction of the FIA. This is likely to be take place during the first phase of implementation of the FIA, which is due to be completed by the middle of 2002. Once all the bodies regulated by the Code are subject to the FIA, the Code will cease to have effect.

14.2.2 Access to information

The Code provides access to:

- Facts and analysis of major policy decisions
- Internal guidelines concerning dealings with the public
- Reasons for administrative decisions
- Information under the Citizen's Charter concerning public services.

In addition, upon specific request, information relating to policies, actions and decisions relating to each category can be obtained under the Code.

Facts and analysis of major policy decisions
Facts and analysis that the Government consider relevant and important in framing major policy proposals and decisions will normally be made available when policies and decisions are announced.

---

[1]The list of public bodies can be found at www.parliament.ombudsman.org.uk/pca/govdepts.htm.

Internal guidelines concerning dealings with the public

Explanatory material on the dealings by government departments or public bodies with the public, including any relevant rules, procedures, internal guidance to officials, and similar administrative manuals, are available except where publication could prejudice any matter that should be kept confidential under Part II of the Code.

Reasons for administrative decisions

Reasons for administrative decisions are generally made available to those who are affected by them. There are a few areas where well-established convention or legal authority limits the commitment under the Code to give reasons – for example, decisions on citizenship applications under Section 44(2) of the British Nationality Act 1981, decisions on merger and monopoly cases, or whether to take enforcement action.

Information under the Citizen's Charter concerning public services

The Code provides access to full information concerning how public services are run, how much they cost, who is in charge, and which complaints and redress procedures are available. It also provides full information where possible concerning which services are provided, which standard of service can be expected, targets and the results achieved.

The Code also provides a framework for requests for information. There is no requirement under the Code that pre-existing documents, as distinct from information, must be made available on request. In addition, the Code does not require a government department or public body to acquire information it does not possess, nor to provide information that is already published or provided as part of an existing service.

14.2.3 Limits on access to information

Part II of the Code sets out several categories of information that will be disclosed unless the harm likely to arise from disclosure would outweigh the public interest in making the information available. The categories are:

- Defence, security and international relations
- Internal discussion and advice
- Communications with the Royal household
- Law enforcement and legal proceedings
- Immigration and nationality
- Effective management of the economy and collection of tax
- Effective management and operations of the public service
- Public employment, public appointments and honours
- Voluminous or vexatious requests
- Publication
- Research, statistics and analysis
- Privacy of an individual

- Commercial confidences by a third party
- Information given in confidence
- Statutory and other restrictions.

Harm or prejudice includes both actual harm or prejudice and the risk or reasonable expectation of harm or prejudice. In such cases, it is necessary for the authority asked to disclose information to consider whether any harm or prejudice arising from disclosure will be outweighed by the public interest in making information available.

Defence, security and international relations
This category includes information whose disclosure would harm national defence or security, information which if disclosed would harm the conduct of international relations or affairs, and information received in confidence from foreign governments, foreign courts or international organizations.

Internal discussion and advice
Information cannot be disclosed if it would 'harm the frankness and candour of internal discussion'. This includes information such as the proceedings of Cabinet and Cabinet committees, internal opinions, advice, recommendations, consultation and deliberations, projections and assumptions relating to internal policy analysis, analysis of alternative policy options, and information relating to rejected policy options and confidential communications between departments, public bodies and regulatory bodies.

Communications with the Royal Household
This includes information relating to confidential communications between Ministers and the Queen or other members of the Royal household, as well as information relating to confidential proceedings of the Privy Council.

Law enforcement and legal proceedings
This category covers information:

- Whose disclosure could prejudice the administration of justice, including fair trial, legal proceedings or the proceedings of any tribunal, public inquiry or other formal investigations whether actual or likely, or whose disclosure is and has been, or is likely to be, addressed in the context of such proceedings
- Whose disclosure could prejudice the enforcement or proper administration of the law, including the prevention, investigation or detection of crime, or the apprehension or prosecution of offenders
- Relating to legal proceedings or the proceedings of any tribunal, public inquiry or other formal investigation which have been completed or terminated, or relating to investigations which have or might have resulted in proceedings
- Covered by legal professional privilege
- Whose disclosure would harm public safety or public order, or would prejudice the security of any building or penal institution

- Whose disclosure could endanger the life or physical safety of any person, or identify the source of information or assistance given in confidence for law enforcement or security purposes
- Whose disclosure would increase the likelihood of damage to the environment, or rare or endangered species and their habitats.

Immigration and nationality

This category includes information relating to immigration, nationality, consular and entry clearance cases. However, some information can be obtained (although not through access to personal records) where there is no risk that disclosure would prejudice the effective administration of immigration controls or other statutory provisions.

Effective management of the economy and collection of tax

This category concerns information in respect of which disclosure would harm the ability of the Government to manage the economy, would prejudice the conduct of official market operations, or could lead to improper gain or advantage. Information in respect of which disclosure would prejudice the assessment or collection of tax, duties or National Insurance contributions, or assist tax avoidance or evasion, will not be provided if the harm likely to arise from disclosure outweighs the public interests in making the information available.

Effective management and operations of the public service

This category includes information whose disclosure could lead to improper gain or advantage, or would prejudice the competitive position of a department or other public authority or authority; negotiations or the effective conduct of personnel management, or commercial or contractual activities, as well as the awarding of discretionary grants. It also includes information whose disclosure would harm the proper and efficient conduct of the operations of a department or other public body or authority, including NHS organizations, or of any regulatory body.

Public employment, public appointments and honours

This category includes:

- Personnel records relating to public appointments as well as employees of public authorities, including those relating to recruitment, promotion and security vetting
- Information, opinions and assessments given in confidence in relation to public employment and public appointments made by ministers of the Crown, by the Crown on the advice of ministers, or by statutory office holders
- Information, opinions and assessments given in relation to recommendations for honours.

Voluminous or vexatious requests

The Code limits access to those whose requests for information are vexatious or manifestly unreasonable or are formulated in too general a manner, or which because of the amount of information to be processed or the need to retrieve information from files not in current use would require unreasonable diversion of resources.

Publication

Information that is or will soon be published will generally not be provided. Note also that information whose disclosure, where the material relates to a planned or potential announcement or publication, could cause harm, for example of a physical or financial nature, will not be provided unless public interest outweighs the harm that is likely to arise from disclosure.

Research, statistics and analysis

Information relating to incomplete analysis, research or statistics, where disclosure could be misleading or deprive the holder of priority of publication or commercial value, will not be disclosed.

This category also includes information held only for preparing statistics or carrying out research, or for surveillance for health and safety purposes, including food safety, and which relates to individuals, companies or products that will not be identified in reports of that research or surveillance, or in published statistics.

Privacy of an individual

Information will not be provided if it will amount to unwarranted disclosure to a third party of personal information about any person including a deceased person, or any other disclosure that would constitute or could facilitate an unwarranted invasion of privacy. This is supported and reinforced by the Data Protection Act 1998 and the Article 8 right to privacy incorporated into English law by the Human Rights Act 1998.

Commercial confidences by a third party

Information relating to commercial confidences, trade secrets or intellectual property whose unwarranted disclosure would harm the competitive position of a third party will not be disclosed.

Information given in confidence

In the context of the law of confidence, the Code limits access to:

- Information given in confidence by a person who gave the information under a statutory guarantee that its confidentiality would be protected or by a person who was not under any legal obligation, whether actual or implied, to supply it and has not consented to its disclosure.
- Information whose disclosure without the consent of the supplier would prejudice the future supply of such information.
- Medical information provided in confidence if disclosure to the subject would harm their physical or mental health, or should only be made by a medical practitioner.

Statutory and other restrictions

The Code limits access to information whose disclosure is prohibited by or under any enactment, regulation, European Community law or international agreement, and information whose release would constitute a breach of Parliamentary Privilege.

14.2.4 Applications for information

Application

The Home Office provides a form for applicants to request information, which is available on its web site.[2] This form can be used to request information from any government departments, agencies and public bodies that come under the jurisdiction of the Parliamentary Ombudsman.

It is not compulsory for applicants to use the proposed form. However, in practice, use of the form will make it easier for the department, agency or public authority concerned to respond to the request promptly and efficiently. The more precise the request, the better the response is likely to be. Applicants should be as specific as possible about the decision, law or policy they seek information in respect of, and, if possible, should give names, dates and places.

Delay

Information will be provided as soon as practicable. The target for a response to simple requests for information is 20 working days from the date of receipt of the request. This target may need to be extended when significant search or collation of material is required. Where information cannot be provided under the terms of the Code, an explanation will normally be given.

Fees

Each government department, agency and public authority makes its own arrangements for fees. Details of fees are available on request. Fee schemes may include a standard charge for processing simple requests for information. Where a request is complex and requires extensive searches of records, or processing or collation of information, an additional fee reflecting reasonable costs may be charged.

14.2.5 Enforcement

Any complaint that information that should have been provided under the Code has not been provided or that an unreasonable fee has been charged should be made in the first instance to the government department, agency or public authority concerned.

---

[2]The web site is at www.homeoffice.gov.uk.

If the applicant is not satisfied with the response from the government department, agency or public authority, he may make a further complaint to the Parliamentary Ombudsman via a Member of Parliament. Complaints will be investigated at the Ombudsman's discretion in accordance with the procedures provided in the Parliamentary Commissioner Act 1967.

Because the Parliamentary Ombudsman is an independent officer of Parliament, he has the power to see the papers relevant to each case. He will decide whether the government department, agency or public authority was justified in refusing to provide access to the information south. The Parliamentary Ombudsman has produced his own leaflet,[3] which explains how he is able to help the public in these and other matters.

14.3 The Freedom of Information Act 2000

14.3.1 General principles

The FIA goes a good deal further than the Code. When in force, it will provide a general, statutory right of access to all types of recorded information held by public authorities. The FIA will also place a number of obligations on public authorities to ensure that information held by them is easier to access. Two codes of practice issued under the FIA will provide guidance to public authorities concerning responding to requests for information and associated matters[4] and concerning records management.[5]

The FIA also sets out the exemptions to the general right of access.

The FIA will be brought into full force by 30 November 2005. Implementation will be gradual. Different types of public authority will be phased in over the next five years. Once the FIA is fully implemented, it will have a massive impact. Secrecy will be out and transparency will be in. Individuals and organizations will have the right to request access to information that was previously denied.

14.3.2 Authorities subject to the Freedom of Information Act 2000

The Home Secretary, Jack Straw, stated that as a result of the FIA:

> . . . for the first time people will have a statutory right of access to information held by fifty thousand public authorities.

[3]The leaflet is available from www.parliament.ombudsman.org.uk/parly.htm.
[4]See the Draft Code of Practice On the Discharge of the Functions of Public Authorities Under Part I of the Freedom of Information Act 2000 at www.homeoffice.gov.uk/foi/dftcp00.htm.
[5]See the Draft Code on the Management of Records under Freedom of Information at www.pro.gov.uk/recordsmanagement/FreedomofInformationdefault.htm.

The FIA is intended to have wide application across the public sector at national, regional and local level. A large number of authorities, bodies and offices will fall within the scope of the FIA. Schedule 1 to the Act sets out a list of public authorities that will be subject to the FIA, including:

- Government departments
- Local authorities
- NHS bodies (hospitals, doctors, dentists, pharmacists and opticians)
- Schools, colleges and universities
- The police
- The House of Commons and the House of Lords
- The Northern Ireland Assembly
- The National Assembly for Wales.

Schedule 1 also includes a long list of other public bodies ranging from various official advisory and expert committees to regulators and organizations such as the Post Office, National Gallery, and the Parole Board. Other public authorities can be named at a later date.

The FIA also provides that certain organizations can be named as public authorities for the purpose of certain relevant parts of their work. Public authorities can be designated in one of the following ways:

- By order of the Secretary of State designating any body or the holder of any office that satisfies certain specified conditions (Section 4(1)).
- By order of the Secretary of State in respect of any body that satisfies certain conditions and appears to exercise functions of a public nature or provides any service which is a function of a public authority under a contract with that authority (Section 5).
- An entity that falls under the definition of a publicly-owned company for the purposes of the FIA (Section 6).
- By specification in relation to the principal authorities of national and local government, the armed forces, the national health service, education services, the police and other public bodies and offices (Schedule 1).

The fact that a public authority 'holds' information does not extend to holding that information on behalf of another person or authority. For example, the right to access would not extend to a Member of Parliament's constituency papers just because they were held in his government department. However, it does extend to information held elsewhere on behalf of an authority, for example in a private repository.

14.3.3 Access to information

The FIA provides a statutory right of access to all types of information, whether personal or non-personal. Furthermore, a person now has the right under the FIA to be told whether certain information exists. However, personal information concerning third parties cannot be released in breach of the Data Protection Act 1998 or the Human Rights Act 1998.

The right to access will not be exercisable until the relevant authority is brought under the scope of the FIA. However, when the FIA is in force it will be fully retrospective.

14.3.4 Exemptions

Although the FIA creates a general right of access to information, it also sets out no less than 23 exemptions where that right is either disapplied or disqualified. Apart from vexatious or repeated requests, to which a public authority is not required to respond, there are two general categories of exemption:

1. Where the public authority must consider whether disclosure is required in the public interest
2. Where there is no duty to consider the public interest.

Qualified exemptions – disclosure is in the public interest

Certain information will only be disclosed if it is in the public interest to do so. The public interest exemption applies to most of the 23 exemptions under the FIA. Where a public authority considers that the public interest in withholding information outweighs the public interest in disclosing the information, it must inform the applicant of its reasons unless to do so would mean actually releasing the exempt information. A public authority does not have to confirm or deny it holds the requested information if it is exempt from disclosure.

Information intended for future publication

Section 22 of the FIA exempts information that is intended to be published where it is reasonable that the information should not be disclosed until the intended date of publication. Examples of the type of information covered by this exemption include information relating to research projects that it would be inappropriate to publish until the project had been completed, or statistical information that is usually published to a specific timetable, for example annually or quarterly. Similarly, where a publication scheme states that a public authority will publish information on specified dates or at specified intervals, the authority will normally be able to rely on this exemption in relation to particular requests for such information.

National security

Under Section 24 of the FIA, information is exempt if it is required to safeguard national security. A certificate signed by a Minister of the Crown is conclusive proof that such information should be exempt.

Defence

Section 26 of the FIA exempts information which, if disclosed, could prejudice the defence of Great Britain or any colony or the capability, effectiveness or security of the armed forces.

International relations

Section 27 of the FIA exempts information if disclosure could prejudice relations between the United Kingdom and any other state, international organization or international court, the interests of the United Kingdom abroad or the promotion or protection by the United Kingdom of those interests. This section exempts confidential information (as defined by Section 27(3) of the FIA) obtained from a state or international organization or international court.

Relations within the United Kingdom

Section 28 of the FIA excludes information that could prejudice relations between any two administrations in the United Kingdom. An 'administration' is defined in Section 28(2) of the FIA as the government of the United Kingdom, the Scottish administration, the Executive Committee of the Northern Ireland Assembly, or the National Assembly for Wales.

The economy

Section 29 of the FIA exempts information that, if disclosed, could prejudice the economic interests of the United Kingdom or the financial interests of any administration in the United Kingdom.

Investigations and proceedings conducted by public authorities

Section 30 of the FIA excludes information held by a public authority for the purposes of a criminal investigation or criminal proceedings conducted by it. This section also exempts information relating to the obtaining of information from confidential sources, in other words informers, if it was obtained or recorded in the context of criminal investigations and proceedings, as well as the investigations in Section 31 of the FIA relating to law enforcement and civil proceedings that arise from such investigations.

Law enforcement

Section 31 of the FIA exempts the following:

1. Information that, if disclosed, could prejudice specified law enforcement matters
2. Information that could prejudice investigations or proceedings by a public authority that may lead to a prosecution, or civil proceedings brought by a public authority arising out of such investigations or proceedings:
   - Investigations into circumstances justifying regulatory action under any enactment
   - Regulatory investigations relating to unfitness or incompetence of company directors
   - Investigation of persons in regulated professions or involved in activities that require a licence
   - Investigations into accidents
   - Action relating to charity management
   - Action relating to health and safety.

Audit functions

Section 33 of the FIA exempts the disclosure of information that could prejudice the exercise by any public authority of its auditing functions. This relates to the audit of the accounts of other public authorities, or examinations into the efficiency, economy and effectiveness with which they use their resources to discharge their public functions.

Formulation of government policy

Section 35 of the FIA exempts information held by a government department or by the National Assembly for Wales if it relates to the formulation or development of government policy, ministerial communications, advice by law officers or the operation of a ministerial private office. Once a decision as to government policy has been taken, any statistical information used to provide an informed background to that decision cannot be exempted, although it may be exempt under Section 36 of the FIA.

Prejudice to effective conduct of public affairs

Section 36 of the FIA exempts information held by government departments which does not fall under Section 35 of the FIA relating to the formulation of government policy and information held by other public authorities if, in the reasonable opinion of a qualified person as defined in Section 36(5) of the FIA, its disclosure could:

- Prejudice the maintenance of the convention of collective ministerial responsibility
- Prejudice the work of the Executive Committee of the Northern Ireland Assembly or the National Assembly for Wales
- Inhibit the free and frank provision of advice or exchange of views
- Otherwise prejudice the effective conduct of public affairs.

However, information held by the House of Commons or the House of Lords can be withheld regardless of public interest.

Communications with the Royal family

Section 37 of the FIA exempts information relating to the award of any honour or dignity by the Crown or to any communications with the Royal family or household.

Health and safety

Section 38 of the FIA exempts information that, if disclosed, could endanger the physical or mental health or safety of any individual.

Environmental information

Section 39 of the FIA exempts environmental information that is to be made available to the public pursuant to regulations under the Convention on Access to Information, Public Participation in Decision Making and Access to Justice in Environmental Matters signed in Aarhus on 25 June 1998.

Personal information

Under Section 40 of the FIA, a public authority must consider whether it is in the public interest to disclose certain personal information. This includes information concerning a third party under the Data Protection Act 1998.

Legal professional privilege

Section 42 of the FIA exempts information covered by legal professional privilege.

Commercial interests

Section 43 of the FIA exempts information if it constitutes a trade secret and information that could prejudice the commercial interests of any person, including the public authority holding the information.

Absolute exemptions – no duty to consider the public interest

Certain categories of information can be withheld by public authority absolutely without having to consider whether disclosure is in the public interest. Public authorities are under no obligation to confirm or deny that they hold such information if it is subject to absolute exemption.

Information accessible by the applicant by other means

Section 21 of the FIA exempts information if it is reasonably accessible to the applicant by other means – for example, books and pamphlets published by a public authority, or birth, marriage and death certificates.

Information available by virtue of other legislation or through a voluntary system is deemed to be reasonably accessible to the applicant and is therefore exempt, even if it is only available on payment of a fee. However, information that is available on inspection will only be exempt under this section if it is reasonably accessible to the applicant.

Information supplied by, or relating to, bodies dealing with security matters

Section 23 of the FIA exempts information directly or indirectly supplied by, or relating to, certain bodies dealing with security matters as specified in Sections 23(3) and (4) of the FIA. The FIA provides a certification process. A certificate signed by a Minister of the Crown is conclusive of proof that the exemption is justified. There is a separate appeals mechanism against such certificates.

Court records

Section 32 of the FIA exempts information that is held, recorded or obtained by a public authority contained in documents:

- Filed with, or placed in the custody of, a court ('court' is defined in Section 32(4) of the Act in the same terms as Section 19 of the Contempt of Court Act 1981, and therefore includes tribunals and other bodies exercising the judicial powers of the State, as well as coroners' courts).

- Served upon, or by, the public authority for the purposes of such proceedings.
- Which a court has created for the purpose of such proceedings for example bench memoranda.

This exemption does not apply to any other information held by a public authority, even though the information may relate to, and be deployed in connection with, court proceedings.

Parliamentary privilege

Section 34 of the FIA exempts information if disclosure would infringe the privileges of either House of Parliament. The Speaker of the House of Commons and the Clerk of the Parliaments in the House of Lords must sign certificates as conclusive evidence that the exemption applies.

Prejudice to effective conduct of public affairs

Section 36 of the FIA exempts information held by the House of Commons and the House of Lords which is not exempt by virtue of Section 35 of the Act concerning the formulation of government policy regardless of public interest if the Speaker of the House of Commons or the Clerk of the Parliaments in the House of Lords signs a certificate stating that in his reasonable opinion disclosure could:

- Prejudice the maintenance of the convention of collective ministerial responsibility
- Prejudice the work of the Executive Committee of the Northern Ireland Assembly or the National Assembly for Wales
- Inhibit the free and frank provision of advice or exchange of views
- Otherwise prejudice the effective conduct of public affairs.

Personal information

Under Section 40 of the FIA a public authority can refuse to disclose personal information without considering the public interest if the information relates to the applicant himself. This is because the information is covered by the provisions of the Data Protection Act 1998. A public authority can also refuse to disclose personal information without considering the public interest if the information concerns a third party and disclosure would breach one of the data protection principles set out in Data Protection Act 1998, Schedule 1.

14.3.5 Applications for information

Application

There is no compulsory form. However, the request must be in writing. It can be made by email. Any individual or organization may request information, regardless of the purpose of the application. Although an applicant will have to identify himself for the purpose of the application, the identity of the applicant is otherwise of no concern to a public authority except in the case of vexatious or repeated requests.

Where possible, the information must be provided by the public authority to the applicant in the manner requested. This may be in the form of a copy or a summary. The applicant may ask to inspect the record itself.

Delay

A response must be provided promptly and in any event within 20 working days or another period as provided for under regulations to be no longer than 60 working days. If a fee is charged, the period of 20 working days will be extended by up to three months until the fee is paid.

Where a public authority is not able to reach a decision in respect of the public interest in disclosure within 20 working days, it must reach a decision within a reasonable period. In such circumstances, the authority is still required to issue a notice to the application that an exemption applies within the 20 working days limit.

A public authority may ask for further information it reasonably requires in order to identify and locate the information requested.

Fees

A fee may be charged for dealing with the request. The FIA provides that the Secretary of State may make regulations governing fees to be charged by authorities which will be set out in the Secretary of State's *Fees Regulations*. Public authorities must notify the applicant that a fee is payable and that it is exempt from having to disclose information until the fee has been paid.

14.3.6 Enforcement

The FIA will be enforced by the newly established Information Commissioner. The Information Commissioner also issues practice recommendations on compliance with the FIA and the codes issued under it. A newly established Information Tribunal, formerly the Data Protection Tribunal, will oversee the decisions of the Information Commissioner.

The Information Commissioner will oversee the FIA, as well as the Data Protection Act 1998. In the future, the Data Protection Commissioner will therefore become the Information Commissioner. Because the FIA and the Data Protection Act 1998 both relate to information policy, this double supervisory role should allow the Information Commissioner to provide a coherent approach to the handling of and access to information.

An applicant who is not given access information to the information requested from a public authority must first follow the public authority's complaints procedure. If the applicant is still dissatisfied, he may apply to the Information Commissioner. The Information Commissioner is required to make a decision unless the applicant:

- Has not exhausted the authority's own complaints system
- Has delayed too long before complaining
- Is vexatious or frivolous
- Withdraws or abandons the complaint.

Following his decision, the Information Commissioner may serve one or more types of notice.

Decision notice

Under Section 50 of the FIA the Information Commissioner may issue a decision notice. A decision notice states that the Information Commissioner has made a decision concerning the complaint, and sets out steps the applicant or the public authority must follow in order to comply with the FIA.

Information notice

Under Section 51 of the FIA the Information Commissioner may serve an information notice. An information notice enables the Information Commissioner to obtain the information from a public authority, including unrecorded information he requires in order to deal with a complaint or to reach a determination on whether an authority has complied with the FIA. The Information Commissioner can specify the time for the authority to comply with the request and the form in which the information should be provided.

Enforcement notice

Under Section 52 of the FIA the Information Commissioner may serve an enforcement notice on a public authority if the public authority has failed to comply with any of the requirements of the FIA. The notice requires the authority to take such steps within a specified time as may be specified in order to comply with the requirements of the FIA. For example, the notice can require the disclosure of certain information in the public interest.

When serving a notice, the Information Commissioner must explain the appeals mechanism. Notices can be appealed to the Information Tribunal. The decision of the Information Tribunal can be appealed to the High Court.

Under Section 53 of the FIA, notices are subject to 'executive override'. This means that a Cabinet Minister may sign a ministerial certificate, which overrides the Information Commissioner's notice. In order to obtain executive override of a notice, a public authority must obtain a certificate from the minister within 20 days of receipt of the notice. There is no right of appeal against a ministerial certificate.

15 Official Secrets

John Wadham

15.1 Introduction

Sections 1 and 2 of the Official Secrets Act ('OSA') 1911 were rushed through Parliament in just one day, amidst the widespread public hysteria over national security that dominated the period leading up to the First World War. It is perhaps not surprising, given the speed and circumstances in which the Official Secrets Act found its way on to the statute books, that both sections attracted a great deal of criticism over the years. In particular, Section 2 was the focus of regular and damning attacks from judges, politicians and the media. In the 1970s the Franks Committee recommended its abolition after three defendants were acquitted in a case that became known as the 'ABC' case, involving the publication of an army document in the *Sunday Telegraph*.

Recognizing the force of these attacks, the government published a White Paper in July 1988 setting out its proposals for the reform of Section 2. Based upon these proposals, the Official Secrets Act 1989 received the Royal Assent some 10 months later, although Section 1 of the 1911 OSA remains in force.

Section 1 of the 1911 OSA provides for the offence of 'espionage'. Section 2 of the 1989 OSA provides for offences relating to the specific disclosure of official information.

The restriction of freedom of expression by the OSA 1911 and the OSA 1989 is considered to be justified in order to protect national security. However, it has been said that:

> Inconvenient or embarrassing revelations, whether for the Security Services, or for public authorities, should not be suppressed. Legal proceedings directed towards the seizure of the working papers of an individual journalist, or the premises of a newspaper or television programme publishing his or her reports, or the threat of such proceedings, tends to inhibit discussion.
> *(R (on the application of Bright) v Central Criminal Court (2000))*

The government also frequently brings actions for breach of confidence as an effective alternative to a prosecution under the Official Secrets Acts. Breach of confidence is considered at Chapter 6.

15.2 Section 1 of the Official Secrets Act 1911: Spying

15.2.1 General principles

Section 1 of the 1911 OSA states:

> If any person for any purpose prejudicial to the safety or interests of the State:
>
> (a) approaches, inspects, passes over or is in the neighbourhood of, or enters any prohibited place within the meaning of this Act, or
>
> (b) makes any sketch, plan, model or note which is calculated to be or might be or is intended to be directly or indirectly useful to an enemy, or
>
> (c) obtains, collects, records or publishes or communicates to any other person any secret official code word or pass word, or any sketch, plan, model, article or note, or other document or information which is calculated to be, or might be, or is intended to be directly or indirectly useful to an enemy . . .
>
> . . . [he] shall be guilty of an offence.

The maximum sentence is 14 years' imprisonment. The meaning of 'prohibited place' is set out at extreme length in Section 3 of the 1911 OSA. It effectively includes every government and military building, however insignificant, as well as all means of communications (for example roads and railways) and essential services (for example gas and electricity stations).

15.2.2 Areas of risk for the media

As far as the media are concerned, the most likely area of danger in Section 1 is Section 1(c), which concerns obtaining or communicating secrets.

However, the prosecution in any trial for an offence under this section would be required to establish 'a purpose prejudicial to the interests of the state'.

In 1978, charges under Section 1(c) were brought against two journalists, Duncan Campbell and Crispin Aubrey, and a former soldier, John Berry, in the 'ABC' case. Information was published in the magazine *Time Out* concerning signals intelligence and defence installations. The prosecution alleged that the publication of the information in the magazine was for a 'purpose prejudicial to the interests of the state'.

On the fifteenth day of the trial, the judge made it known that he considered the charges to be 'oppressive'. The following morning the charges were withdrawn on the instructions of the Attorney General. However, the judge did not close the door on future prosecutions against the media:

> I find it impossible to say that Section 1 can only be applied to cases of spying or sabotage.

However, he suggested that Section 1 charges should be brought only in the clearest and most serious cases.

Since the ABC case, there have been no further prosecutions against members of the media. In recent years, the government has increasingly relied on the civil remedy of breach of confidence to prevent the media communicating allegedly secret material, for example the *Crossman Diaries* and *Spycatcher* litigation (see Chapter 6). However, that does not mean that the media should discount the risk of prosecution under Section 1 of the 1911 OSA. There is always a risk of prosecution if information is published which is considered to be for a 'purpose prejudicial to the interests of the state'.

15.3 The Official Secrets Act 1989: specific disclosure of official information

15.3.1 Objectives of the 1989 Official Secrets Act

The 1989 OSA was introduced to replace Section 2 of the 1911 OSA, which, during its 80-odd years of life, had probably been the subject of more criticism than any other law on the statute book. It was the generality of Section 2 that the Franks Committee and other critics found most objectionable. Section 2 of the 1911 OSA penalized the disclosure of any information obtained by a person holding office under the Crown or by a government contractor in the course of his duties, no matter how trivial the information, and irrespective of the harm likely to arise from its disclosure.

According to the 1988 White Paper, the central objective of the government's new legislation was to provide a better definition of when the disclosure of official information is an offence:

> The objective of the Government's proposals is to narrow the scope of the present law so that the limited range of circumstances in which the unauthorized disclosure of official information needs to be criminal is clearly defined. This will ensure that no one need be in doubt in what circumstance he would be liable to prosecution, and enable the courts to enforce the law without any overdue burden of proof being placed either on the defence or the prosecution.

The principal yardstick adopted to justify the imposition of criminal sanctions for wrongful disclosure is the degree of harm to the public interest that may result. It will therefore not be enough that disclosure is undesirable, a betrayal of trust, or an embarrassment to the government. Where the harm arising from improper disclosure is not sufficient to warrant recourse to the criminal law, the government said in the White Paper that it would be content to rely upon the Civil Service disciplinary code or upon the civil law of confidence to protect its interests.

15.3.2 General principles

The criminal law in relation to official secrets under the 1989 OSA now applies to six clearly defined categories of information only. Other classes of official information, such as Cabinet documents and advice to ministers, will not be specifically protected. The White Paper stated:

> Documents of this kind will be protected by the proposals if their subject matter merits it, but their coverage *en bloc* would fuel suspicions that information was being protected by the criminal law merely for fear of political embarrassment.

Under the 1989 OSA, liability for disclosure falls on those who improperly disclose information in one of the six categories provided for in Sections 1 to 6 of the 1989 OSA 'knowing or having good reason to know that to do so is likely to harm the public interest'. With the exception of Section 1, which regulates security and intelligence matters, and Section 4, which regulates special investigation powers, the prosecution also has to prove that the disclosure was in fact damaging. Section 5 of the 1989 OSA is most relevant to the media. The prosecution has to prove that the person who disclosed the information knew that harm to the public interest was likely to result. The question is ultimately one for the jury.

The possible defence of disclosure in the public interest was rejected by the legislators and is not found in the 1989 OSA. It was considered that the question of criminality should not depend on motivation but instead on the nature and degree of harm caused by the defendant. The defence of disclosure after some prior publication was also rejected because it was said that newspaper or broadcast stories may carry little weight in themselves but could be damaging if they were confirmed by a government official. However, in *R v Shayler (2001)* the Court of Appeal suggested that if the material was already in the public domain, a prosecution should not ordinarily be authorized.

The usual criminal law concepts apply to the 1989 OSA. For example, a member of the media who incited, encouraged or paid a government official to disclose secrets might also be prosecuted for the offence of inciting or aiding and abetting an offence under Section 1 of the 1989 OSA, even if the disclosure never resulted in publication. A member of the media found guilty of such an offence would be in the same position as the government official, and would not have recourse to the statutory defence under Section 5 of the 1989 OSA. However, in *R v Shayler (2001)* the Court of Appeal suggested that:

> It would have to be an extreme case on the facts for a prosecution for incitement to be justified having regard to the structure of the [1989 Act] which attaches such importance to the status of the individual charged.

In *R v Shayler (2001)* the Court of Appeal also confirmed that the usual defence of 'necessity' applies to the 1989 OSA. It will not be a criminal offence if a disclosure is necessary to prevent:

> . . . the imminent (if not immediate) threats to the life and limb of members of the general public as a result of the security services' alleged abuses and blunders.

However, there must be a close nexus between the disclosure and possible injury to members of the public.

The maximum penalty under the 1989 OSA is two years' imprisonment. A number of civil servants, police officers and military personnel have been convicted and have received sentences of up to one year in prison. No journalist or member of the media has ever been convicted under the 1989 OSA.

Tony Geraghty, the author of *The Irish War*, was prosecuted under the 1989 OSA, but before the case proceeded to trial the Attorney General discontinued the prosecution. No reasons were given. The evidence against Geraghty was as strong (or as weak) as the evidence against Nigel Wylde, a computer consultant employed by the Ministry of Defence, who was prosecuted for supplying him with information. It has to be assumed that the prosecution was discontinued because the Attorney General did not want to be seen to continue a prosecution against an author in the face of increasing criticism from others in the media. The prosecution of Nigel Wylde was subsequently discontinued just before his trial when Duncan Campbell, the 'C' in the 'ABC' case, gave expert evidence on behalf of the defence team that all the information was already in the public domain.

15.3.3 Impact of the Human Rights Act 1998

The Human Rights Act 1998 may change the way the 1989 OSA is interpreted. The Human Rights Act 1998 incorporates the Article 10 European Convention on Human Rights right to freedom of expression into English law. Any interference with the Article 10 freedom of expression can only be justified if the interference is regulated by law, is a 'proportionate' response, and is for the purpose of:

> . . . national security, territorial integrity or public safety, for the prevention of disorder or crime, for the protection of health or morals, for the protection of the reputation or rights of others, for preventing the disclosure of information received in confidence, or for maintaining the authority and impartiality of the judiciary.
>
> (Article 10(2))

As a result, the 1989 OSA cannot create a criminal offence that restricts freedom of expression unless it is a proportionate response to any damage caused or any threat to national security. When considering whether an offence has been committed, the court must weigh up the damage caused against the public interest in disclosure. It seems unlikely that the offence under Section 1 of the 1989 OSA will satisfy this balancing test because of the absence of the requirement of proof of damage.

However, in *R v Shayler (2001)* the Court of Appeal held that Section 1 and Section 4 of the 1989 OSA were compatible with Article 10. In that case, it was alleged that David Shayler, who worked for MI5, had disclosed information about his previous work to the *Mail on Sunday*. A series of stories was published by the newspaper in August 1997. Shayler left for Europe and spent four months in prison in France, but the attempt to extradite him failed. He returned to England voluntarily in August 2000, where he was arrested and prosecuted. Although both he and the newspaper were subject to an injunction and a claim for damages, the journalists were never arrested or prosecuted.

Although the court accepted that it was necessary to scrutinize the reason for imposing criminal sanctions on the disclosure of information, it held that Shayler could not rely on the public interest in disclosure. The court took the view that the alternative remedies available to Shayler, including disclosing malpractice to the police, meant that disclosure to the press was not necessary for the purposes of Article 10. At the time of writing, Shayler is awaiting judgment from the House of Lords.

15.3.4 Protected categories of information

The six areas of information covered by the 1989 OSA are:

1. Security and intelligence matters
2. Defence
3. International relations
4. Information useful to criminals
5. Interception and phone-tapping
6. Information entrusted in confidence to other states or international organizations.

The 1989 OSA broadly applies to three categories of person who has disclosed information:

1. Those in the security and intelligence services whose primary function is to keep secrets (MI5, MI6 and GCHQ)
2. Crown servants and government contractors who from time to time deal with sensitive information
3. Those who have received protected information from someone who belongs to either of the first two categories – in other words someone not connected to the government, for example the media.

In order to establish criminality Sections 1 to 6 of the 1989 OSA lay down a complicated sliding scale of culpability, which is contingent upon which of the three categories the disclosure falls into. For example, in the case of a member of the security services, all the prosecution would need to prove is the disclosure itself. In the case of a crown servant or government contractor, the prosecution needs to prove that the disclosure was, or was likely to be, damaging. In the case of a person in the third category, the prosecution must establish that he was aware of the protected nature of the information disclosed, knew that it came from a 'classified' source, and envisaged that the disclosure was or would be damaging. This requires the greatest amount of evidence.

It can be seen that the first four Sections of the 1989 OSA cover only Crown or government employees and contractors. Section 5 has direct application to journalists or anybody else who, having received the sort of information or material described in Sections 1 to 4, goes on to make unlawful and damaging disclosure of it.

In the future, each of these provisions must be interpreted in accordance with the provisions of the Human Rights Act 1998.

Section 1: Security and intelligence matters

Section 1 applies to 'any information, document or other article relating to security or intelligence' which is disclosed without lawful authority by any person who is or has been:

- A member of the security or intelligence services, or a person who has been notified by a Minister of the Crown that he is subject to Section 1 as if he were a member of those services
- A Crown servant or government contractor.

An unauthorized disclosure by a person within the first category is automatically an offence. The only available defence (with the exception of 'necessity', see part 15.3.2 above) is to establish that the accused 'did not know and had no reasonable cause to believe' that the material disclosed related to security or intelligence. This defence will be available only infrequently.

Those within the second category will commit an offence if the unauthorized disclosure is 'damaging' within the meaning of the 1989 OSA, in other words if a person causes or is likely to cause damage to the work of, or any part of, the security and intelligence services. As with the first category, it is a defence for the accused to prove that he did not know or have reasonable cause to believe that the information related to security or intelligence. It is also a defence for the accused to show that he neither knew nor had reasonable cause to know that the disclosure would be damaging.

Section 2: Defence

This section only applies to Crown servants and government contractors, both past and present. As with security and intelligence, unauthorized disclosure of any information, document or other article 'relating to defence' is a criminal offence if it is damaging.

In this context, a disclosure is 'damaging' if it:

- Damages the capability of the armed forces
- Leads to loss of life or injury to members of the armed services
- Leads to serious damage to the equipment or installations of the armed forces
- Endangers the interests of the United Kingdom abroad
- Relates to information that, if disclosed without authority, is likely to have any of the above effects.

Information 'related to defence' is given a very wide definition, and includes the size, development, operations and training of the armed forces, the development and production of weapons and other equipment, military planning, and defence policy and strategy.

Again, it is a defence for the accused under Section 2 to prove that he did not know or have reasonable cause to believe either that the information related to defence or that the disclosure would be damaging.

Section 3: International relations

Like Section 2, Section 3 applies only to present or former Crown servants or government contractors who make damaging disclosures. In this case, the protected material is any information, document or other article either relating to international relations or which is both confidential and was obtained from a foreign state or an international organization.

The disclosure will be 'damaging' if it:

- Endangers the interests of the United Kingdom abroad
- Seriously obstructs the promotion or protection by the United Kingdom of those interests
- Endangers the safety of British citizens abroad
- Relates to information that, if disclosed without authority, would be likely to have any of the above effects.

'International relations' is defined as the relations between states and/or international organizations, and includes any matter concerning a foreign state or international organization that is capable of affecting the United Kingdom's foreign affairs.

Once again, the accused will escape liability upon proof that he neither knew nor had reasonable cause to believe that the information was protected under this Section or that the disclosure would be damaging.

Section 4: Crime and special investigation powers

Information of use to criminals and information about telephone-taps and other forms of interception are covered by Section 4. The Section applies only to persons who are, or have been, Crown servants or government contractors.

In relation to the general 'of use to criminals' category, criminal liability is incurred if the unauthorized disclosure:

- Results in the commission of an offence
- Facilitates an escape from legal custody, or prejudices the safekeeping of persons in legal custody
- Impedes the prevention or detection of offences or the apprehension or prosecution of suspected offenders
- Is likely to have any of the above consequences.

A person charged with unlawful disclosure of such information will establish a valid defence if he can prove that he neither knew nor had reasonable cause to believe that the disclosure would have any such effect.

The second leg of Section 4 makes it an offence to disclose without lawful authority:

- Any information obtained through a telephone-tap or other form of interception authorized by a warrant issued under the Regulation of Investigatory Powers Act 2000
- Any information obtained through actions that are authorized by a warrant issued under Section 3 of the Security Service Act 1989
- Any information, document or other article relating to the telephone-tap or other form of interception under either of the two Acts above.

In order to protect both the effectiveness of the interception and the security of that which is being intercepted, the OSA 1989 protects the practice – in other words the person who is being 'bugged' and how the person is being bugged – as well as the content.

Alongside security and intelligence matters, this class of information is given the highest level of protection by the 1989 OSA. In order to secure a conviction, the prosecution need prove only an unauthorized disclosure (but see 'necessity' at part 15.3.2 above). The only defence then available to the accused is that he did not know and had no reasonable cause to believe that the information disclosed fell within the protected category.

Section 5: Information resulting from unauthorized disclosure

The first four Sections of the 1989 OSA are aimed at those employed by or contracted to the crown or the government. It is considered to be a fundamental principle of state and military security that public servants entrusted with sensitive information honour the commitment to confidentiality and/or secrecy that is a part of their contract of employment. Sections 1 to 4 serve, where appropriate, to add the sanction of the criminal law to that contractual commitment.

However, where protected information has been passed on without authority and used to the detriment of the state, the criminal sanction extends beyond the public servant who breached security to the person who received the information. For such a person, a specific offence is created by Section 5 of the 1989 OSA. In addition, it is possible to be charged with inciting or aiding and abetting an offence under Section 1 to 4 of the 1989 OSA.

Section 5 directly impacts on those in the media. It is an offence for any person to disclose without lawful authority any information, document or other article that:

- Falls within the protected classes to which Sections 1 to 4 apply
- Has come into his possession as a result of unauthorized disclosure by those persons to whom Sections 1 to 4 apply
- Has come into his possession as a result of unauthorized disclosure by someone to whom the information was properly entrusted in confidence by a Section 1 to 4 person.

In order to secure a conviction under Section 5, the burden of proof imposed upon the prosecution is of the highest order. It must be proved that the disclosure was damaging within the meaning laid down in the other Sections of the 1989 OSA and that the accused person disclosed the information knowing or having reasonable cause to believe that:

- It fell within the protected categories described in Sections 1 to 4
- It had come into his or her possession as a result of an unauthorized disclosure as described in the second or third categories above
- The disclosure would be damaging.

Section 6: Information entrusted in confidence to other states or international organizations

Section 3 protects confidential information obtained from a foreign state or international organization. Section 6 affords protection to information travelling in the opposite direction – in other words, sensitive material that the United Kingdom entrusts in confidence to the governments or government departments of other countries.

Like Section 5, Section 6 also impacts upon those outside government service. It can therefore be used against the media. In one respect it is wider than Section 5, since for the offence to be committed it is not necessary that the information came from a Crown servant or government contractor.

Section 6 makes it an offence for a person to make a damaging disclosure without lawful authority of any information, document or other article that:

- '. . . relates to security or intelligence, defence or international relations'
- Has been communicated in confidence by or on behalf of the United Kingdom to another state or to an international organization.

The prosecution must prove that:

- The information came into the accused's possession without the authority of the relevant foreign state or international organization to whom it was entrusted and without that state or international organization having previously made it available to the public

- The accused knew or had reasonable cause to know that the information fell within the protected classes set out in the categories above and that the disclosure would be damaging.

15.3.5 Definitions

For the purpose of Section 6, the terms 'damaging', 'security or intelligence', 'defence' and 'international relations' have the same meanings as in Sections 1 to 3 of the 1989 OSA.

15.3.6 Official direction

Under Section 8 of the 1989 OSA, the authorities can issue an 'official direction' for the return of any document or other article that is covered by Sections 1 to 6. Failure to comply with such a direction is a criminal offence.

15.4 The Defence Advisory Notice system

Apart from the formal system of secrecy enforcement operated through the Official Secrets Act 1911 and the Official Secrets Act 1989, the government and the media have an alternative voluntary system of dealing with sensitive information relating to national security in the form of the Defence, Press and Broadcasting Advisory Committee and 'Defence Advisory Notices', or DA Notices, previously known as D-notices.

The Defence, Press and Broadcasting Advisory Committee is chaired by the Permanent Under Secretary of State for Defence. It consists of members representing the Home Office, the Ministry of Defence and the Foreign and Commonwealth Office, as well as 13 members nominated by the media. It meets about twice a year to review existing DA Notices.

DA Notices are the method by which the Government advises the media that the publication of a certain kind of information would be damaging to the national interest or put lives at risk. The Defence, Press and Broadcasting Advisory Committee circulates DA Notices in the form of a formal letter to newspaper editors and their equivalents in television and radio broadcasting. There are currently five DA Notices in place, which are mostly concerned with defence plans, equipment and installations, and security or intelligence. The text of the DA Notices can be found on the Defence, Press and Broadcasting Advisory Committee's web site.[1] DA Notices do not have the force of law, and prosecutions do not usually follow from their breach.

[1]The web site can be found at www.dnotice.org.uk.

The secretary of the Defence, Press and Broadcasting Advisory Committee can also be contacted voluntarily by a member of the media who wishes to check that his stories will not damage national security. Although this can be a sensible arrangement, it suffers from two potential drawbacks. The journalist or broadcaster may feel that the process constitutes a form of vetting by the government. Furthermore, once the secretary of the Defence, Press and Broadcasting Advisory Committee has had sight of the story, the risk of a government injunction to stop the publication increases. However the Defence, Press and Broadcasting Advisory Committee's web site states:

> All discussions between the media and the Secretary are carried out in confidence and government departments do not subsequently initiate police or legal action unless they have information from some other source . . .

> . . . The Secretary therefore makes every effort to point out to the media any material which he thinks might be in breach of an injunction or which might be an offence under some Act, but he is not himself a legal expert and therefore sometimes advises consulting the Treasury Solicitor for expert legal advice in order to head off possible police or legal action.

In some instances the Secretary will himself contact journalists, broadcasters, authors or publishers to offer advice, or the Defence, Press and Broadcasting Advisory Committee will issue a specific notice if it is thought that published material may threaten or damage national security. None have been issued in recent years.

16 Parliamentary Proceedings and Elections

Tom Cassels and Rebecca Handler

16.1 Introduction

Members of Parliament and the proceedings of Parliament are cloaked with certain traditional rights and privileges that are aimed at safeguarding the freedom and independence of the individuals involved and the dignity of the institution. Foremost among these privileges are:

- Complete freedom of speech or 'absolute privilege', which protects debates and official proceedings in the House of Commons and the House of Lords
- The power of each House to regulate its own procedures, including the power to punish members and outsiders for breach of privilege known as 'contempt of Parliament'.

The freedom of members of Parliament to speak on any matter without the fear of legal consequence extends to reports of Parliamentary proceedings, and is protected by Article 9 of the Bill of Rights 1688:

> The freedom of speech and debates or proceedings in Parliament ought not to be impeached or questioned in any court or place out of Parliament.

Fair and accurate reports of Parliamentary proceedings and extracts from Parliamentary papers reported in the broadcast media or in newspapers are subject to 'qualified privilege'. This means that the motives behind the publication can be examined. Chapter 1 deals with defamation and the public policy defences of absolute privilege and qualified privilege.

Political elections have not always been the largely civilized affairs they are today. Widespread corruption and malpractice used to be regular features of Parliamentary elections. To stamp out such tendencies, detailed laws were introduced to regulate and control every aspect of electioneering. Election campaigns are now heavily regulated to prevent corruption and malpractice. While most of the regulation is aimed at controlling the actions of direct participants in elections, such as voters, candidates and organizers, the power of the media to influence the electoral process is acknowledged by regulation under the Representation of the People Act 1983 in the areas of false statements about candidates and election expenses.

16.2 Parliamentary proceedings

16.2.1 Privilege

Statements made in the course of proceedings in Parliament or in a committee of either House are absolutely privileged against civil actions. Members of Parliament may not be sued for libel in respect of any defamatory allegation or imputation made during official Parliamentary proceedings.

There are, of course, numerous examples of MPs who have used the absolute privilege afforded to them to 'punish the unpunishable' or make allegations which, if said in public outside the chamber of the House of Commons, would probably result in an action for defamation. The spies Kim Philby and Anthony Blunt were exposed by being named in the House of Commons. The MP Geoffrey Dickens named suspected sex offenders on a number of occasions in the House of Commons.

However, the media should take care when reporting such accusations. The publication of fair and accurate accounts of Parliamentary debates and extracts from Parliamentary papers is protected only by qualified privilege. The media can report a potentially defamatory statement made during proceedings in Parliament as long as the report is fair and accurate. However, if the claimant can show that the report was made maliciously, qualified privilege will be no defence.

Parliamentary privilege may be invoked to prevent the publication of evidence, including the publication of draft reports, taken by a Select Committee before it has been reported to the House in cases where publication has not been authorized by the Select Committee or, if it is no longer in existence, by the Speaker.

There is some doubt as to whether there is privilege against criminal prosecution for statements made in Parliament. The Contempt of Court Act 1981 expressly allows a defence for reports of judicial proceedings but omits a similar provision in respect of Parliamentary proceedings. On the other hand, the statutory offence of inciting racial hatred specifically excludes from prosecution anything said in Parliament.

16.2.2 Contempt

Contempt of Parliament is any act or words that disrupt or impede the proper working of either House or disrupt, intimidate or wrongly influence MPs in discharge of their duty.

There is no statutory definition of what will constitute contempt of Parliament. Between 1998 and 2000, Neil Hamilton and Mohammed Al-Fayed were embroiled in a high profile dispute, following allegations that Hamilton had corruptly demanded and accepted from Al-Fayed various benefits in return for tabling parliamentary questions. This became known as the 'Cash for Questions' affair (*Hamilton v Al-Fayed (1999); Hamilton v Al-Fayed (2000)*). As a result, a Joint Committee was set up to examine the question of Parliamentary privilege. The Joint Committee's report concluded that contempt should be defined by statute because the possible penal sanctions made it important for the elements of contempt and the possible punishments to be clearly understood. The report also recommended that Parliament's power to punish those in contempt of Parliament should be transferred to the court, in order to achieve the clarity of procedure and judgment that it currently lacks (*House of Lords Paper 43–1 (1998–1999)*).

However, the recommendations of the Joint Committee have not yet been implemented. It is only possible to assess what can and cannot be published by reference to previous examples.

Misbehaviour

Conduct that disrupts proceedings, for example shouting or throwing things from the strangers' gallery, is punishable as contempt.

Disrupting, obstructing or influencing

This is the broadest category of contempt, and encompasses any conduct that has a tendency to impede the proper functioning of either House or its members.

- In 1957, during the aftermath of the Suez crisis, the *Sunday Express* and *Romford Recorder* published articles that suggested that MPs were gaining improper advantages in relation to the rationing of petrol. Both editors were summoned to the House of Commons and reprimanded for contempt.
- In 1947, Gerry Allighan MP was expelled from the House of Commons for contempt after writing an article alleging that members were receiving payments for passing confidential information about Parliamentary business to journalists. It subsequently emerged that Allighan himself was one of those who had been 'leaking' material.
- In 1957, the *Sunday Graphic*, incensed at a Parliamentary question tabled by Arthur Lewis MP which suggested that money raised for the Hungarian Relief Fund should go to help Egyptian victims of the Suez bombing campaign, published his home telephone number and invited its readers to ring him. It was held to be a contempt.

Like judges, MPs are nowadays more resilient and accustomed to strident criticism than they used to be. It is highly unlikely that robust but honest attacks by the media on Parliament or its Members would now lead to findings of contempt, although action might easily be taken over reports which appear to be malicious. A Member of Parliament may waive absolute privilege for the purposes of defamation proceedings (*Hamilton v Al-Fayed (1999)*).

Either House may consider a report of its proceedings in a newspaper or other publication to be a breach of its privilege if it is obviously inaccurate or untrue. Because such conduct may disrupt, obstruct or influence the functioning of Parliament, it may be punishable as contempt.

Improper disclosure and breach of embargo

Action for contempt of Parliament is most frequently seen in relation to improper disclosure and breach of embargo, where liability for contempt has arisen after the publication of 'leaked' details of confidential Parliamentary business.

- In 1967, Tam Dalyell MP was reprimanded for disclosing to the *Observer* details of evidence given to a Select Committee of the House of Commons that was investigating chemical warfare research at Porton Down
- In 1972, the *Daily Mail* revealed advance information about proposed increases in the civil list. It was held to be in contempt
- In 1975, the *Economist* published material from a leaked Select Committee report. It was held to be in contempt.

16.2.3 Procedure

In cases of suspected breach of privilege or contempt, the matter is first referred by an individual MP to the Speaker for a ruling on whether there is a *prima facie* case. If the Speaker rules that there is a case to answer, the issue is placed before the all-party Committee of Privileges.

After private deliberations, during which the accused and/or witnesses may be called but otherwise have no right to be present, the Committee decides whether a contempt has occurred. If the Committee concludes that a contempt has occurred, the offender is reported to a sitting of the whole House with a recommendation as to punishment.

The guilty party may be reprimanded, banished, suspended from Parliament or imprisoned.

16.3 Elections

16.3.1 False statements about candidates

Section 106 of the Representation of the People Act 1983 makes it an offence for:

> Any person who . . . before or during an election, for the purpose of affecting the return of any candidate at the election, makes or publishes any false statement of fact in relation to the personal conduct or character of the candidate . . . unless he can show that he had reasonable grounds for believing, and did believe the statement to be true.

The offence may be committed by the maker of a false statement or by anyone (for example, a newspaper, television or radio station) who publishes it.

There are four elements that need to be proved by the prosecution:

1. The statement was one of fact rather than opinion
2. It referred to the personal character or dealings of an individual candidate
3. It was politically motivated and was made in order to affect the chances of the candidate being elected, and
4. It was false.

Mere falsity is sufficient. The statement does not have to be false *and* damaging, although it is unlikely that any candidate would take action in respect of a statement that he did not consider to be damaging in some respect. In this respect, the law places election candidates in a more favourable position than other victims of untruths. In an action for defamation it is necessary to establish defamation as well as falsity in order to stand any chance of obtaining an injunction.

Even if the jury is satisfied that all four elements exist, the maker or publisher of the false statement has a defence to the charge if he can establish that at the relevant time he believed the statement to be true and had reasonable grounds for that belief.

Section 106 provides that an injunction may be granted by the High Court or County Court against the maker of such a false statement, preventing them from repeating a 'false statement of a similar character about a candidate'.

Section 10 of the Defamation Act 1952, which remains in force under the Defamation Act 1996, specifically excludes 'defamatory statements published by, or on behalf of, a candidate in any election to a local government authority or to Parliament' from the protection of the defence of qualified privilege.

16.3.2 Election expenses

The provision and payment of expenses incurred by an election candidate is strictly controlled by law. Sections 72 to 76 of the Representation of the People Act 1983 state that payment of all election expenses must be made through the candidate's election agent. Section 75 makes it an offence to incur expenses with a view to procuring the election of a Parliamentary or Local Government candidate except with his agent's authorization.

Consequently, it is illegal for well-wishers or supporters of a candidate to advertise in order to enhance his chances of election. However, the law allows media support by editorial comment, publication of a particular candidate's views or disparagement of his opponents as long as it is not paid for.

Similarly, advertising aimed at advancing a particular candidate is not permitted. However, the law allows advertising directed at advancing the general interests of a political party. The following are examples of the distinction:

- In *R v Tronoh Mines Ltd & Others (1952)* it was held that newspaper advertisements condemning the financial policies of the Labour Party, which appeared during an election, were not illegal because they did not relate to any particular constituency. The court ruled that the law:

. . . does not prohibit expenditure, the real purpose or effect of which is general political propaganda, even although that general political propaganda does incidentally assist a particular candidate among others.

- The same conclusion was reached in *The Labour Party v News Group Newspapers (1987)*. An organization calling itself the Committee for a Free Britain had, in the middle of an election campaign, placed anti-Labour Party advertisements, which focused on the views of 'Betty Sheridan from Haringey' and 'Mark Jenks from Mansfield'. The Labour Party sought an injunction to restrain their republication. The judge found that because the particular wording of the advertisements 'only made sense in the national context there was no breach of Section 75 of the Act'.

Where expense is incurred primarily to oppose rather than support a candidate, it will be illegal. In *DPP v Duffield & Another (1976)* and *DPP v Luft & Another (1977)*, money was spent on publicity and literature encouraging people in three individual constituencies not to vote for National Front candidates. The House of Lords confirmed that if the dominant motive is to oppose one candidate, it inevitably follows that expense is intended to secure the election of one or other of his opponents.

16.3.3 Broadcasting controls

Section 93 of the Representation of the People Act 1983 places complicated controls on programmes broadcast during an election that concentrate on a particular constituency.

Candidates are given significant powers to control programmes about their own constituency. Their rights can be summarized as follows:

- Every candidate in the relevant constituency must consent to the transmission of a programme
- All candidates who take an active part in the programme have 'copy control' – in other words, the right to edit in or edit out their own contributions to the broadcast.

The law therefore gives candidates significant powers to control or, if they wish, disrupt programmes about their constituency. However, either because candidates are too busy electioneering or because they are grateful for the opportunity to receive television or radio coverage, there seem to be few major disputes over programme contents.

PART VII
Media Regulation

17 Professional Regulatory Bodies

Tom Cassels

17.1 Introduction

There are numerous occasions where a person has a valid complaint about something that has been published or broadcast about him, but has no recourse to the law. For example, articles can be distressingly inaccurate but not in a way that gives the subject of the story a legal cause of action. There are other occasions where the subject of a feature has a right to sue, but either cannot afford to do so or prefers to avoid the aggravation of litigation.

In such cases an alternative avenue of complaint is provided by the Press Complaints Commission in respect of newspapers, and the Broadcasting Standards Commission, the Independent Television Commission and the Radio Authority in respect of television and radio broadcasts.

Regulatory bodies are often used as mediators in situations where publication of an offending story would be a breach of the regulatory body's relevant code. For example, Princes William and Harry have been treated with respect following the death of the Princess of Wales partly as a result of a request for restraint by Lord Wakeham, the former chairman of the Press Complaints Committee.

The importance of regulatory bodies and their codes of practice is likely to grow as a result of the incorporation into English law of the European Convention on Human Rights Article 8 right to privacy and the Article 10 right to freedom of expression by the Human Rights Act 1998. In addition, Section 12 of the Human Rights Act 1998 requires the court to have regard to the provisions of any relevant privacy code when considering the right to freedom of expression.

17.2 The press: history of self-regulation

For those that believe media excess is a modern phenomenon, a study of the newspaper industry's regulatory history is an enlightening experience. Outrage at the perceived misbehaviour of the press has been with us for as long as newspapers themselves.

At least once every decade since the Second World War, parliamentarians have threatened legislative controls and the industry has responded with tightened self-regulation and resolutions of good behaviour. The first of the post-war parade of professional regulatory bodies came into existence at around the time Queen Elizabeth II was crowned.

When it was established in 1953, the first self-regulatory body of the Press, it must be said, had all the appearances of an 'unwanted' baby. Those who brought it into the world, the proprietors and journalists of the newspaper industry, had spent the previous four years filibustering in the apparent hope that the self-regulatory body called for in 1949 by the first Royal Commission on the Press could be avoided.

However, the climate changed drastically in 1953 when a Private Members' Bill that would have had the effect of imposing outside control was introduced into Parliament. Not for the last time, the newspaper industry reacted swiftly when faced with the threat of statutory regulation. The result was the General Council of the Press.

Although it was enough to fend off Parliamentary interference, the Council, in its early days, was a poor imitation of what the Royal Commission had seen as necessary – i.e. a voluntary body that would administer a 'code of conduct in accordance with the highest professional standards'. Lack of proper funding and the absence of any lay membership on the Council, along with a noticeable absence of enthusiasm from the press itself, made it fairly ineffective.

Reforms in the shape of an independent chairman, increased finances and a 20 per cent lay membership were squeezed out of the industry in 1962 after the second Royal Commission on the Press attacked the Council's poor record and once again raised the threatening spectre of a statutory body of control.

Although the performance of what by then was known as the Press Council improved drastically, the last Royal Commission, which reported in 1977, still found much to criticize. Once again, funding and lay membership were increased. From 1977, the stature of the Council grew year by year, as indeed did the amount of work with which it dealt. Although it stopped short of laying down the comprehensive code of conduct that was suggested by the last Commission, it issued Declarations of Principle on privacy, payments and financial journalism which defined the limits of acceptable behaviour in these important areas.

In the late 1980s, however, a clamour for legislative moves against the Press once again found a large level of support at the Palace of Westminster. Public and parliamentary disquiet had been fed by a stream of complaints about breach of privacy, harassment of individuals and their families, inaccurate reporting and intrusion. Some of the complaints were true and some were false, but their overall effect was to stir the politicians into real action.

In the 1988–1989 Parliamentary Session, two separate Private Members' Bills, one on privacy and the other concerning an enforceable right of reply, won considerable support and made it through the committee stages of the House of Commons.

Early in 1989, with the writing fairly clearly on the wall, the editors of all national newspapers met at the Newspaper Publishers Association in London and emerged with a written declaration that:

> We, having given due consideration to criticism of the Press by Parliament and public, accept the need to improve methods of self-regulation. Accordingly, we declare today our unanimous commitment to a common Code of Practice to safeguard the independence of the Press from threats of official control.

Like Neville Chamberlain, the editors quickly found that 'peace in our time' was not quite so easy. For the Government it was too little, too late.

A few months later, the Secretary of State for National Heritage set up a committee under David Calcutt QC to:

> . . . consider what measures (whether legislative or otherwise) are needed to give further protection to individual privacy from the activities of the Press and improve recourse for the individual citizen.

The Report of the Calcutt Committee on Privacy and Related Matters was published in June 1990. Although it recommended against the introduction of a statutory right of privacy, it effectively placed the press on probation:

> The press should be given one final chance to prove that voluntary self-regulation can be made to work.
>
> *(Paragraph 14.38)*

The government let it be known immediately that it accepted Calcutt's findings. Writing in the *Times* on 22 June 1990, the Home Secretary, David Waddington, stated that the newspaper industry had a 12-month period 'to put its house in order or face tough statutory controls'.

Calcutt recommended that the existing Press Council should be disbanded and, in its place, a Press Complaints Commission should be set up. That Commission should:

- Concentrate on providing an effective means of redress for complaints against the press
- Be given specific duties to consider complaints of unjust or unfair treatment by newspapers or periodicals and of infringement of privacy through published material or the behaviour of reporters
- Publish, monitor and implement a comprehensive code of practice for the guidance of both the press and the public
- Operate a hot-line for complaints on a 24-hour basis
- In certain circumstances, recommend the publication of an apology or a reply in favour of a successful complainant

- Have an independent chairman and no more than 12 members, with smaller complaints committees
- Have clear conciliation and adjudication procedures, with a fast-track procedure for the correction of significant factual errors
- Not operate a waiver of legal rights as a required prerequisite to having a complaint heard.

Finally, Calcutt recommended that:

If the industry wishes to maintain a system of non-statutory self-regulation, it must demonstrate its commitment, in particular by providing the necessary money for setting up and maintaining the Press Complaints Commission.

The industry took the warnings to heart. Within a few months of the Calcutt Report, a Press Standards Board of Finance had been established. It eventually decreed that the Press Complaints Commission should have an annual budget of £1½ million, a fund that, of course, would be provided by the newspaper industry. In its last year of existence, the Press Council's budget was £600 000.

In October 1990, Lord McGregor of Durris, who in 1977 chaired the Third Royal Commission on the Press, was appointed the first Chairman of the proposed Press Complaints Commission.

By mid-December a Code of Practice was issued, and two days after Christmas the names of the Commission's 16 members were announced. They included seven current editors of newspapers or magazines, the executive Vice-Chairman of *Times Newspapers*, a former editor-in-chief of the Press Association, and a former Northern Ireland Secretary.

Public confidence in the effectiveness of press self-regulation was firmly established by 1995. That year, the *News of the World* published a picture of Countess Spencer, the stepmother of the Princess of Wales, in clear breach of the Code of Practice. Rupert Murdoch, whose Fox Corporation owned the *News of the World*, publicly condemned the editor. This condemnation dispelled any doubts in the mind of the public as to whether the Code of Practice was taken seriously by the press. Since then, the public has been able to complain in the confidence that they will be taken seriously by the party against whom they are complaining.

17.3 The Press Complaints Commission

17.3.1 Structure

The cornerstone of the newspaper industry's system of self-regulation is the Press Standards Board of Finance Ltd (Presbof). Presbof was incorporated as the representative body of the entire press in the immediate aftermath of the Calcutt report into privacy and related matters published in June 1990 (see Chapter 8). Its constituent members are the:

- Newspapers Publishers Association
- Newspaper Society
- Periodical Publishers Association
- Scottish Newspapers Publishers Association
- Scottish Daily Newspaper Society.

In other words, all of the trade associations for the newspaper and magazine industry.

The stated purposes of Presbof are to:

- Co-ordinate and promote self-regulation within the industry
- Finance the Press Complaints Commission (the 'PCC')
- Provide a ready means of liaison between the PCC and the industry
- Monitor and review the Code of Practice through a Code Committee.

Below Presbof there exists an Appointments Commission charged with finding and appointing suitable members of the PCC, and a Code Committee consisting almost entirely of editors, the function of which is to review and, if necessary, amend or extend the Code of Practice.

17.3.2 How complaints are dealt with

Figure 17.1 illustrates the step-by-step passage of complaints. At the outset complainants are also told that the PCC will apply the following principles:

- All complaints are judged against the Code of Practice. If there is no *prima facie* breach of the Code, the PCC tells the complainant that it can take the matter no further.
- The objective of the PCC is to achieve a speedy resolution of the grievance. To that end, it will normally deal only with complaints which are lodged within one month of publication of the relevant story or, if the complainant first wrote to the editor, within one month of the editor's reply.
- The PCC will not usually entertain complaints from third parties, in other words anyone not directly involved in the published piece. In such circumstances, however, it frequently writes to those who are concerned in the story asking if they wish to co-operate in the complaint. If not, the matter goes no further. The PCC justifies this principle on the grounds of practicality in that if the subject of the story does not wish to give his or her side of things, the evidence is bound to be one-sided.
- The PCC will not deal with a complaint if litigation in respect of a story is either in progress or about to commence. At the conclusion of the PCC procedure there is, however, nothing to prevent the complainant issuing proceedings.

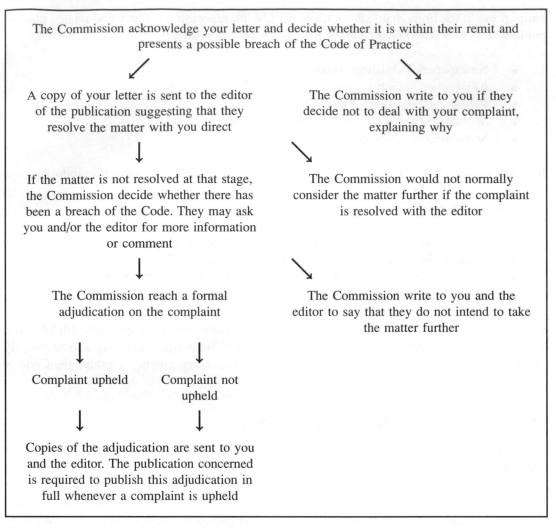

Figure 17.1 How your complaint is dealt with

17.3.3 Code of Practice

All members of the press have a duty to maintain the highest professional and ethical standards. In doing so, they should have regard to the provisions of the Code of Practice and to safeguarding the public's right to receive information.

Editors are responsible for the actions of journalists employed by their publications. They should also satisfy themselves as far as possible that material accepted from non-staff members is obtained in accordance with the Code of Practice.

While recognizing that this involves a substantial element of self-restraint by editors and journalists, it is designed to be acceptable in the context of a system of self-regulation. The Code of Practice applies in the spirit as well as in the letter.

It is the responsibility of editors to co-operate as swiftly as possible with PCC enquiries. Any publication that is criticized by the PCC under one of the following clauses is *duty bound* to print the adjudication that follows in full and with due prominence.

1. Accuracy

1. Newspapers and periodicals should take care not to publish inaccurate, misleading or distorted material.
2. Whenever it is recognized that a significant inaccuracy, misleading statement or distorted report has been published, it should be corrected promptly and with due prominence.
3. An apology should be published whenever appropriate.
4. A newspaper or periodical should always report fairly and accurately the outcome of an action for defamation to which it has been a party.

2. Opportunity to reply

A fair opportunity for reply to inaccuracies should be given to individuals or organizations when reasonably called for.

3. Comment, conjecture and fact

Newspapers, while free to be partisan, should distinguish clearly between comment, conjecture and fact.

4. Privacy

Intrusions and enquiries into an individual's private life without his or her consent, including the use of long-lens photography to take pictures of people on private property without their consent, are not generally acceptable, and publication can only be justified when in the public interest.

Private property is defined as any private residence, together with its garden and outbuildings, but excluding any adjacent fields or parkland. In addition, hotel bedrooms but not other areas in a hotel, and those parts of a hospital or nursing home where patients are treated or accommodated, are included.

5. Listening devices

Unless justified by public interest, journalists should not obtain or publish material obtained by using clandestine listening devices or by intercepting private telephone conversations.

6. Hospitals

1. Journalists or photographers making enquiries at hospitals or similar institutions should identify themselves to a responsible executive and obtain permission before entering non-public areas.

2. The restrictions on intruding into privacy are particularly relevant to enquiries about individuals in hospital or similar institutions.

7. Misrepresentations

1. Journalists should not generally obtain or seek to obtain information or pictures through misrepresentation or subterfuge.
2. Unless in the public interest, documents or photographs should be removed only with the express consent of the owner.
3. Subterfuge can be justified only in the public interest and only when material cannot be obtained by any other means.

8. Harassment

1. Journalists should neither obtain nor seek to obtain information or pictures through intimidation or harassment.
2. Unless their enquiries are in the public interest, journalists should not photograph individuals on private property (as defined in the note to Clause 4) without their consent; should not persist in telephoning or questioning individuals after having been asked to desist; should not remain on their property after having been asked to leave; and should not follow them.
3. It is the responsibility of editors to ensure that these requirements are carried out.

9. Payment for articles

Payment or offers of payment for stories, pictures or information should not be made directly or through agents to witnesses or potential witnesses in current criminal proceedings or to people engaged in crime or to their associates, which includes family, friends, neighbours and colleagues, except where the material concerned ought to be published in the public interest and the payment is necessary for this to be done.

10. Intrusions into grief or shock

In cases involving personal grief or shock, enquiries should be carried out and approaches made with sympathy and discretion.

11. Innocent relatives and friends

Unless it is contrary to the public's right to know, the press should generally avoid identifying relatives or friends of persons convicted or accused of crime.

12. Interviewing or photographing children

1. Journalists should not normally interview or photograph children under the age of 16 on subjects involving the personal welfare of the child in the absence of or without the consent of a parent or other adult who is responsible for the children.
2. Children should not be approached or photographed while at school without the permission of the school authorities.

13. Children in sex cases

1. The press should not, even where the law does not prohibit it, identify children under the age of 16 who are involved in cases concerning sexual offences, whether as victims, or as witnesses or defendants.
2. In any press report of a case involving a sexual offence against a child:
   2.2 the adult may be identified
   2.3 the term 'incest' where applicable should not be used
   2.4 the offence should be described as 'serious offences against young children' or similar appropriate wording
   2.5 the child should not be identified
   2.6 care should be taken that nothing in the report implies the relationship between the accused and the child.

14. Victims of crime

The press should not identify victims of sexual assault or publish material likely to contribute to such identification unless, by law, they are free to do so.

15. Discrimination

1. The press should avoid prejudicial or pejorative reference to a person's race, colour, religion, sex or sexual orientation, or to any physical or mental illness or handicap.
2. It should avoid publishing details of a person's race, colour, religion, sex or sexual orientation, unless these are directly relevant to the story.

16. Financial journalism

1. Even where the law does not prohibit it, journalists should not use for their own profit financial information they receive in advance of its general publication, nor should they pass such information to others.
2. They should not write about shares or securities in whose performance they know that they or their close families have a significant financial interest, without disclosing the interest to the editor or financial editor.
3. They should not buy or sell, either directly or through nominees or agents, shares or securities about which they have written recently or about which they intend to write in the near future.

17. Confidential sources

Journalists have a moral obligation to protect confidential sources of information.

18. The public interest

Clauses 4, 5, 7, 8 and 9 create exceptions that may be covered by invoking the public interest. For the purposes of this code, that is most easily defined as:

1. Detecting or exposing crime or a serious misdemeanour.
2. Protecting public health and safety.
3. Preventing the public from being misled by some statement or action of an individual or organization.

In any cases raising issues beyond these three definitions the PCC will require a full explanation by the editor of the publication involved, seeking to demonstrate how the public interest was served.

17.4 Broadcasting: semi self-regulation

Television and radio in the twenty-first century is one of the most sophisticated industries known to the world. Unfortunately, in the United Kingdom the system by which broadcasting is regulated has been left behind by the technology. The regulation system is unwieldy and far from efficient. Apart from the Broadcasting Standards Commission, there is the Independent Television Commission and the Radio Authority. All have authority to handle complaints.

However, this is all about to change. On 12 December 2000, the government published a communications White Paper designed to bring coherence to the regulation of the converging industries of communications and broadcast media. The White Paper proposes a new super-regulator called the Office of Communications (Ofcom), which will bring together the Broadcasting Standards Commission, the Independent Television Commission, the Radio Authority, the Radiocommunications Agency, and Oftel. According to the government, Ofcom will:

> . . . promote competition in telecommunications and broadcasting [and] regulate television and radio by means of a new framework which will allow flexibility for industry whilst fully meeting the expectations of viewers and listeners and maintaining high levels of quality and diversity.

The government has indicated that Ofcom will be 'independent' but will work closely with the Department of Trade and Industry and the Department for Culture, Media and Sport.

Pending the establishment of Ofcom, expected to take place in 2003, regulation of broadcast media remains in the hands of the bodies described below.

The Broadcasting Act 1996 gives the government power over television and radio. The Broadcasting Standards Commission is accountable to Parliament. As such, regulation of broadcasting is not a 'self-regulating' authority like that of the Press Complaints Commission.

17.5 The Broadcasting Standards Commission

17.5.1 History

Broadcasting companies in Britain managed for many years to escape the widespread public distrust with which the press have historically been associated. Although they have never been above criticism – for example, Winston Churchill complained about political bias at the BBC as long ago as 1953 – somehow both the BBC and independent television and radio were always regarded as being above the more criticized practices of the popular newspapers.

It is perhaps for that reason that the broadcasting industry had no equivalent of the Press Complaints Commission until 1981. Up to that time the BBC, the Independent Broadcasting Authority (the governing body of independent television) and the Radio Authority each ran their own complaints tribunal, the adjudications of which were usually printed in one or other of the magazines produced by these organizations, in other words the *TV Times* or the *Listener*.

However, in 1977 the Annan Committee on the Future of Broadcasting recommended the establishment of a statutory body that would sit in public in order to investigate and decide upon complaints from the public. The result in 1981 was the establishment of the Broadcasting Complaints Commission (the 'BCC').

When the relevant legislation was passing through Parliament, a chorus of protest was heard from the broadcasting industry. The proposed BCC was described variously as a 'potential monster' (Colin Shaw, Deputy Director of the IBA), a 'pain in the neck' (Alasdair Milne, Managing Director of BBC television), and a 'threat to editorial enterprise' (Sir Hugh Greene, former Director General of the BBC). Despite the much-publicized fears of these eminent broadcasters, the BCC did not have a major impact upon the industry in the powers bestowed upon it by Parliament and in the way it exercised them.

A Broadcasting Standards Council was also established. This considered complaints about the portrayal of violence and of sexual conduct, and about matters of taste and decency. It had the same wide jurisdiction as the BCC.

In 1996, the BCC and the Broadcasting Standards Council were replaced. By Part V of the Broadcasting Act 1996, the Broadcasting Standards Commission (the 'BSC') was established. The BSC is an amalgamation of the BCC and the Broadcasting Standards Council. It is the only organization created by United Kingdom legislation that covers all television and radio broadcasting.

17.5.2 Function

The BSC's function is to:

- Produce codes of conduct relating to standards and fairness
- Consider and adjudicate on complaints, and
- Monitor, research and report on standards and fairness in broadcasting.

The jurisdiction of the BSC extends to all terrestrial and satellite television and radio broadcasting, including text, cable and digital services in the United Kingdom. It therefore has jurisdiction over BBC television, BBC radio, ITV, Channel 4, Channel 5, independent radio, and all licensed cable and satellite programme services.

17.5.3 Codes of conduct

The codes of conduct on standards and fairness give guidance on good practice, which all broadcasters and their regulators are required to reflect. The codes set out the principles to be observed and the practices to be followed:

- To avoid unjust or unfair treatment in programmes
- To avoid the unwarranted infringement of privacy in programmes or in connection with their preparation, and
- In connection with the portrayal of violence and sex.

17.5.4 Complaints

The BSC considers complaints relating to:

- Standards. This includes the portrayal of violence, sex and other issues of taste and decency, such as bad language. The code and any research are considered alongside the material complained of and its context
- Fairness. Only people with a direct interest in a broadcast can complain about unfair treatment or unwarranted infringement of privacy. The BSC studies written exchanges of evidence and may hold a hearing.

The decisions of the BSC are published regularly. Broadcasters must report any action taken by them as a result of a decision made by the BSC. The BSC can also require broadcasters to publish any decision in a newspaper or magazine, or 'on air'.

17.5.5 Monitoring

The BSC monitors the standards of United Kingdom broadcasting and reports on the attitude of the public towards standards and fairness issues. It may also report to the Department for Media, Culture and Sport.

17.6 The Independent Television Commission

The Independent Television Commission (the 'ITC') was established by the Broadcasting Act 1990 to govern the licensing and regulating of independent television, teletext, and licensed cable and satellite services in the United Kingdom. It replaced the Independent Broadcasting Authority.

The ITC is governed by the Broadcasting Act 1990 and the Broadcasting Act 1996. Amongst its extensive statutory powers, the ITC has the authority to lay down and enforce codes of practice in order to maintain what it considers to be proper standards in respect of politically sensitive material, good taste, decency and the portrayal of violence.

Any satellite service that is broadcast into the United Kingdom from any non-United Kingdom supplier does not fall within the scope of the ITC. The codes only apply to broadcasters who hold an ITC licence.

From the public's point of view, the most significant of the existing codes is the ITC programme code, which covers matters such as taste, decency, the portrayal of violence, privacy, impartiality, charitable appeals and religious programmes.

There are also ITC codes covering advertising standards and practice to prevent advertisements that are misleading, offensive or likely to encourage dangerous or anti-social attitudes or behaviour, and programme sponsorship to protect editorial independence and prevent sponsor credits from intruding unacceptably on programmes.

The ITC's powers are fairly wide. Apart from directing that an apology or correction should be broadcast by an offending channel, it can also order the company involved not to repeat the programme. In more serious cases the company can be given a formal warning that it is in breach of its licence, be fined (often in large amounts), or have its licence shortened or, in extreme circumstances, even revoked altogether.

The ITC, of course, has no jurisdiction over the BBC.

17.7 The Radio Authority

The Radio Authority is a statutory body, set up by the government, which derives its powers from the Broadcasting Act 1990 and the Broadcasting Act 1996. It licenses and regulates all commercial radio services comprising of national, local, cable, national FM subcarrier, satellite and restricted services. It will also license national and local digital radio services over the next few years.

The Radio Authority is responsible for planning frequencies, appointing licensees and regulating programming and advertising. It is required to publish codes, to which licensees must adhere, covering programming, advertising and sponsorship, and engineering. It also regulates ownership. It can apply sanctions, including broadcast apologies and/or corrections, fines, and the shortening or revocation of licences.

The Radio Authority does not license or regulate any BBC radio services.

17.8 Other broadcast bodies

Apart from the BSC and ITC, complaints can also be directed to the BBC Viewer and Listener Correspondence in respect of BBC TV and radio. The BBC's internal guidelines for producers[1] is a useful source of material on which to base complaints concerning BBC broadcasts.

Grievances can also be addressed to the Radiocommunications Agency, which deals with enquiries and complaints about domestic interference and reports of unlicensed broadcasting or pirate radio, and Oftel, the regulator for the United Kingdom telecommunications industry, which was set up under the Telecommunications Act 1984.

[1]The web site is at www.bbc.co.uk/info/editorial/prodgl/index.shtml.

18 Advertising

Tom Cassels and Rebecca Handler

18.1 Introduction

Today there are very few people, particularly amongst those working in the media, who underestimate the power of advertising. Since commercial television was introduced in the 1950s the advertising industry has grown massively, and it is well known that large companies are prepared to spend millions of pounds each year publicizing their products. Because a large part of these advertising budgets is devoted to buying space on television and in newspapers, the media are among the many beneficiaries.

In 1961, the advertising industry recognized that there was a need for unified control over the content and presentation of non-broadcast advertisements. The industry therefore devised and developed a self-regulatory system and published the first edition of the Code of Advertising Practice (the 'Code'). It also established the Advertising Standards Authority (the 'ASA') to supervise the system and apply the Code to ensure that advertisements are legal, decent, honest and truthful. The ASA is a self-regulatory body, independent from the government and the advertising industry.

The only major areas of advertising not directly subject to the Code are television and radio commercials. Television advertisements are regulated by the Independent Television Commission. Radio advertisements are regulated by the Radio Authority. Both have their own sets of rules, which are similar to those imposed by the Code, and are considered in Chapter 17.

18.2 The Code of Advertising Practice

18.2.1 Aims and functions

The Code is the body of rules by which the overwhelming majority of advertisements produced by the United Kingdom advertising agencies are regulated. Essentially, the Code is a set of principles and guidelines on the content of advertisements.[1] The system of advertising control works in three ways:

[1]A complete guide to the ASA and the Code can be found at www.asa.org.uk.

1. Advice: the Code is used as a 'pre-publication guide' for advertisers, agencies and publishers in order to ensure compliance with its provisions
2. Resolving complaints: the Code is used as a 'rulebook' by which the ASA adjudicates complaints by members of the public, consumer groups and companies who are misled or offended by an advertisement
3. Research: spot checks are made each week by the ASA using the rules of the Code as guidelines. The ASA can take action to have an advertisement withdrawn or changed without having to wait for a complaint.

All advertisements and promotions in the non-broadcast media are covered by the Code. These include:

- Press: national, regional, magazines and free newspapers
- Outdoor: posters, transport, aerial
- Direct marketing: letters, leaflets, brochures, catalogues, circulars, mailing lists
- Cinema commercials
- Sales promotions: packaging, front page, reader offers, competitions and prize draws
- Internet: advertisements in 'paid for space' including banner and pop-up, commercial emails and sales promotions, but not general product information on web site 'home pages'
- Other electronic media, including advertisements on computer games, videos and CD-Roms.

The ASA estimates that some 30 million press advertisements are published in the United Kingdom each year. The ASA carries out around 10 000 spot checks each week, and receives about 12 000 complaints each year.

18.2.2 Current edition

The Code is currently in its tenth edition, which came into force on 1 October 1999, with Addendum 1 added on 23 April 2000.

18.2.3 The rules of the Code

1. The basic principle of the Code is that an advertisement should be:
   - Legal: it must not break the law or incite others to break the law.
   - Decent: it should not cause offence. Particular care should be taken to avoid causing offence on the grounds of race, religion, sex, sexual orientation or disability. However, the fact that a particular product may be offensive to some people is not in itself a valid ground for objection to an advertisement for that product.

- Honest: it must not take unfair advantage of consumers by 'exploiting their credulity or inexperience'; and
- Truthful: it must not mislead, either expressly or though ambiguity. Particular care must be taken with political advertisements, the quotation of prices and the use of testimonials.

2. Advertisements should be 'prepared with a sense of responsibility to consumers and society'. In practice, this means that advertisers should not play on fear without good reason, or condone violence and antisocial behaviour. Care should be taken not to exploit or infringe the privacy of consumers, and to avoid portraying or referring to individuals without their permission. Care should also be taken to avoid showing or advocating dangerous behaviour, for example excessive drinking or smoking. Special care should be taken with advertisements directed at children.

3. Advertisements must abide by the principles of 'fair competition generally accepted in business', and should not denigrate the products of rivals or exploit the goodwill of others. Advertisements should be wary of imitating other advertisements.

4. The Code sets out additional rules for advertising products whose nature requires that special care be taken to protect the interests of consumers. These include advertisements containing health claims, employment and business opportunities, financial services and products, and advertising aimed at children.

An appendix to the Code establishes a separate 'Cigarette Code', which is also administered by the ASA and contains the body of principles developed in conjunction with the tobacco industry to govern the advertising of cigarettes and tobacco products.

18.2.4 The complaints procedure

The procedure adopted by the ASA for handling complaints about breaches of the Code is very similar to that used by the Press Complaints Commission (see Chapter 17).

As the ASA has no legal authority, the handling of complaints relies upon what it calls a 'self-regulatory system'.

Complaints should be made in writing to the ASA by letter or email. An initial assessment is made to ensure that the complaint falls within the remit of the Code and that there is a case to answer. If it is within the necessary remit, the complaint will be investigated. Only one complaint is necessary for an investigation to be launched.

The complaint is submitted to the advertising company, who is asked to comment on the complaint in writing and provide evidence that no breach of the Code has occurred if it disputes the claim. Under the Code, particular emphasis is placed on preserving and supplying all evidential matter and documentary evidence in support of the advertisement.

If the matter is particularly serious, the ASA will ask for the relevant advertisement to be withdrawn until the investigation is concluded.

When all the available evidence and comments of the parties are gathered in, the advertisement is assessed and an adjudication is made. An advertiser found to be in breach of the Code will be asked to undertake not to repeat the breach and to amend or withdraw the offending advertisement.

18.2.5 Sanctions

Following adjudication, the ASA may carry out the following to ensure that advertisements that break the Code are amended or withdrawn:

- Persuasion: the ASA first asks that the offending advertisement be withdrawn
- Refusal of further advertising space: the ASA can ask publishers and media owners to refuse more space for an advertisement until it has been changed
- Adverse publicity: the ASA publishes the outcome of all adjudications weekly on the web site, plus a regular hard copy summary
- Withdrawal of trading privileges: trading privileges, financial discounts and other incentives can be withdrawn
- Legal proceedings: persistent offenders can be referred to the Office of Fair Trading, which can seek an injunction through court proceedings.

Usually, it is not necessary for the ASA to take any action beyond informing the advertising company that it has breached the Code. The majority of companies will withdraw their advertisement from circulation in order to avoid damaging their reputation by circulating an advertisement that is offensive or misleading, prejudicing their good name or losing clients' money through the production of advertisements which cannot be used.

PART VIII

The Law under the European Convention on Human Rights

19 The Human Rights Act 1998

Hugh Tomlinson QC

19.1 Introduction

The Human Rights Act 1998 (the 'HRA') came into effect on 2 October 2000. It is designed to 'give further effect' to the rights and freedoms enshrined in the European Convention on Human Rights (the 'Convention') and to make them enforceable in the courts of the United Kingdom. It is now unlawful for 'public authorities', including courts, to act in a way that is incompatible with Convention rights. A number of these rights, including the right to freedom of expression (Article 10) and the right to respect for private life (Article 8), are of particular importance for the media. The law of defamation is potentially subject to substantial change as a result of the HRA. In addition, the HRA is likely to lead to further significant revisions of the principles governing court reporting and the development of a tort of invasion of privacy.

19.2 The basic scheme of the Human Rights Act 1998

19.2.1 General principles

The Convention is an international treaty, under the terms of which the United Kingdom is bound to secure to everyone within its jurisdiction the rights and freedoms that are set out (Article 1 of the Convention). It was designed, in the aftermath of the Second World War, to protect the individual against State interference with their fundamental rights and freedoms. Although the United Kingdom accepted the right to individual petition under the Convention in 1966, the Convention was not enforceable in the English courts.

The HRA was designed to 'give further effect' to the Convention without disturbing the sovereignty of Parliament. The HRA does not directly incorporate the Convention into English law, but gives effect to it by requirements relating to the interpretation of legislation and the actions of public authorities.

The operation of the HRA can be approached by considering eight questions:

1. Who is bound by the HRA?
2. How does the HRA take effect?

3. When does the HRA take effect?
4. Who can bring a claim under the HRA?
5. How can a claim be brought?
6. When can a claim be brought?
7. What happens if a claim is successful?
8. Can the HRA have any effect on disputes involving 'private' bodies or individuals?

19.2.2 Who is bound by the HRA?

The HRA only has direct application to 'public authorities'. It has no direct application to private bodies.

Public authorities are not fully defined. By Section 6(3) HRA, a 'public authority' includes a court, a tribunal that exercises functions in relation to legal proceedings, and any person certain of whose functions are functions of a public nature. In other words, the HRA envisages three different types of public authorities:

1. Public bodies that are obviously public authorities ('*standard* public authorities')
2. Bodies that carry out some public functions ('*functional* public authorities')
3. Courts and tribunals.

Standard public authorities

A standard public authority must not act incompatibly with Convention rights in any of its functions, whether or not they are 'private' in nature. In other words, the Convention applies to matters such as employment and contracting with private bodies.

The only public bodies that are certain to be treated as standard public authorities under the HRA are those that are obviously governmental in character, such as central government, local government and the police. It seems likely that bodies such as the Broadcasting Complaints Commission will also be treated as a standard public authority.

Functional public authorities

A functional public authority does not act unlawfully under Section 6(5) HRA where the particular act being challenged is 'of a private nature'.

The range of bodies that will be treated as functional authorities is less clear. The government has expressed the view that functional authorities include the privatized utilities Railtrack, the National Society for the Prevention of Cruelty to Children, the BBC, the Independent Television Commission (but not the independent television companies), the British Board of Film Classification and the Press Complaints Commission. It has, however, been held that 'public' in Section 6(3)(c) HRA is used in the sense of 'governmental' (*R (Heather) v The Leonard Cheshire Foundation (2001)*). This has the effect of restricting the range of bodies that are subject to the HRA.

Courts and tribunals

The position in relation to a 'court or tribunal' is the same as that for standard public authorities.

19.2.3 How does the HRA take effect?

The HRA provides for the Convention to be given effect in two ways. First, by the interpretation of existing legislation:

> So far as it is possible to do so . . . legislation . . . must be read and given effect in a way which is compatible with Convention rights.

> (Section 3(1) HRA)

The courts will take a purposive approach and will 'read in' Convention rights unless the language of the statute clearly prevents the courts doing so. Section 3 HRA must be used in a way that respects the will of the legislature and preserves the integrity of statute law (*R v Lambert (2001)*). However, it has been accepted that it will sometimes be necessary under Section 3 HRA to adopt an interpretation that is linguistically strained, not only by reading down the express language of the statute but also by the implication of provisions (*R v A (No 2) (2001)*).

Secondly, the HRA imposes a requirement on public authorities to act in accordance with the Convention:

> It is unlawful for a public authority to act in a way which is incompatible with a Convention right.

> (Section 6(1) HRA)

However, this does not apply if the public authority could not have acted differently as a result of a provision of primary legislation (Section 6(2)(a) HRA), or if the public authority is acting 'to give effect or enforce statutory provisions which cannot be interpreted in a way which is compatible with the Convention' (Section 6(2)(b) HRA).

It should be noted that the HRA is intended to preserve Parliamentary sovereignty. The courts cannot 'strike down' primary legislation, although they can declare that a statute is incompatible with Convention rights (Section 4 HRA). If such a declaration is made there is a 'fast track' procedure for amending legislation (Section 10 HRA).

Actions of a public authority that are incompatible with Convention rights will be unlawful unless one of the two 'exceptions' in Section 6(2) HRA is made out. The public authority must show either that:

- As a result of a provision of primary legislation, it could not have acted differently (Section 6(2)(a) HRA), or
- It was acting so as to 'give effect to or enforce' a statutory provision that cannot be read in a way that is compatible with Convention rights (Section 6(2)(b) HRA).

19.2.4 When does the HRA take effect?

In general, the HRA applies to any acts committed after the relevant provisions of the legislation came into force on 2 October 2000.

However, Section 22(4) HRA has introduced an element of retrospectivity. A defendant to proceedings brought by a public authority can rely on a Convention right even though the act in question took place *before* the HRA itself came into force. In this context, proceedings brought by a public authority will include an appeal by either party in such proceedings.

19.2.5 Who can bring a claim under the HRA?

Section 7(1) HRA allows proceedings against a public authority only by a 'victim' as defined by the Convention (Section 7(7) HRA), even for the purposes of judicial review (Section 7(3) HRA).

'Victim' is defined in Article 34 of the Convention as:

> . . . any person, non governmental organization or group of individuals claiming to be the victim of a violation.

It is uncertain whether local authorities or public bodies such as the BBC will be able to establish they are victims for the purposes of bringing proceedings under the HRA.

The provisions of Section 7 HRA mean that:

- Companies have human rights, although perhaps not in areas such as liberty or freedom of conscience where a company has no interest to be infringed
- A victim must show he is *personally* affected by Convention rights – this may include potential victims or an indirect victim, but not a pressure group.

19.2.6 How can a claim be brought?

Under Section 7(1) HRA a 'victim' claiming a public authority has acted unlawfully under Section 6(1) HRA may:

- Bring proceedings in the appropriate court or tribunal, and
- Rely on Convention rights in any proceedings.

The policy under the HRA is to avoid procedural technicalities. The proposed rules of court under the HRA do not seek to place procedural limits on claims.

19.2.7 When can a claim be brought?

Under Section 7(5) HRA proceedings must be brought within one year, or such longer period as the court or tribunal considers equitable having regard to all the circumstances.

However, Section 7(5) HRA does not apply where a stricter time limit already exists. For example, in judicial review applications the provision of Civil Procedure Rules Schedule 1 53.4(1) remains in force, with the result that an application for judicial review on the grounds of or incorporating a claim under the HRA must be made promptly and in any event within three months.

19.2.8 What happens if a claim is successful?

Powers of the court

Section 8 HRA defines the powers that courts or tribunals have in relation to the HRA. Section 8(1) HRA states:

> In relation to any act (or proposed act) of a public authority which the court finds (or would be) unlawful, it may grant such relief or remedy, or make such order, within its powers as it considers just and appropriate.

The breadth of these powers is the justification for the refusal by the Government to enact in the HRA Article 13 of the Convention, which grants the right to an effective remedy of Convention rights.

Many civil cases under the HRA will be brought as judicial review proceedings. Relief for judicial review has always been discretionary, and the broad power on the court to grant such relief that it considers just and appropriate under section 8(1) HRA ensures that relief will continue to be discretionary in HRA cases.

Damages

Damages may only be awarded by a court that has *power* to award damages or compensation in civil proceedings (Section 8(2) HRA).

Section 8(3) HRA states that no award for damages shall be made unless the award is necessary to afford just satisfaction taking account of *all* the circumstances of the case including, in particular:

- Any other relief or remedy granted
- The consequences of any decision in respect of that unlawful act.

Section 8(4) HRA requires that:

> In determining –
>
> (a) whether to award damages, or
> (b) the amount of an award,

the court must take account of the principles applied by the European Court of Human Rights in relation to the award of compensation under Article 41 of the Convention.

Article 41 provides that:

If the Court [of Human Rights] finds that there has been a violation of the Convention or the protocols thereto, and if the internal law of the High Contracting Party concerned allows only partial reparation to be made, the Court shall, if necessary, afford just satisfaction to the injured party.

However, damages cannot be awarded in respect of judicial acts done in good faith, other than damages to compensate a person for detention under Article 5(5) of the Convention (Section 9(3) HRA).

Declaration of incompatibility

If a court is satisfied that primary legislation is incompatible with the Convention it may make a declaration of that incompatibility (Section 4(2) HRA). To date only two such declarations have been made, in relation to a provision of the Consumer Credit Act 1974 (*Wilson v First County Trust (2001)*) and relation to provisions of the Mental Health Act 1983 (*R v Mental Health Review Tribunal ex parte H (2001)*).

There is a fast track for the amendment of primary legislation to bring it into line with the Convention if such a declaration is made (Section 10 HRA).

19.2.9 Can the HRA have any effect on disputes between 'private' bodies or individuals?

As stated above, the HRA is only directly binding on public authorities. In other words, it has only *vertical* application (only applying to the relationship between individuals and the State).

However, because courts and tribunals are public authorities (Section 6(3)(a) HRA) they will act unlawfully under Section 6(1) HRA if they act in a way that is incompatible with Convention rights. This means that the HRA has potential *horizontal* application (extending to the regulation of relations between private individuals or bodies, allowing Convention rights to be invoked by them in private law disputes).

In *Douglas v Hello! Ltd (2001)*, the Court of Appeal suggested that as a result of the HRA the courts were under a positive duty to develop the common law in accordance with the Convention. Furthermore, it is clear the HRA requires courts to interpret statutes to ensure compatibility with Convention rights even in cases in which no public body is a party (*Wilson v First County Trust (2001)*). In addition, the HRA makes special provision in relation to measures that might affect the exercise of the Convention right to freedom of expression (Section 12 HRA), and it is clear that, at least in this area, it has horizontal effect.

19.3 The Convention rights

19.3.1 General principles

Substantive rights

The HRA incorporates most of the substantive rights of the Convention. For the purposes of the media, the most important rights are:

- The right to respect for private and family life (Article 8 of the Convention)
- Freedom of thought, conscience and religion (Article 9 of the Convention)
- Freedom of expression (Article 10 of the Convention).

Most Convention rights impose negative obligations in the sense that the state is required to *abstain* from interfering with a specific human right. However, sometimes the Convention requires public authorities to take positive steps to *protect* rights. These include the right to life, the prohibition from inhuman treatment, the right to respect for private life, the right to freedom of religion, thought and conscience, the right to freedom of expression, freedom of assembly, the right to possession of property and the right to education.

The positive obligations accepted by the Court fall into three categories:

1. The obligation to change a law or administrative practice
2. The obligation to provide financial assistance, and
3. The obligation to intervene in the relationship between individuals in order to protect 'private' violations of rights protected by the Convention.

Breach of qualified rights

However, some rights, including the rights in Articles 8, 9 and 10, are 'qualified rights'. In other words, they are subject to a list of 'exceptions' or restrictions.

When it is claimed that there has been a breach of a qualified right:

1. The claimant must satisfy the burden of proving on the balance of probabilities that there is a breach of the right *on the face of it*; if so
2. The public authority must prove, on the balance of probabilities, that it is entitled to restrict the qualified right by showing that:
    - It has acted 'in accordance with the law
    - The aim of the restriction in question is one of those identified in the particular Convention right as a being a 'legitimate' restriction, and
    - The restriction on the Convention right is 'necessary in a democratic society'. The nearest paraphrase of 'necessary' is 'really needed', in other words the interference must correspond to a pressing social need and be proportionate to the aim pursued.

Waiver

Convention rights can be 'waived'. This is likely to be particularly important in relation to fair trial rights and the rights of employees of standard public authorities. However, such waiver is only effective if it is established in an unequivocal manner and is attended by the minimum safeguards commensurate with the importance of the right. Under the HRA the waiver will have to be:

- Clear and unequivocal
- Made in the absence of constraint, and
- Made in 'full knowledge' of the nature and extent of the right.

In addition, the court may refuse to accept that a right has been waived if there are compelling policy considerations to the contrary.

19.3.2 Right to respect for private life (Article 8)

Article 8 states:

1. Everyone has the right to respect for his private and family life, his home and his correspondence.
2. There shall be no interference by a public authority with the exercise of this right except such as is in accordance with the law and is necessary in a democratic society in the interests of national security, public safety or the economic well-being of the country, for the prevention of disorder or crime, for the protection of health or morals, or for the protection of the rights and freedoms of others.

The concept of 'private life' in Article 8 is open-ended. It does not just include the notion of an 'inner life', but also 'the right to establish and develop relationships with other human beings'. It does not exclude the activities of a professional or business nature (*Niemetz v Germany (1992)*).

The right to respect for private life includes:

- The right to personal identity (*Gaskin v United Kingdom (1989)*) or sexual identity (*Cossey v United Kingdom (1990)*)
- The right to personal sexuality (*Dudgeon v United Kingdom (1981)*)
- The collection of personal information (*Z v Finland (1997)*)
- The right to physical and moral integrity (*A v United Kingdom (1998)*)
- The right to choose mode of dress and appearance (*Sutter v Switzerland (1984)*).

A businessman's or professional's office may constitute a 'home' for the purposes of Article 8 (*Niemetz v Germany (1992)*). Interference with the home also includes blighting the environment, such as the noise generated by aircraft and serious environmental pollution (*Hatton v United Kingdom (2001)*).

In *X and Y v Netherlands (1985)*, the European Court of Human Rights made clear that:

> ... although the object of Article 8 is essentially that of protecting the individual against arbitrary interference by the public authorities, it does not merely compel the State to abstain from such interference: in addition to this primary negative obligation, there may be positive obligations inherent in an effective respect for family life. These obligations may involve the adoption of measures designed to secure respect for private life even in the sphere of the relations of individuals between themselves.

As a result, there is a strong argument that the HRA places the English courts under a duty to develop the law to protect privacy.

19.3.3 Freedom of expression (Article 10)

General principles
Article 10 states:

1. Everyone has the right to freedom of expression. This right shall include freedom to hold opinions and to receive and impart information and ideas without interference by public authority and regardless of frontiers. This Article shall not prevent States from requiring the licensing of broadcasting, television or cinema enterprises.
2. The exercise of these freedoms, since it carries with it duties and responsibilities, may be subject to such formalities, conditions, restrictions or penalties as are prescribed by law and are necessary in a democratic society, in the interests of national security, territorial integrity or public safety, for the prevention of disorder or crime, for the protection of health or morals, for the protection of the reputation or rights of others, for preventing the disclosure of information received in confidence, or for maintaining the authority and impartiality of the judiciary.

It has been repeatedly made clear by the European Court of Human Rights that freedom of expression 'constitutes one of the essential foundations of a democratic society and one of the basic conditions for its progress and for each individual's self fulfilment'.

Content of expression
Freedom of expression is applicable to 'information' or 'ideas' that are favourably received or regarded as inoffensive or as a matter of indifference. It is also applicable to information or ideas that offend, shock or disturb the State or any sector of the population, because without such pluralism, tolerance and broadmindedness there is no 'democratic society'.

Means of expression

Article 10 protects not only the content of expression, but also the specific means by which an opinion is expressed.

An extensive range of media for the production, transmission and distribution of information and ideas, including speech, print, radio and television broadcasting, artistic creations, film and electronic information systems, are protected under Article 10 HRA.

Even if the person who provides the means is not the holder of the opinion, he is protected. For example, the organizers of an exhibition of paintings were held to be exercising their freedom of expression in relation to the paintings (*Muller v Switzerland (1988)*).

The wide scope of expression makes it impossible to formulate general rules for the assessment of the need for protection of particular exercises of the freedom, or the extent to which a government might limit them. Instead a number of factors, including the kind of expression, the medium through which it is delivered and the audience to which it is directed, must be taken into account in order to determine the extent of protection that the court might allow a particular item of expression. 'Expression' is not restricted to verifiable, factual data, but also includes opinions, criticism and speculation, whether or not they are objectively 'true' (*Lingens v Austria (1986)*).

Restrictions

The freedom is subject to some restrictions set out in Article 10(2). These must be construed strictly, and the need for any restrictions must be established convincingly (see, for example, *Zana v Turkey (1997)*).

Much of the European Court of Human Rights case law relating to Article 10 has been concerned with the scope of such restrictions. The cases emphasize the need to 'balance' freedom of expression with the public interest, although in practice the European Court of Human Rights has engaged in a quite complex process of consideration of a multitude of factors.

In the absence of 'bright lines' of distinction (*Observer & Guardian v United Kingdom (1991)*) the matter becomes one of appreciation for the court, which will look at:

- The type of expression involved
- The duties and responsibilities attached to the particular exercise of the freedom
- The means of the communication
- The audience to which it is directed, and
- The significance of the interference and the purpose for which it is imposed.

Types of expression

Different types of expression have been given different levels of protection by the European Court of Human Rights.

278

Political

Under Article 10, 'political expression' has the highest importance. The expression of politicians, and in particular the views of the opposition, are therefore given utmost protection (*Castells v Spain (1992)*), while politicians must also be tolerant of sharp criticism of themselves (*Lingens v Austria (1986)*).

Artistic

Artistic expression receives less protection than political speech. In *Muller v Switzerland (1988)*, paintings depicting activities involving homosexuality and bestiality were on public display without warnings. It was held that the duties and responsibilities of the artist imposed on him special considerations of restraint rather than opportunities of freedom. A similar approach was taken in *Otto-Preminger-Institut v Austria (1994)*, which upheld decisions to seize and forfeit a film to be exhibited by the applicant in circumstances where showing it would result in 'justified indignation' among a local population on the grounds of religion.

Commercial

Commercial expression is treated as being of less importance than either political or artistic expression. In *Markt Intern and Beerman v Germany (1989)*, it was held that an injunction against a trade magazine that prohibited it from publishing information about an enterprise operating in its market sector was justified. As commercial speech, it was found to be subject to different standards of control than other kinds of expression, illustrated by reference to the truth of items published. The European Court of Human Rights said that even if statements in the publication were true, they could be prohibited under certain circumstances such as a duty to respect the privacy of others or the confidentiality of certain commercial information.

Duties and responsibilities

Article 10(2) provides that the exercise of the freedom of expression carries with it duties and responsibilities that bear some relation to the restrictions that may be imposed on the freedom.

Press and television

The press and television are media to which the European Court of Human Rights has attached great importance in relation to the effective enjoyment of freedom of expression in matters of political and public concern. The case of *Observer and Guardian v United Kingdom (1991)* makes it clear that the role of the press is that of a 'public watchdog', which must impart information and ideas on political issues and other areas of public interest just as the public has a right to receive them.

The Convention protects the operation of the press in drawing attention to political issues. In particular, the European Court of Human Rights has given support to the right of journalists to protect their sources. The general position in relation to the freedom of expression of the press was analysed by European Court of Human Rights in *Bergens Tidende v Norway (2001)*, in which it was said that:

By reason of the 'duties and responsibilities' inherent in the exercise of freedom of expression, the safeguard afforded by Article 10 to journalists in relation to reporting on issues of general interest is subject to the proviso that they are acting in good faith in order to provide accurate and reliable information in accordance with the ethics of journalism.

Other areas

The necessity of public interference in a democratic society requires that it have as its objective the furtherance of one or more of the public aims set out in Article 10(2). Some of these grounds correspond to the limitations found in other provisions of the Convention (national security, public safety and prevention of disorder or crime), while the rest are specific to Article 10.

The classification or identification of the objective for which the interference has been imposed may be crucial to the outcome of a case.

Broadcasting

Article 10 does not prevent the state from having a licensing system for broadcasting, television and cinema enterprises. However, the licensing power requires justification under Article 10(2) (*Groppera Radio AG v Switzerland (1990)*). Limitations on broadcast transmissions, particularly the regulation of content, cannot be founded on the licensing power alone, but must also meet the test of necessity for one of the purposes expressly provided in Article 10(2).

A state monopoly on broadcasting which prohibits other operators from establishing cable television has been held to be incompatible with the Convention as being unnecessary in a democratic society (*Informationsverein Lentia v Austria (1993)*).

United Kingdom violations

The absence of a clear 'right of expression' in English law has meant that United Kingdom applications based on Article 10 have regularly come before the European Commission and Court of Human Rights. However, it should be noted that the European Court of Human Rights has found the United Kingdom to be in violation of Article 10 on only six occasions:

- The 'Thalidomide' contempt case (*Sunday Times v United Kingdom (1979)*)
- The two 'Spycatcher' cases (*Sunday Times v United Kingdom (No 2) (1991); Observer & Guardian v United Kingdom (1991)*)
- The 'Tolstoy' libel damages case (*Tolstoy Miloslavsky v United Kingdom (1995)*)
- The case on the disclosure of sources by journalists (*Goodwin v United Kingdom (1996)*)
- The 'SPUC' election leaflet case (*Bowman v United Kingdom (1998)*).

19.1 The HRA and the right to privacy

19.4.1 Section 12

The 'right to privacy' in Article 8 of the Convention gave rise to serious concerns on the part of the press when enactment of the HRA was initially proposed. It led Lord Wakeham, the Chairman of the Press Complaints Commission, to seek amendments to the Human Rights Bill. These were eventually accepted by the Government and are now contained in Section 12 HRA, which provides that, when a court is considering the grant of relief that 'might affect the exercise of the Convention right of freedom of expression':

> The court must have particular regard to the importance of the Convention right to freedom of expression.
>
> (Section 12(4) HRA)

Where the proceedings relate to 'journalistic material' or conduct connected with it, the court must take into account the extent to which it is in the public interest for the material to be published and 'any relevant privacy code' (Section 12(4)(b) HRA).

The effect of the Section 12 HRA is not entirely clear, and on one view it adds nothing to the pre-HRA approach of the English courts. However, it has been held that it:

> ... puts beyond question the direct applicability of at least one article of the Convention as between one private party to litigation and another – in the jargon, its horizontal effect.
>
> (*Douglas v Hello! (2001)*)

As Section 12(4) HRA directs attention to 'any relevant privacy code', it is likely that any newspaper that breaches paragraph 3 of the Press Complaints Commission's Code of Practice (see Chapter 17) would have its claim to freedom of expression 'trumped' by privacy considerations (*Douglas v Hello! (2001)*).

19.4.2 Tort of privacy?

The HRA has already begun to give a decisive impetus to the development of a tort of privacy in English law. In *Douglas v Hello! (2001)* the Court of Appeal considered whether Michael Douglas and Catherine Zeta-Jones were entitled to an interim injunction restraining *Hello!* magazine from publishing pictures of their wedding, the exclusive rights to which had been sold to *OK!* magazine. The matter was dealt with as a claim in breach of confidence. However, the Court of Appeal said that the law had:

> ... reached a point at which it can be said with confidence that the law recognizes and will appropriately protect a right of personal privacy.

It was said that 'the law no longer needed to construct an artificial relationship of confidentiality between intruder and victim'. Instead, the right to privacy could be substituted for this element of the tort. However, on the facts an injunction was refused because damages were an adequate remedy for the claimants who had, in effect, 'sold' their privacy rights.

In *Venables v News Group Newspapers Ltd (2001)* the applicants, who had been convicted of murdering the infant James Bulger, were granted injunctions against the whole world to prevent the publication of information that might lead to their identification. The court considered that such relief constituted an 'extension of the law of confidence', which was warranted by the 'exceptional circumstances' of the case. In particular, the court was concerned that as a result of the widespread hatred of the applicants and the many threats to their lives, the publication of information that might lead to their identification posed a real risk to their lives.

Most recently, in *A v B and C (2001)* the court granted an injunction to restrain a tabloid newspaper from publishing 'kiss and tell stories' concerning the adulterous affairs of a professional footballer. It was a breach of confidence for the women to provide the information in their possession to the newspaper with a view to its publication in the media. It would be a breach of confidence for the paper to publish it. The case was, again, dealt with on the basis of conventional 'breach of confidence' principles. Nevertheless, it illustrates an important shift in favour of the protection of privacy resulting from the HRA. It seems likely that the HRA will, over the next few years, provide the impetus for the English courts to develop a full tort of 'invasion of privacy'.

19.5 Other areas of impact on the media

19.5.1 General principles

The HRA has an impact on the media in a number of other ways:

- Where the media is subject to regulation by governmental bodies, the HRA will have a direct 'vertical' impact – it will restrict the range of permissible interferences with freedom of expression by public authorities.
- Where the courts seek to control the reporting of proceedings, they are now obliged to take into account the right to freedom of expression and impose the minimum restrictions necessary.
- Where the media are involved in 'private law' disputes with individuals or organizations, the HRA will have an indirect, 'horizontal' impact – for example, the principles of the law of defamation (see Chapter 1) have already begun to show significant changes in the light of the HRA.

19.5.2 Freedom of expression

The HRA has given further impetus to the recent recognition of the fundamental importance of freedom of expression in the common law. It is now clear that restrictions on freedom of expression in the public interest must be 'strictly proved':

> . . . if those who seek to bring themselves within paragraph 2 of article 10 are to establish 'convincingly' that they are – and that is what they have to establish – they cannot do so by mere assertion, however eminent the person making the assertion, nor by simply inviting the court to make assumptions; what is required . . . is proper evidence.　　　　　　　　　　　　　　　　　　　*(Kelly v BBC (2001))*

It has been suggested that, because the Convention right to freedom of expression is qualified in favour of the reputation and rights of others (which includes the right to respect for private life under Article 8), when considering an injunction against the media, 'privacy' and 'reputation' rights are as relevant as freedom of expression (*Douglas v Hello! (2001)*).

19.5.3 Media regulation

The media are, of course, subject to substantial statutory and non-statutory regulation. Bodies such as the Independent Television Commission and the Broadcasting Standards Commission (see Chapter 17) are public authorities for the purposes of the HRA and must, therefore, act in a way that is compatible with the Article 10 rights of the media. It is likely that the Press Complaints Commission will also be held to be a public authority for HRA purposes, and it must, therefore, also act compatibly with Convention rights.

19.5.4 Defamation

The courts have been generally cautious in applying Convention principles to the law of defamation. In *Branson v Bower (2000)* it was said that:

> It is important, however, to recognize that the European Convention has not been directly incorporated into English law. The courts must take these matters into account when applying domestic law but they should not be regarded as bypassing our long-established principles. We should use European jurisprudence to assist us in testing, from time to time, whether our own laws are consistent with the rights guaranteed under the Convention. European decisions, however, are often difficult to apply by analogy because they are tied to their own facts . . . In this jurisdiction it happens that we have a civil law of defamation that is sophisticated and highly developed and includes a range of defences for the media.

Nevertheless, the law of defamation does involve considerable interference with the freedom of expression of the media, and is potentially subject to radical revision in the light of the approach taken by the European Court of Human Rights. The impact of Article 10 on a number of aspects of the law of defamation has been considered in the case law since 2 October 2000:

- Publication: the rule that each separate communication of defamatory words gives rise to a separate cause of action has been held to be consistent with Article 10, even when it is applied to publication on the Internet (*Loutchansky v Times Newspapers (2001)*).

- Justification: the requirement that the defendant prove the truth of a defamatory allegation has been held to be compatible with Article 10(2), meeting 'the legitimate purpose' recognized by Article 10(2) of protecting people from the publication of damaging and unjustified falsehoods (*Berezovsky v Forbes (2001)*).

- Reference: the test as to whether the words complained of in fact refer to the claimant is objective and, at common law, the liability for 'unintentional defamation' is strict. However, it has been held that the application of this principle to 'lookalike' photographs is incompatible with Article 10 (*O'Shea v MGN (2001)*).

- Fair comment: the common law of fair comment appears to be consistent with Article 10 (see *Branson v Bower (2001)*). It appears that 'freedom of speech' considerations limit the basis on which the defence can be rebutted by a plea of 'malice' (*Cheng v Paul (2001)*).

- Qualified privilege: it has been said that the principles of qualified privilege in English law are compatible with Article 10 (*Loutchansky v Times Newspapers (2001)*). However, in *Saad Al-Fagih v HH Saudi Research & Marketing (2001)* the Court of Appeal found that the media were entitled to qualified privilege in a case where they had neutrally reported defamatory remarks made by one politician about another without checking them. This approach is consistent with recent European case law (*Thoma v Luxembourg (2001)*), and represents a very considerable liberalizing of the position from the point of view of the press. Qualified privilege has also been found to exist in a case of a story that was written in accordance with the standards of ethical journalism of the country of primary publication (*Lukowiak v Unidad Editorial SA (2001)*). The precise limits of qualified privilege remain controversial, and this is the subject of a number of pending appeals.

- Remedies: it has been held that the combination of Articles 6 and 10 does not give a claimant a right to seek a 'declaration of falsity' (*Loutchansky v Times Newspapers (2001)*).

A number of areas remain to be considered, including the common law rule that a defendant cannot, in mitigation of damage, lead evidence of specific acts of misconduct (the rule in *Scott v Sampson (1882)*) or of other defamatory publications to the same effect. The result of this rule is that a defendant cannot, in practice, lead evidence as to the claimant's actual reputation or the reputation he deserves. It is arguable that this rule is incompatible with Article 10.

19.5.5 Reporting of proceedings

The HRA is likely to encourage a greater openness in the approach taken by the courts in relation to the reporting of proceedings. The Convention was a decisive influence on the radical change in practice in relation to hearings in private under the Civil Procedure Rules, which govern civil litigation.

It seems likely that the remaining restrictions on reporting family proceedings that do not involve children will be substantially relaxed. In *Clibbery v Alan (2001)*, the court considered the conflict between the Article 10 rights of a party who wished to publicize Family Division proceedings concerning property which had taken place in private, and the Article 8 rights of the other party who wished the proceedings to remain private. It was held that a blanket prohibition on disclosure was not 'necessary in a democratic society', there was no 'pressing social need' for such a rule, and it would not be proportionate to the legitimate aim of protecting Article 8 rights.

PART IX

The Law in Other Jurisdictions

20 The Law in Scotland

Rosalind McInnes

20.1 Introduction

There is much about the law of Scotland that is comfortingly familiar to media organizations and media lawyers in England. The Defamation Acts of 1952 and 1996, the Copyright Designs and Patents Act of 1988, the Data Protection Act 1998, the Contempt of Court Act 1981 and the Human Rights Act 1998 are all United Kingdom-wide statutes. It has also been said that the law of confidence is the same in both countries (*Osborne v BBC (1999)*).

However, differences in history, procedure and culture have resulted in a need for those in England to exercise caution when considering the law of Scotland. The Scottish 'civil law' legal system is based on Roman law, and is fundamentally different from the 'common law' English legal system. Moreover, recent years have seen devolutionary sentiment and the creation of the Scottish Parliament increase the scope for legislation in Scotland that takes into account the different traditions of the Scottish legal system. The Regulation of Investigatory Powers (Scotland) Act 2000 and the draft Freedom of Information (Scotland) Bill are prime examples.

Media organizations and journalists should always seek advice from a Scottish lawyer when considering issues relating to the law of Scotland. This chapter sets out the three areas where the greatest risk is involved: defamation, reporting restrictions, and contempt of court.

20.2 Defamation

20.2.1 Definition of defamation

One of the older and more influential formulations for defamation in Scottish law is:

> ... the imputation of something which is criminal, dishonest, or immoral in the character or actions of the person aggrieved ...
>
> (*McLauchlan v Orr, Pollock & Co (1894)*)

However, modern Scottish commentators tend to favour the English definition:

> . . . would the words tend to lower the plaintiff in the estimation of right-thinking members of society generally?
>
> *(Sim v Stretch (1936))*

Cultural differences within Scotland may influence the meaning of 'society'. In 1990, the *Stornoway Gazette* paid damages to the local MP, Calum MacDonald, in respect of a letter that criticized him for not voting in favour of legislation intended to prevent the promotion of homosexuality. Although such an allegation would probably not have been considered defamatory in most parts of Scotland, it clearly was in the Western Isles.

However, the Scottish courts are increasingly unlikely to accept the views of 'splinter groups' of society. In the case of *Bell v Bell's Trustee (2001)* it was held that it was of no assistance to the pursuer, or claimant, to say that:

> . . . an allegation is damaging in the section of society to which he belongs if it is not also disparaging in the view of society as a whole.

20.2.2 Innuendo

As in England, innuendo may found an action for defamation.

In *Russell v Stubbs (1913)*, the appearance of the name of the pursuer on a list of debtors with a note attached to the list implied nothing other than the fact that the name appeared on the court books and was not capable of bearing the innuendo that the pursuer was impecunious. In *Stein v Beaverbrook Newspapers Limited (1968)*, the innuendo that the pursuer was a hypocrite was held to have been properly inferred from a reference that the pursuer had campaigned against chequebook journalism whilst engaging in it himself. In *Morrison v Ritchie (1902)*, the innuendo arose from a newspaper announcement of the birth of twins to a couple who had married the previous month.

20.2.3 Class actions

As in England, members of a class of persons can sue if the class is sufficiently well defined for the defamation to be held to apply to them as individuals.

In *Macphail v Macleod (1895)* it was established that a particular minister could not sue on an attack against ministers generally, but could sue on a charge of drunkenness against the ministers in his presbytery. In *Baigent v BBC (1999)* a total award of £60 000 was made to three members of a family, none of whom had been individually mentioned, in respect of a programme to which the family as a whole took objection.

20.2.4 Onus and standard of proof

The onus (or burden) of proof rests with the defender, the equivalent of the defendant, where he raises the defence of *veritas*, the equivalent of the English defence of justification.

The standard of proof is 'the balance of probabilities'. In *Wray v Associated Newspapers Limited and Another (2000)* it was held that where the 'sting' of the defamation comprised an allegation of commission of a crime, the standard of proof would remain the balance of probabilities but the court would:

> . . . require strong evidence in support of their truthfulness. I should emphasize that by using the phrase 'strong evidence' I am accepting at once that the standard is the balance of probabilities, but the weight necessary to tip that balance in favour of the Defenders, has to be considerable.

20.2.5 Statute

The Defamation Acts of 1952 and 1996 apply, in large part, in the same way as they do in England. Sections 5 to 11 of the Defamation Act 1996 do not apply to Scotland. Changes as a result of devolution were made by Schedule 8 of the Scotland Act 1998.

20.2.6 Differences between Scottish and English law

There are some striking differences between the law of defamation in Scotland and in England.

No criminal defamation
In Scotland, defamation is exclusively a civil wrong or 'delict', the equivalent of tort. There is no such thing as criminal libel.

Publication not required
A defamatory statement is actionable in Scottish law even if no third party hears it.

Libel and slander indistinguishable
There is no practical distinction in Scottish law between oral and written defamation. 'Libel' and 'slander' are sometimes used interchangeably.

Defence of *in rixa*
Words spoken in the heat of the moment in a quarrel may lend themselves to the defence of *in rixa* (*Carroll v BBC (1997)*).

Time limits

The one-year limitation period for issuing a libel action introduced by the Defamation Act 1996 does not apply to Scotland. A person has three years in Scotland in which to raise such an action (Prescription and Limitation (Scotland) Act 1973 as amended 1985).

Experience in England after the introduction of the Defamation Act 1996 may suggest that actions out of time are rarely an issue. However, it may be an option for an English claimant who is out of time in England to sue in Scotland.

No exemplary or punitive damages

Scottish law does not countenance exemplary or punitive damages (*Stein v Beaverbrook Newspapers Ltd (1968)*), although persisting in proclaiming the truth of an allegation by pleading *veritas* may give rise to aggravated damages (*Baigent v BBC (2000)*).

Procedure

Defamation actions may be raised in the sheriff courts throughout Scotland or in the Court of Session in Edinburgh.

If a defamation action is raised and the pursuer dies, a trustee can carry on the action under Section 3 of the Damages (Scotland) Act 1993. Otherwise, as in England, it is not possible to 'defame the dead'.

A Scottish civil jury of 12 jurors hears a defamation case, as opposed to the 15 jurors who hear a criminal trial, unless the court regards this as inappropriate. For example, in *Shanks v BBC (1993)* it was held that an issue involving company frauds would be best heard before a judge. A motion for jury trial was rejected. Despite the relative generosity of Scottish juries to successful defamation pursuers, jury trial remains uncommon in Scotland.

No bar on prior restraint

Unlike the position in England, in Scotland it is currently still possible to stop publication of a defamatory statement even if the pursuer is offering to prove its truth. As recently as 1990, the Court of Session granted an 'interdict', the equivalent of an injunction, in favour of Sheriff Ewan Stewart against the broadcast of a *Focal Point* documentary which claimed that he was unfit for judicial office. However, the interdict was successfully recalled within days.

As a result of Section 12 of the Human Rights Act 1998, it is now unlikely that an interdict would be granted in a defamation action except in extraordinary circumstances. However, even a doomed application for an interdict made at the eleventh hour has the potential to cause a media organization inconvenience. Because defamation actions are comparatively rare in Scotland, some sheriffs may still grant interdicts *ex parte*, in other words without the presence of the defendant, if they are not adequately addressed on the human rights arguments.

For this reason, those who may be the subject of such an application in Scotland should lodge a 'caveat' in the Court of Session and in any sheriff court where an application may be made.

Caveats are documents that may be cheaply and easily lodged, last for a year, and are renewable. Their effect is that the caveat holder is warned in advance of an order sought against him and has the chance to oppose it.

20.2.7 Privilege

Privilege exists at common law and by statute in Scotland. Of most importance to journalists is the absolute statutory privilege in respect of fair and accurate contemporaneous reporting of a public court of justice. Unlike the position in England, litigants in Scotland only have qualified privilege.

Absolute privilege

Absolute privilege covers:

- Statements made in the Westminster and Holyrood Parliaments
- Reports authorized by Parliament
- Statements made in court by a judge, advocate (the equivalent of a barrister), solicitor or witness concerning the particular proceedings.

Qualified privilege

Qualified privilege at common law in Scotland is similar to that in England, and includes giving employee references and the reporting of suspected crime or cruelty to the appropriate authorities. If the statement can only be made in the media, in theory the publication and the individual journalist are protected (*Waddell v BBC (1973)*).

A much diluted form of the United States public figure defence along the lines of *Sullivan v New York Times (1964)* has been seen in a number of Scottish cases (*Langlands v Leng (1916); Waddell v BBC (1973); Mutch v Robertson (1981)*). In *Wray v Associated Newspapers Limited and Another (2000)* the court made it clear that if the allegations had related to the MP's political actions rather than to his domestic life, a different approach would have been in order.

20.2.8 Damages

Juries in Scotland are generous to defamation pursuers. In *Winter v News Scotland (1991)*, a prison wardress at Glenochil Prison sued the *Sun* for alleging she had sexual intercourse with an inmate while on duty. She was awarded the then historic sum of £50 000 by a jury for injury to feelings by publication in the court of session. In 1999, the *Sun* was again sued for defamation by Father Noel Barry, a Catholic priest, and Annie Clinton, a primary school headmistress, for allegations of sexual impropriety. The jury awarded Annie Clinton £125 000 and Noel Barry £45 000. The disparity between the two figures presumably arose because the *Sun* led with evidence of Noel Barry's inappropriate relationship with a former nun (*Barry v News Group Newspapers Ltd (1999)*).

Predictably, defamation actions that involve commercial entities as the pursuer have yielded the highest awards. In *Capital Life v Sunday Mail (1979)* the Capital Life Assurance Company was awarded £327 000 excluding interest and 'expenses', in other words costs, in respect of a defamatory statement that they had engaged in unlawful business practices.

However, even without such features awards have been increasing at what is a worrying rate for the media. In *Baigent v BBC (1999)* a total award of £186 000 was made to five family members who ran a nursing home in Lanarkshire in the wake of a documentary saying that the elderly residents were poorly treated. In *Wray v Associated Newspapers and Another (2000)* the MP Jimmy Wray was awarded damages of £60 000 after a newspaper reported his former wife's claims that he had physically abused her. The judge conceded that the figure chosen was 'instinctive'. In contrast, Anton Gecas unsuccessfully sued Scottish Television in 1992 in respect of a programme that alleged he was involved with the death squad extermination of Jewish civilians. The court said that if it had found in Gecas's favour it would have awarded £20 000 in respect of the allegations.

Awards of damages at these levels, whether granted by judge or jury, have proved resistant to appeal.

20.3 Reporting restrictions

20.3.1 Defamation

Since the introduction of the Defamation Act 1996, fair and accurate contemporaneous reporting of a public court of justice in Scotland is granted absolute privilege for the purposes of defamation actions.

Such reports need not be full:

> There is no duty on a reporter in a report of a law suit to make his report exhaustive, it is . . . sufficient if the reporter gives the result of the litigation truly and correctly.
>
> (Duncan v Associated Newspapers (1929))

However, the report must give equal prominence to both sides (*Wright and Greig v Outram (1890)*).

The publisher has the onus of proof as to whether the report is fair and accurate (*Hope v Outram (1909)*).

In *Cunningham v Scotsman Publications (1987)* the court held that privilege applies to documents 'referred to and founded upon before the court with a view to advancing a submission which is being made', even if the whole document is not read.

However, the 'record' (pronounced with the emphasis on the second syllable), the parties' collected written pleadings which form the basis for any hearing of evidence or argument in the case, is not itself privileged until its contents are referred to expressly or by implication in open court.

In short, even if a journalist obtains from one of the parties, or a helpful solicitor or a clerk, a set of the pleadings in the case, they should only be quoted with care at an early stage in the case.

20.3.2 Contempt of Court Act 1981

The privilege granted to court reporting for contempt purposes is as set out in Section 4 of the Contempt of Court Act 1981.

Section 4(2) Orders

Order for reporting restrictions under Section 4(2) of the Contempt of Court Act 1981 are quite commonly sought in Scotland.

Orders under Section 4(2) have been granted in relation to hearings:

- That deal with the impact of prejudicial publications (*Robb v Caledonian Newspapers (1995)*)
- Where evidence has been given in the course of a plea in bar of trial (*HMA v Little (1999)*)
- Where separate trials have been set with linked charges or defendants
- Where the accused is particularly psychologically vulnerable (*Scottish Daily Record and Sunday Mail Petitioners (1998)*).

The media have no direct right to appeal a Section 4(2) Order in Scotland, since the terms of Section 159 of the Criminal Justice Act 1988 do not extend to Scotland.

However, it is accepted that the media nonetheless have a right of challenge. In 1999, Kim Galbraith was convicted of murdering her husband. The trial was very widely reported. Galbraith appealed, and sought a Section 4(2) Order prohibiting all reporting until the appeal was determined or until the end of any second trial. The Scottish media were, unusually, given prior notice by the court of the application, and invited to address the court. They opposed the application.

The court refused to grant the order:

> . . . as we have explained, the main thrust of [the] argument was that, unless the Section 4(2) Order were made, the appeal proceedings in this case would prompt a barrage of articles containing comment from Mr Galbraith's relatives and others

which would be hostile to the appellant and would poison the minds of any potential jurors in a retrial. It is plain, however, that a report of this kind would go beyond a simple report of the proceedings . . . In that event, the court would have power to deal with the matter in terms of Section 2(2) [of the Contempt of Court Act 1981] and in an appropriate case, to punish the publisher. That is the mechanism which Parliament has provided for protecting the course of justice from the effect of publications of that kind. The court's power in Section 4(2) is not intended to be used to deal with such publication but to deal, rather, with reports of its proceedings which are fair and accurate and should nonetheless be postponed. It would accordingly be an abuse of this particular power to pronounce an order . . . not for the purpose of warding off an anticipated consequence of the fair and accurate reporting of the appeal proceedings but for the purpose of warding off prejudicial comment which those proceedings might prompt.

(Galbraith v HMA (2000))

Since *Galbraith*, the Scottish supreme courts have developed a practice of advising various media organizations of the existence of an order and giving them a chance to oppose it before the Order is made final. A generally more cautious attitude towards reporting restrictions has developed in the wake of the case.

Interim interdict

An interim interdict (or interlocutory injunction), which prevents material from being broadcast or published, is apparently still available, even where publication would not amount to contempt (*Muir v BBC (1997)*).

Children

As in England, there are restrictions on the identification of children in proceedings. Section 47 of the Criminal Procedure (Scotland) Act 1995 restricts reporting of particulars, including photographs, calculated to reveal the identities of people under 16 involved in criminal proceedings as the accused or alleged victim. The court may also impose restrictions in relation to the identity of other child witnesses, although this is not done automatically.

The court may also restrict reporting in relation to children involved in civil proceedings under Section 46 of the Children and Young Persons (Scotland) Act 1937 as amended by the Broadcasting Act 1990. Section 44 of the Children (Scotland) Act 1995 prohibits publication of matters in respect of proceedings within the 'children's hearing' system.

In the past, the Scottish court has treated photographs as a statutory breach even when the photographs were not thought to identify the child (*McArdle v Orr (1994)*).

Only living children are protected by reporting restrictions (*Caledonian Newspapers Ltd, Petitioners (1995)*).

296

20.4 Contempt of court

20.4.1 General principles

The Contempt of Court Act 1981 (the 'CCA') was designed in part to harmonize the law of contempt of court on both sides of the border. The last couple of years have seen a greater similarity of approach between Scotland and England. The Scottish media have benefited from the successive stewardship of the Scottish Supreme Courts of Lord Hope and Lord Rodger, both of whom have shown a visionary regard for freedom of expression and the role of the media.

However, the Scottish media continue to operate within a law of contempt that is considerably less liberal than that enjoyed by its southern counterparts. Moreover, Scottish contempt law is still the riskiest area of involvement for a non-Scottish media organization. The Scottish courts impose some of the strictest rules against pre-trial publicity in the world.

20.4.2 Plea in 'bar of trial'

The situation in which a newspaper is found to be in contempt, but the trial of the subject of the newspaper story goes ahead, has a long pedigree in Scottish law. A successful plea in 'bar of trial', in other words that the trial should not go ahead because of the damaging effects of publicity, is rare in Scottish law. Quashing a conviction on the basis of such publicity, as happened in the case of the Taylor sisters in England (*R v Taylor & Taylor (1993); R v Solicitor-General ex parte Taylor & Taylor (1994)*) is unknown.

In 1989, the *Daily Express* was fined £30 000 by a Scottish court for contempt of court in respect of a story checked in Manchester by an English barrister (*HMA v News Group Newspapers (1989)*). The newspaper had published an article under the headline 'Hit Man Guns Down Red Defector'. Although the article did not name the arrested man, the court held:

> ... [he] could readily and sufficiently be identified in general from the text of the article ... The story was told in a sensational way and we do not for one moment accept that the article did not tend to suggest that the guilt of the arrested person might be presumed ... It described the victim as a Yugoslavian political exile ... Under the headline it contained assertions of fact about the incident itself, including the statement 'He was blasted by a fusillade of shots fired from a parked car ... The car, believed to be a black-coloured Metro, raced away'.

> [We] were astonished that the publishers of the Scottish *Daily Express* have attempted to defend their article, which in our opinion was a disgraceful one, perhaps one of the clearest examples of contempt of court which could be envisaged.

The court went on to say that it was unfortunate, given the extent to which the Scottish legal system depends on the absence of pre-trial publicity, that advice about publication was given by an English lawyer rather than a Scottish one. Despite the excoriation of the *Express* by the court, the prosecution of the arrested man continued. He was ultimately convicted.

The double standard involved and the disparity with English law have been criticized by media lawyers in Scotland. In recent years, the Scottish courts have begun to develop a greater regard for consistency in this area.

20.4.3 Identification

A striking difference between Scotland and England is the rarity with which pictures of criminal suspects may be published in Scotland. Although such a publication is usually only a contempt of court where an issue of identification arises, it is best to assume that identification will be an issue in the average Scottish case.

In March 1992, the BBC was found guilty of contempt for broadcasting a couple of seconds of footage of accused murderer Paul Ferris being led from a police van into court. The court observed:

> It is clearly essential that witnesses are not materially influenced in any way. It follows that in any case where the question of identification may arise it is clear that the publication in the press or television of any film, photograph, or even an artist's likeness during a trial or after a warrant has been issued, causes a potential risk to the administration of justice . . . There is only one safe route for the media to follow and it is this – do not publish any picture of an accused person in Scotland until a trial is finished or the charge has been dropped by the Lord Advocate. It has been made clear in many cases that any breach of this rule is liable to be dealt with by this court as contempt.

In recent years there have been occasions where the Scottish media have published photographs of an accused in the course of his trial. However, each instance has been exceptional in one way or the other. Photographs were printed of Mohammed Sarwar, the Govan MP, prior to his acquittal of electoral offences (*HMA v Scotsman Publications (1999)*). Photographs were also printed of the two men accused of the Lockerbie bombing. By the time the case came to trial, although identification was very clearly an issue, images of the accused had been shown around the world over a period of almost 10 years. Photographs were also printed of Sister Marie Docherty, a nun found guilty of physical child abuse in Aberdeen in September 2000. However, it had been made explicit that identification would not be treated as an issue in the case.

Printing pictures of witnesses who have completed their evidence will not, under normal circumstances, pose a risk. However, there may be a risk if a defence of 'incrimination' is raised – in other words, if the accused states that another person is responsible for the crime.

20.4.4 Strict liability rule

Complainant

In Scotland, the accused himself, the Lord Advocate and the judge or sheriff may bring proceedings for contempt. This potential for a three-sided attack may partly explain the greater caution of the Scottish media in contempt matters.

Active proceedings

When proceedings are 'active', the strict liability rule applies as it does in England.

Criminal proceedings

Criminal proceedings become active in Scotland from:

- The moment of arrest without warrant
- The grant of a warrant to arrest
- The grant of a warrant to cite, or
- Service of an indictment or of a document specifying the charge.

There is no equivalent of the 'oral charge' in Scotland.

Criminal proceedings are concluded by:

- Acquittal or sentence
- Any other verdict, finding, order or decision that puts an end to the proceedings, or
- Discontinuance or operation of law.

When the Crown in Scotland abandons or 'deserts' a trial, it may do so either for the time being or absolutely. Only absolute, or express, abandonment brings the proceedings to an end. *Express Newspapers* were fined £50 000 (*Express Newspapers plc (1999)*) for reporting fully on a case that had been deserted for the time being, under the misapprehension that this meant that the matter was entirely concluded.

Civil proceedings and criminal and civil appeal proceedings

For most Scottish civil actions, the 'closing of the Record', in other words the period by which the parties' written pleadings are supposed to be complete, is the significant date when proceedings become 'active'.

In the case of a motion or application to the court, for example for interim interdict, the trigger is the point at which the motion is enrolled or the application made.

In any other case, the relevant point is when the date for a hearing is fixed or when a hearing is allowed (Schedule 1 Paragraph 14 of the CCA).

Given the comparative rarity of the civil jury in Scotland and the assumption that those acting in a judicial capacity, even trained lay justices (*Aitchison v Bernardi (1984)*), are substantially immune from being influenced by media comment, civil proceedings and criminal and civil appeal proceedings are unlikely to give rise to contempt difficulties.

Substantial risk of serious prejudice

Under Section 2(2) of the CCA, strict liability will arise in respect of 'a publication which creates a substantial risk that the course of justice in the proceedings in question will be seriously impeded or prejudiced'.

In *HMA v News Group Newspapers (1989)*, the court held:

> In our opinion, which fortunately coincides with opinions expressed in English cases, there can be no contempt unless there is some risk, greater than a minimal one, that the course of justice in the proceedings in question will be seriously impeded or prejudiced. The adverb 'seriously' does not require translation. It must be given its familiar and ordinary meaning.

In that case, 'substantial' was taken as meaning:

> . . . material or . . . greater than minimal risk that the course of justice in the proceedings . . . would be . . . seriously impeded or prejudiced.

In contrast, 'seriously' was held to require a real impediment or prejudice to the course of justice.

In *HMA v Caledonian Newspapers Ltd (1995)*, the court observed:

> We do not agree . . . that the strict liability rule imposes a very high test . . .

> In the case of criminal proceedings . . . the impediment or prejudice will be regarded as serious if it may affect the outcome of the trial in regard to such matters as the evidence of witnesses or the evaluation of the jury of the evidence . . .

> If, as in . . . probably most . . . criminal trials upon indictment, it is the outcome of the trial or the need to discharge the jury . . . that is put at risk, there can be no question that that which . . . is put at risk is as serious as anything could be.

The court agreed that the public policy underlying the strict liability rule was that of deterrence.

Risk

It is probably impossible, on either side of the border, to set out exhaustively the ways in which contempt of court may be committed. However, certain criteria regularly arise in connection with the assessment of risk.

Link to accused

Where the publication or broadcast does not link the accused with the charges, there may be no contempt (*Robb v Caledonian Newspapers (1995)*).

Public domain

It is not a defence that other newspapers have already released the same or similar information in recent history. Repetition may be regarded as especially dangerous.

Curing prejudice

The ability of the judge or sheriff to direct the jury so as to 'cure' any prejudice caused is not traditionally regarded by the Scottish courts as an adequate defence unless the directions would, in any event, be appropriate in the circumstances (*HMA v Scottish Media Newspapers (2000)*). The difference between a general and a specific direction might not be that material.

Jury

The absence of a jury is a matter of vital significance in assessing risk. Scottish sheriffs sit alone in many criminal cases. It is generally considered to be the case that they and other judges are capable of ignoring media comment.

In *Al Megrahi & Khalifa Fhima v Times Newspapers (1999)*, the two men accused of the Lockerbie bombing argued that the *Times* newspaper was in contempt of court in respect of an article and editorial in which the *Sunday Times* claimed Colonel Ghadaffi had personally ordered the bombing of the PanAm flight. The editorial, headed 'The Guilt of Ghadaffi', stated:

> It would be an odd sort of justice that found [Ghadaffi's] cat's paws guilty of murder and let the real villain off the hook ... but even if the suspects are convicted (and it is conceivable that a verdict in Scottish law of not proven or even not guilty might be found after all this time), what will the Government do then? Lift sanctions against a regime convicted of mass murder.

The two men claimed, not unreasonably, that this article assumed their guilt. However, because the trial was without a jury and before a panel of senior Scottish judges, they were unable to put forward the normal arguments. The court found that the *Sunday Times* pieces did not constitute a contempt. However, there was some suggestion by the court that judges may in certain circumstances be 'subconsciously' influenced or influenced by the publication of, for example, details of previous convictions. It is thought that these suggestions primarily reflect the particular concerns of the Lockerbie trial.

Time of trial

The presumed shortness of public memory is a major factor in determining whether or not there will be a finding of contempt. The risk steadily increases as the trial approaches. Scottish law has relatively short timescales in which an accused is brought to trial, known as the '110-day' and '40-day' rules. An accused may not be detained for a total period of more than 110 days by virtue of a warrant committing him for trial for any offence except to be placed on trial. An accused may not be detained for a period of more than 40 days after the bringing of a complaint against him in court. Extensions of the 110-day period may be granted only by a High Court judge. Extensions of the 40-day period may be granted by a sheriff. As a result of these rules, trials can move quickly in Scotland and time is not quite as great a healer for contempt purposes.

The further the circulation of the publication and the more intense its circulation in the area around the trial itself, the greater the risk.

Public figures

The celebrity of the accused can be a double-edged sword for the media. It may permit them to use a photograph of the accused during the currency of the trial. Mohammed Sarwar's celebrity status as an MP was probably the single deciding factor in the *Scotsman* recently being held in contempt (*HMA v Scotsman Publications (1999)*). On the other hand, the fact that the accused is an offender of some notoriety does not mean that it is safe to remind the general public of this fact yet again.

There are some signs that the courts in Scotland are beginning to recognize that an article relating to a well-known public figure may not tell potential jurors anything of which they are not already aware. In *HMA v Scottish Media Newspapers (2000)* the court considered a front-page article in the *Evening Times* about the arrest of a Scottish actor, Iain McColl, for allegedly threatening a sheriff officer with an axe. The article referred to the actor's debts, his 'well-documented history of personal setbacks, including drink problems', the fact that his neighbours had complained about disturbances at his home, and to his claim to have 'beaten his demons'. The court observed that the case was unlikely to come to trial until around nine months after publication, and said:

> Where personalities, whether from the world of politics, sport or entertainment, are tried by a jury, the jurors may often know more about their way of life and the background to any charge than they would in an ordinary case. That in itself may mean that the judge presiding at any trial would think it appropriate to give a more pointed direction about the need for a jury to reach their verdict solely on the evidence led in court. Nothing in the article would in our view significantly affect the decision whether to give such a direction.

Subject matter

Suggestions in the publication that the accused is guilty or that he only has a technical or legal defence are clearly capable of creating a risk, even if the implication is not direct. In

HMA v Scotsman Publications (1999) the court accepted that the average reader, reading allegations that witnesses in a trial were being intimidated, would assume that the accused or supporters of the accused were behind any such intimidation. The court observed:

> Where, in the context of the criminal prosecution, particularly one involving charges of election fraud and attempting to pervert the course of justice, there is reference to fear and intimidation, the ordinary reader is likely to assume that the accused is ultimately the person whose intimidation is to be feared . . . I have to say that in my opinion there could hardly be a more prejudicial suggestion in advance of a trial than the one in question.

The reporting of previous convictions is extremely dangerous, as is the reporting of alleged confessions (*X v Sweeney (1982)*).

Implications that a witness other than the accused is dishonest may also amount to contempt. The *Daily Record* was found in contempt in 1999 for prejudicing a 'children's hearing', which takes place without a jury, by carrying an article the day before an eight-year-old child was due to give evidence about allegations of parental ill-treatment. The newspaper argued that it was unlikely an eight-year-old would read the article or understand it sufficiently to let it colour her version of events in court. However, the court said that it was satisfied that there would have been a substantial risk of the story impairing or prejudicing the evidence of the child and her two siblings, because the day before the three children were due to give evidence one of them had been branded a liar in the newspaper. That was held to create a risk of prejudice.

In the significant decision of *Cox & Griffiths, Petrs (1998)*, the *Daily Record* described the movement of a number of high-risk prisoners from one prison to another under heavy security precautions and quoted a police insider and a prison source on the security measures involved. The trial judge held the article to be a contempt of court and imposed a fine of £1500 each on the editor and the reporter. On appeal, it was held the article did not give rise to a substantial risk of serious prejudice to the course of justice. The court accepted that although there may have been a risk of prejudice, potential members of the jury did not need a 'germ-free atmosphere'. The court held that risk of prejudice had to be weighed against freedom of speech.

20.4.5 Common law contempt

There is one somewhat unusual instance of common law contempt of court finding in Scotland that was quashed on appeal. In February 1997, a freelance journalist was found guilty of common law contempt in court and fined £750 after he misheard evidence in a crowded courtroom during a drugs trial and filed an incorrect report. Despite the reporter's submission that he did not have the necessary intent to impede or prejudice the administration of justice, the court held that the report was so reckless that it was not necessary to establish intention. On appeal, it was held that the trial judge had applied the incorrect test.

20.4.6 Statutory defences

Scottish decisions on the statutory defences of innocent publication under Section 3 of the CCA and discussions in good faith of public affairs under Section 5 of the CCA are scant.

Section 3
A somewhat unorthodox use was made of the Section 3 defence by the newspapers that printed the copy of a freelance journalist who radically misheard the evidence and was found guilty of the common law offence of contempt (see part 20.4.5 above).

Section 5
There was a brief discussion of the Section 5 defence in the Lockerbie case. The court observed that there were questions about its applicability, particularly if material that was said to be 'incidental' incorporated specific reference to the trial concerned.

Generally, the construction of the Section 5 defence in Scotland is characterized as 'much narrower' than it is in England. In 1997, the BBC made a programme about brutality in prisons. A prison warder who was due to be tried for an alleged assault successfully obtained an interdict which stopped the programme from going out until after his trial. The BBC argued that the programme was a discussion in good faith of public affairs and fell under the Section 5 defence. The Scottish court held that it would not consider a Section 5 defence before a publication had actually occurred. In other words, the court held that the defence could only be used by a person who was accused of committing contempt. It could not be used by a person to publish a controversial article or programme (*Muir v BBC (1997)*). The European Commission on Human Rights declined to intervene in the case.

21 The Law in the United States of America

Estelle Overs

21.1 Introduction

The American legal system is one of the most important in the world today. It affects legal, business, technological and political issues throughout the globe.

The American legal system is based on English law. However, it has evolved into a two-tier federal legal system. Each of the 50 states making up the union of the United States of America has independent legal authority and its own laws and constitution. Co-existing with the laws and constitution of each individual state is the separate unified system of federal law, specifically granted to the federal government of the union of the United States of America by the United States Constitution (the 'Constitution'). Federal law can either be made by judges sitting in federal courts or passed as law by Congress. The Constitution provides that whenever there is a conflict between state law and federal law, federal law will prevail.

The Constitution is an important source of law in the United States. It provides citizens with a number of 'rights' that limit the power of the government over their actions. Some of the rights apply only to the federal government. Some apply to both state and the federal governments. A few limited rights even apply to actions between individuals. The Bill of Rights, which is set out in the first ten Amendments to the Constitution, is the most important source of limitation on the federal government's power. Most of the rights in the first ten Amendments are also applicable to state governments. Until the incorporation of the European Convention on Human Rights under the Human Rights Act 1998, there was no equivalent source of 'rights' in English law.

Freedom of speech and freedom of the press are rights granted under the First Amendment, and are therefore considered to be 'fundamental' principles. However, these freedoms are not absolute. State governments and the federal government can legislate in respect of them, although such legislation is subject to constitutional challenge in the courts.

This chapter sets out state-based law as followed by the majority of the states, as well as federal law passed under the authority of the Constitution. Unlike the position in England, civil actions in the United States are often heard by a judge and jury. The term 'plaintiff' is used instead of 'claimant' in the United States.

21.2 Defamation

Freedom of speech and freedom of the press are uninhibited by reason of the First Amendment to the Constitution. However, over the last 40 years the courts have attempted to provide protection for those whose reputation has been damaged by defamatory speech.

It is generally considered to be more difficult for a plaintiff to issue proceedings for defamation in the United States than it is in England. This is because a plaintiff in the United States has a considerable number of legal hurdles to overcome in order to prove all elements of the tort, particularly if the defamatory statement involves a 'matter of public concern'. Many defamation actions in the United States are determined at an early stage in the proceedings by a finding of summary judgment in favour of the defendant or settle before they reach trial.

Media organizations and journalists should be aware that there is no guarantee it is safe to publish a story in England just because it did not attract a defamation lawsuit in the United States.

21.2.1 Elements of the tort

The law of defamation in the United States is divided into two parts: the common law elements and the Constitutional requirements. Where a defamatory statement involves a *private* person and a *private* matter, the *common law* tort elements are applied. Where a defamatory statement involves a '*matter of public concern*', the plaintiff, whether a private person or a public official or figure, must prove two additional *Constitutional* requirements.

The elements of the common law tort of defamation are defamatory language:

- Of or concerning the plaintiff
- Which is published by the defendant to a third person, and
- Which causes damage to the plaintiff's reputation.

If the defamatory statement involves a 'matter of public concern', the Constitution requires the plaintiff prove two additional elements:

- Falsity of the statement, and
- Fault on the part of the defendant.

Defamatory language

Defamatory language includes any words, pictures or other forms of direct or indirect remark that tend adversely to affect the reputation of the plaintiff. Only a living person may be defamed.

Publication

Publication takes place when the defamatory statement is communicated, either intentionally or negligently, to a third person. It is the intent to publish, not the intent to defame, which is important.

Although each publication of a defamatory statement is a separate publication for the purpose of awarding damages, most American courts have adopted the 'single publication' rule under which all copies of a newspaper, magazine or book are treated as one publication. However, damages are still calculated by looking at the total effect of the published defamatory statement on all those who read it.

A 'primary publisher' such as a newspaper or television station will be held responsible to the same extent as the author of the defamatory statement. For example, the *Washington Post* would be liable to the plaintiff to the same extent as the journalist who wrote the defamatory story published in its pages.

A 'republisher', in other words someone who repeats a defamatory statement, will be held liable on the same basis as a primary publisher even if the republisher repeats the source or makes it clear it does not believe the statement. If the *New York Times* published the defamatory story previously published in the *Washington Post*, it would be liable on the same basis as the *Washington Post* and the journalist who wrote the article, even if it had stated that the article was republished or acknowledged that the article was not truthful.

Matter of public concern

Where the defamation relates to a 'matter of public concern', the plaintiff must also prove the falsity of the statement (*Philadelphia Newspapers, Inc v Hepps (1986)*) and fault on the part of the defendant.

The type of fault the plaintiff must prove depends on the status of the plaintiff:

- A private person must prove negligence regarding the falsity of the statement
- A 'public official' (*Sullivan v New York Times (1964)*) or a 'public figure' (*Associated Press v Walker (1967)*) must prove malice.

The definition of 'public figure' is very broad. It encompasses someone who has achieved 'pervasive fame or notoriety' such as a famous film star or celebrity sports star, business and community leaders and politicians, or someone who has 'voluntarily assumed a central role in a public controversy' such as a well-known environmental or political activist (*Gertz v Robert Welsh, Inc (1974)*).

Malice

Malice was defined in the well-known case *Sullivan v New York Times (1964)* as knowledge on the part of the defendant that the statement was false, or a reckless disregard as to its truth or falsity. In that case, the *New York Times* published an advertisement by a civil rights group that alleged that the plaintiff, the Commissioner for Public Affairs in a city in Alabama, had assisted in the expulsion and harassment of black students and the wrongful arrest of Dr Martin Luther King. The plaintiff sued the *New York Times* over the allegations. Many of the allegations turned out to be false. At trial, the jury found in favour of the plaintiff. However, the United States Supreme Court reversed the decision. The court held that the First Amendment of the Constitution allowed the harsh criticism of public officials, even if the criticisms were proved to be false. The court held that in such circumstances it was necessary for the plaintiff to show 'actual malice' on the part of the publisher.

21.2.2 Libel and slander

Like the English law, defamatory language is placed into two categories. *Libel* is the written or printed form of defamatory language. Most courts include scripted television and radio programmes and electronic media within the category of libel. *Slander* is spoken defamation. Some courts class ad-libbed television and radio programmes as slander. The distinction is relevant only as to proof of damages.

21.2.3 Defences

Consent
A defendant may raise the complete defence of consent to all allegations of defamation.

Truth
In common law cases the defendant may raise truth, which is the equivalent of justification in English law, as a complete defence.

Absolute privilege
Absolute privilege may protect a defendant who reports a defamatory statement made during judicial proceedings, by legislators during debate, by government officials exercising the functions of their office or in a 'compelled broadcast'. A 'compelled broadcast' is one in which a radio or television station must allow the speaker airtime or a newspaper must print a public notice. This usually involves presidential or political candidates during elections.

Qualified privilege
Qualified privilege can be invoked in respect of reports of official or public proceedings or meetings. However, it can be lost if the plaintiff can prove malice on the part of the defendant. Although it provides a defence in relation to accurate reports of false statements, it does not provide a defence for inaccurate reports.

21.3 Copyright

21.3.1 General principles

Copyright protection in the United States is governed by federal law under the Copyright Act 1976 as amended. The Copyright Act 1976 protects works created after 1 January 1978.

Copyright protects original works of authorship that are expressed in a 'tangible' form, in other words written down or recorded. For copyright to exist in a work, it will usually fall within one of the following categories:

- Literary, musical and dramatic works
- Pictorial, graphic, and sculptural works
- Motion pictures and other audiovisual works
- Sound recordings.

The categories are not exhaustive. Like the law of copyright in the United Kingdom, the categories can be considered broadly. For example, computer programs can be registered as 'literary works'. Compilations and derivative works can also be copyrighted.

Copyright does not protect ideas, news, information, names, works that have not been expressed in a 'tangible form' (such as improvisation or performances that have not been written down or recorded) or 'common property' such as calendars and height and weight charts.

Like the position under the law of the United Kingdom, joint authors of a work will be co-owners of the copyright in the work unless there is an agreement to the contrary.

Freelancers retain some copyright in their work. In the case of *New York Times Co Inc v Tasini (2001)* the Supreme Court held that articles written for the *New York Times* by freelancers could not be licensed by the newspaper for inclusion in electronic databases because in the absence of an express transfer of copyright the newspaper acquired copyright in the articles only for the purpose of 'reproducing and distributing the contribution as part of that particular collective work, any revision of that collective work and any later collective work in the same series' (Section 201(c) of the Copyright Act 1976). The court held that inclusion of freelance articles in electronic databases was a separate work and not a 'reproduction, distribution, revision or the same series'.

21.3.2 Publication

Protection under the Copyright Act 1976 is available to both published and unpublished works. Under the previous legislation, publication and notice of copyright was necessary in order to obtain federal copyright protection. Publication remains relevant for works published after 1 January 1978 because all works published in the United States must be deposited with the Library of Congress in Washington.

21.3.3 Domicile and nationality

Unpublished works

Copyright protection is available for all unpublished works, regardless of the domicile or nationality of the author.

Published works

Copyright protection can be secured for published works if the author is a national or resident of the United States or a national or resident of a country that is a party to an international treaty.

The United States grants authors from other jurisdictions reciprocal protection of copyright as a result of its ratification of the two main international treaties on copyright, the Berne Convention as amended by the World Intellectual Property Organization (WIPO) Treaty 1996 in respect of new information and communication technologies and the Universal Copyright Convention. The WIPO is a specialized agency of the United Nations that has taken a leading role in developing global policy and co-ordinates and administers international treaties relating to intellectual property protection.

21.3.4 Notice and registration

It is not necessary to place a notice on or register an original work in order to obtain copyright protection. Copyright is secured automatically as soon as a work is expressed in a 'tangible' form, in other words written down or recorded. Although notice was a requirement under the Copyright Act 1976 it was abolished when the United States became a signatory in 1989 to the Berne Convention.

However, it is prudent to place a notice on a work and register with the Copyright Office at the Library of Congress in Washington. Use of a notice and registration informs the public that the work is protected by copyright, identifies the copyright author and ensures that copyright infringers cannot claim to be ignorant of the existence of copyright in the work. The formula ©, the name of the copyright owner and date of first publication should be placed on the work. In addition, registration is necessary for works of United States origin before proceedings for infringement may be filed in court.

21.3.5 Duration

Works created on or after 1 January 1978

Works expressed in tangible form on or after 1 January 1978 are protected from the moment of creation for the author's life plus 70 years.

Works created before 1 January 1 1978

The duration of protection for works created before 1 January 1978 is dependent on whether the work was published and registered.

Not published or registered
The duration of copyright will generally be the same as works created on or after 1 January 1978.

Published or registered
Copyright commences on the date of publication, or the date of registration if unpublished, plus 28 years. Renewal is automatic during the twenty-eighth year for an extra period of 67 years, making the total period of protection 95 years.

21.3.6 Infringement

Copyright is infringed though copying. Infringement actions can only be brought in a federal court, not a state court. Registration is necessary for works of United States origin before proceedings for infringement may be filed.

21.3.7 Remedies

The principal remedy for infringement is an injunction, either in preliminary or permanent form. Damages are also available which are designed to compensate the plaintiff's loss and prevent the defendant from making a profit. The court can order the impounding and destruction of infringing material, as well as the equipment used to manufacture it.

The court also has the discretion to award the winning party the costs of the proceedings. Unlike the English legal system, in the United States the costs of proceedings are not presumed to be awarded to the winner.

21.3.8 Cyber-crime convention

The Council of Europe, a political organization founded in 1949 which develops agreements to standardize the social and legal practices of member countries, has drawn up a convention on cyber-crime[1] that prohibits the reproduction and distribution of copyright protected material. The convention was adopted on 8 November 2001 and will be legally effective when at least five countries ratify it, a process expected to take up to two years. Although the United States is not a member state, it has been invited to become involved with the convention.

---

[1]The convention can be found at http://conventions.coe.int/treaty/en/projects/cybercrime.htm.

21.4 New media

The United States is at the forefront of the development of law and legislation in relation to new media.

21.4.1 Online defamation

Unlike the liability imposed upon newspapers and broadcasters, providers of 'interactive computer services' are not liable for publishing or for failing to edit, withhold or restrict access to defamatory material written by others. The situation is different in England. Section 230(c) of the Communications Decency Act 1996 provides:

> No provider or user of an interactive computer service shall be treated as the publisher or speaker of any information provided by another information content provider.

'Information content provider' is defined in Section 230(e)(3) as:

> . . . any person or entity that is responsible, in whole or in part, for the creation or development of information provided through the Internet or any other interactive computer service.

The legislation was enacted by Congress in recognition of the difficulties faced in regulating content on the Internet because of the speed with which information can be communicated and to overrule the case of *Stratton Oakmont Inc v Prodigy Services Co (1995)* in which Prodigy, an Internet service provider, was found liable for defamation. It was also enacted in an effort to avoid the development of self-regulation of content on the Internet as part of an government policy to encourage Internet service providers to develop blocking and filtering technologies to allow parents to control access by children to inappropriate material online.

The effect of Section 230 of the Communications Decency Act 1996 was felt in the case of *Blumenthal v Drudge (1998)*. Sidney Blumenthal was an assistant to President Bill Clinton. He brought a defamation action in the District Court of Columbia against Matt Drudge, the author of an online gossip column called 'The Drudge Report', in which Drudge alleged that Blumenthal had assaulted his wife and that the assault been 'covered up'. Blumenthal also brought an action against AOL because it made 'The Drudge Report' available to its subscribers. Although the court was of the view that AOL had editorial control over the article and should have exercised such editorial control, it was bound by the provisions of Section 230 and held that AOL was immune from suit.

Although Internet service providers cannot be sued for defamation, they can be ordered to divulge the identities of anonymous individuals who post defamatory statements on sites hosted by them. In 2000, a Florida state court ordered Yahoo! and AOL to hand over the identities of individuals alleged to have posted defamatory messages on bulletin boards hosted by them concerning the plaintiff, Eric Hvide. The plaintiff had issued proceedings against anonymous defendants called 'John Doe 1 through 8, persons presently unknown to the plaintiff but whose true identities will be included in the amendments hereto when those identities are discovered' (*Eric Hvide v John Does (2000)*).

The case generated considerable controversy as a result of the implications for the loss of anonymity on the Internet. The American Civil Liberties Union, a non-profit organization 'dedicated to preserving the principles of individual liberty embodied in the Bill of Rights', filed briefs in the proceedings to address the issues involved in balancing the right of the plaintiff to protect his reputation and the First Amendment right of the defendants to speak anonymously. In October 2000, the Court of Appeals in Florida upheld the order for disclosure against Yahoo! and AOL.

There have been several cases where companies and individuals have issued proceedings for online defamation against defendants alleged to have posted defamatory statements on the Internet. In 1999, a San Diego company called ZiaSun Technologies sued four people for allegedly posting false information about the company in Internet chatrooms. The company sought an injunction preventing the defendants from posting further messages. The defendants raised truth as a defence. In January 2000, a federal court granted the first ever preliminary injunction against Internet defamation (*ZiaSun Technologies Inc v Floyd Schneider (2000)*). The case was subsequently settled out of court.

21.4.2 Copyright

Existing works

The Digital Millennium Copyright Act 1998 (the 'DMCA') is the most comprehensive reform of United States copyright law for several years. It updates the Copyright Act 1976 in the digital age by making it illegal to offer technology that circumvents copyright protection systems. It also implements the WIPO Copyright Treaty 1996.

Several high-profile Internet copyright infringement lawsuits have been brought under the provisions of the Copyright Act 1976 and the DMCA by the Recording Industry Association of America (RIAA) and the Motion Picture Association of America (MPAA).

RIAA v Napster

In December 1999, the RIAA brought proceedings for a preliminary injunction against Napster, the well-known music file swapping service. The RIAA accused Napster of facilitating the direct infringement of copyright in music recordings by allowing users to exchange compressed files of copyright protected music through its online service. Following a finding of infringement, the court issued a preliminary injunction against Napster that effectively shut the service down (*A&M Records Inc v Napster Inc (2000)*).

In February 2001 the Court of Appeals upheld the injunction. However, it prevented the closure of the Napster service by remitting the injunction to the trial judge to be drafted in narrower terms. The Court of Appeals held that the injunction must only prevent the exchange of music files whose owners notified Napster of copyright infringement. In August 2001 the RIAA applied to the court for an order for summary judgment against Napster on the issue of liability.

MPAA v 2600

In 2000, the MPAA brought proceedings against an Internet 'hacker' magazine called *2600* for breach of the anti-circumvention provisions of the DMCA. The magazine posted a software code known as DeCSS on its web site which allowed users to bypass the anti-copying features on DVD discs. The MPAA alleged the code was used to illegally copy and distribute copyrighted films on the Internet. The magazine claimed its conduct should be excused under an exemption in the DMCA for 'fair use' which allows people to make copies for personal use without the permission of the author and claimed the anti-circumvention provisions of the DMCA violated its right to free speech under the First Amendment. However, the Federal Court issued a preliminary injunction in January 2000 preventing the magazine from publishing the DeCSS code on the basis that it promoted copyright theft.

Although the magazine complied with the injunction by removing DeCSS from its web site, it created links to other web sites that posted the code. The MPAA returned to court. In August 2000 the injunction was expanded to prohibit the links and a final order and permanent injunction was granted (*Universal City Studios Inc v Reimerdes (2000)*).

In May 2001, with the support of a digital rights organization, computer programmers and law professors, *2600* appealed the injunction. The United States Government Justice Department intervened in support of the injunctions and the Screen Actors Guild filed briefs in support of the MPAA. The issues raised by the case are so important that the decision by the appeal court is likely to be subject of an appeal to the Supreme Court.

Linking and framing

The courts have not decided whether linking and framing infringe copyright. Two important cases that raised the issue settled before the court could clarify the legal issues by giving judgment. There is an argument that placing restrictions on the use of links and framing interferes with the First Amendment right to freedom of speech.

In 1997, Ticketmaster sued Microsoft for infringing its trademark by linking from a city guide web site to a page inside Ticketmaster's web site, known as a 'deep link'. Ticketmaster claimed the deep link prevented it controlling visitors to its web site and reduced advertising revenue because it bypassed its 'home page' (*Ticketmaster Corporation v Microsoft Corporation (1997)*). Microsoft relied on the First Amendment. The case reached a settlement in February 1999, the terms of which remain confidential. However, Microsoft did remove the deep link and now links to Ticketmaster's home page.

In 1997, the *Washington Post* and other news services sued a web site called TotalNews for infringement of their trademarks and breach of copyright in respect of the frames used by TotalNews to deep link to pages in their web sites. TotalNews carried no original content of its own. The case settled on the basis that TotalNews would no longer use frames but would instead link to the web sites of the plaintiffs, although TotalNews could not claim any endorsement by or affiliation with the plaintiffs (*Washington Post Company v TotalNews (1997)*).

Domain names

Civil proceedings

The Anticybersquatting Consumer Protection Act 1999 protects domain names under the laws of trademarks and passing off. It provides a civil remedy against any person who registers or uses a domain name that is identical to or confusingly similar to the trademark of another person, with the intent to profit from the goodwill of that person. Under this Act the court may order the forfeiture or cancellation of the domain name or transfer it to the owner of the trademark, and award damages to the plaintiff.

Claims can also be brought under the Federal Trademark Dilution Act 1995. In the case of *Panavision International v Toeppen (1998)*, the Court of Appeals upheld an order under that Act that the defendant transfer the domain names panavision.com and panaflex.com to the plaintiff, the owners of registered trademarks in Panavision and Panaflex, the well-known camera and photographic equipment. At trial, the court heard that the defendant did not use the web sites to provide any service. The panavision.com web site displayed an aerial view of a town in Illinois called Pana and the panaflex.com web site contained only the word 'hello'. The Court of Appeals took into account the fact that the defendant had registered hundreds of domain names using the well known trademarks of other companies and had stated his intention of selling or licensing the domain names to the true owners.

ICANN registration and dispute resolution

Several web companies and registries offer domain name registration services. However, the so-called 'top level' domain names such as .com, .net and .org can only be registered by registrars accredited by the Internet Corporation for Assigned Names and Numbers (ICANN), a United States non-profit organization that works with WIPO.

If a dispute arises in relation to a domain name that has been registered by an ICANN accredited registrar, an application can be issued for an adjudication under ICANN's Uniform Administrative Dispute Resolution Policy (UDRP). Under the UDRP, the dissatisfied party must obtain a court order in civil proceedings for a ruling as to which party is entitled to the domain name registration. Once the ruling has been obtained, the ICANN accredited registrar will implement it.

If the dispute arises from a registration that is alleged to have been made abusively, such as 'cybersquatting', the UDRP provides an expedited administrative procedure that allows the dispute to be resolved without the cost and delay of litigation by one of ICANN's approved dispute resolution service providers. The disputed domain name does not have to be a registered trademark in order to fall within the remit of UDRP. Julia Roberts and Madonna were recently granted relief against cybersquatting in recognition of their 'character' or 'personality' rights.

21.4.3 Data protection

The United States does not have data protection equivalent to the Data Protection Act 1998 in the United Kingdom, but instead relies on a combination of legislation and self-regulation. The United States Department of Commerce and the European Commission have entered into a voluntary data protection system called the International Safe Harbor Privacy Principles.[2] The United States government has encouraged companies processing data online in the United States to register and comply with the Safe Harbor provisions in order to avoid prosecution by European authorities under European privacy laws.

21.4.4 Reporting restrictions

It is difficult to regulate reporting restrictions in the United States because of the First Amendment to the Constitution which protects freedom of speech. The Internet has impacted upon the problems that may arise from this protection. In 1995, the Canadian courts imposed reporting restrictions on the Canadian media in respect of the trial in Canada of a husband and wife called Barnardo and Homolka who were charged with the sexual abuse and murder of children. However, a huge amount of detail about the case was posted on the Internet in the United States and leaked into Canada. Although this posed a serious threat to the trial, the Canadian authorities found it impossible to regulate the flow of information and prosecute for contempt of court because of the sheer volume of information crossing the border.

21.4.5 Obscenity and racial hatred

Obscenity

The Communications Decency Act 1996 was designed to regulate indecent and obscene speech on the Internet and to prevent the transmission of such material to children. However, there was considerable opposition to this Act by civil liberties and Internet groups. In *Reno v American Civil Liberties Union (1997)* the American Civil Liberties Union successfully challenged the Communications Decency Act in the Supreme Court as an unconstitutional restraint on free speech. The Supreme Court held that using federal law to regulate the Internet in order to compensate for a lack of blocking and filtering technology amounted to a 'total ban' which violated the First Amendment freedom of speech right of adults to receive and view such material. Part of the Act was struck down, although Section 230, which legislates in respect of online defamation remains in force.

[2]The Safe Harbor web site can be found at www.export.gov/safeharbor.

Racial hatred

It is not possible to access the Internet without an Internet service provider. As a result, Internet service providers have been targeted by individuals and action groups in relation to racial hatred. In 2001, AOL was sued in an Illinois district court for breach of its terms of service by a Muslim who alleged that the company failed to remove anti-Islamic hate speech posted in Muslim-interest Internet chat rooms after he had repeatedly alerted the company to its presence.

Problematic issues arise where material posted on the Internet is accessed in other countries. In 2000, an anti-racism group in Paris sought an injunction in a French court against Yahoo! prohibiting Internet users in France from accessing a web site hosted by Yahoo! that auctioned Nazi memorabilia. Although the site was not available on Yahoo!'s French-language portal yahoo.fr, it was available on Yahoo.com. Yahoo.com is based in the United States but is easily accessible to Internet users in France. Yahoo! defended the proceedings on the grounds that the Yahoo.com service is governed by the law of the United States, and, as a result auctions of Nazi material could not be prevented because of the constitutional right to freedom of speech in the United States.

The French court held that Yahoo! had to respect French laws prohibiting the exhibit or sale of objects that incite racial hatred. It granted the injunction. Yahoo! issued proceedings in United States on the issue of whether foreign countries have jurisdiction over the domestic activities of United States companies and material published on American web sites. A United States judge ruled that he could hear the case. On 7 November 2001, a District Judge in California held that the First Amendment right to freedom of speech was the dominant legal consideration and ruled that the order made by the French court was inconsistent with United States law. However, the anti-racism group has appealed the judgment. The case will have a considerable impact on the issue of foreign jurisdiction over unlawful material on the Internet.

Convention on cyber-crime

In an effort to develop co-ordinated law on the possession on obscene material on the Internet, the Council of Europe has drawn up a convention on cyber-crime which was adopted on 8 November 2001. Although the United States is a non-member state, it has been invited to become involved with the convention.

21.5 Invasion of privacy

21.5.1 General principles

Unlike the English law, the law of the United States has a well established tort of invasion of privacy which encompasses both common law principles and constitutional requirements relating to privacy.

The right of privacy is a personal right and does not extend to members of the plaintiff's family or survive after the death of the plaintiff. It does not apply to companies.

The tort includes four different kinds of wrong:

1. Appropriation of the plaintiff's picture or name. The plaintiff must show unauthorized use by the defendant of the plaintiff's picture or name for the defendant's commercial advantage. However, liability is usually limited to use in advertisements or the promotion of products or services – for example, the unauthorized use of a film star's photograph to endorse food or clothing.
2. Intrusion upon the plaintiff's affairs or seclusion. The plaintiff must show an act of prying or intrusion by the defendant in the plaintiff's private matters that would be objectionable to a reasonable person – for example, electronic surveillance or taking a zoom lens photograph of a film star in his bedroom. Taking a photograph of a person in a public place such as a restaurant would be not actionable.
3. Publication of facts placing plaintiff in a false light. The plaintiff must show the defendant has published facts about the plaintiff that place the plaintiff in a false light in the public eye. For liability to arise, there must be publicity rather than mere 'publication' as required by defamation. The false light must be a view the plaintiff does not hold or an action the plaintiff did not take. It must also be objectionable to a reasonable person – for example, a television report that alleges a liberal politician supports the death penalty. If the matter is in the public interest, the plaintiff must prove malice.
4. Public disclosure of private facts about a plaintiff. The plaintiff must show that the defendant disclosed to the public private information about the plaintiff – for example, the publication by a national magazine of the medical records of a famous singer. The public disclosure must be objectionable to a reasonable person.

21.5.2 Defences

Consent
Consent is a good defence, although some states require that the consent must be in writing.

Truth
Truth is not a good defence to most invasion of privacy actions. However, a broadcaster or newspaper cannot be sued for publishing a true fact that is part of the public record or a record released to the public.

21.5.3 Anti-terrorism legislation

The terrorist attacks on New York and Washington on 11 September 2001 are likely to have a significant impact on the law of privacy in the United States.

Combating Terrorism Act 2001

In immediate response to the attacks of 11 September, on 13 September 2001 the Senate unanimously approved the Combating Terrorism Act 2001 (*Amendment SA 1562 to HR 2500*) in order to 'enhance the capability of the United States to deter, prevent, and thwart domestic and international acts of terrorism against United States nationals and interests'.

The Combating Terrorism Act 2001 greatly extends the powers of surveillance by federal and state governments. It broadens the definition of wiretaps to include the monitoring of communications over the Internet. It allows prosecutors to authorize surveillance for 48 hours without the approval of a judge. It allows United States and state attorneys to authorize the installation of FBI Internet surveillance systems. It also expands the circumstances in which wiretaps can be authorized without a warrant to include 'threats to public health and safety or national security' and 'attacks on the integrity or availability of protected computers'.

Under this Act, the government will be able to monitor of the addresses of web sites visited by an Internet user, the terms he types into search engines and the names and addresses – but not the content – of his email correspondence.

Although the Combating Terrorism Act 2001 is designed to combat terrorism, it will also allow the government to authorize a wiretap without warrant in respect of any suspected 'computer hacking' offence. This power and the speed with which the Act was passed has caused concern in some quarters in the United States. The lack of any constitutional right to challenge it is also causing concern. Because privacy is a common law right derived from the Due Process Clause of the Fifth Amendment to the Constitution and the Equal Protection Clause of the Fourteenth Amendment, it is not guaranteed directly by the Constitution and is not subject to constitutional challenge.

USA Patriot Act 2001

On 25 October 2001 the Senate passed by 98 votes to 1 the Uniting and Strengthening America by Providing Appropriate Tools Required to Intercept and Obstruct Terrorism (USA PATRIOT) Act 2001 (*HR 3162*) in order to 'deter and punish terrorist acts in the United States and around the world, to enhance law enforcement investigatory tools and for other purposes'. This Act became public law on 26 October 2001 when it was signed by President George W. Bush.

The USA Patriot Act 2001 increases criminal sentences for acts of terrorism or for those who harbour or finance terrorists or terrorist organizations and makes it a crime for individuals or groups to possess substances that can be used as biological or chemical weapons. The Treasury Department is given power to order domestic banks to investigate the sources of large overseas private banking accounts and to impose sanctions on other countries that refuse to provide banking information to United States investigators.

Law enforcement officials may seek court orders to place 'roving wiretaps' on an individual suspected of involvement in terrorism in order that any telephone, rather than one specific telephone, used by that person may be monitored. They may also subpoena the addresses and times of email messages sent by those suspected of terrorism. National security investigators will be able to obtain a court order in order to place wiretaps on terrorist suspects if foreign intelligence operations are a 'significant' rather than the only purpose of the investigation.

The surveillance powers for wiretapping telephones and computers provided by the USA Patriot Act 2001 have 'sunset clauses' and will expire in 2005. However, any information obtained in that period under the provisions of the Act may be used in court proceedings after 2005. The Act also provides that the United States government may be sued for information that is 'leaked' as a result of the increased wiretapping and surveillance powers.

21.6 Reporting restrictions

The First Amendment to the Constitution prohibits Congress from interfering with freedom of speech or freedom of the press. The free flow of ideas is considered to be an important function in a democratic society and the rights under the First Amendment are considered to be 'fundamental'. As a general rule, the press has no greater freedom to speak than a member of the public.

However, these freedoms are not absolute. State governments and the federal government can legislate in respect of them although such legislation is subject to constitutional challenge in the courts. When considering the lawfulness of such regulation, the courts will balance the importance of the fundamental rights with the purpose the government is trying to achieve. The court will only uphold the law if it is 'necessary to achieve a compelling government purpose'.

Access to court proceedings

The First Amendment guarantees the public and the press the right to attend criminal trials and pretrial proceedings. The guarantee probably also applies to civil trials. However, the right may be outweighed if the trial judge finds that there is a 'compelling interest' in holding the hearing or part of the hearing in private, such as the need to protect children who are victims of sex offences.

Regulation of broadcasting

The courts will not interfere so readily with legislation by state and federal governments in respect of radio and television broadcasting. This is because the broadcast media do not have as many opportunities to bring news and information to the public as the press. The right of the public to receive information of public concern is more important than the right of the broadcast media to broadcast what they please.

21.7 Contempt of court

The law of contempt is similar to the law in the United Kingdom. It is generally defined in both federal- and state-based law as disobedience of a court order or an act of disrespect in the face of the court such as disorderly or disruptive behaviour or behaviour that obstructs the administration of justice. Punishment can include a fine or a period of imprisonment.

As in the United Kingdom, contempt is usually used to compel a person to comply with a court order or to punish a person who has violated an order – for example, the imprisonment of Susan McDougal for 18 months for refusing to testify before the 'Whitewater' grand jury investigation into President Clinton.

21.8 Protection of journalistic sources

Most state courts hold that journalists have a constitutional qualified privilege not to reveal confidential sources, following the decision of the Supreme Court in *Branzberg v Hayes (1972)*.

Many of the states have also passed state legislation called 'shield laws' which protect journalists against being compelled to reveal their sources. Shield laws can be 'absolute' providing protection except in exceptional circumstances or 'qualified' whereby disclosure can be ordered if there is a compelling need for the information.

21.9 Obscenity and racial discrimination

21.9.1 Obscenity

Obscenity is a description or a depiction of sexual conduct that when taken as a whole by the average person:

- Appeals to the prurient interest in sex
- Portrays sex in a patently offensive way, and
- Does not have any serious literary, artistic, political or scientific value (*Miller v California (1973)*).

The Supreme Court has held that obscenity is not protected speech under the First Amendment to the Constitution (*Roth v United States (1957)*). This means that state governments are able to legislate to prohibit the dissemination of obscene material without unlawfully interfering with the First Amendment right to freedom of speech. However, any legislation in respect of obscenity must not be too vague or too broad, or it will be struck down by the courts on that basis. For example, a state law prohibiting the sale of any book that 'tended to corrupt the morals of youth' was held invalid because it was too broad (*Butler v Michigan (1957)*). The issue of whether material is obscene is a question of fact for the jury.

State governments cannot make private possession at home of obscene material, except for child pornography, a crime because of the constitutional right to personal privacy. However, the protection does not extend beyond a person's home and he can be convicted of offences relating to importation, distribution and exhibition of obscene materials.

21.9.2 Racial discrimination

Due Process and Equal Protection

Grossly unreasonable discrimination by federal and state governments will violate the Due Process Clause of the Fifth Amendment to the Constitution and the Equal Protection Clause of the Fourteenth Amendment to the Constitution.

Private persons are not subject to the Due Process Clause or the Equal Protection Clause as they only apply to government action. However, Congress has passed laws under the Thirteenth Amendment to the Constitution and the Commerce Clause to prevent discrimination by private persons.

Thirteenth Amendment

The Thirteenth Amendment to the Constitution states that slavery shall not exist in the United States. The Thirteenth Amendment applies to both government and private action and gives Congress the power to pass laws that prohibit any 'badge of slavery', such as school segregation and hiring on the basis of race.

Commerce Clause

The Commerce Clause of the Constitution allows Congress to legislate in respect of commercial activities between the states that make up the union of the United States. Because almost any action can be considered to be connected with commercial activity, Congress has used the Commerce Clause to pass legislation preventing racial discrimination such as the Civil Rights Act 1964 which bans discrimination in public facilities and public education and the Civil Rights Act 1991 which bans discrimination in federal and private workplaces.

21.10 Freedom of information

The Freedom of Information Act 1966 provides that any person has the right to request access to federal records or information.

Upon receipt of a written request, a federal government agency must disclose the requested record to the applicant unless the record falls within one of the exceptions set out in the Freedom of Information Act 1966. The right of access is enforceable upon obtaining a court order.

This Act does not provide a right of access to records held by Congress, the courts, state or local government agencies or private persons or organizations.

Each state has its own laws governing public access to state and local records.

20 The Law in Scotland

Rosalind McInnes

20.1 Introduction

There is much about the law of Scotland that is comfortingly familiar to media organizations and media lawyers in England. The Defamation Acts of 1952 and 1996, the Copyright Designs and Patents Act of 1988, the Data Protection Act 1998, the Contempt of Court Act 1981 and the Human Rights Act 1998 are all United Kingdom-wide statutes. It has also been said that the law of confidence is the same in both countries (*Osborne v BBC (1999)*).

However, differences in history, procedure and culture have resulted in a need for those in England to exercise caution when considering the law of Scotland. The Scottish 'civil law' legal system is based on Roman law, and is fundamentally different from the 'common law' English legal system. Moreover, recent years have seen devolutionary sentiment and the creation of the Scottish Parliament increase the scope for legislation in Scotland that takes into account the different traditions of the Scottish legal system. The Regulation of Investigatory Powers (Scotland) Act 2000 and the draft Freedom of Information (Scotland) Bill are prime examples.

Media organizations and journalists should always seek advice from a Scottish lawyer when considering issues relating to the law of Scotland. This chapter sets out the three areas where the greatest risk is involved: defamation, reporting restrictions, and contempt of court.

20.2 Defamation

20.2.1 Definition of defamation

One of the older and more influential formulations for defamation in Scottish law is:

> . . . the imputation of something which is criminal, dishonest, or immoral in the character or actions of the person aggrieved . . .
>
> (*McLauchlan v Orr, Pollock & Co (1894)*)

However, modern Scottish commentators tend to favour the English definition:

> . . . would the words tend to lower the plaintiff in the estimation of right-thinking members of society generally?
>
> *(Sim v Stretch (1936))*

Cultural differences within Scotland may influence the meaning of 'society'. In 1990, the *Stornoway Gazette* paid damages to the local MP, Calum MacDonald, in respect of a letter that criticized him for not voting in favour of legislation intended to prevent the promotion of homosexuality. Although such an allegation would probably not have been considered defamatory in most parts of Scotland, it clearly was in the Western Isles.

However, the Scottish courts are increasingly unlikely to accept the views of 'splinter groups' of society. In the case of *Bell v Bell's Trustee (2001)* it was held that it was of no assistance to the pursuer, or claimant, to say that:

> . . . an allegation is damaging in the section of society to which he belongs if it is not also disparaging in the view of society as a whole.

20.2.2 Innuendo

As in England, innuendo may found an action for defamation.

In *Russell v Stubbs (1913)*, the appearance of the name of the pursuer on a list of debtors with a note attached to the list implied nothing other than the fact that the name appeared on the court books and was not capable of bearing the innuendo that the pursuer was impecunious. In *Stein v Beaverbrook Newspapers Limited (1968)*, the innuendo that the pursuer was a hypocrite was held to have been properly inferred from a reference that the pursuer had campaigned against chequebook journalism whilst engaging in it himself. In *Morrison v Ritchie (1902)*, the innuendo arose from a newspaper announcement of the birth of twins to a couple who had married the previous month.

20.2.3 Class actions

As in England, members of a class of persons can sue if the class is sufficiently well defined for the defamation to be held to apply to them as individuals.

In *Macphail v Macleod (1895)* it was established that a particular minister could not sue on an attack against ministers generally, but could sue on a charge of drunkenness against the ministers in his presbytery. In *Baigent v BBC (1999)* a total award of £60 000 was made to three members of a family, none of whom had been individually mentioned, in respect of a programme to which the family as a whole took objection.

Appendix A Glossary of Legal Terms

Actus reus   The physical act, which usually in conjunction with the required mental element, constitutes a crime.

Antecedents   A person's past history. Usually used in the context of a defendant who has pleaded or been found guilty in a criminal court. His antecedents, in other words history, personal circumstances and any previous convictions are read to the court prior to sentence being passed.

Arraignment   In criminal procedure, the formal process of putting the charge to the accused in court and calling for his plea.

Arrest   Detaining someone or depriving him of his liberty. An arrest can be achieved by words alone – for example, 'you are under arrest'.

Bail   The sum put up by the accused or another person to ensure the accused's appearance at his trial.

Bankruptcy   The circumstances in which a person is adjudged insolvent by the court and his remaining property is administered for the benefit of his creditors.

Bind over   An order placing a person under a legal obligation to the court, usually to be of good behaviour or to keep the peace.

Burden (or onus) of proof   The obligation of establishing, through evidence, a matter of fact or state of mind to the satisfaction of the court. See also standard of proof.

Care order   An order of the court placing a child or young person under the control and guardianship of the local authority.

Cause of action   A legal right that may be enforced through the courts.

Civil Procedure Rules   The new rules for conducting civil litigation introduced in April 1999. Under the Rules, parties are encouraged to avoid going to court to resolve their dispute except as a last resort.

Claimant   The new term for plaintiff under the Civil Procedure Rules. Known as a 'pursuer' under the law of Scotland and a 'plaintiff' under the law of the United States of America.

Common law   The body of law derived from judicial precedents or custom, as opposed to statute.

Constitution   The written laws of the United States Constitution which, amongst other things, grant federal law to the federal government of the union of the United States and provide citizens with a number of 'rights' that limit the power of the federal and state governments over their actions. There is no written equivalent in the law of England and Wales.

Contact order An order of the court allowing a person to have contact with a child who lives with another person, previously called visitation rights.

Contempt of court Wilful disregard of the authority of the court or interference with its processes.

Contract A legally enforceable agreement, in other words an exchange of promises supported by consideration given by each side. A contract may be oral or in writing.

Copyright The exclusive right to produce copies and control an original literary, dramatic, musical or artistic work, sound recording, film, broadcast or cable programme or the typographical arrangement of a published edition.

Corroboration Independent facts or testimony that support an existing piece of evidence.

County court The most junior court in all civil proceedings with the exception of family cases, which may be heard in the magistrates' court. The county courts are responsible for dealing with the bulk of civil litigation in England and Wales. Cases are decided by a district judge (often a solicitor) or a circuit judge (usually a barrister) both of whom sit alone, with the exception of civil actions against the police which may be heard before a circuit judge and a jury.

Court of Appeal Hears appeals from the Crown Court, the County Court and the High Court. The Master of the Rolls heads the Civil Division and the Lord Chief Justice heads the Criminal Division. Sits with at least two and usually three judges. Decisions are made by a majority.

Cross examination The second phase of a witness's examination in court, in other words the answers given to questions asked by the other side's lawyer. Leading questions may be asked during cross-examination.

Crown court The primary court hearing indictable criminal offences. Cases may be heard by a High Court judge, a circuit judge or a recorder. May also hear appeals from the magistrates' court.

Damages The monetary sum ordered by the court to be paid by the defendant to the successful claimant in civil proceedings. Damages usually represent compensation for loss, but may be a form of punishment by the court if exemplary damages are awarded.

Decree absolute The final and irrevocable order of divorce by the court which leaves the parties free to remarry. Unless cause is shown why the order should not be made, it will follow automatically several weeks after a decree nisi.

Decree nisi The first stage of a formal divorce. A provisional decree of divorce which will later (usually after about six weeks) be made absolute unless cause is shown why it should not be so made.

Disclosure The process in civil litigation of formally exchanging lists of relevant documents in the possession of each party and allowing them to be inspected. Known as 'discovery' prior to the Civil Proceedings Rules.

Examination in chief The first phase of a witness's examination in court, in other words the answers given to the initial set of questions asked by the lawyer who calls him into the witness box. Leading questions may not be asked during examination in chief.

326

Ex parte application   An application to the court where one side only is present. Often encountered in circumstances where emergency injunctions are sought. May be less frequent in the future as a result of Section 12 of the Human Rights Act 1998 which prevents hearings made in the absence of the defendant. Now known as a hearing 'without notice' under the Civil Procedure Rules.

Fair dealing   A defence against infringement of copyright which acknowledges the wider interest of freedom of speech by allowing the use of copyrighted material for certain worthy purposes.

Hearsay evidence   Matters that were not seen or heard directly by the person giving evidence, for example 'Z told me that he saw Y take drugs' as opposed to, 'I, myself, saw Y take drugs'.

High court   The most senior court of trial for civil litigation. Divided into the Queen's Bench Division, the Chancery Division and the Family Division. Cases are presided over by a single judge. There are also Divisional Courts of each of the Divisions which hear appeals and exercise a supervisory jurisdiction over inferior courts. Such cases are presided over by two or three judges.

House of Lords   The final court for appeals. It is unusual for a case to be taken as far as the House of Lords unless a major point of law is involved. A minimum of three judges hear cases although the usual number is five. Decisions are made by a majority.

Impeachment   A term used in the law of the United States of America meaning the casting of an adverse reflection of the truthfulness of a witness. Also used to describe the bringing of criminal charges against the President, the Vice President and all officers of the United States for treason, bribery and other crimes and misdemeanours.

In camera   A legal hearing or trial held in private and from which the public is excluded. Reporting of such cases is limited. Now known as a hearing 'in private' under the Civil Procedure Rules.

Information   A charge or complaint made before a magistrate, usually on oath, to institute criminal proceedings.

Injunction   An order of the court instructing a person to do ('mandatory') or more usually to refrain from doing ('prohibitory') a certain act. May be for a short period of time ('interim') or permanent ('final'). Known as an 'interdict' under the law of Scotland.

Intellectual property rights   The legal protection provided in respect of things that are created by a person's skill, labour and investment of time and money.

Inter partes application   A hearing where both parties are heard by the court (as opposed to an ex parte application). Now known as a hearing 'on notice' under the Civil Procedure Rules (as opposed to a hearing 'without notice').

Justification   Truth as a defence to a defamation action. Known as 'veritas' under the law of Scotland and 'truth' under the law of the United States of America.

Leading questions   Questions asked during a witness's examination in court that suggest the answer desired. Leading questions may not be asked during examination in chief.

Legal professional privilege   All confidential communications between a lawyer and his client, and all communications between a lawyer or his client and a third party, which come into existence for the dominant purpose of pending or actual litigation.

Libel   Defamation in writing or some other permanent form such as a tape or video recording. Defamation in radio and television broadcasts and computer-generated transmissions is defined by statute as libel.

Limitation period   The time period prescribed by statute within which a person must bring his claim.

Magistrates' court   The most junior and most numerous of the criminal courts. Magistrates deal with summary and triable either way criminal offences. Most magistrates are lay persons with no legal qualifications. Magistrates also hear family cases in civil proceedings.

Mens rea   The mental element of a crime – 'a guilty mind'.

Obiter dictum   The opinion of a judge not forming part of his decision.

Passing off   The law that prevents a person representing the marks, packaging or other features of goods of another as his own.

Patent   The legally registered and enforceable grant to an inventor of a scientific development of the sole right to make, use or sell his invention for a certain period.

Pre-action protocols   Regulations contained in the Civil Procedure Rules which outline the steps each party should take to seek information from and provide information to the other about a prospective legal claim.

Precedents   Judicial decisions that act as authorities for the purpose of deciding later cases.

Public domain   The circumstances in which copyright in a work has expired and anyone is free to deal with the work as they choose without the need to pay a licence fee or obtain permission from the owner.

Ratio decidendi   The legal reasoning behind a judge's decision.

Recognizance   The monetary bond entered into before the court by which a person binds himself to do a certain thing, usually to turn up for his trial.

Re-examination   The final phase of a witness's examination in court, in other words the re-questioning by the lawyer who called him into the witness box. Re-examination may only deal with matters that arose during cross examination. Leading questions may not be asked.

Remission of sentence   The part of a sentence of imprisonment from which a prisoner is automatically released from serving unless he is of bad behaviour.

Residence order   An order of the court allowing a person to have a child live with him, previously called custody.

Slander   Spoken defamation or defamatory language in some other temporary form.

Standard of proof   The satisfaction of the court, through evidence, of a matter of fact or state of mind. In civil cases, a fact can be held established if the evidence renders it more probable than not. In criminal cases, a fact can be held established if the evidence satisfies beyond a reasonable doubt. See also burden of proof.

Statute   The body of principles of rules and law laid down as a result of Parliamentary legislation, as opposed to common law.

Subpoena   An order by the court requiring a person to come before it at a stated time and place and ordering that he will be subject to a penalty if he does not comply. Now known as a 'witness summons' under the Civil Procedure Rules.

Summing up   The judge's address to the jury at the end of a case. The judge sums up the evidence and the arguments of the prosecution and the defence. After the summing up, the jury is sent out to consider its verdict.

Surety   A person who assumes legal responsibility for the fulfilment of another's obligation. Also a person who puts up bail for another.

Tort   A civil wrong or injury arising from an act or failure to act for which an action for damages (other than arising from a breach of contract) may be brought. Known as 'delict' under the law of Scotland.

Tortfeasor   A person who commits a civil wrong or injury for which damages may be claimed at law.

Trademark   A mark that identifies a product or service and prevents a person from taking unfair advantage of the goodwill of an established business. Trademarks use the symbol ™ if the trademark is not registered, or ® if the trademark is registered, to demonstrate protection.

Trustee in bankruptcy   The person to whom the property of a person adjudged to be bankrupt is passed and who administers that property for the benefit of the bankrupt's creditors.

Ultra vires   Beyond the legal power of authority of a person, corporation or agent.

Ward of court   A minor or person legally incapable of handling his own affairs who is placed under the control and protection of the court.

Warrant   An authorization granted by a magistrate allowing the police to arrest a person or search or seize property.

Without prejudice communications   Communications between the parties to litigation which explore settlement. They are privileged on public policy grounds of encouraging parties to settle their differences, rather than to litigate before the court.

Appendix B Professional Bodies

Advertising Standards Authority
2 Torrington Place
London WC1E 7HW

www.asa.org.uk
Telephone: 020 7580 5555

American Bar Association
Service Center
541 North Fairbanks Court
Chicago, IL 60611
United States of America

www.abanet.org
Telephone: 001 312 988 5522

Bar Council of England and Wales
3 Bedford Row
London WC1R 4DB

www.barcouncil.org
Telephone: 020 7242 0082

Broadcasting Standards Commission
7 The Sanctuary
London SW1P 3JS

www.bsc.org.uk
Telephone: 020 7808 1000

Council of Europe
Palais de l'Europe
Avenue de l'Europe
67000 Strasbourg
France

www.coe.int
Telephone: 00 33 3 90 21 20 33

Court Service
Southside
105 Victoria Street
London SW1E 6QT

www.courtservice.gov.uk
Telephone: 020 7210 2266

Department of Trade and Industry
Enquiry Unit
1 Victoria Street
London SW1H 0ET

www.dti.gov.uk
Telephone: 020 7215 5000

Defence, Press and Broadcasting Advisory
Committee (DA Notices)
Secretary of the Defence, Press and Broadcasting
Advisory Committee
Room 704
Ministry of Defence
Metropole Building
Northumberland Avenue
London WC2N 5BP

www.dnotice.org.uk
Telephone: 020 7218 2206

European Court of Human Rights
European Union
Rue de la Loi 175
B1048
Brussels Belgium

www.echr.coe.int
www.europa.eu.int
Telephone: 00 32 2 285 81 11

Equity
Guild House
Upper Saint Martin's Lane
London WC2H 9EJ

www.equity.org.uk
Telephone: 020 7379 6000

Faculty of Advocates (Bar of Scotland)
Advocates Library
Parliament House
Edinburgh EH1 1RF

www.advocates.org.uk
Telephone: 0131 226 5071

Her Majesty's Stationery Office (HMSO)
St.Clements House
2–16 Colegate
Norwich NR3 1BQ

www.hmso.gov.uk
Telephone: 01603 723020

Independent Television Commission
33 Foley Street
London W1W 7TL

www.itc.org.uk
Telephone: 020 7255 3000

Information Commissioner
Wycliffe House
Water Lane
Wilmslow
Cheshire SK9 5AF

www.dataprotection.gov.uk
Telephone: 01625 545 700

Internet Corporation for Assigned Names and Numbers (ICANN)
4676 Admiralty Way, Suite 330
Marina del Rey, CA 90292–6601
United States of America

www.icann.org
Telephone: 001 310 823 9358

International Federation of Journalists
IPC-Residence Palace
Rue de la Loi 155
B-1040 Brussels, Belgium

www.ifj.org
Telephone: 00 32 2 235 22 00

Law Society of England and Wales
The Law Society's Hall
113 Chancery Lane
London WC2A 1PL

www.lawsociety.org.uk
Telephone: 020 7242 1222

Law Society of Scotland
26 Drumsheugh Gardens
Edinburgh EH3 7YR

www.lawscot.org.uk
Telephone: 0131 226 7411

Library of Congress Copyright Office (United States)
101 Independence Avenue, SE
Washington, DC 20559–6000
United States of America

www.loc.gov/copyright
Telephone: 001 202 707 3000

Mechanical-Copyright Protection Society (MCPS)
29–33 Berners Street
London W1P 4AA

www.mcps.co.uk
Telephone: 020 7580 5544

Musician's Union
60–62 Clapham Road
London SW9 0JJ

www.musiciansunion.org.uk
Telephone: 020 7582 5566

National Union of Journalists
Headland House
308 Grays Inn Road
London WC1X 8DP

www.gn.apc.org/media/nuj.html
www.nuj.org.uk
Telephone: 020 7278 7916

Office of Communications (Ofcom)
Department of Trade and Industry
Enquiry Unit
1 Victoria Street
London SW1H 0ET

www.ofcom.gov.uk
Telephone: 020 7215 5000

Office of Telecommunications
50 Ludgate Hill
London EC4M 7JJ

www.oftel.gov.uk
Telephone: 020 7634 8700

Official Solicitor
81 Chancery Lane
London WC2A 1DD

www.offsol.demon.co.uk
Telephone: 020 7911 7127

Parliamentary Ombudsman
Millbank Tower
Millbank
London SW1P 4QP

www.ombudsman.org.uk
Telephone: 0845 015 4033

Performing Right Society (PRS)
29–33 Berners Street
London W1P 4AA

www.prs.co.uk
Telephone: 020 7580 5544

Phonographic Performance Limited
1 Upper James Street
London W1R 3HG

www.ppluk.com
Telephone: 020 7534 1000

Press Complaints Commission
1 Salisbury Square
London EC4Y 8JB

www.pcc.org.uk
Telephone: 020 7353 1248

**Producers Alliance for Cinema and Television
(PACT)**
45 Mortimer Street
London W1N 7TD

www.pact.co.uk
Telephone: 020 7331 6000

Radio Authority
Holbrook House
14 Great Queen Street
Holborn
London WC2B 5DG

www.radioauthority.org.uk
Telephone: 020 7430 2724

Royal Courts of Justice
Strand
London WC2A 2LL

(no web site)
Telephone: 020 7936 6000

Safe Harbor
(United States Department of Commerce)
US Department of Commerce
1401 Constitution Avenue, NW
Washington, DC 20230
United States of America

www.export.gov/safeharbor
Telephone: 001 202 482 4883

World Intellectual Property Organization
(WIPO)
PO Box 18, CH-1211 Geneva 20
Switzerland

www.wipo.org
Telephone: 00 41 22 338 9111

Writers Guild of Great Britain (WGGB)
430 Edgware Road
London W2 1EH

www.writersguild.org.uk
Telephone: 020 7723 8074

Appendix C Specimen Agreements

1. Interview Agreement (Fee Payable)

2. Interview Agreement (No Fee Payable)

3. Contributors Release (Television)

4. Confidentiality Agreement

5. Moral Rights Waiver
   (a) By Individual
   (b) By Personal Representative(s)
   (c) With Assignment of Reversionary Copyright
   (d) By Personal Representative(s) for Film
   (e) Notice of Assertion of Right to be Identified

6. Assignment of Copyright

These specimen agreements are for illustrative purposes only. Law and practice evolve quickly and previous understandings of the law can change radically. These examples are not a substitute for legal advice.

Before acting on any of the following specimen agreements you should first consult with a lawyer with the appropriate qualifications and expertise.

Specimen agreement 1:
Interview Agreement (Fee Payable)

To: [Interviewee]

From: [Company or Producer]

Date:

Dear

[Interview] [Name of programme]

This agreement confirms the understanding between us relating to the interview to be given by you and transmitted and/or recorded by us ('the interview') which we propose but do not undertake to broadcast, exhibit and/or otherwise exploit.

1. You agree to the recording and/or broadcasting and/or live relay of the interview and hereby grant to us all consents necessary to enable us to make the fullest use of the interview throughout the world in perpetuity by any and all means in any and all media, whether now known or hereafter developed or discovered, without liability (save as specifically hereinafter provided) or acknowledgement to you and the right to issue publicity concerning the interview and for such purpose to use and reproduce your name and photograph and recordings of the interview.

2. In recognition of the needs of film and television production, we shall be entitled to edit, copy, add to, take from, adapt or translate the interview as we see fit and you irrevocably waive the benefits of any provision of law known as 'moral rights' under the Copyright Designs and Patents Act 1988 or any similar laws of any jurisdiction.

3. You warrant and undertake to us that you are fully entitled to give the interview to us and that no contribution by you to the interview (whether by way of inflection or gesture or otherwise) will infringe the copyright or any other right of any person, breach any contract or duty of confidence, constitute a contempt of court, be defamatory or be calculated to bring any broadcaster into disrepute.

4. [Optional clause] You undertake to us that you will not prior to _____ give to any person any interview or make, give or release any statement for publication by any means or medium relating to [the subject matter of the interview].

5. [Optional clause] You agree to indemnify us against all and any costs, claims, expenses and liabilities (including, without limitation, reasonable legal fees resulting from breach by you of any of the agreements, warranties and/or undertakings on your part contained in this agreement.

6. In consideration of the above and your agreement that we may record an [exclusive] interview with you [of approximately _____ minutes' duration] we hereby agree to pay to you in full and complete satisfaction of our obligations to you the sum of [£] (receipt of which is hereby acknowledged).

7. This agreement may be freely assigned or licensed by us.

8. This agreement is to be governed by and construed in accordance with English law.

Yours sincerely   Agreed and Accepted by

_____   _____
For and on behalf of   [Interviewee]
[Company]

Specimen agreement 2:
Interview Agreement (No Fee Payable)

To: [Interviewee]

From: [Company or Producer]

Date:

Dear

[Interview][Name of programme]

We write to confirm our agreement that, in consideration of our arranging to film and record the interview to be given by you and transmitted and/or recorded by us ('the interview') which we propose but do not undertake to broadcast, exhibit and/or otherwise exploit:

1. You agree to the recording and/or broadcasting and/or live relay of the interview and hereby grant to us all consents necessary to enable us to make the fullest use of the interview throughout the world in perpetuity by any and all means in any and all media, whether now known or hereafter discovered or developed, without liability or acknowledgement to you and the right to issue publicity concerning the interview and for such purpose to use and reproduce your name and photograph and recordings of the interview.

2. In recognition of the needs of film and television production, we shall be entitled to edit, copy, add to, take from, adapt or translate the interview as we see fit and you irrevocably waive the benefits of any provision of law known as 'moral rights' under the Copyright Design and Patents Act 1988 or any similar laws of any jurisdiction.

3. You warrant and undertake to us that you are fully entitled to give the interview to us and that no contribution by you to the interview (whether by way of inflection or gesture or otherwise) will infringe the copyright or any other right of any person, breach any contract or duty of confidence, constitute a contempt of court, be defamatory or be calculated to bring any broadcaster into disrepute.

4. [Optional clause] You undertake to us that you will not prior to _____ give to any person any interview or make, give or release any statement for publication by any means or medium relating to [the subject matter of the interview].

5. [Optional clause] You agree to indemnify us against all and any costs, claims, expenses and liabilities (including, without limitation, reasonable legal fees resulting from breach by you of any of the agreements, warranties and/or undertakings on your part contained in this agreement.

338

6. This agreement may be freely assigned or licensed by us.

7. This agreement is to be governed by and construed in accordance with English law.

Yours sincerely   Agreed and Accepted by

_____   _____
For and on behalf of   [Interviewee]
[Production Company]

Specimen agreement 3:
Contributor's Release (Television)

Producer   [   ]

Producer's Registered Office   [   ]

Contributor's Name   [   ]

Contributor's Address   [   ]

Contributor's Telephone Number   [   ]

Programme   [   ]

Description of Contribution   [   ]

Date of Recording Contribution   [   ]

In full and final consideration (the sufficiency of which I hereby accept and acknowledge) of the Producer granting me a credit in the Programme (the manner and size of which the Producer shall determine) (if my Contribution or any element thereof is actually incorporated in the final edited version of the Programme), I hereby consent to the filming and recording of my Contribution to the Programme, subject to the following terms and conditions:

1. I acknowledge that the Producer has fully explained the nature and content of the Programme.

2. I acknowledge that the copyright (if any) and all other rights in my Contribution vest in and are hereby assigned to the Producer (to the extent necessary by present assignment of future copyright) and that the Producer shall have the unfettered right to deal with my Contribution or any part of it as the Producer sees fit. Accordingly my Contribution or any part of it may be exhibited or otherwise exploited in all media and means whether now known or yet to be invented (the 'Media') throughout the world and universe as known and yet to be discovered (the 'Territory') for the full period of copyright and all renewals, revivals, reversions and extensions of this period (the 'Period'). I hereby waive such rights in my Contribution as a I now have or hereafter may acquire in relation thereto under Sections 77 and 80 of the Copyright, Designs & Patents Act 1988, and any so called 'moral rights' of authors.

3. I acknowledge that my Contribution may involve my participation in risky or dangerous activities and confirm that I am aware of the dangers thereof and consent to participate in such activities. I warrant that I do not suffer from any physical disability or health condition which may make my participation inadvisable. I agree and accept that I will participate at my own risk.

4. The Producer will not be liable to me or my legal representatives for any loss or damange or injury to me or my property caused in connection with the Programme unless caused by negligence of the Producer.

5. The Producer may without further consent use my name, likeness, biography, photographs of me and recordings of interviews with me in publicity for and promotion of the Programme in the Media throughout the Territory during the Period.

6. I confirm that the subject matter of my Contribution is truthful, that I have not misled the Producer in any way, that I have disclosed to the Producer all matters which are relevant to my Contribution, and that my Contribution is not defamatory or otherwise calculated to bring the Producer into disrepute, and that it does not contain anything which is an infringement of copyright.

7. I acknowledge that my Contribution or extracts of it may be included by the Producer in programming not directly associated with the Programme and accordingly consent to participation in all aspects of programming, that are or could reasonably be associated with or involved in the type or nature of the Producer's programming.

8. I confirm that I will participate in the filming of the Programme on the date/s agreed and acknowledge that the Producer has incurred costs in arranging for the filming of my Contribution.

9. I agree to indemnify the Producer from and against any and all costs, proceedings, claims, damages and losses including legal fees, howsoever suffered or incurred by the Producer as a result of any breach by me of any of the terms of this Release form.

10. I acknowledge that I may receive or acquire confidential information about the Producer as a result of my Contribution, and agree not to divulge any information about the Producer's programming or about the Producer which may have the effect of damaging the business or reputation of the Producer, its programming or its employees including but not limited to giving information directly or indirectly to newspapers, television or other media.

11. I hereby confirm that I shall not seek to enforce any rights to equitable remuneration in respect of any rental and lending rights which may accrue pursuant to legislation save insofar as the said legislation provides for separate payments relating thereto to be collected on my behalf by the relevant national collection agencies (in which case any claim shall be against such collecting agency) or insofar as the said legislation provides for separate and specific payment relating thereto to be paid to the Producer for and on my behalf.

12. This Release form is the whole and only agreement relating to my Contribution and shall be governed by and construed in accordance with the laws of England and Wales the courts of which shall be the courts of competent jurisdiction.

_____

Contributor's signature

_____

Date of signature

Specimen agreement 4:
Confidentiality Agreement

THIS AGREEMENT is made the   day of   [insert year]

BETWEEN:

(1)   [Company name], a company incorporated under the laws of [   ], and registered under number [   ], whose registered office is at [address] (the 'Recipient') and

(2)   [Entity Name], a company incorporated under the laws of [   ], and registered under number [   ], whose registered office is at [address] (the 'Discloser')

hereinafter collectively referred to as the 'Parties' and individually as the 'Party'.

WHEREAS:

(1)   The Parties are considering entering into a [commercial] transaction with each other in relation to [details of potential transaction], (the 'Transaction')

(2)   As a preparatory step to developing the Transaction the Recipient may receive or have access to Confidential Information (as defined in clause 1 of this Agreement) from the Discloser

(3)   The Discloser wishes to protect such Confidential Information.

NOW IT IS HEREBY AGREED AS FOLLOWS:

1. DEFINITION OF CONFIDENTIAL INFORMATION

'Confidential Information' is defined as all information which is furnished by the Discloser or any of its directors, officers, employees, shareholders, lawyers, accountants, financial advisors or other agents ('Representatives') in oral, written, magnetic, electronic or other form to the Recipient or any of the Recipient's Representatives, regardless of whether specifically identified as confidential, together with any and all proprietary data, trade secrets, know-how, ideas, principles, concepts, analyses, compilations or other documents concerning the Discloser which are acquired by the Recipient or Recipient's Representatives.

2. SCOPE

The Parties agree that this Confidentiality Agreement sets forth the way in which the disclosure, circulation and use of Confidential Information between the two Parties will take place. The Recipient hereby agrees that Confidential Information will be used solely for the purposes of evaluating the transaction and shall not be used for any purpose other than as specified in this Agreement.

3. OBLIGATIONS OF THE RECIPIENT

3.1 The Recipient shall take any and all measures necessary to ensure the confidentiality of Confidential Information.

3.2   The Recipient shall not disclose Confidential Information to any third party other than the Recipient's Representatives who strictly need to know such Confidential Information for the purpose of evaluating the Transaction.

3.3   The Recipient shall not disclose, and shall direct its Representatives not to disclose, to any person the fact that discussions or negotiations are taking place concerning a possible Transaction, or any of the terms, conditions or other facts with respect to any such Transaction. The term 'person' shall be interpreted to include without limitation any individual, government body, partnership, corporation or other entity.

3.4   The Recipient shall immediately notify the Discloser of any event that could compel the Recipient to disclose Confidential Information to third parties. The Recipient shall not disclose such Confidential Information without providing the Discloser with advance notice and shall disclose only that portion of Confidential Information that is legally required to be disclosed. The Recipient shall make reasonable efforts to obtain a protective order or other reliable assurance that any Confidential Information required to be disclosed is treated confidentially.

3.5   If the Recipient has reason to believe or has knowledge that Confidential Information has been accessed by or disclosed to unauthorized individuals or third parties, such belief or knowledge shall be immediately communicated in writing to the Disclosure.

3.6   The Recipient shall not store or reproduce Confidential Information in any form, unless strictly necessary for the purpose of evaluating the Transaction. This prohibition includes, but is not limited to, a ban on the copying of documents containing Confidential Information, unless strictly necessary for the purpose of evaluating the Transaction.

4. OWNERSHIP AND USE OF CONFIDENTIAL INFORMATION

4.1   The Confidential Information shall remain the property of the Discloser. Specifically, nothing in this Agreement shall be construed as granting or conferring (either directly or indirectly) to the Recipient or the Recipient's Representatives any right, title or licence of use in respect of any Confidential Information.

4.2   Any documents, disks, audio tapes, compact discs, video tapes or other storage devices containing Confidential Information, shall be promptly deleted (in the case of electronic delivery of Confidential Information), destroyed (in the case of physical delivery of Confidential Information) or returned by the Recipient upon the Discloser's request and/or upon the termination or completion of negotiations related to the transaction. Notwithstanding the return or destruction of any Confidential Information and materials based on the Confidential Information, the Recipient will continue to be bound by its obligations of confidentiality and other obligations hereunder.

5. TERM OF AGREEMENT

The Recipient's obligations to protect Confidential Information shall subsist from the date of this agreement and shall survive for two (2) years from the date of receipt of such Confidential Information.

6. EXCEPTIONS

The Recipient shall not be liable for disclosure of any Confidential Information if such Confidential Information:

(a) is now or hereafter comes into the public domain without breach of this Agreement and through no fault of the Recipient, or

(b) was known to the Recipient prior to the effective date of this Agreement, and the Recipient can prove this from its written records, or

(c) was received from a third party legally entitled to disclose such Confidential Information, or

(d) was disclosed by the Recipient with the prior written approval of the Discloser.

7. LIABILITY

If the Recipient breaches this Agreement, the Discloser may at its option elect to institute proceedings in court to obtain damages and/or to obtain injunctive relief and/or to enforce specific performance of this Agreement. Such remedies shall not be deemed to be the exclusive remedies for a breach of this Confidentiality Agreement but shall be in addition to all other remedies available at law or equity.

8. MISCELLANEOUS

8.1 This Agreement contains the entire understanding relative to the protection of the Confidential Information covered by this Agreement and supersedes all prior and collateral communications, reports and understandings, if any, between the Parties regarding such Confidential Information.

8.2 No amendment, modification, waiver, change or addition hereto shall be effective or binding on either party unless the same is in writing and signed by both Parties.

8.3 Each party agrees that no failure or delay by the other party to this Agreement in exercising any right, power or privilege hereunder shall operate as a waiver hereof nor shall any single or partial exercise thereof preclude any other or further exercise of any right, power or privilege hereunder.

8.4 No waiver or modification of this Agreement will be binding upon either party unless made in writing and signed by a duly authorized representative of the Parties.

8.5 This Agreement shall be governed by and construed in accordance with English law. The Parties expressly waive any right to any forum to which they may otherwise be entitled and submit to the jurisdiction of the Courts of England for the settlement of any claim or matter arising under this Agreement.

SIGNED by	)	SIGNED by	)
	)		)
duly authorized to sign	)	duly authorized to sign	)
for and on behalf of	)	for and on behalf of	)
[Company Name]	)	[Entity Name]	)

Specimen agreement 5:
Moral Rights Waiver

(a) By Individual

From: [individual] of [address] (the 'Author')

To: [publisher] of [address] (the 'Publisher')

Dated:

Dear

Re: [title] (the 'Work')

1. The Author asserts the Author's right to be identified in relation to the Work on the title page and cover in the following form: [state form of identification required] and the Publisher undertakes to comply with such request and to require all sub-publishers and other licensees to honour this right. The Author acknowledges that no casual or inadvertent failure by the Publisher or by any third party to comply with this provision shall constitute an infringement of this right and in the event of any infringement the Author agrees that the Author shall not seek injunctive relief and the sole remedy of the Author shall be a claim for damages.

2. The Author acknowledges that it is necessary for the purposes of publication for the Publisher to have the right to make alterations of the text of the Work in order to make corrections and conform the text to the Publisher's house style and also for the purpose of authorizing translations of the Work and for removing any material which might in the opinion of the Publisher be actionable at law or which might damage the Publisher's reputation or business interests and also for the purpose of complying with the advice of the Publisher's legal advisers and for other general copy-editing purposes and the Author consents to the exercise by the Publisher of such rights and agrees that the product of such exercise shall not be capable of being considered a distortion mutilation or derogatory treatment of the Work.

OR

The Author irrevocably and unconditionally waives all rights to which the Author may be entitled pursuant to Sections [77], 80 and 85 of the Copyright, Designs and Patents Act 1988 and any other moral rights provided for under the laws now or in future in force in any part of the world in relation to the exploitation by the Publisher its successors assigns and licensees of the Work.

Yours faithfully

Signed by [Author]

We confirm and agree the above and agree to be bound by it.

SIGNED by [name]   )
For and on behalf of   )
[name of Publisher]   )

(b) By Personal Representative(s)

From: [moral rights owner] of [address]

To: [publisher] of [address]

Dated:

Dear

[title] (the 'Work')
By [name of author] [the 'Author']

1. In consideration of your undertaking in paragraph 2 I/we warrant confirm and agree as follows:

EITHER

1.1 By virtue of Clause [insert] of the will of the Author dated [date] all moral rights conferred by Part I Chapter IV of the Copyright, Designs and Patents Act 1988 were by testamentary disposition bequeathed to me/us

OR

1.1 The will of the Author made no provision for the testamentary disposition of the moral rights conferred by Part I Chapter IV of the Copyright, Designs and Patents Act 1988 but pursuant to Clause [insert] of the will of the Author dated [date] all rights of copyright in the Work were by testamentary dispositions bequeathed to me/us and pursuant to the provisions of Section 95(1)(b) of the Copyright, Designs and Patents Act 1988 all moral rights in the work are vested in me/us.

OR

1.1 The Author died intestate and pursuant to Section 95(1)(c) of the Copyright, Designs and Patents Act 1988 all moral rights conferred by Part I Chapter IV of such Act are exercisable by me/us as the Personal Representative(s) of the Author pursuant to [specify method of appointment].

1.2 I/we irrevocably and unconditionally waive all rights to which I/we am/are entitled pursuant to Sections 77, 80 and 85 of the Copyright, Designs and Patents Act 1988 and any other moral rights provided for under the laws now or in future in force in any part of the world in respect of the inclusion and exploitation by you or your successors licensees and assignees of the Work.

2. The Publisher undertakes to pay to me/us the sum of £[insert] [or other payment].

Yours faithfully

SIGNED by [name(s) of   )
moral rights owners]   )
)

We confirm and agree the above and agree to be bound by it.

SIGNED by [name]   )
For and on behalf of   )
[name of Publisher]   )

(c) With Assignment of Reversionary Copyright

From: [right owner(s)] of [address]

To: [publisher] of [address]

Dated:

Dear

[title] [the 'Work'] by [name of author] [the 'Author']

1. In consideration of your undertaking in paragraph 2 I/we warrant confirm and agree as follows:

EITHER

1.1 By virtue of Clause [insert] of the will of the Author dated [date] all rights of copyright in the Work and moral rights conferred by Part I Chapter IV of the Copyright, Designs and Patents Act 1988 (the 'Act') were by testamentary disposition bequeathed to me/us.

OR

1.1 The will of the Author made no provisions for the testamentary disposition of the moral rights conferred by Part I Chapter IV of the Copyright, Designs and Patents Act 1988 (the 'Act') but pursuant to Clause [insert] of the will of the Author dated [date] all rights of copyright in the Work were by testamentary disposition bequeathed to me/us and pursuant to the provisions of Section 95(1)(b) of the Act all moral rights in the Work are vested in me/us.

OR

1.1 The Author died intestate and pursuant to Section 95(1)(c) of the Copyright, Designs and Patents Act 1988 (the 'Act') all moral rights conferred by Part I Chapter IV of the Act are exercisable by me/us as the Personal Representative(s) of the Author pursuant to [specify method of appointment] which vested in me/us all rights of copyright in the Work.

1.2 I/we irrevocably and unconditionally waive all rights to which I/we am/are entitled pursuant to Sections 77, 80 and 85 of the Act and any other moral rights provided for under the laws now or in future in force in any part of the world in respect of the publication and expectation by you your successors assignees and licensees of the Work I/we now assign to you and your successors assignees and licensees absolutely the whole of the reversionary interests in the copyright in the Work throughout the world for the full period of copyright protection including all renewals revivals reversions and extensions now or in the future existing under the laws in force in any part of the world and warrant that I/we are the sole absolute unencumbered legal and beneficial owner(s) of the same.

2. The Publisher undertakes to pay to [name of right owner(s)] the sum of £[insert] [or other payment].

Yours faithfully

SIGNED by [names of)
rights owners])
)

We confirm and agree the above and agree to be bound by it.

SIGNED by [name])
For and on behalf of)
[name of Publisher])

(d) By Personal Representative(s) for Film

From: [name(s) of moral right owner(s)] of [address]

To: [name of company] of [address]

Dated:

Dear

[title] (the 'Work') by [name of author] (the 'Author')

1. In consideration of your undertaking in paragraph 2 [I or we] warrant and agree as follows:

    1.1 By virtue of clause [insert] of the will of the Author dated [date] all moral rights conferred by the Copyright, Designs and Patents Act 1988 were by testamentary disposition bequeathed to [me or us]

OR

    1.1 The will of the Author made no provision for the testamentary disposition of the moral rights conferred by the Copyright, Designs and Patents Act 1988 but pursuant to clause [insert] of the will of the Author dated [date] all rights of copyright in the Work were by testamentary disposition bequeathed to [me or us] and therefore pursuant to the provisions of Section 95(1)(b) of that Act all moral rights in the Work are vested in [me or us]

OR

    1.1 The Author died intestate and pursuant to the Copyright, Designs and Patents Act 1988 Section 95(1)(c) all moral rights conferred by that Act are exercisable by [me or us] as the personal representative(s) of the Author pursuant to [specify manner of appointment]

1.2 [I or we] consent to the incorporation of the Work in the [screenplay or film or sound recording] entitled [name] and irrevocably and unconditionally waive all rights to which [I am or we are] entitled pursuant to the Copyright, Designs and Patents Act 1988 Sections 77, 80 and 84 and any other moral rights provided for under the laws now or in future in force in any part of the world in respect of the inclusion and exploitation by you your successors and licensees of the Work by means of such [screenplay or film or sound recording] in any and all media throughout the world.

2. The company undertakes to pay to [me or us] the sum of £[insert].

Yours faithfully

[signature(s) of personal representative(s)]

We confirm and agree the above and agree to be bound by it.

[signature on behalf of company]

(e) Notice of Assertion of Right to be Identified

From: [name of author or director] of [address]

To: [name of company] of [address]

Dated:

Dear

[title] [directed] by [name of author or director] (the 'Work')

1. I am the [author or director] of the Work.

2. This letter constitutes a notice in accordance with the provisions of the Copyright, Designs and Patents Act 1988 Section 78(2)(b) of the assertion of the right granted pursuant to Section 77(1) of that Act (the right of the author of a copyright literary, dramatic, musical or artistic work and the director of a copyright film to be identified as author or director of the work.

3. Pursuant to the provisions of the Copyright, Designs and Patents Act 1988 Section 77(8) I have the right to specify the form of identification which you are obliged to use. Such form is as follows: [specify form of identification].

349

4. The provisions of the Copyright, Designs and Patents Act 1988 Section 77 detail the circumstances in which I am entitled to be identified and a copy of that section is enclosed for your ease of reference.

Yours faithfully

[signature of author or director]

Enc.

Enclosure
Section 77 Copyright, Designs and Patents Act 1988

77. Right to be identified as author or director

1. The author of a copyright literary, dramatic, musical or artistic work, and the director of a copyright film, has the right to be identified as the author or director of the work in the circumstances mentioned in this section; but the right is not infringed unless it has been asserted in accordance with section 78.

2. The author of a literary work (other than words intended to be sung or spoken with music) or a dramatic work has the right to be identified whenever
   (a) the work is published commercially, performed in public, broadcast or included in a cable programme service; or
   (b) copies of a film or sound recording including the work are issued to the public;

   and that right includes the right to be identified whenever any of those events occur in relation to an adaptation of the work as the author of the work from which the adaptation was made.

3. The author of a musical work, or a literary work consisting of words intended to be sung or spoken with music, has the right to be identified whenever
   (a) the work is published commercially;
   (b) copies of a sound recording of the work are issued to the public; or
   (c) a film of which the sound-track includes the work is shown in public or copies of such a film are issued to the public;
   and that right includes the right to be identified whenever any of those events occur in relation to an adaptation of the work as the author of the work from which the adaptation was made.

4. The author of an artistic work has the right to be identified whenever
   (a) the work is published commercially or exhibited in public, or a visual image of it is broadcast or included in a cable programme service;

(b) a film including a visual image of the work is shown in public or copies of such a film are issued to the public;

(c) in the case of a work of architecture in the form of a building or a model for a building, a sculpture or a work of artistic craftsmanship, copies of a graphic work representing it, or of a photograph of it, are issued to the public.

5. The author of a work of architecture in the form of a building also has the right to be identified on the building as constructed or, where more than one building is constructed to the design, on the first to be constructed.

6. The director of a film has the right to be identified whenever the film is shown in public, broadcast or included in a cable programme service or copies of the film are issued to the public.

7. The right of the author or director under this section is

(a) in the case of commercial publication or the issue to the public of copies of a film or sound recording, to be identified in or on each copy or, if that is not appropriate, in some other manner likely to bring his identity to the notice of a person acquiring a copy,

(b) in the case of identification on a building, to be identified by appropriate means visible to persons entering or approaching the building, and

(c) in any other case, to be identified in a manner likely to bring his identity to the attention of a person seeing or hearing the performance, exhibition, showing, broadcast or cable programme in question;

and the identification must in each case be clear and reasonably prominent.

8. If the author or director in asserting his right to be identified specifies a pseudonym, initials or some other particular form of identification, that form shall be used; otherwise any reasonable form of identification may be used.

9. This section has effect subject to Section 79 (exceptions to right).

Specimen agreement 6:
Assignment of copyright

This DEED OF ASSIGNMENT is made the day of [insert year]

BETWEEN:

[Name of owner of copyright] (the 'Assignor') and
[Name of the acquirer of copyright] (the 'Assignee).

WHEREAS:

(1) The Assignor owns all Rights in the Work
(2) The Assignor wishes to assign all such Rights to the Assignee; and
(3) The Assignee wishes to accept such an assignment on the following terms.

IT IS AGREED:

1. DEFINITIONS
   In this Assignment the following words shall have the following meanings:
   - 'Rights': all copyright (and all rights of a like nature anywhere in the world) in the Work together with all the Assignor's rights and interests in such copyright, including (without limitation) all rights of action and remedies in relation to past infringements
   - 'Work': [describe the work for example a book, script, article].

2. ASSIGNMENT
   In consideration of the sum of [insert] [plus VAT] paid by the Assignee to the Assignor, the Assignor hereby with full title guarantee assigns the Rights to the Assignee for the full period of copyright in the Work.

3. FURTHER ASSURANCE
   The Assignor will at the reasonable request of the Assignee:
   (a) do all acts and execute and swear all documents that are reasonably necessary to vest absolute legal and beneficial ownership of the Rights in the Assignee or to perfect the Assignee's title thereto anywhere in the world; and
   (b) give to the Assignee such reasonable assistance as the Assignee may request in evidencing the Assignee's title to the Rights anywhere in the world.

4. WARRANTIES AND CONFIRMATIONS
   The Assignor warrants and confirms that:
   (a) the Assignor is the sole, legal and beneficial owner of the Rights and has full power to enter into this Assignment
   (b) the Assignor has not previously assigned or granted any licences in respect of any of the Rights or otherwise encumbered any of the Rights

(c) the Work is the original, sole [or joint] work of the Assignor

(d) the Work is not defamatory

(e) the Assignor has waived irrevocably all moral rights which may exist in the Rights anywhere in the world; and

(f) the Assignor will not hereafter use or permit the use of the Work without the licence of the Assignee.

5. INDEMNITY

The Assignor will keep the Assignee indemnified from and against all loss, costs, demands, damages and expenses suffered or incurred in respect of or arising out of any breach or non-performance or alleged breach as non-performance of any of the above warranties on the part of the Assignor.

6. GOVERNING LAW

This Deed of Assignment is subject to and shall be construed in accordance with English law and the parties hereby irrevocably submit to the exclusive jurisdiction of the English Courts in relation thereto.

Executed as a DEED by the Assignor and the Assignee the day and year appearing above.

Signed on behalf of the Assignor as a
DEED by [Assignor]

Signed on behalf of the Assignee as a
DEED by [Assignee]

Bibliography

The following books, periodicals, codes and internet legal services provide further information on the areas of law considered in this book.

Books

Alberstat, P. (2000). *Independent Producers' Guide to Film and TV Contracts*. Focal Press.

Besenjak, C. (2001). *Copyright Plain and Simple* (United States law), 2nd edn. Career Press.

Bonnington, A., McInnes, R. and McKain, R. (2000). *Scots Law for Journalists*, 7th edn. W. Green/Sweet & Maxwell.

Braithwaite, N. (ed.) (1995). *The International Libel Handbook: A Practical Guide for Journalists*. Butterworth-Heinemann.

Carey, P. and Verow, R. (1998). *Media and Entertainment: The Law and Business*. Jordans.

Clayton, R. and Tomlinson, H. (2000). *The Law of Human Rights*. Oxford University Press.

Eady, D. and Smith, A. (2000). *Arlidge, Eady and Smith On Contempt*, 2nd edn. Sweet & Maxwell.

Fairley, D. and McInnes, R. (2000). *Contempt of Court in Scotland*. CLT Professional Publishing.

Milmo, P. (ed.) (1997). *Gatley on Libel and Slander*, 9th edn. Sweet & Maxwell.

Morrison, A. (ed.) (1996). *Fundamentals of American Law*. Oxford University Press.

Pritchard, J. (2001). *The New Penguin Guide to the Law*, 4th edn. Penguin Books.

Robertson, G. and Nicol, A. (1992). *Media Law*, 3rd edn. Penguin Books.

Wadham, J. and Crossman, G. (eds) (2000). *Your Rights: The Liberty Guide*, 7th edn. Pluto.

Wadham, J. and Mountfield, H. (2000). *Blackstone's Guide to the Human Rights Act 1998*, 2nd edn. Blackstone Press Ltd.

Wadham, J., Griffiths, J. and Rigby, B. (2001). *Blackstone's Guide to the Freedom of Information Act*. Blackstone Press Ltd.

Bibliography

Periodicals

The Civil Court Practice 2001. Butterworths.
Entertainment and Media Law Reports. Sweet & Maxwell.
Entertainment Law Review. Sweet & Maxwell.
European Human Rights Law Review. Sweet and Maxwell.

Codes

British Codes of Advertising and Sales Promotion (www.asa.org.uk).
Broadcast Standards Commission Codes of Guidance: Fairness & Privacy and Standards (www.bsc.org.uk).
ITC Code of Advertising Standards and Practice (www.itc.org.uk).
ITC Programme Code (www.itc.org.uk).
National Union of Journalists Code of Conduct (www.nuj.org.uk).
Press Complaints Commission Code of Practice (www.pcc.org.uk).
Radio Authority Advertising and Sponsorship Code (www.radioauthority.org.uk).
Radio Authority News and Current Affairs Code (www.radioauthority.org.uk).
Radio Authority Programme Code (www.radioauthority.org.uk).

Internet legal services

United Kingdom law

Butterworths (www.butterworths.com)

Law Direct: free legal information service.
LEXIS-NEXIS: access to legal, news and business information services.
NewLawOnline: reporting of legal decisions from the High Court, Court of Appeal, House of Lords and European Court of Justice.

Sweet & Maxwell (www.smlawpub.co.uk)

WestLawUK: cases, legislation, journals and commentary.

United States law

American Bar Association (www.lawtechnology.org/lawlink/home.html)

American Bar Association Legal Technology Resource Center: quick access to websites with important legal information.

Index

Lists of cases and statutes, including page references, are in pages xix to xxx. Page numbers below followed by an asterisk denote entries in the glossary, or, in the case of organizations, their contact details. Page numbers followed by an *n* refer to footnotes giving web site addresses.

Absolute privilege, *see under* Privilege
Account of profits:
　breach of confidence, 103
　copyright infringement, 60
Acts of Parliament, *see table of statutes in pages*
　xxvii–xxx
Actus reus, 325*
Advertising, 263–6
　British Codes of Advertising and Sales Promotion,
　　354
　election expenses, 244–5
　on Internet, 264
　ITC Code of Advertising Standards and Practice,
　　261, 354
　overview, 263
　Radio Authority Advertising and Sponsorship
　　Code, 354
　see also Code of Advertising Practice
Advertising Standards Authority, 263, 263*n*, 330*
　see also Code of Advertising Practice
Aggravation, in defence to libel, 13–14
Agreements:
　specimen, 335
　　assignment of copyright, 351–2
　　confidentiality agreement, 342–4
　　contributor's release (television), 340–1
　　interview agreement (fee payable), 336–7
　　interview agreement (no fee payable), 338–9
　　moral rights waiver, 345–50
American Bar Association, 330*, 354
American Civil Liberties Union, 313
Analysis information, 217
Annan Committee, 259
Antecedents, 325*
Anti-terrorism legislation, USA, 318–20
Appeals, active period, 172

Arbitration proceedings, reporting restrictions, 161–2
Arraignment, 325*
Arrest, 325*
　reporting, 170–1
Artistic expression, 279
Artistic works, and copyright, 46–7
　copyright ownership, 50
　definition, 46
　duration of copyright, 58
　moral rights, 61–3
　originality, 47–8
Assignments of copyright, 80, 83
　specimen agreement, 335, 351–2
Attorney General, role in contempt of court
　　proceedings, 177–8
Audiovisual works, copyright, USA, 309
Audit functions information, 223
Authorship:
　false attribution of, 61
　joint, 46, 50
　　USA, 309

Bail, 325*
　media coverage and, 171
Bankruptcy, 325*
　trustee in bankruptcy, 329*
Bar Council of England and Wales, 330*
BBC:
　internal guidelines for producers, 261–2, 262*n*
　Viewer and Listener Correspondence, 261
　see also Broadcasting
Berne Convention (on copyright), 43, 61, 64, 74, 310
Bibliography, 353–4
Bill of Rights, USA, 305
Bind over, 325*

Index

Blackmail, withholding of names, 141
Blanket bans:
    breach of confidence, 89
    on reporting, 140, 156
Blasphemous libel, 34–6
    definition, 34–5
    mental element, 35
    penalties, 35
    recent prosecutions, 35–6
    religious protection, extent of, 36
Blasphemy, *see* Blasphemous libel
Books, bibliography, 353
Breach of confidence, 89–103
    blanket bans, 89
    confidential information, 90–2
    criteria for establishing, 90
    v. defamation, 103
    defences to, 97–101
        consent, 98
        iniquity, 98–100
        public domain, 98
        public interest, 98–100, 100–1
    and official secrets, 228, 230
    overview, 89–90
    prior restraint, 197–200
    and privacy, 116–17
    procedure, 101–3
        the action, 101
        interim injunctions, 89–90, 101–3
    remedies, 103
        account of profits, 103
        damages, 103
        delivery up, 103
    see also Confidence
Breach of copyright, *see* Copyright infringement
British Codes of Advertising and Sales Promotion, 354
    see also Code of Advertising Practice
Broadcasting:
    Annan Committee, 259
    during elections, 245–6
    European Convention on Human Rights, 280
    regulation in USA, 320
    semi self-regulation, 258, 261–2
    see also Broadcasts; Programme Codes
Broadcasting Complaints Commission, 259
Broadcasting Standards Commission, 249, 258–60,
    283, 330*
    Codes of Guidance
        fairness and privacy, 112, 260, 354
        standards, 112, 260, 354
    complaints, 260
    function, 259

history, 258–9
    monitoring, 260
    as a public authority, 128
Broadcasting Standards Council, 259
Broadcasts:
    'compelled broadcasts', USA, 308
    copyright, 48–9
        copyright ownership, 51–2
        duration of copyright of, 59
        infringement, 54
        live events, 49
    see also Broadcasting
Brutality, as obscenity, 206
Bulletin boards, Internet defamation, 67
Burden (onus) of proof, 325*

Cabinet, *see under* Government
Cable programmes, copyright, 49
    copyright ownership, 51–2
    duration of copyright of, 59
Calcutt Committee (Government Committee on
        Privacy and Related Matters), xxxiii–xxxiv
    report on privacy, 120–3, 251–2
        general principles, 120–2
        post-Calcutt, 122–3
Care order, 325*
Cases, *see table of cases in pages xvii–xxiv*
Cause of action, 325*
Caveats (Scottish law), 292–3
Children:
    children's hearing in Scotland, 296, 303
    interviews and photographs, 256
    reporting restrictions, 142–7
        cases involving indecency or immorality, 147
        employment tribunals, 163
        legislation, 142–3, 146–7, 153
        legitimacy and maintenance proceedings, 144
        in magistrates'/crown courts, 145, 146
        Scottish law, 296
        in sex cases, 257
        wardship proceedings, 143–4
        youth and other courts, 144–5
    see also Family proceedings
Cigarette Code, advertisement practice, 265
Citizen's Charter, 214
Civil court judgments, on Internet, 135, 135n
Civil law system, in Scotland, 289
Civil libel, *v.* criminal libel, 38
Civil Procedure Rules, 134, 136, 158, 172, 325*
    and human rights legislation, 273, 284
Civil proceedings, active period, 172

Claimant, 325*

Code of Advertising Practice, 263–6, 263*n*
  aims and functions, 263–4
  Cigarette Code, 265
  complaints procedure, 265–6
  current edition, 264
  rules, 264–5
  sanctions, 266

Code of Practice on Access to Government
    Information, 105, 212, 213–19
  access to information, 213–14
    limits on, 214–18
  applications and fees for information, 218, 218*n*
  enforcement, 218–19
  general principles, 213
  public bodies subject to, 213, 213*n*

Codes of practice, 354
  see also individual codes of practice

Comment, *see* Fair comment

Commercial expression, 279

Commercial interests, 217, 224

Common law, 325*
  development of, xxxi

Communications:
  global nature of, xxxii
  interception of, 118, 121, 122, 127–8
  legal professional privilege, 30, 97, 191, 224, 327*
  Office of Communications (Ofcom), 332*
  surveillance, 127–8
  'without prejudice' communications, 30, 329*

Complaints:
  Broadcasting Standards Commission, 260
  Code of Advertising Practice, complaints
      procedure, 265–6
  see also Press Complaints Commission

Computer programs/databases, copyright, 45
  infringement of, 55
  USA, 309

Confidence:
  breach of, *see* Breach of confidence
  law of, 44
    English *v.* other countries', 91–2
  obligation of, 92–7
    agreement terms, 92–3
    Cabinet members, 97
    confider–confidant relationships, 95–7
    government employees, 93–4
    media sources, 97
    private employees, 93
    third parties, 97
    and 'whistle blowing', 94–5

Confidential information, 121, 217

Confidentiality:
  effect of passage of time, 92
  exceptions during arbitration proceedings, 161–2
  information having necessary quality of, 90–2
  material made available on disclosure, 156
  and the public domain, 91, 98
  specimen agreement, 335, 342–4

Consent:
  to breach of confidence, 98
  to defamation (USA), 308
  to invasion of privacy (USA), 318
  to publication of defamatory matter, 25

Constitution, 325*

Contact order, 326*

Contempt of court, 166–83, 326*
  active proceedings, 169–72
    appeals, 172
    arrests, reporting of, 170–1
    civil proceedings, 172
    criminal proceedings, 169–72
    inquests, 172
    retrials, 172
  Attorney General role, 177–8
  civil contempt, 166
  common law contempt, interfering with
      pending/imminent proceedings, 180–1
  contempt in the face of the court, 182
  criminal contempt, 166
    prior restraint, 201
  defences to strict liability contempt, 178–80
    discussion of public affairs, 179–80
    fair and accurate contemporary reports, 179
    innocent publication, 178–9
  definition, 166, 326*
  failing to comply with a court order, 182
  v. freedom of expression, 167
  injunctions, 183
  jurors, interviews with, 159–60
  legislation, 166, 167–80
    protection of journalistic sources, 185–8
    scope of, 180
  misreporting, 179
  negligence, 179
  overview, 166–7
  penalties, 183
  scandalizing the court, 182
  in Scotland, *see under* Scottish law
  strict liability, 168–9
  strict liability rule, 166, 168, 176
    applying to publications, 168, 169, 173
    in civil proceedings, 172
    role of Attorney General, 177–8

Index

Contempt of court (*Cont.*)
  substantial risk of serious prejudice, 173–7
    anticipating verdict, 177
    circulation of publication, 177
    civil proceedings, 177
    content of publication, 175
    date of hearing, 174–5
    defendant's character and record, 176
    district judge trials, 174
    'fade factor', 175
    judge alone trials, 174
    jurors, undermining/intimidation of, 177
    jury trials, 174
    lay magistrate hearings, 174
    parties, undermining/intimidation of, 177
    photographs, 175
    place of trial, 175
    in Scottish law, 300–3
    type of court, 173–4
    witnesses, undermining/intimidation of, 177
  tape recorders in court, 160–1
  third-party contempt, 183
  USA, 321
  use of documents disclosed during proceedings, 182
Contempt of Parliament, 240, 241–3
  breach of embargo, 243
  definition, 241–2
  disrupting, obstructing, influencing, 242
  improper disclosure, 243
  inaccurate/untrue reporting of proceedings, 242
  misbehaviour, 242
  procedure, 243
Contract, 326*
Contracts of employment, duty of confidence, 93
Contributor rights, 84–5
Contributor's release (television), specimen agreement, 335, 340–1
Convictions, spent convictions and malice, 14, 15
Cookies (software), data protection, 75
Copying, 53–4, 54, 58
Copyright, 43–64, 326*
  artistic works, *see* Artistic works
  assignments, 80, 83
    specimen agreement, 335, 351–2
  Berne Convention, 43, 61, 64, 74, 310
  breach of, *see* Copyright infringement
  broadcasts, 48–9, 51–2, 54, 59
  cable programmes, 49, 51–2, 59
  categories of work, 44
  copying, 53–4, 54, 58
  and criticism, 55, 56

derivative works, 48
digital media, 63–4
dramatic works, *see* Dramatic works
duration of, 58–9
European Copyright Directive, xxxii, 63–4, 63*n*, 73, 73*n*
expiry of, 59
extracts, 53
false attribution of authorship, 61
films (motion pictures), 49, 51–2, 59, 309
general principles, 44
infringement of, *see* Copyright infringement
as intellectual property right, 43
international conventions, 74
joint ownership, 46, 50, 309
legislation, 43
length of work, 45
Library of Congress Copyright Office (USA), 332*
literary works, *see* Literary works
Mechanical-Copyright Protection Society (MCPS), 332*
moral rights, 61–3, 70, 82
  waiver of, 82, 335, 345–50
musical works, *see* Musical works
new media, *see under* New media
no copyright, 58
older works, 59
originality, 47–8
  'sweat of the brow' test, 47
overview, 43–4
ownership, 50–3
  formalities, 53
  joint, 46, 50, 309
  transfer of, 52
parodies, 53–4
pastiches, 53
photographs, 50–1, 81
published editions, 49
reviews, 55, 56
rights clearance, *see* Rights clearance
Rome Convention, 43
secondary, 48
sound recordings, 48–9, 51–2, 59, 309
spoken words, 82
  recordings, 45, 57, 82
underlying rights, 48, 49
underlying works, 81
Universal Copyright Convention, 43, 53, 69, 74
USA law, *see under* United States of America
video recordings, 49
see also World Intellectual Property Organization

Copyright Directive (EU), xxxii, 63–4, 63*n*, 73, 73*n*
  digital media, 63–4
  exemptions, 64
  prohibition on exploitation, 64
Copyright infringement, 53–5, 57, 81
  adaptations, 54–5
  broadcasts, 54
  copying, 53–4, 54
  criminal offences, 60–1
  defences to, 55–8
    educational purposes, 58
    fair dealing, 55–6
    incidental inclusion, 57, 81
    libraries, 58
    public interest, 58
    spoken words, 57, 82
  public performances, 54
  remedies, 59–60
    account of profits, 60
    damages, 59–60
    delivery up, 60
    flagrant damages, 60
    infringement damages, 59
    injunctions, 59
  sale, hire and importation, 55
Copyright Office, Library of Congress, Washington, 310, 332*
Copyright Regulations 1995, 43
Correspondence, interception of, 118, 121, 122
Corroboration, 326*
Costs:
  in defamation cases, 32–3
    early settlement, 33
    failure to accept offer, 33
    statement in open court, 33
Council of Europe, 74, 78–9, 330*
County court, 326*
Court, as a public authority, 138
Court of Appeal, 326*
Court proceedings:
  in camera, 133, 327*
  judgments, copies of, 134–5
  open court rule, 134–8
    exceptions, 133
    general principles, 134
    obtaining information, 134–5
  overview, 133–4
  proceedings held in chambers, 137–8
  proceedings held in private, 133, 135–7
    publication of information, 136–7
  trial within a trial, 140
  see also Magistrates' courts; Reporting restrictions

Court records, 224
Court reports, qualified privilege, 21, 23–4
Court Service, 135*n*, 330*
Criminal convictions, and defence to libel, 14–15
Criminal investigations, documents, qualified privilege, 24
Criminal libel, 34, 37–9
  v. civil libel, 38
  defences to, 38–9
  definition, 38
  penalties, 39
Criminal proceedings, active period, 169–72
  arrest, 170–1
  bail, 171
  commencement of, 169–70
  conclusion of, 171–2
  warrants, 171
Criminals, and defamation, 5
Criticism:
  and copyright, 55, 56
  and fair comment, 16, 18
Cross examination, 326*
Crown Court, 326*
Custody, *see* Residence order
Cyber-crime convention, 74, 74*n*, 78, 311, 311*n*, 317
Cybersquatting, 72
  USA, 315–16

D-notices, *see* Defence Advisory Notice system
DA Notices, *see* Defence Advisory Notice system
Damages, 326*
  breach of confidence, 103
  breach of copyright, 59–60
  in defamation cases, *see under* Defamation
  under human rights legislation, 273–4
Data, definition, 107
Data controllers:
  definition, 106–7
  disproportionate effort, 109, 110
  obligations on, 105, 107–10
    compliance with Schedules and Data Protection Order, 109–10
    data protection principles, 108
    fair and lawful processing, 108–9
    notification procedure, 108
  see also Data protection; Personal data
Data protection:
  cookies (software), 75
  legislation, 74–6, 104–13
    criminal offences, 113
    definitions, 106–7

Data protection (*Cont.*)
  legislation (*Cont.*)
    exemptions, 112–13
    general principles, 105–6
    history, 105
    overview, 104–5
  privacy statements on web sites, 75
  Safe Harbor Privacy Principles, 75, 316, 316*n*
  see also Data controllers; Personal data
Data Protection Commissioner, 104, 106, 108, 108*n*, 112
Data Protection Directive (EU), 127
Data Protection (Processing of Sensitive Personal
    Data) Order 2000, 110
Data Protection Tribunal, 106
Debt, allegations about, and defamation, 7
Decree absolute, 326*
Decree nisi, 326*
Defamation, 3–33
  application of human rights principles, 283–4
  v. breach of confidence, 103
  categories, 4–5
  damages, 30–2
    aggravated, 13, 32
    compensatory, 32
    exemplary, 32
    general principles, 30–1
    libel *v.* slander, 4–5
    in Scotland, 292, 293–4
    types of, 31–2
  and death, 5
  declaration of falsity, 284
  defamatory language, definition, 6–8
  definition, 3
  and election candidates, 244
  English law *v.* Scottish law, 291–2
  general principles, 3–11
  identification of claimant, 10
  innocent dissemination, 25–6
  legal aid not available, 4
  legal procedure, 26–30
    the action, 27–9
    applications for ruling on meaning, 29
    costs, 32–3
    damages, 30–2
    evidence, 29
    forum non conveniens, 26–7
    injunctions, 28
    jurisdiction, 26–7
    limitation period, 27
    pre-action protocols, 28
    protection of information sources, 29–30
    service outside jurisdiction, 26
    summary disposal, 29
    trial, 30
  and malice, 18–20
  malicious falsehood, 5, 121
  meaning of words, 8–9
  MPs' waiver of absolute privilege, 242
  offer to make amends, 8, 24–5
  overview, 3
  and privacy, 118–19
  and privilege, 118–19
  proof of, 4
  publication of an image, 118
  publication of defamatory statements, 10–11
  in Scotland, *see under* Scottish Law
  USA law, *see under* United States of America
  who may be sued?, 6
  who may sue?, 5–6
  see also Internet defamation; Libel; Slander
Defamation cases, prior restraint, 196–7
Defence, national, 215, 221, 234–5
Defence Advisory Notice system, 238–9
Defence, Press and Broadcasting Advisory
    Committee, 238–9, 238*n*, 331*
Delict (Scotland), *see* Tort
Delivery up:
  after breach of confidence, 103
  after copyright infringement, 60
Department of Commerce (USA), 334*
Department of Trade and Industry, 330*
Derivative works, copyright, 48
Digital media, copyright, 63–4
Direct marketing, 111
Disclosure (discovery), 326*
Divorce:
  decree absolute, 326*
  decree nisi, 326*
  reporting restrictions, 153–4
Doctor and patient, obligation of confidence, 96–7
Documents, privileged, 29–30
Domain names, Internet, xxxii, 72, 315–16
Dramatic works:
  copyright, 45
    adaptations, 54
    broadcasting, 54
    copyright ownership, 50
    duration of copyright, 58
    moral rights, 61–3
    originality, 47
    public performances, 54
    published editions, 49
    USA, 309
  types of, 45

E-commerce Directive (EU), xxxii, 68n, 73, 77–8
  Internet defamation, 68–9
Elections, 243–6
  broadcasting controls, 245–6
  expenses, 244–5
    advertising, 244–5
    opposing/supporting candidates, 245
  false statements about candidates, 243–4
Email:
  intercepting, 127
  Internet defamation, 67
  see also Communications
Employees:
  copyright ownership, 52
  obligation of confidence, 93
    Government employees, 93–4
Employment contracts, duty of confidence, 93
Employment tribunals, reporting restrictions, 162–4
Environment Information Regulations 1992, 113
Environmental information, access to, 113, 223
Equity (actors' union), 83, 331*
Espionage, 228
  and protection of journalistic sources, 189
European Convention for the Protection of the
    Individual, 105
European Convention on Human Rights, 269,
    275–80
  breach of qualified rights, 275–6
  compatibility/incompatibility of primary legislation
    with, 123, 271, 274
  fair and public trial, 133
  freedom of expression, see under Freedom of
    expression
  general principles, 275–6
  incorporated into English law, xxxii–xxxiii
  protection of rights, 275
  and reporting restrictions, 138
  right to respect for private life, 269, 276–7
  substantive rights, 275
  victim, definition, 272
  waiver of rights, 276
  see also Human rights legislation
European Court of Human Rights, 331*
European Directives:
  Copyright Directive, xxxii, 63–4, 63n, 73, 73n
  Data Protection Directive, 127
  E-commerce Directive, xxxii, 68–9, 68n, 73, 77–8
  Rental and Lending Rights Directive, 85
European Union On-Line web site, 68n, 73n
Ex parte injunctions/application, 102, 327*
Examination in chief, 326*
Expression, freedom of, see Freedom of expression

Faculty of Advocates (Bar of Scotland), 331*
'Fade factor', 175
Fair comment, 284
  as defence to libel, 15–20
  and malice, 15, 18, 284
Fair dealing, 327*
  copyright clearance, 81
  as defence to copyright infringement, 55–6
Falsehood, malicious, 5, 121
Family life:
  privacy, 121
  right to respect for, 275
Family proceedings, reporting, 285
  see also Children
Fidelity, employees' duty of, 93
Films (motion pictures), copyright, 49
  copyright ownership, 51–2
  definition, 49
  duration of copyright of, 59
  USA, 309
Financial journalism, 257
Football fixtures, copyright, 45
Forum non conveniens, 26–7
Fraud, reporting restrictions, 154–5
Freedom of conscience, 275
Freedom of expression, 102–3, 117, 232, 275
  v. contempt of court, 167
  European Convention on Human Rights, 89, 277–80
    broadcasting, 280
    content of expression, 277
    duties and responsibilities, 279–80
    general principles, 277
    means of expression, 278
    restrictions, 278
    types of expression, 278–9
    UK violations, 280
  human rights legislation, 269, 282–3
  v. privacy, 114–15, 117
Freedom of information, 212–27
  legislation, 212, 219–27, 219n
    access to information, 220–1
    applications and fees for information, 225–6
    authorities subject to, 219–20
    enforcement, 226–7
    exemptions, 221–5
    general principles, 219
    personal information disclosure, 224, 225
  local government, 212
  overview, 212
  USA, 322–3
  see also Code of Practice on Access to
    Government Information

Freedom of Information (Scotland) Bill, 289
Freedom of the press, USA, 305, 306
Freedom of religion, 275
Freedom of speech:
    and malice, 284
    USA, 305, 306, 316, 317, 321
Freedom of thought, 275
Freelancers, copyright:
    new media, 69–70
    USA, 309

General Council of the Press, 250
Ghost writers, 50
Government:
    Cabinet members, obligation of confidence, 97
    cabinet proceedings, 215
    formation of policy, information about, 223
    information prejudicial to effective conduct of
        public affairs, 223, 225
    management of economy, 216, 222
Government Committee on Privacy and Related
    Matters, see Calcutt Committee
Government employees, obligation of confidence,
    93–4
Government information, see Code of Practice on
    Access to Government Information
Government institutions, and defamation, 6
Graphic works, copyright, USA, 309
Groups, defamatory statements about, 6

Hacking, 75, 78
Harassment, 117, 118, 256
Health and safety information, 223
Hearing in private, see In camera
Hearing on notice, see Inter partes application
Hearing without notice, see Ex parte
    injunctions/application
Hearsay evidence, 327*
Her Majesty's Stationery Office (HMSO), 331*
High Court, 327*
HMSO (Her Majesty's Stationery Office), 331*
Homosexuality, allegation of, and defamation, 7
Honours, 216
Hospitals, journalists' enquiries at, 255–6
House of Lords, 327*
Human rights legislation, 123–6, 269–85
    as between 'private' bodies or individuals, 270, 274
    claims under
        claimants, 272
        damages, 273–4
        declaration of incompatibility, 274

powers of courts and tribunals, 273
    procedure, 272
    timing of, 273
defamation, 283–4
effecting provisions of, 271, 272
freedom of expression, see under Freedom of
    expression
general principles, 123–4, 269–70
    private parties, 124
media regulation, 283
operation of, 269–70
privacy, right to, 281–2
privacy, tort of?, 281–2
public authorities bound by, 123–4, 270–1
    courts and tribunals, 271
    functional, 270
    standard, 270
recent decisions, 124–6
reporting of proceedings, 284–5
waiver of Convention rights, 276
see also European Convention on Human Rights
Husband and wife, obligation of confidence, 95

ICANN, see Internet Corporation for Assigned
    Names and Numbers
Identity cards, 128
Image, publication of, 118, 119, 120
    see also Photographs
Immigration, 216
Immorality, reporting restrictions, 147
Impeachment, 327*
Implication, 9
In camera, 133, 327*
In rixa defence, 291
Incidental inclusion, and copyright, 57, 81
Incompetence, professional, allegations of, 7
Incorporated bodies, and defamation, 5–6
Indecency:
    indecent displays, 209–10
    reporting restrictions, 147, 151, 153
    see also Obscenity
Independent Television Commission (ITC), 249,
    260–1, 283, 331*
    Code of Advertising Standards and Practice, 261,
        354
    Programme Code, 261, 354
Information, 327*
    confidential, 121, 217
    freedom of, see Freedom of information
    sources of, see Journalistic sources
Information Commissioner, 106, 226–7, 331*

'Information superhighway', xxxi
Information Tribunal, 106
Infringement of Privacy (consultation paper), 123
Injunctions, 183, 327*
    see also Interdicts
Innuendo, 8, 9
    in Scottish law, 290
Inquests, 162, 172
Integrity, author's rights of, 62–3, 82
Intellectual property rights, 43, 44, 327*
    see also Copyright; New media; Rights clearance
Inter partes application, 327*
Interdicts (Scotland), 327*
    interim (interlocutory injunctions), 296, 299
    see also Injunctions
Interlocutory injunctions, 296, 299
International Convention for the Protection of
    Performers, Producers of Phonograms and
    Broadcasting Organizations 1961 (Rome
    Convention), 43
International Federation of Journalists, 332*
International relations, 215, 222, 235, 237–8
Internet:
    advertisements, 264
    civil court judgments published on, 135, 135*n*
    copyright infringement lawsuits, USA, 313–14
    defamation, *see* Internet defamation
    domain names, xxxii, 72, 315–16
    E-commerce Directive (EU), xxxii, 68–9, 68*n*, 73,
        77–8
    existing legal principles, xxxii
    global nature of, 65
    legal services, 354
    legislation, 65
    linking and framing, 71
        USA, 314–15
    reporting restrictions, USA, 316
    research on, 71
    service providers, 66–7, 73, 77, 77–8
        and copyright, 64, 69
    surveillance (USA), xxxiv
    web sites:
        codes of practice, 354
        legal services, 354
        personal data, 75
        privacy statements on, 75
        professional bodies, 330–4
    world wide web, 66
    see also New media
Internet Corporation for Assigned Names and
    Numbers (ICANN), xxxii, 72, 332*
    USA, 315–16

Internet defamation, 66–9
    bulletin boards, 67
    E-commerce Directive (EU), xxxii, 68–9, 68*n*, 73,
        77–8
    email, 67
    general principles, 66–7
    jurisdiction, 68, 78
    newsgroups, 66–7
    USA, 69, 312–13
    world wide web, 66
Interviews:
    with jurors, reporting restrictions, 159–60
    performers' rights, 82–3
    specimen agreement:
        fee payable, 335, 336–7
        no fee payable, 335, 338–9
ITC, *see* Independent Television Commission

Joint authorship/ownership, 46, 50
    USA, 309
Journalistic sources, protection of, 29–30, 184–92
    case law, 192
    code of practice, 257
    and contempt of court, 185
    and espionage, 189
    excluded and special procedure material, 191, 192
    general principles, 185
    interests of justice, 185–7
    interests of national security, 187–8
    overview, 184
    police powers, 189–92
    prevention of disorder/crime, 188–9
    in USA, 321
Judicial proceedings:
    reports of, privilege, 21, 23–4
    statements during course of, 21
Jurors:
    interviews with, reporting restrictions, 159–60
    undermining/intimidation of, contempt of court,
        177
Jury trials, 174
    in Scotland, 292, 301
    in USA, 305
Justification, 327*
    as defence to libel, 11–15
        aggravation, 13–14
        criminal convictions and, 14–15
        meaning of statement, 12
        partial, 13
        substantial, 12–13
    see also Veritas

Law enforcement information, 215–16, 222
Law Society of England and Wales, 332*
Law Society of Scotland, 332*
Lawyer and client, obligation of confidence, 97
Leading questions, 327*
Leave (consent to publication), defamation and, 25
Legal aid availability:
    defamation actions, 4
    malicious falsehood actions, 5
Legal proceedings, information about, 215–16
Legal professional privilege, 30, 97, 191, 224, 327*
Legal services, on Internet, 354
Legitimacy proceedings, reporting restrictions, 144
Letters (correspondence), interception of, 118, 121, 122
Libel, 328*
    blasphemous libel, 34–6
    consent to publication, 25
    criminal libel, 37–9
        v. civil libel, 38
    defences to, 11
        fair comment, 15–20
        innocent dissemination, 25–6
        justification, 11–15
        leave and licence, 25
        offer of amends, 8, 24–5
        privilege, 20–4
    definition, 4, 328*
    meaning of words, 8–9
    seditious libel, 34, 36–7
    v. slander, 4
        in Scotland, 291
    sting of libel, 12–13
    USA, 308
    see also Defamation; Slander
Libraries, copying by, 58
Library of Congress, Washington, 309
    Copyright Office, 310, 332*
Licence (consent to publication), defamation and, 25
Licences:
    copyright licence, 84
    synchronization licence, 86
Licensing justices, reporting restrictions, 164
Limitation period, 328*
    defamation claims, 27
Listening devices, 117–18, 122
    journalists' use of, 255
    see also Surveillance
Literary works, copyright, 44–5
    adaptations, 54
    broadcasting, 54
    copyright ownership, 50
    definition, 44
    duration of copyright, 58
    ghost writers, 50
    moral rights, 61–3
    originality, 47
    public performances, 54
    published editions, 49
    USA, 309
Local government institutions, and defamation, 6
Logarithmic tables, copyright, 45

Magistrates' courts, 328*
    committal proceedings, reporting restrictions,
        148–50
        general principles, 148
        legislation, 148–9
        offences triable either way, 149–50
        summary offences, 149–50
    licensing justices, 164
    young offenders in, 145, 146
Maintenance proceedings, reporting restrictions, 144
Malice:
    and defamation, 18–20
    and fair comment, 15, 18, 284
    and freedom of speech, 284
    liability for malice of others, 19–20
    and qualified privilege, 22, 24
    and spent convictions, 14, 15
    USA, 307–8
Malicious falsehood, 5, 121
Mechanical-Copyright Protection Society (MCPS),
    86, 332*
Media regulation, 283
    broadcasting, see Broadcasting Standards
        Commission; Independent Television
        Commission; Radio Authority
    press, see Press Complaints Commission
    regulatory bodies, 249–62
    see also New media
Media sources, obligation of confidence, 97
Medical disciplinary hearings, reporting restrictions,
    165
Medical records:
    access to, 113
    obligation of confidence, 96–7
Mens rea, 168, 328*
Mental health review tribunals, reporting restrictions,
    164
Misrepresentation, by journalists, 256
Moral rights, 61–3, 82
    integrity, 62–3, 82
    paternity, 62, 82

rights clearance, 70
waiver of, 70, 82
    specimen agreement, 335, 345–50
Motion pictures, *see* Films
Multimedia, *see* New media
Multimedia products, rights clearance, 70–1
Musical works:
    copyright, 45–6
        adaptations, 54–5
        broadcasting, 54
        copyright ownership, 50
        duration of copyright, 58
        extracts, riffs and hooks, 53
        joint ownership, 46, 50
        moral rights, 61–3
        originality, 47, 48
        parodics and pastiches, 53–4
        public performances, 54
        published editions, 49
        separate for tunes and lyrics, 46
        USA, 309
    rights clearance, 86
        commissioning music, 86
        live performers, 86
        pre-existing songs and recordings, 86
Musicians' Union, 86, 332*

Names, prevention of publication of, 141–2
National defence, 215, 221, 234–5
National security, 155–6, 215, 221, 224, 234
National Union of Journalists, 332*
    Code of Conduct, 112, 354
Nationality, 216
New media, xxxi–xxxii, 65–79
    copyright, 69–74
        employees, 69–70
        European directives, 73
        formalities, 69
        freelancers, 69–70
        general principles, 69
        international conventions, 74
        original works, 69
        pre-existing works, 70–1
        registration, 69
        rights clearance, 70–1
        sub-contractors, 69–70
        third party contributions, 70–1
    copyright infringement, 71
    obscenity, 77–8
    overview, 65
    racial hatred, 77–8

reporting restrictions, 76–7
    USA, *see under* United States of America
    see also Internet; Internet defamation; Media
        regulation
News reporting, and copyright, 55
Newsgroups, Internet defamation, 66–7
Newspaper employees, copyright ownership, 52
Newspapers, letters and emails to, copyright, 45
Nurses' disciplinary hearings, reporting restrictions,
    165

Obiter dictum, 328*
Obscenity:
    contemporary standards, 208
    defences, 209
    definitions, 206–8
    general principles, 205–6
    intention irrelevant, 208
    on Internet, cyber-crime convention, 317
    legislation, 205–9
    likely readers/audience, 207–8
    new media, 77–8
    penalties, 209
    publication, 208
    USA, 316, 321–2
    see also Indecency
Ofcom (Office of Communications), 258, 332*
Offences:
    summary offences, 149–50
    triable either way, 149–50
Office of Communications (Ofcom), 258, 332*
Office of Telecommunications (Oftel), 262, 333*
Official secrets, 228–39
    and breach of confidence, 228, 230
    Defence Advisory Notice system, 238–9
    legislation, 227–38, 230–8
        crime and investigation powers, 235–6
        defences to, 231, 232, 236
        definitions, 238
        general principles, 231–2
        and human rights, 232–3
        international relations, 235, 237
        national defence, 234–5
        objectives, 230–1
        official direction, 238
        penalties, 232
        protected categories of information, 233–8
        protected documents, 231
        security and intelligence matters, 234
        spying, 229–30
        unauthorized disclosure, 236–7

Official secrets (*Cont.*)
overview, 228
paper hearing, 156
reporting restrictions, 155–6
withholding of names, 141
Official Solicitor, 333*
Oftel (Office of Telecommunications), 262, 333*
Ombudsman, *see* Parliamentary Ombudsman
Onus (burden) of proof, 325*
Open court rule, *see under* Court proceedings
Opinion, *see* Fair comment
Opticians' disciplinary hearings, reporting
restrictions, 165
Organizations, 330–4*
Originality, and copyright, 47–8
'sweat of the brow' test, 47

PACT (Producers Alliance for Cinema and
Television), 83, 333*
Paper hearing, 156
Parliamentary Ombudsman, 213, 219, 219*n*, 333*
public bodies subject to investigation by, 213,
213*n*
Parliamentary proceedings, 240–3
contempt of, *see* Contempt of Parliament
overview, 240
privilege, 225, 240, 241
Parliamentary reports, qualified privilege, 21, 23
Parliamentary statements, absolute privilege, 20–1
Parodies, copyright, 53–4
Passing off, xxxii, 44, 328*
Pastiches, copyright, 53
Patents, 44, 328*
Paternity, author's right of, 62, 82
PCC, *see* Press Complaints Commission
Performers' rights, 70, 82–3
interviews, 82–3
Performing Right Society (PRS), 86, 333*
Periodicals, 354
Personal data:
Data Protection (Processing of Sensitive Personal
Data) Order 2000, 110
definition, 104, 107
disclosure of, 217, 224, 225
processing, 107
right of access to, 104–5, 110, 112
right to assessment, 112
right to compensation, 111
right to prevent automated decision taking, 111,
112
right to prevent processing, 110–11, 112
damage or distress, 110–11
direct marketing, 111
right to rectification, blocking, erasure, destruction,
111, 112
sensitive, 107, 110
on web sites, 75
see also Data controllers; Data protection
Personal files, access to, 113
Personality rights, 119, 120
Pharmacists' disciplinary hearings, reporting
restrictions, 165
Phonographic Performance Limited (PPL), 86, 333*
Photographs:
aerial photography, 118
and contempt of court in Scotland, 298
children, 296
copyright ownership, 50–1
in court, 161
of defendants, 175
and fair dealing, 81
unauthorized, breach of confidence, 90, 116
see also Image
Pictorial works, copyright, USA, 309
Plaintiff (USA), *see* Claimant
Planning enquiries, reporting restrictions, 164
Political expression, 279
Political parties, and defamation, 6
Pools coupons, copyright, 45
Pornography, 209
Practice Direction (Contempt Reporting Restrictions)
1982, 140
Pre-action protocols, 328*
Precedents, 328*
Prejudice, in Scottish law, 300, 301, 303
Presbof (Press Standards Board of Finance), 252,
252–3
Press:
duties and responsibilities under European
Convention on Human Rights, 280
freedom of (USA), 305, 306
self-regulation, 249–52
Press Complaints Commission (PCC), 122, 200, 249,
251–2, 333*
Code of Practice, 100, 112, 252, 253, 254–8, 354
accuracy, 255
children, interviews and photographs, 256
children in sex cases, 257
comment, conjecture, fact, 255
confidential sources, 257
discrimination, 257
editors' responsibilities, 254–5, 256, 258
financial journalism, 257

harassment, 256
hospitals, 255–6
innocent friends and relatives, 256
intrusions into grief or shock, 256
listening devices, 255
misrepresentation/subterfuge, 256
opportunity to reply, 255
payment for articles, 256
privacy, 255
public interest, 257–8
sexual assault victims, 257
complaints procedure, 253–4
as a public authority, 128, 283
structure, 252–3
Press conferences, reports of, qualified privilege, 24
Press Council, 250, 251, 252
Press Standards Board of Finance (Presbof), 252, 252–3
Priest and parishioner, obligation of confidence, 97
Prior restraint, 195–201
breach of confidence, 197–200
applications for interim injunctions, 199–200
general principles, 198
non-confidential material, 197–8
public domain, 198
compliance, 196
contempt proceedings, 201
defamation, in Scottish law, 292–3
defamation cases, 196–7
applications for interim injunctions, 196–7
defendants, 196
general principles, 195–6
interim injunction applications, 195
applications without notice, 195
invasion of privacy, 200
Privacy, xxxiii–xxxiv
common law rights, 115–20
breach of confidence, 116–17
defamation, 118–19
trademarks, 119–20
trespass, 117–18, 121
v. freedom of expression, 114–15, 117
the future, 126–30
communication surveillance and interception, 127–8
companies, 126–7
impact on the media, 128
a 'Privacy Act', 128–30
Government Committee on Privacy and Related Matters, see Calcutt Committee
individuals' right to, 124
Infringement of Privacy (consultation paper), 123

invasion of, 106
prior restraint, 200
USA, see under United States of America
PCC Code of Practice, 255
right to, 114–30, 281–2
background, 114–15
conflicting Articles, 117
tort of?, xxxiv, 114, 115–16, 281–2
see also Breach of confidence; Confidence; Data protection; Human rights legislation; Personal data
Private life, right to respect for, 269, 276–7
Private study, and copyright, 55
Privilege:
absolute, 20–1
Scotland, 293
USA, 308
and defamation, 118–19
as defence to libel, 20–4
judicial proceedings:
reports of, 21, 23–4
statements during course of, 21
legal professional privilege, 30, 97, 191, 224, 327*
Parliamentary proceedings, 20–1, 225, 240, 241
qualified, 22–4
and defamation, 284
Scotland, 293
USA, 308, 321
Privileged documents, 29–30
Privy Council, 215
Producers Alliance for Cinema and Television (PACT), 83, 333*
Professional bodies, 330–4*
Programme Codes:
Independent Television Commission (ITC), 261, 354
Radio Authority, 354
Prohibited places, 229
Proof, standard of, 328*
Public appointments, 216
Public authorities, 216, 222
bound by human rights legislation, 270–1
duty to observe right to privacy, 123–4
Public domain, 328*
confidentiality and, 91, 98
after copyright expiry, 59
Public interest:
absolute exemptions to disclosure of information, 224
in defence to copyright infringement, 58
in defence to libel, 16
PCC Code of Practice, 257–8

Public meetings, reports of, qualified privilege, 24
Public services information, 216
Publication:
    prevention of, *see* Prior restraint
    state restriction on, *see* Freedom of information;
        Obscenity; Official secrets; Parliamentary
        proceedings
Pursuer (Scotland), *see* Claimant

Qualified privilege, *see under* Privilege
Questions, leading, 327*

Racial discrimination, USA, 322
Racial hatred, 210–11
    defences, 211
    definitions, 211
    general principles, 210
    'holocaust denial', 211
    new media, 77–8
    statements made in Parliament, 241
    USA, 317
Radio, *see* Broadcasting; Media regulation
Radio Authority, 249, 259, 261, 333*
    Advertising and Sponsorship Code, 354
    News and Current Affairs Code, 354
    Programme Code, 354
Radiocommunications Agency, 262
Railway timetables, copyright, 45
Ratio decidendi, 328*
Recognizance, 328*
Recordings, *see* Sound recordings; Spoken words;
    Tape recordings
Re-examination, 328*
Regulatory bodies, 249–62
    see also Media regulation; *and individual
        regulatory bodies*
Rehabilitation periods, 15
Religion:
    freedom of, 275
    see also Blasphemous libel
Remission of sentence, 328*
Rental and Lending Rights Directive (EC), 85
Rental rights, 85
    equitable remuneration, 85
Reporting restrictions, 133–65
    arbitration proceedings, 161–2
    blanket bans, 140, 156
    breach of, 134
    children, *see under* Children
    crown courts, 146, 149–50, 154–5, 158–9, 159

divorce cases, 153–4
employment tribunals, 162–4
fraud, 154–5
immorality, 147
indecency, 147, 151, 153
inquests, 162
interviewing jurors, 159–60
legitimacy proceedings, 144
licensing justices, 164
magistrates' courts, *see* Magistrates' courts
maintenance proceedings, 144
material made available on disclosure, 156
medical disciplinary hearings, 165
mental health review tribunals, 164
names of parties, 141–2
new media, 76–7
nurses' disciplinary hearings, 165
official secrets, 155–6
opticians' disciplinary hearings, 165
pharmacists' disciplinary hearings, 165
photography in court, 161
planning enquiries, 164
postponement of reporting, 138–41
    discretion of court, 140
    general principles, 138–40
    terms of the order, 140–1
Practice Direction (Contempt Reporting
    Restrictions) 1982, 140
press challenges to, 156–8
    appeal under Criminal Justice Act 1988, 158–9
    appeal under Youth Justice Act 1999, 159
    application to originating court, 157–8
    judicial review, 158
in Scotland, *see under* Scottish law
sexual offences, *see* Sexual offences
sketches in court, 161
summary offences, 149–50
tape recorders, 160–1
USA, 316, 320
veterinary surgeons' disciplinary hearings, 165
wardship proceedings, 143–4
see also Court proceedings
Reputation, protection of, 119
    see also Blasphemous libel; Defamation; Libel;
        Slander
Research:
    and copyright, 55
    on the Internet, 71
    research information, 217
Residence order, 328*
Retrials, active period, 172
Reviews, copyright, 55, 56

Ridicule, exposure to, 8
Rights clearance, 80–6
  contributor rights, 84–5
  copyright, 81–2
    fair dealing, 81
    incidental inclusion, 81
    spoken words, 82
  copyright assignments, 80, 83
    specimen agreement, 335, 351–2
  licences, 80, 84
    exclusive, 84
  moral rights, waiver of, 70, 82
    specimen agreement, 335, 345–50
  multimedia products, 70–1
  music, 86
    commissioning music, 86
    live performers, 86
    pre-existing songs and recordings, 86
  overview, 80
  performers' rights, 70, 82–3
    interviews, 82–3
  rental rights, 85
  territory, 84–5
  types of right, 81
  use and exploitation, 84–5
  use fees, 81, 83
Rome Convention (on copyright), 43
Royal Courts of Justice, 333*
Royal household, 215, 223
Rumours, and defamation, 9

Safe Harbor, 334*
  international privacy principles, 75, 316, 316n
Scandalum Magnatum, 37
Scottish law, 289–304
  Children.
    children's hearing, 296, 303
    reporting restrictions, 296
  civil law system, 289
  contempt of court, 295–304
    active proceedings, 299
    appeal proceedings, 300
    bar of trial, 295, 297–8
    civil proceedings, 299–300
    common law contempt, 303–4
    complainants, 299
    criminal proceedings, 299, 300
    general principles, 297
    identification, 298
    and juries, 301
    photographs, 298

    prejudice, 300, 301, 303
    public figures, 302
    reporting restrictions, 295–6
    risk of serious prejudice, 300–3
    statutory defences, 304
    strict liability rule, 299–303
    subject matter, 302–3
    time of trial, 302
  defamation, 289–94
    class actions, 290
    criminal defamation, 291
    damages, 292, 293–4
    defence of *in rixa*, 291
    definition, 289–90
    v. English law, 291–2
    innuendo, 290
    jury trials, 292
    libel and slander indistinguishable, 291
    prior restraint, 292–3
    privilege, 293
    procedure, 292
    proof, onus and standard of, 291
    publication not required, 291
    record (written pleadings) and privilege, 295
    reporting restrictions, 294–5
    statutes applying, 291
    time limits, 292
  Freedom of Information Bill, 289
  interim interdicts (interlocutory injunctions), 296, 299
  overview, 289
  reporting restrictions
    children, 296
    contempt of court, 295–6
    defamation, 294–5
  UK-wide statutes, 289
Sculptural works, copyright, USA, 309
Secondary copyrights, 48
Security, national, 155–6, 215, 221, 224, 234
Seditious libel, 34, 36–7
Sentence, remission of, 328*
September 11th, xxxiv, 318–19
Sexual offences, 150–3
  legislation, 151, 153
  PCC Code of Conduct, 257
  reporting restrictions, 150, 151–2, 257
    defence to breaching anonymity, 152–3
    employment tribunals, 163
    general principles, 150–1
    levels of protection, 151–2
    lifting the prohibition, 152
  shorthand writers, copyright, 50

Sexual relationships, obligation of confidence, 95–6
Shield laws, USA, 321
Sketches, made in court, 161
Slander, 328*
    definition, 4, 328*
    v. libel, 4
        in Scotland, 291
    USA, 308
    see also Defamation; Libel
Sound recordings, copyright, 48–9
    copyright ownership, 51–2
    definition, 48
    duration of copyright, 59
    spoken word recordings, 45, 57, 82
    USA, 309
Speech, freedom of, *see* Freedom of speech
Spent convictions, and malice, 14, 15
Spoken words, copyright, 82
    recordings, 45, 57, 82
Spying, 229–30
Standard of proof, 328*
Statistical information, 217
Statute(s), 328*
    see also table of statutes in pages xxvii–xxx
Strict liability, *see under* Contempt of court
Study, *see* Private study
Subpoena, 328*
Subterfuge, by journalists, 256
Summary offences, 149–50
Summing up, 329*
Surety, 329*
Surveillance, 127–8
    Internet (USA), xxxiv
    see also Listening devices
Synchronization licences, 86

Tape recordings, made in court, 160–1
Teacher and pupil, obligation of confidence, 97
Telephone calls:
    intercepting, 127
    see also Communications
Television:
    contributors to, specimen agreement, 335, 340–1
    duties and responsibilities under European
        Convention on Human Rights, 279–80
    satellite services, 261
    see also Broadcasting; Media regulation
Television listings, copyright, 45
Terrorism, xxxiv, 126
    USA anti-terrorism legislation, 318–20
Test cases, xxxi

Third parties:
    contributions to new media, 70–1
    obligation of confidence, 97
Third-party contempt, 183
Thought, freedom of, 275
Tobacco products, advertisement practice, 265
Tort, 329*
Tortfeasor, 329*
Trademarks, xxxii, 44, 329*
    Internet domain names, 72
    personal names as, 119–20
    and privacy, 119–20
    USA, 315
Trespass, 117–18, 121
Trial within a trial, 140
Trustee in bankruptcy, 329*
Truth (USA), *see* Justification

Ultra vires, 329*
Uniform Administrative Dispute Resolution Policy
    (UDRP), 72, 315–16
United States of America (USA), law in, 305–23
    anti-terrorism legislation, 318–20
    Bill of Rights, 305
    contempt of court, 321
    copyright, 309–11
        common property, 309
        copying, 311
        cyber-crime convention, 311, 311*n*
        domain names, 315–16
        domicile and nationality, 310
        duration, 310–11
        existing works, 313–14
        freelancers, 309
        general principles, 309
        infringement, 311
        joint authors, 309
        linking and framing, 314–15
        new media, 313–17
        notice and registration, 310
        publication, 309
        published works, 309, 310
        reciprocal protection of, 310
        remedies, 311
        'tangible form', 309, 310
        unpublished works, 310
    cyber-crime convention, 311, 311*n*, 317
    defamation, 306–8
        absolute privilege, 308
        common law torts, 306
        consent to, 308

defamatory language, 306
defences, 308
elements of the tort, 306–8
Internet service providers, 69
libel, 308
malice, 307–8
matter of public concern, 306, 307
online, 69, 312–13
publication, 307
qualified privilege, 308
slander, 308
truth, 308, 313
federal law, 305
freedom of information, 322–3
freedom of the press, 305, 306
freedom of speech, 305, 306, 316, 317, 321
invasion of privacy, 317–20
anti-terrorism legislation, 318–20
consent, 318
defences, 318
general principles, 317–18
Internet surveillance, xxxiv
tort of, 317–18
truth, 318
journalistic sources, protection of, 321
shield laws, 321
jury trials, 305
legal services on Internet, 354
new media, 312–17
copyright, 313–17
data protection, 316
domain names, 315–16
ICANN registration and disputes, 315–16
linking and framing, 314–15
obscenity, 316
online defamation, 69, 312–13
racial hatred, 317
reporting restrictions, 316
obscenity, 316, 321–2
overview, 305

racial discrimination, 322
reporting restrictions, 320
access to court proceedings, 320
broadcasting regulation, 320
Internet, 316
state law, 305
US Constitution, 305
wiretapping, 319, 319–20
Universal Copyright Convention, 43, 53, 69, 74
USA, see United States of America
Use fees, 81, 83

Veritas (Scotland), 291, 292, 327*
see also Justification
Veterinary surgeons' disciplinary hearings, reporting
restrictions, 165
Video recordings, copyright, 49
Violence, as obscenity, 206
Visitation rights, see Contact order

Ward of court, 329*
Wardship proceedings, reporting restrictions, 143–4
Warrants, 329*
media coverage and issue of, 171
WGGB (Writers Guild of Great Britain), 83, 334*
'Whistle blowing', 94–5
WIPO, see World Intellectual Property Organization
'Without prejudice' communications, 30, 329*
Witness summons (subpoena), 328*
World Intellectual Property Organization (WIPO),
xxxii, 63, 72, 74, 334*
Copyright treaty, 310, 313
Internet regulation, 65
World wide web, see Internet; Internet defamation
Writers' Guild of Great Britain (WGGB), 83, 334*

Youth courts, reporting restrictions, 144–5

 **Focal Press**

www.focalpress.com

Join Focal Press on-line

As a member you will enjoy the following benefits:

- · an email bulletin with **information on new books**
- · a regular **Focal Press Newsletter**:
  - o featuring a selection of new titles
  - o keeps you informed of **special offers, discounts and freebies**
  - o alerts you to **Focal Press news and events** such as author signings and seminars
- · complete access to **free content** and reference material on the focalpress site, such as the focalXtra articles and commentary from our authors
- · a **Sneak Preview** of selected titles (sample chapters) *before* they publish
- · a chance to have your say on our **discussion boards** and **review books** for other Focal readers

Focal Club Members are invited to give us feedback on our products and services.
Email: worldmarketing@focalpress.com – we want to hear your views!

Membership is **FREE**. To join, visit our website and register. If you require any further information regarding the on-line club please contact:

> Lucy Lomas-Walker
> Email: lucy.lomas-walker@repp.co.uk
> Tel: +44 (0) 1865 314438
> Fax: +44 (0)1865 314572
> Address: Focal Press, Linacre House,
> Jordan Hill, Oxford, UK, OX2 8DP

Catalogue

For information on all Focal Press titles, our full catalogue is available online at www.focalpress.com and all titles can be purchased here via secure online ordering, or contact us for a free printed version:

USA
Email: christine.degon@bhusa.com
Tel: +1 781 904 2607

Europe and rest of world
Email: jo.coleman@repp.co.uk
Tel: +44 (0)1865 314220

Potential authors

If you have an idea for a book, please get in touch:

USA
editors@focalpress.com

Europe and rest of world
focal.press@repp.co.uk